Deniz-Osman Tekin

Von Sèvres nach Lausanne

Die Neuordnung Südosteuropas

Deniz-Osman Tekin

VON SÈVRES NACH LAUSANNE

Die Neuordnung Südosteuropas

ibidem-Verlag
Stuttgart

Bibliografische Information der Deutschen Nationalbibliothek
Die Deutsche Nationalbibliothek verzeichnet diese Publikation in der Deutschen Nationalbibliografie; detaillierte bibliografische Daten sind im Internet über http://dnb.d-nb.de abrufbar.

Bibliographic information published by the Deutsche Nationalbibliothek
Die Deutsche Nationalbibliothek lists this publication in the Deutsche Nationalbibliografie; detailed bibliographic data are available in the Internet at http://dnb.d-nb.de.

Coverabbildung: Deportation of the Armenians in the Baghdad railway.
Quelle: http://commons.wikimedia.org/wiki/File:Armenian_genocide3.jpg.
Armenians killed during the Armenian Genocide.
Quelle: http://commons.wikimedia.org/wiki/File:Morgenthau336.jpg

∞

Gedruckt auf alterungsbeständigem, säurefreien Papier
Printed on acid-free paper

ISBN-13: 978-3-8382-0580-9

© *ibidem*-Verlag
Stuttgart 2015

Alle Rechte vorbehalten

Das Werk einschließlich aller seiner Teile ist urheberrechtlich geschützt. Jede Verwertung außerhalb der engen Grenzen des Urheberrechtsgesetzes ist ohne Zustimmung des Verlages unzulässig und strafbar. Dies gilt insbesondere für Vervielfältigungen, Übersetzungen, Mikroverfilmungen und elektronische Speicherformen sowie die Einspeicherung und Verarbeitung in elektronischen Systemen.

All rights reserved. No part of this publication may be reproduced, stored in or introduced into a retrieval system, or transmitted, in any form, or by any means (electronical, mechanical, photocopying, recording or otherwise) without the prior written permission of the publisher. Any person who does any unauthorized act in relation to this publication may be liable to criminal prosecution and civil claims for damages.

Printed in Germany

*Toprağından sürülmüş
bütün halklara...*

Inhalt

Glossar 9

1. Einleitung 15
2. Südosteuropa – Heterogenität eines Raumes 19
    2.1. Der Terminus *Südosteuropa* 19
    2.2. Naturräumliche Betrachtung 24
    2.3. Anmerkungen zur Kulturgeographie 27
3. Die Geschichte Südosteuropas 31
    3.1. Die Vielvölkerstaaten 31
        3.1.1. Das Russische Reich 31
        3.1.2. Die Habsburger Monarchie Österreich-Ungarn 35
        3.1.3. Das Osmanische Reich 37
    3.2. Vom Berliner Kongress nach Sèvres 41
        3.2.1. Südosteuropa bis zur Jahrhundertwende 41
        3.2.2. Der Erste Balkankrieg 46
        3.2.3. Der Fall Kosovo 51
        3.2.4. Der Zweite Balkankrieg 52
        3.2.5. Der Erste Weltkrieg 55
        3.2.6. Der Vertrag von Sèvres (1920) 62
    3.3. Von Sèvres nach Lausanne 64
        3.3.1. Der nationale Widerstand Mustafa Kemals und die *Megali Idea* 64
        3.3.2. Der Vertrag von Lausanne (1923) 66
4. Sieg oder Niederlage? – Die Verträge von Sèvres und Lausanne aus türkischer Perspektive 69

5. Flucht, Vertreibung, Zwangsumsiedlungen und der Vertrag von Lausanne 83

    5.1. Nationen, Ethnien, Minderheiten – Definitorische Grundlagen 83

    5.2. Südosteuropa – Eine Bilanz 90

    5.3. Die armenische Tragödie: *Meds Yeghern* 97

    5.4. Lehrstück Lausanne? Die vertragliche Regelung des Bevölkerungsaustausches 107

6. Zusammenfassung: Brüche und Kontinuitäten in einem Raum 117

7. Quellen- und Literaturverzeichnis 121

8. Anhang 129

    8.1. Zeittafel 129

    8.2. Der Vertrag von Sèvres vom 19. August 1920 132

    8.3. Der Vertrag von Lausanne vom 24. Juli 1923 187

    8.4. Konvention über die Regime der Meerengen vom 24. Juli 1923 208

    8.5. Konvention über den Austausch der griechischen und türkischen Bevölkerung vom 30. Januar 1923 214

Glossar

Alföld	Ungarische Tiefebene
Amselfeld (Kosovo polje)	Hochebene im heutigen Kosovo mit symbolischer Bedeutung für den serbischen Nationalismus: Niederlage der serbischen Fürstentümer gegen die Osmanen am St. Veitstag (28. Juni 1389) leitete Untergang des mittelalterlichen serbischen Reiches ein.
Aschkenasische Juden	Juden Mittel-, Nord- und Osteuropas und ihre Nachfahren.
Atatürk	s. Mustafa Kemal
Balkanisierung	Meist abwertend verwendetes Schlagwort für Zerstückelung politischer, wirtschaftlicher und organisatorischer Einheiten. Bezieht sich auf die Kleinstaatenwelt, die nach der Auflösung der Vielvölkerstaaten in Südosteuropa entstanden war.
Berliner Kongress	Zusammenkunft der europäischen Mächte und des Osmanischen Reiches vom 13.06. bis 13.07.1878 in Berlin zur Verhandlung einer Friedensordnung auf der Balkanhalbinsel. Die geschaffene Neuordnung führte zu neuen Spannungen.
Byzanz	Oströmischer Nachfolgestaat des Römischen Imperiums. Russen, Ukrainer, Serben, Bulgaren, Makedonier und Rumänen wurden vom byzantinisch-orthodoxen Christentum geprägt.
Catena Mundi	"Weltkette"; irrtümliche Vorstellung einer Gebirgskette, die von den Pyrenäen bis nach Mesembria, einer Stadt am Schwarzen Meer, reiche.
Çete	"Freischärler" oder "Bande"
Dersim	Name eines Gebietes im Osten der Türkei, das mehrheitlich von Kurden und Zaza bewohnt wird. Von der türkischen Regierung gegen den Willen der einheimischen Bevölkerung 1937 in Tunceli umbenannt. Dersim war stets Schauplatz großer Aufstände. Der letzte ereignete sich 1937/38. Hierbei kam es zu staatlich angeordneten Massakern an der Bevölkerung Dersims. Noch heute sticht Dersim mit seinem oppositionellen Charakter hervor.

Eisernes Tor	Durchbruchstal der Donau zwischen dem serbischen Erzgebirge und dem Banater Gebirge.
Entente	Gegner der Mittelmächte im Ersten Weltkrieg unter der Führung Frankreichs und Großbritanniens.
Friede von Karlowitz	Am Ende des "Großen Türkenkrieges" 1699 geschlossener Frieden zwischen dem Osmanischen Reich auf der einen und Österreich, Polen und Venedig auf der anderen Seite. Drängte das Osmanische Reich nach Südosteuropa zurück.
Großwesir	Vom Sultan eingesetzter Regierungschef.
Güneş Dil Teorisi (türk.)	"Sonnensprachtheorie"; Theorie der türkischen Nationalisten, der zufolge Türkisch die 'Ursprache' sei, aus der sich alle anderen entwickelt haben. Erhielt Unterstützung von Mustafa Kemal.
Hohe Pforte	Osmanisches Außenministerium in der Sultansresidenz in Istanbul/Konstantinopel. Sinngemäß Synonym für die osmanische Regierung.
Hrant Dink (1954-2007)	Armenischer Journalist, geboren in Malatya (Türkei). Herausgeber der armenisch-türkischsprachigen Zeitung Agos.
Illyrer	Historisches Volk des Altertums im heutigen Dalmatien und Albanien.
Ismet Inönü Pascha (1884-1973)	Eig. Mustafa Ismet (ab 1934) Inönü. Engster Berater Mustafa Kemals. Führte die Truppen während des nationalen Widerstandes der Türken und vertrat sie bei den Friedensverhandlungen in Lausanne. Erster Ministerpräsident und zweiter Präsident der Türkei.
İttihat ve Terakki Cemiyeti (türk.)	"Komitee für Einheit und Fortschritt"; mächtigste politische Organisation der Jungtürken. Gegründet 1889. Regierte ab 1908 mit kurzen Unterbrechungen bis 1918 und war treibende Kraft beim Völkermord an den Armeniern. Mustafa Kemal trat der Organisation 1907 bei.
Izmir	Türkischer Name einer Stadt im Westen der Türkei (ehemals griechischer Name: Smyrna).
Jungtürken	Nationalistische Bewegung der Türken im Osmanischen Reich. Entmachteten unter Enver Pascha 1908 den Sultan.

Karst	Geomorphologie: Unterirdische und oberirdische Geländeformen, die durch Lösungsvorgänge an geeigneten Gesteinen (z.B. Kalk, Gips oder Steinsalz) entstehen.
k. u. k. Regierung	Abkürzung für 'kaiserlich und königlich'; gemeint ist die Österreichisch-Ungarische Monarchie.
Kemalismus	Staatsideologie des türkischen Staates formuliert von Mustafa Kemal. Zu den sechs Prinzipen des Kemalismus gehören Republikanismus, Populismus (im Sinne einer klassenübergreifenden Gesellschaftskooperation), Laizismus, Revolutionismus, Nationalismus und Etatismus.
Khanat von Kazan'	Tatarischer Nachfolgestaat der Goldenen Horde (historisches mongolisches Teilreich), der sich im 15. Jahrhundert entwickelte und ca. 115 Jahre existierte.
Kranker Mann am Bosporus	Von Zar Nikolaus I. geprägter Begriff. Bezog sich auf das Osmanische Reich, das ständig Krisenerscheinungen zeigte und letztendlich an seiner Reformunfähigkeit unterging.
Küçük Kaynarca	1774 geschlossener Vertrag, der den russisch-osmanischen Krieg von 1768-74 beendete.
Magyaren (ung.)	Eigenbezeichnung der Ungarn
Megali idea (griech.)	"Große Idee"; maximale Territorialforderung der griechischen Nationalisten im 19. Jahrhundert mit dem Ziel der Wiederherstellung der byzantinischen Grenzen.
Millet	Selbstverwaltungsstatus der nicht muslimischen Religionsgemeinschaften im Osmanischen Reich.
Mustafa Kemal (1881-1938)	Gründer und erster Staatspräsident der Türkei. Erhielt 1934 den Ehrennamen "Atatürk" (Vater der Türken). Aktivitäten in der jungtürkischen Bewegung.
Mittelmächte	Kriegsbündnis zwischen dem Deutschen Reich, Österreich-Ungarn, dem Osmanischen Reich und Bulgarien im Ersten Weltkrieg. Ihre Gegner waren in der Entente zusammengeschlossen.
Osmanismus	Idee im Osmanischen Reich, welche die Gleichheit aller Bürger des Reiches vor dem Gesetz, ungeachtet der ethnischen oder religiösen Zugehörigkeit, vorsah.
Pascha, Paşa (türk.)	Titel der höchsten Beamten und Militärs im Osmanischen Reich.

Philhellenismus	Bewegung, welche aus der Verherrlichung des antiken Griechenland und des Kampfes für die Unabhängigkeit vom Osmanischen Reich entstand.
PKK	Abkürzung für *Partiya Karkerên Kurdistan* (Arbeiterpartei Kurdistans). 1978 im Südosten der Türkei gegründete Guerillaorganisation, die 1984 mit dem Ziel eines unabhängigen kurdischen Staates den bewaffneten Kampf gegen die Türkei aufnahm. Inzwischen tritt die PKK für einen Autonomiestatus innerhalb der Türkei ein.
Puszta	Steppe in Ungarn
Sandžak	"Fahne". Bezeichnung einer Verwaltungseinheit im Osmanischen Reich, wie beispielsweise der Sandžak Novi Pazar auf dem Balkan.
Sepharden	Juden, die auf der Iberischen Halbinsel lebten und Ende des 15. Jahrhunderts, nach Abschluss der Reconquista Spaniens, vertrieben wurden. Flohen zum größten Teil in das Osmanische Reich.
Smyrna	s. Izmir
St. Veitstag	s. Amselfeld
Talat Pascha	Führender Kopf der *İttihat ve Terakki Cemiyeti*. Einer der Hauptverantwortlichen für den Völkermord an den Armeniern 1915.
Tanzimat	Reformperiode im Osmanischen Reich in der Mitte des 19. Jahrhunderts.
Tertiär	Geologischer Zeitabschnitt der Erdneuzeit; vor ca. 65 bis ca. 2 Millionen Jahren.
Transhumanz	Saisonal bedingte halbnomadische Fernweidewirtschaft.
Venezianische Republik	Vom 7./8. Jahrhundert bis 1797 Wirtschaftsmacht mit zeitweise stärkster Seemacht des Mittelmeeres. Besetzung während des Italienfeldzugs Napoleons am 13.05.1979 und Zuteilung an Österreich.
Vidovdan	s. St. Veitstag
Vilayet	Größerer Herrschaftsbereich (Provinz) im Osmanischen Reich.

Ergänzt durch:

- Hatschikjan, Magarditsch/Troebst, Stefan [Hrsg.]: Südosteuropa. Gesellschaft, Politik, Wirtschaft, Kultur. Ein Handbuch, München, 1999, S. 551f.
- Weithmann, Michael W. [Hrsg.]: Der ruhelose Balkan. Die Konfliktregionen Südosteuropas, München, 1993, S. 313ff.

1. Einleitung

"The collapse of the Ottoman Empire at the onset of the twentieth century provided the backdrop for a hundred years of genocide and ethnic cleansing in southeastern Europe and Anatolia."[1] (Norman Naimark)

Nach dem Ende des Zweiten Weltkrieges erlebte Europa eine lange Phase des Friedens, die mit dem Zusammenbruch der Sowjetunion endete. Der Südosten Europas verwandelte sich in einen Schauplatz kriegerischer Auseinandersetzungen.

Die Bürgerkriege im ehemaligen Jugoslawien lenkten die Blicke der Öffentlichkeit auf diese Region. Begriffe wie *ethnische Säuberung* oder *Zwangsumsiedlung* hielten Einzug in den allgemeinen Sprachgebrauch. Ziel der Konfliktparteien war nämlich die Errichtung ethnisch-homogener Nationalstaaten. Ganze Landstriche wurden von Menschen anderer Sprachen, Konfessionen und Kulturen 'gesäubert' – dabei ist Vielfalt in jederlei Hinsicht gerade für diesen Raum charakteristisch.

In der gesellschaftspolitischen Debatte ist es fast schon selbstverständlich geworden, die gegenwärtigen Konflikte als Folge historischer Ereignisse zu sehen. Doch sind die Informationsdefizite, die den öffentlichen Diskurs bestimmen, offenkundig.

Der Hass der Völker sei tief verwurzelt und würde immer wieder zum Vorschein treten – ein Hass, der sich quer durch die Halbinsel entlang der hellenischen und lateinischen Welt und später der Konfessionsgrenze ziehe. Samuel Huntington prophezeite in diesem Zusammenhang sogar einen *Zusammenprall der Zivilisationen*[2].

---

[1] Naimark, Norman: Fires of Hatred. Ethnic Cleansing in Twentieth-Century Europa, Cambridge, 2001, S. 17.
[2] Huntington, Samuel Phillips: The Clash of Civilizations and the Remaking of World Order, New York, 1998.

Das *lange 19. Jahrhundert*, wie Eric Hobsbawm die Zeit von 1789 bis 1914 bezeichnete, war in der Tat äußerst konfliktreich – eine Zeit großer Veränderungsprozesse. Industrialisierung, Säkularisierung, Entwicklung der bürgerlichen Gesellschaft und besonders die Nationenbildung waren Kennzeichen dieser Periode. Für Südosteuropa war zur Wende vom 18. zum 19. Jahrhundert in erster Linie die Nationenbildung ein entscheidender Faktor. Über Jahrhunderte war es zwischen dem Reich der Romanows, der Habsburger Monarchie und dem Osmanischen Reich aufgeteilt. Diese Mächte waren jedoch nicht in der Lage, die ethnische und kulturelle Vielfalt der Region zusammenzuhalten, so dass diese Vielvölkerstaaten mit ihren feudalen oder halbfeudalen und stark autoritären Herrschaftsstrukturen nach und nach zusammenbrachen.

Vor allem dem Zusammenbruch des Osmanischen Reiches folgte ein Wettstreit um die Aufteilung seiner ehemaligen Gebiete. Neue Nationen formierten sich, neue Staaten entstanden. Die Neuordnung der ehemals osmanischen Gebiete auf europäischem Boden scheint noch heute nicht abgeschlossen zu sein.

Die verschiedenen kriegerischen Auseinandersetzungen, welche die Region über die Jahrhunderte erschütterten, mündeten in Friedensverträgen, die neue Grenzen festlegten. Die neuen Grenzziehungen waren für die beteiligten Konfliktparteien jedoch nie zufriedenstellend, so dass jede Grenzveränderung eine Forderung nach Revision oder Korrektur mit sich brachte. Die Grenzpolitik wirkte sich gravierend auf die ethnische und kulturelle Zusammensetzung der einzelnen Staaten aus. Aus Mehrheiten wurden Minderheiten – und umgekehrt. Minderheiten galten in den neugestalteten Staaten als Störfaktor für den inneren und äußeren Frieden und die Sicherheitspolitik. Das Resultat waren ethnische Säuberungen ganzer Regionen in Form von Zwangsumsiedlungen, Vertreibung und Flucht. Daneben gibt es eine Reihe von Beispielen für systematische Deportationen ganzer Bevölkerungsgruppen, die oft in Völkermorden endeten. Um solche Exzesse zu vermeiden, wurden vertraglich geregelte gegenseitige Bevölkerungstransfers zwischen den Konfliktparteien vorgeschlagen. Der mit dem Lausanner Vertrag festgeschriebene Bevölkerungsaustausch zwischen Griechenland und der Türkei ist der erste prominente Fall für einen völkerrechtlich legitimierten Austausch und galt lange Zeit als Präzedenzfall in der internationalen Politik.

Diese Studie setzt sich mit der Neuordnung des südosteuropäischen Raumes vom 19. Jahrhundert bis zur Mitte des 20. Jahrhunderts und den damit einhergehenden Konsequenzen für die betroffenen Menschen auseinander. In vier Kapitel gegliedert, beginnt sie mit einem allgemeinen geographischen Überblick, in dem unter anderem definiert wird, was unter dem Begriff Südosteuropa zu verstehen ist. Im zweiten Teil werden die historischen Grenzveränderungen dargestellt. Zunächst wird auf die drei Vielvölkerstaaten, die über den südosteuropäischen Raum herrschten, eingegangen, um anschließend die Entwicklung des Raumes vom Berliner Kongress über Sèvres nach Lausanne aufzuzeigen, die gerne mit dem Begriff *Balkanisierung* umschrieben wird. Im Vordergrund der Ausführungen steht die sich in kürzester Zeit mehrmals verändernde Landkarte der Region. Das darauffolgende Kapitel beschäftigt sich mit der Bewertung der Verträge von Sèvres und Lausanne im türkischsprachigen Diskurs[3]. Im Anschluss wird die Problematik der Minderheiten beleuchtet. Neben definitorischen Grundlagen und der Wanderungsbilanz für Südosteuropa werden an zwei ausgewählten Beispielen die praktischen Auswirkungen der ethnischen Homogenisierungspolitik diskutiert. Ziel dieser Studie ist es, die Aufteilung und Neuordnung der ehemals osmanischen Gebiete darzustellen und der Frage nachzugehen, welche Folgen dies für die Landkarte, Politik und Ethnien der Region hatte. Anschließend wird hinterfragt werden, ob vertraglich geregelte Bevölkerungstransfers die ethnischen Konflikte, die vermeintlich aus den neuen Grenzziehungen resultieren, hätten verhindern können.

---

[3] Dabei muss an dieser Stelle insbesondere auf eine textnahe Übersetzung der türkischen Quellen hingewiesen werden.

2. Südosteuropa – Heterogenität eines Raumes

2.1. Der Terminus *Südosteuropa*

Noch immer besteht kein tragfähiger Konsens über die Definition des Begriffes Südosteuropa im wissenschaftlichen Diskurs. Je nach Fachrichtung oder auch Nationalität des jeweiligen Wissenschaftlers sind inhaltliche oder geographische Umschreibungen dessen, was unter Südosteuropa zu verstehen sei, unterschiedlich. Selbst die Benennung der Region divergiert zwischen *Südosteuropa*, *Balkan*, *Balkanhalbinsel* oder, wie unter anderem Karl Kaser diese Region umschreibt, *südöstliches Europa*. Kaser rechtfertigt seine Definition durch das Fehlen einer *südosteuropäischen Geschichte* als solche – nach historisch-anthropologischer Perspektive besäße der Südosteuropa-Begriff keine klar definierten oder definierbaren Grenzen und der Raum stelle, mit Ausnahme bestimmter Epochen, keine Geschehenseinheit dar. Da der Begriff *südöstliches Europa* keine Definition und Abgrenzung erfordere, bevorzugt Kaser diese Begrifflichkeit. Er lehnt oben genannte Definitionen grundsätzlich ab, da diese nicht zwingend notwendig seien sowie den Anschein erweckten, es gäbe eine gesamteuropäische Geschichte mit jeweiligen Unterabteilungen. Ebenso sinnlos sei es, einen "geographischen Rahmen festzulegen und diesen mit historischen Daten aufzufüllen – dem Auffüllen eines Swimming-Pools ähnlich. Historische Verläufe, Prozesse und Kulturen im südöstlichen Europa waren gewöhnlich entweder klein- oder großräumiger als der Umfang dieses Swimming-Pools."[4] Grenzdefinitionen verleiten nach Kaser ebenfalls dazu, diese als Kulturgrenzen zu akzeptieren, jedoch zeigt die historisch-anthropologische Perspektive, dass eine Kultur von benachbarten Kulturen bereichert wird – durch die Globalisierung trifft dies inzwischen noch sehr viel stärker zu. Zusammengefasst ist es nach Kaser nicht sinnvoll, "von einem Konzept der 'Geschichte Südosteuropas' auszugehen,

---

[4] Kaser, Karl: Südosteuropäische Geschichte und Geschichtswissenschaft, 2. Aufl., Wien, 2002, S. 23.

sondern von einem, das den Aspekt betont, europäische Geschichte im südöstlichen Europa erforschen zu wollen"[5].

Konrad Clewing und Oliver Jens Schmitt beschreiben die Region als einen historischen Raum, der als Geschehenseinheit aufgefasst werde, jedoch keine starren Grenzen besitze, die über Zeiten hinweg unverrückt bestünden. Daher gehen sie von breiten Übergangszonen zu benachbarten Kulturlandschaften aus, "ob nun im Nordwesten in Richtung des deutschsprachigen Mitteleuropa, im Nordosten in den west- und ostslawischen Raum, im Westen in den italienisch geprägten Bereich der Adria und im Südosten nach Vorderasien"[6]. Einzig zu den Meeren hin besitze der Raum feste Grenzen – im Westen zur Adria und dem Ionischen Meer, im Osten zum Schwarzen Meer, im Süden zur Ägäis.

Eine rein geographische Begriffsdefinition wäre sicherlich möglich, indem zu den Meeren im Westen, Süden und Osten natürliche Grenzen nach Norden hin, etwa Gewässer oder Gebirge, festgelegt würden. Eine solche Definition blendet jedoch einen entscheidenden Faktor aus: den Menschen. Geographie und historische Geschehen stehen in enger Beziehung zueinander.

> "Beide Disziplinen behandeln – mit unterschiedlichen Methoden und Intentionen – denselben Gegenstand: Mensch in Zeit und Raum. Während die einen immer wieder dazu tendieren, den Raum ohne die Menschen, verfallen die anderen dazu, die Menschen ohne den Raum zu sehen."[7]

Die menschliche Gesellschaft ist ein Produkt vieler Faktoren, weshalb es notwendig ist, die Gesamtheit von Wirkungen zu erfassen. In der zweiten Hälfte des letzten Jahrhunderts ging man von einem einfachen geographischen Determinismus aus, der die Menschen zu passiven Anpassungsprodukten an geographische Konstanten degradierte. Heute liegen uns elaborierte Erklärungsmodelle und Studien vor, die zeigen, dass die Wechselbeziehungen äußerst komplex und kontextbezogen sind.[8] Dies ist auch Grund dafür,

---

[5] Ebd., S. 23.
[6] Clewing, Konrad/Schmitt, Oliver Jens: Südosteuropa: Raum und Geschichte, in: Clewing, Konrad/Schmitt, Oliver Jens [Hrsg.]: Geschichte Südosteuropas. Vom frühen Mittelalter bis zur Gegenwart, Regensburg, 2011, S. 2.
[7] Kaser, Karl: Südosteuropäische Geschichte und Geschichtswissenschaft, 2. Aufl., Wien, 2002, S. 26.
[8] Vgl.: Ebd., S. 26.

weshalb "Raumbegriffe, so betont der Forschungszweig, der sich mit ihrem Konstruktcharakter und oft auch deren Dekonstruktion beschäftigt, [...] nicht ewig und überzeitlich gültig, also nicht naturgegeben, sondern von Menschen gemacht"[9] sind. So wechselte sich die Darstellung Russlands aus westeuropäischer Sicht vom *europäischen Norden* im 18. Jahrhundert zum Zarenreich im *Osten* im 19. Jahrhundert. Nach 1945 wurden im westlichen Europa schließlich alle Länder der Sowjetunion als Osten wahrgenommen, selbst jene, die historisch nur geringe Anbindung an den ostslawischen Raum besaßen und sich eher in Mittel- oder Zentraleuropa verorteten, wie zum Beispiel Ungarn oder die Tschechoslowakei.[10] Während Wien, die Hauptstadt Österreichs, im Kalten Krieg zum Westen und Prag, die Hauptstadt der Tschechoslowakei, als zum Osten gehörig empfunden wurde, zeigt ein Blick auf die Landkarte, dass Wien östlicher als Prag liegt.

Raumentwürfe für jene Region liegen schon seit dem Altertum vor. Unter dem Einfluss der antiken Geographen fassten die Byzantiner und Gelehrten des Mittelalters den Raum bereits im 6. Jahrhundert als einheitliche Halbinsel zwischen Adria und dem Schwarzen Meer auf. Im Norden wurde die Region, aus dieser Sicht, durch die Donau abgegrenzt. Man war von der Bifurkation der Donau überzeugt und glaubte, die Donau münde neben dem Schwarzen Meer auch in die Adria. Obwohl Skymnos, ein Geograph der Insel Chios, bereits in der Mitte des 2. Jahrhunderts vor unserer Zeitrechnung an dieser Auffassung zweifelte, blieben richtige und falsche Vorstellungen mehrere Jahrhunderte nebeneinander bestehen. Sehr viel länger überdauerte der Irrtum des antiken Geographen Strabon, der glaubte, dass sich der *Haimos*, das ist der antike Name des heutigen Balkans, vom Schwarzen Meer beginnend ununterbrochen bis zur Adria erstreckt. Römische Geographen konnten diesen Irrtum nicht beseitigen und byzantinische Geographen übernahmen diesen Fehler, ohne in Zweifel zu geraten.[11] Die Überzeugung, die sogenannte *Catena Mundi* ziehe durch die ganze Halbinsel, um sie nach Nor-

---

[9] Clewing, Konrad/Schmitt, Oliver Jens: Südosteuropa: Raum und Geschichte, in: Clewing, Konrad/Schmitt, Oliver Jens [Hrsg.]: Geschichte Südosteuropas. Vom frühen Mittelalter bis zur Gegenwart, Regensburg, 2011, S. 7.
[10] Vgl.: Ebd., S. 7.
[11] Vgl.: Kaser, Karl: Südosteuropäische Geschichte und Geschichtswissenschaft, 2. Aufl., Wien, 2002, S. 20f.

den abzuriegeln, verstärkte den Irrtum der Vorstellung einer geographischen Einheit. Verwendet wurden daher Bezeichnungen wie *Haimos-* oder *Haemushalbinsel*[12] oder *Hellenische* oder *Griechische Halbinsel*. Daneben tauchen auch die Bezeichnungen *Byzantinische Halbinsel, Römische Halbinsel* oder *Illyrer Halbinsel* auf. Letzterer, weil lange Zeit der Glaube vorherrschte, dass es sich bei den Bewohnern der Halbinsel um direkte Nachfahren der Illyrer handelte.

In den folgenden Jahrhunderten gehörten *Europäische Türkei* und *Europäisches Osmanisches Reich* zum Sprachrepertoire der Geographen.[13] Dass es sich bei Südosteuropa nicht um eine einheitliche Halbinsel handelte, widerlegte erst in der Mitte des 19. Jahrhunderts der aus Hessen stammende Gelehrte und Diplomat Johann Georg von Hahn.[14] Andere Autoren erwähnen hier auch den Namen des französischen Geographen Ami Boué, der an der vermeintlich vom Schwarzen Meer bis zur Adria verlaufenden Gebirgskette zweifelte.[15] Die Gebirgskette *Catena Mundi* war Jahrhunderte lang in Karten eingezeichnet und hatte sich tief in die Raumwahrnehmung in Europa eingegraben. Da bis in das 19. Jahrhundert hinein Reisen in das von den Osmanen beherrschte Südosteuropa kaum möglich und nur wenigen vorbehalten waren und die osmanischen Machthaber die Reiserouten bestimmten, blieben weite Teile der Region und ihrer morphologischen Strukturen unbekannt.[16] Mit Beginn des 19. Jahrhunderts dominierte bis zum Berliner Kongress im Jahre 1878 der Begriff *Europäische Türkei*, nachdem die Osmanen weite Teile Südosteuropas erobert hatten.

Heute finden wir die paradoxe Situation vor, dass die Halbinsel im Südosten Europas nach einem Gebirge benannt wird, das für die Topographie nicht prägend ist. "Die Bezeichnung beruht also auf einem Fehler, der vor über

---

[12] Vgl.: Clewing, Konrad/Schmitt, Oliver Jens: Südosteuropa: Raum und Geschichte, in: Clewing, Konrad/Schmitt, Oliver Jens [Hrsg.]: Geschichte Südosteuropas. Vom frühen Mittelalter bis zur Gegenwart, Regensburg, 2011, S. 8.

[13] Vgl.: Kaser, Karl: Südosteuropäische Geschichte und Geschichtswissenschaft, 2. Aufl., Wien, 2002, S. 19.

[14] Vgl.: Ebd., S. 8.

[15] Vgl.: Ebd., S. 21.

[16] Vgl.: Clewing, Konrad/Schmitt, Oliver Jens: Südosteuropa: Raum und Geschichte, in: Clewing, Konrad/Schmitt, Oliver Jens [Hrsg.]: Geschichte Südosteuropas. Vom frühen Mittelalter bis zur Gegenwart, Regensburg, 2011, S. 8.

zweitausend Jahren in die Welt gesetzt und bis in das neunzehnte Jahrhundert weitertradiert wurde."[17] Der aus dem türkischen stammende Begriff des Balkan-Gebirges wurde erstmals von dem Geographen August Zeune zu Beginn des 19. Jahrhunderts in seinem 'Versuch einer wissenschaftlichen Erdbeschreibung' verwendet.[18] In der zweiten Hälfte des Jahrhunderts setzte sich dieser Begriff endgültig durch. Diese Kontroverse zeigt, wie schwierig es ist, der Untersuchungsregion eindeutige Grenzen und Begriffe zuzuordnen.

Aus diesen Gründen umfasst diese Studie *Südosteuropa* als kulturgeographischen Begriff, ohne Natur- und Staatsgrenzen, dafür aber mit breiten Übergangszonen der Kulturlandschaften, im Kern die Territorien des heutigen Bulgariens, Griechenlands, Makedoniens, Albaniens, Serbiens, Bosnien und Herzegowinas, Montenegros und des Kosovos, die alle durch die Byzantinischen und Osmanischen Reiche geprägt worden sind. Hinzu kommen die historisch ähnlich geformten rumänischen Regionen wie die Walachei und Moldau als auch Peripherien, die ethnisch und kulturell enge Bindungen an die Kernregion aufweisen. Hierzu gehören die Grenzregionen des historischen Ungarns, somit Dalmatien, Kroatien, Slawonien, die Batschka, das Banat sowie Siebenbürgen, die von großer Bedeutung für die südosteuropäischen Zusammenhänge waren. Die heutige Türkei, als Nachfolgerin des Osmanischen Reiches, wird aufgrund ihres historischen Einflusses auf Südosteuropa nicht nur mit dem kleinen Teil bis zum Bosporus, sondern je nach Relevanz bis weit nach Ostanatolien hinein einbezogen.[19]

---

[17] Kaser, Karl: Südosteuropäische Geschichte und Geschichtswissenschaft, 2. Aufl., Wien, 2002, S. 21.

[18] Vgl.: Clewing, Konrad/Schmitt, Oliver Jens: Südosteuropa: Raum und Geschichte, in: Clewing, Konrad/Schmitt, Oliver Jens [Hrsg.]: Geschichte Südosteuropas. Vom frühen Mittelalter bis zur Gegenwart, Regensburg, 2011, S. 10.

[19] Nach Sundhausen haben die Dardanellen und der Bosporus Anatolien und den Balkan eher verbunden als getrennt. Vgl.: Sundhaussen, Holm: Die Wiederentdeckung des Raums, in: Südosteuropa. Von moderner Vielfalt und nationalstaatlicher Vereinheitlichung, München, 2005, S. 28.

2.2. Naturräumliche Betrachtung

Ein Blick auf die Landkarte zeigt, dass große Teile Südosteuropas gebirgig und schwer zugänglich und somit auch unbewohnbar und unkultivierbar sind.

> "Griechenland gilt zu vier Fünftel (!) als gebirgig, die Staaten des ehemaligen Jugoslawien zu zwei Drittel, ebenso Albanien. Albanien weist eine durchschnittliche Höhe von 708 Metern über dem Meeresspiegel auf, [...] das Doppelte des durchschnittlichen europäischen Niveaus. Bulgarien ist immerhin noch zur Hälfte gebirgig. Lediglich Rumänien und Ungarn werden nicht von Gebirgen dominiert."[20]

Rumänien hat einen Anteil von 30 Prozent an Gebirgen, während in Ungarn nur 2 Prozent des Staatsgebietes auf über 400 Metern Meereshöhe liegen. Ein weiteres Merkmal ist das zerstückelte Relief Südosteuropas. Ursache sind tektonische Vorgänge im Tertiär und Posttertiär.

> "So würde das große ungarische Becken erst in jüngster Tertiärperiode mit Sand, Lehm und Löß gefüllt [...]. Im südöstlichen Europa sind die tektonischen Bassins und Flussläufe klar von der gebirgigen Umgebung abgegrenzt. Solche größere und kleinere Bassins, die zugleich Oasen menschlichen Lebens und menschlicher Aktivitäten bilden, befinden sich mit Ausnahme der Rhodopen in allen Gebirgsmassiven der Region."[21]

Die geographischen Gegebenheiten der Halbinsel haben nicht minder zu den "divergierenden Tendenzen im Zusammenleben der Völker Südosteuropas [beigetragen.DOT], die sich durch die Jahrhunderte und bis in die unmittelbare Gegenwart hinein als stark und geschichtsmächtig erwiesen [...und...DOT] immer wieder den zentrifugalen Kräften einen mächtigen Auftrieb gegeben und Versuche zu großräumigeren Zusammenfassungen herrschaftlicher Gruppierungen erheblich erschwert"[22] haben. Das Dinarische Gebirge, als mächtigster Gebirgszug, durchzogen von Karst und somit äußerst siedlungsfeindlich, ragt schroff und mauerartig auf und trennt den schmalen Küstenstreifen der freundlichen Adria mit den kargen Hochregio-

---

[20] Kaser, Karl: Südosteuropäische Geschichte und Geschichtswissenschaft, 2. Aufl., Wien, 2002, S. 26.
[21] Ebd., S. 26f.
[22] Hösch, Edgar: Geschichte der Balkanländer. Von der Frühzeit bis zur Gegenwart, 5. Aufl., München, 2008, S. 17.

nen des Landesinneren und somit die mediterrane und kontinentale Welt. Mit Breiten von 180 bis 200 Kilometern zieht es sich von den Ausläufern der südlichen Alpen über Kroatien, Bosnien und Herzegowina, Montenegro und Westserbien bis nach Nordalbanien. Der Pindus-Gebirgszug in Nordgriechenland setzt das Dinarische Gebirge von der Meeresenge von Patras bis nach Peloponnes fort und teilt das nördliche griechische Festland in den Epiros im Westen und Thessalien im Osten. Das Rhodopen-Massiv, das Bulgarische Mittelgebirge und der Balkan in Nordbulgarien weisen eine Ost-West-Richtung auf. Das *Alte Gebirge*, die Stara Planina – "im geographischen Sinne – das eigentliche Balkan, [...] zieht sich vom Eisernen Tor über 600 Kilometer lang in einer Breite von 30 bis 50 Kilometern von West nach Ost quer durch Bulgarien, wo es sich am Kap Emine [...] ins Schwarze Meer senkt"[23]. Das Karpatengebirge schließlich führt bis nach Bratislava und umschließt Siebenbürgen mit einem ausgeprägten Bogen.

Diese Gebirgszüge dienten Jahrhunderte lang der Ziegen- und Schafzucht in unterschiedlichster Form. Entweder ähnlich der Alpwirtschaft, wo jedoch die Rinderzucht vorherrscht, oder in Form der Transhumanz, des Voll- und des Halbnomadismus. Besonders die Walachen und Sarakatsanen waren bekannt für die Weide- und Milchwirtschaft. Weiträumige Beckenlandschaften bzw. Ebenen gibt es nur wenige in der Region. Dementsprechend groß ist auch ihre Bedeutung. Das Pannonische Becken, als ausgedehnteste aller Ebenen, wird von der Donau und der Theiß durchflossen und hat eine Fläche von 100 000 km². "Ihre Landschaften sind das flache Alföld mit schwerem Boden und die steppenartige Puszta"[24] und werden zum größten Teil von Ungarn eingenommen. Die Banater Berge trennen das pannonische Tiefland vom Tiefland der Walachei. "Die Donau durchbricht hier beim Eisernen Tor eindrucksvoll das Bergland."[25]

Die Siebenbürgische Ebene ist für Rumänien gemeinsam mit der fruchtbaren Walachischen Ebene, einem weitläufigen Niederungsgebiet am Unterlauf der Donau, von ökonomischer Bedeutung und dient auch als Siedlungsgebiet. So

---

[23] Weithmann, Michael W.: Balkan-Chronik. 2000 Jahre zwischen Orient und Okzident, 3. Aufl., Regensburg, 2000, S. 23.
[24] Ebd., S. 16.
[25] Ebd., S. 17.

wurden auch kriegerische Auseinandersetzungen um die fruchtbaren Ebenen geführt, wie etwa der Dobrudscha-Ebene, südlich des Donaudeltas zwischen Bulgarien und Rumänien gelegen, deren Name vom Fürstengeschlecht der *Dobrotiçi* stammt, die im 14. Jahrhundert hier herrschten. In Bessarabien, zwischen Donau und Karpatenbogen, verläuft die Grenze zur osteuropäischen Steppe. Der Name Bessarabien geht ebenfalls auf ein rumänisches Fürstengeschlecht zurück, der *Bessarab*.[26]

Weitere Ebenen mit großer Bedeutung für die jeweiligen Anrainerstaaten sind das Sofioter Becken, die Thrakische Ebene sowie die Makedonische und Thessalische Ebene, die als Kornkammer Griechenlands gilt. Das südliche Alpenvorland mit den Landschaften Krain, der Untersteiermark und Kras, der Karst sind öde Kalkgebirge, durchsetzt mit Höhlen und Grotten. Im Südosten fällt zwischen der Save und Drau das Hochland ins tiefer gelegene Slawonien ab und zieht sich in die Ebene von Sirmien fort, die bis nach Belgrad reicht, wo Save und Donau zusammenfließen.[27] Gastarbeiterfamilien aus der Türkei werden bei den langen Fahrten von Deutschland in die Türkei zwischen Zagreb und Belgrad einen guten Eindruck dieser flachen und eintönigen Ebene erhalten haben.

> "Bosnien ist das von den Flüssen Bosna und Drina durchstoßene wilde Karstgebirge mit tiefen Schluchten und zerklüfteten Bergrücken. Eine in sich abgeschlossene Binnenlandschaft, die nur über die Täler der Herzegowina Zugang zum Meer hat [...]. Die Herzegowina ist gleichfalls ein öder, zerrissener Hochkarst, der aber von dem Fluss Neretva verkehrsgünstig zur Adria hin durchbrochen wird."[28]

Im Süden grenzt mit Montenegro eine weitaus dramatischere Bergwelt an. Wie ihr Name *Crna Gora*, also *Schwarze Berge*, schon schließen lässt, ist dieses Gebirge unfruchtbar und nur unter schwierigsten Bedingungen bewohnbar. Die kleinen Bergkantone sind nur über mühsame Pässe erreichbar. Dies sollte sich in Eroberungsfeldzügen aus West und Ost bemerkbar machen, wohingegen Belgrad im Osten an einer strategisch günstigen Position liegt und zu den wenigen Plätzen der Erde gehört, die sehr oft belagert worden sind.

---

[26] Vgl.: Ebd., S. 16.
[27] Vgl.: Ebd., S. 18.
[28] Ebd., S. 23f.

Die Landschaft des Sandžaks um Novi Pazar erinnert noch immer an die alte osmanische Verwaltungseinheit dieses Gebietes und bedeutet *Banner* oder *Fahne*.[29] Am südöstlichsten Zipfel Europas erheben sich die Rhodopen zu Hochgebirgshöhen und fallen im Süden zur Ägäis hin nach Thrakien ab. Das von der Sonne ausgebrannte und steinübersäte Ostthrakien ist Staatsgebiet der Türkei, der letzte Rest des Osmanischen Reiches auf europäischem Boden. Die Dardanellen und der Bosporus bilden schließlich die geographischen Grenzen nach Asien.[30] "Die Peripherien dessen, was wir als Südosteuropa bezeichnen, werden von Meer und Inseln gesäumt. Fünf Meere – das Schwarze, das Marmara-, das Adriatische, das Ionische und das Mittelmeer – begrenzen den Subkontinent im Westen, Süden und Südosten. Das größte von ihnen – das östliche Mittelmeer [...]. Den Küsten ist eine Reihe von Inseln und Inselgruppen vorgelagert. Die größeren Inseln – Korfu, Kreta und Zypern – sind sehr gebirgig"[31] und werden wie das Binnenland für Schaf- und Ziegenzucht genutzt. Auf kleineren Inseln, die weit in die Meere ragen, dominiert der Fischfang. Die vom mediterranen Klima geprägten Küstenregionen mit ihrer Vegetation und ihren Lebensmöglichkeiten waren bis in das 20. Jahrhundert von klassischen Produkten wie Oliven, Ölbäumen, Weizen und Wein abhängig.[32]

2.3. Anmerkungen zur Kulturgeographie

Die Umwelt gehört mit zu den Faktoren, die den Menschen und die Gesellschaft bestimmen. Sie bildet die Grundlage der Wirtschaft und prägt letztendlich mit der Interaktion zwischen Ökonomie und Geographie die Mentalität, Denkweise und das alltägliche Leben der Bewohner. Die naturräumliche Gliederung Südosteuropas erklärt einiges. Ein Blick in die Reliefkarte zeigt, dass sich die Physiognomie dieser Region sichtlich von jener des übrigen Europas abhebt. Fast jede Geländeart der Erde ist auf der Halbinsel vorzufinden – offene Küsten, weite Ebenen, trockene Steppen, Hoch- und Waldgebirge,

---

[29] Vgl.: Ebd., S. 20.
[30] Vgl.: Ebd., S. 16ff.
[31] Kaser, Karl: Raum und Besiedlung, in: Hatschikjan, Magarditsch/Troebst, Stefan [Hrsg.]: Südosteuropa. Gesellschaft, Politik, Wirtschaft, Kultur. Ein Handbuch, München, 1999, S. 63.
[32] Vgl.: Ebd., S. 61ff.

breite Tallandschaften, fruchtbare Niederungen und enge Hochtäler. Trotzdem bleiben die lebensunfreundlichen Gebirge dominant und sorgen auf kürzeste Entfernungen für starke Klima- und Vegetationswechsel. Pittoreske Landschaftsformen sind hier auf einem kleinen geographischen Raum geballt. Es fällt schwer, in dieser Wirrnis von Gebirgsketten eine Einheit zu finden.

> "Die Erdoberfläche ist aufgegliedert, wechselt abrupt vom Küstenland ins Hochgebirge, fächert sich auf in einsame Hochlandschaften, die sich wieder in kleine und kleinste Täler aufsplittern, oder sie senkt sich hinab in fruchtbare Talkessel und Flußläufe, und geht dann über in unwirtliche Gebirgsstöcke."[33]

Diese Zersplitterung machte seit jeher größere Reichs- oder Staatsformen für längere Zeiten kaum möglich. Ebenso ließ sie keine Vorherrschaft eines einzelnen Volks zu. Die ineinander verschachtelten Bergketten wirkten nicht nur als räumliche Barrieren, sondern versperrten den Blick auf das Ganze und die gemeinsame Sache. Noch heute unterbrechen strenge Winter die Landverbindungen vieler Regionen – so waren die Völker immer wieder auf abgeschlossene Siedlungsräume angewiesen.

Die Morphologie der Halbinsel verhinderte den Zusammenschluss benachbarter Regionen und somit auch überregionale Herrschaften.

> "Dem geographisch uneinheitlichen vorwiegend gebirgigen Charakter Südosteuropas, den völlig verschiedenen Klima-, Vegetations-, Kultur- und Wirtschaftsgebieten, entspricht der ausgeprägte Partikularismus, die 'Vereinzelung' und der übersteigerte Souveränitätsanspruch seiner Bewohner [...]. Früher äußerte sich das in stammesmäßiger Hinsicht, dann in verschiedenen Konfessionen, in der Neuzeit und der Moderne in der Nationsbildung und in höchst unsicheren Staatsgründungen."[34]

Das Leben der Bevölkerung war bescheiden. Um die wenigen fruchtbaren Äcker- und Weideflächen der Ebenen wurden Kämpfe geführt. Der Durchzug unterschiedlicher Völker und wechselnde Herrscher führten zu hohen Steuerabgaben. Überflutungen der Tallandschaften und Schwemmlandebenen stellten mit der dazugehörigen Malaria-Krankheit eine weitere Bedrohung

---

[33] Weithmann, Michael W.: Balkan-Chronik. 2000 Jahre zwischen Orient und Okzident, 3. Aufl., Regensburg, 2000, S. 13.
[34] Ebd., S. 13.

dar. In den Bergen herrschte zwar eine Brise von Freiheit, jedoch sank dementsprechend auch die Lebensqualität. Wirtschaftliche Grundlage bildeten hier die Viehzucht und das Wanderhirtentum in Form der Transhumanz, dem halbjährlichen Weideflächenwechsel zwischen Gebirge und Tal.

Obwohl West- und Mitteleuropa und der Nahe Osten im Frühmittelalter durch den Übergang in der Landwirtschaft zur Zweifelderwirtschaft mit Fruchtwechsel einen starken Bevölkerungswachstum verzeichnen konnten, blieb die Bevölkerungsdichte in Südosteuropa immer gering. Selbst die Industrialisierung konnte keinen Wandel herbeiführen. Kriegerische Auseinandersetzungen entvölkerten zusätzlich noch weitere Gebiete. Zur ungünstigen Geografie kamen noch Einwanderungswellen und Eroberungszüge, die im Laufe der Geschichte die unterschiedlichsten Völker, Religionen, Sprachen und Kulturen mit sich brachten. Und dennoch muss beachtet werden, dass Südosteuropa "eine ausgesprochene Zwischenlage ein[nimmt.DOT]: Eingebettet, oder besser 'eingekeilt', zwischen Europa und Asien im weitesten Sinne, – zwischen Kontinentaleuropa und dem Nahen Osten. In diesen Großräumen – [...man kann.DOT] sie auch Abendland (Okzident) und Morgenland (Orient) nennen – gab es von alters her mächtige Großreichbildungen, die ihren Einfluß auf die südosteuropäische Randzone geltend machten: im Westen das Heilige Römische Reich Deutscher Nationen, später das Habsburgerreich, im Osten Byzanz und dann das Osmanische Reich [...], [in den letzten Jahrhunderten gesellte sich auch noch das Reich der Romanovs aus dem Norden hinzu.DOT]. Das bedeutete für Jahrhunderte: Feldzüge, Erpressung, Flucht, Umsiedlung und wechselnde Unterwerfung."[35] Diese gemeinsamen historischen Erfahrungen Südosteuropas, Fremdherrschaft und Unterwerfung, unabhängig davon ob diese aus dem Westen oder Osten kam, ließ ein Bewusstsein der nationalen Existenzangst entstehen, die in eine nationale Selbstüberhöhung mit allen Folgen mündete. Gleichzeitig fungierte der Raum aber auch als Brücke zwischen den alten Kulturräumen Europas und des Orients.

> "Orient und Okzident, Mittelmeerraum und Osteuropa, haben hier über tiefe eigene balkanische Wurzeln jeweils ihren Kulturfirnis gelegt [...]. Die unterschiedlichen Kultureinflüsse bilden aber auch die Grundlage für die tiefe konfessionelle

---

[35] Ebd., S. 15.

Teilung in katholische Christen, orthodoxe Christen und Muslims. Und hier verflüchtigt sich der Reiz der multikulturellen Gesellschaft und die gefährlichsten Lunten zum 'Pulverfaß Balkan' treten zutage."[36]

Zusammengefasst können wir also sagen, dass zwei Konstanten die Kulturgeographie Südosteuropas bestimmen: Großräumig die Lage zwischen Orient und Okzident und kleinräumig die verschiedene Landschaftsgliederung, welche die Isolation der Völker verstärkte.[37]

---

[36] Ebd., S. 15.
[37] Vgl.: Ebd., S. 13ff.

3. Die Geschichte Südosteuropas

3.1. Die Vielvölkerstaaten

3.1.1. Das Russische Reich

Die Geschichte des Russischen Reiches beginnt im Jahre 1552 mit dem Einmarsch der Truppen des Moskauer Zaren Ivan IV., dem Schrecklichen, in das Khanat von Kazan'. Hierfür lassen sich nach Andreas Kappeler folgende Gründe aufführen:

> "Mit der Eroberung des Khanats von Kazan' kam erstmals ein eigenständiger Herrschaftsverband mit einer historischen Tradition, einer dynastischen Legitimation und einer Oberschicht, die nicht nur eine andere Sprache sprach, sondern einer fremden Weltreligion und Hochkultur, dem Islam, angehörte, unter russische Herrschaft. Auf der anderen Seite verschleiert die traditionelle Datierung des Übergangs von einem ethnisch relativ geschlossenen zu einem polyethnischen Rußland, daß die Bevölkerung des Moskauer Staats und der anderen ostslawischen Fürstentümer schon seit jeher polyethnisch und multireligiös zusammengesetzt war, daß einige der Nationalitäten der ehemaligen Sowjetunion schon seit dem Mittelalter unter russischer Herrschaft standen."[38]

Jahrhundertelange Eroberung und Expansion ließen ein riesiges Vielvölkerreich entstehen, das sich durch eine große wirtschaftliche, soziale, administrative, aber auch ethnische, konfessionelle und kulturelle Vielfalt auszeichnete – die aufgrund der pragmatischen und administrativen Politik der Herrscher des Russischen Reiches erhalten blieb. Einzig die Loyalität zum Zaren durfte nicht gefährdet werden, andernfalls wurden militärische Mittel eingesetzt.

Die erste allgemeine Volkszählung wurde 1897 durchgeführt, so dass eine ethnische Gliederung für die Jahrhunderte zuvor nur approximativ erfassbar ist. Demnach lag nach Kappeler, der seine Auswertungen auf den sowjetischen Historiker V. M. Kabuzan stützt, der Anteil der Nichtrussen an der Ge-

---

[38] Kappeler, Andreas: Rußland als Vielvölkerreich. Entstehung – Geschichte – Zerfall, 2. Aufl., München, 2008, S. 19.

samtbevölkerung des Russischen Reiches Ende des 16. Jahrhunderts bei etwa 10 Prozent, wobei es sich hierbei hauptsächlich um die Tataren und übrigen Ethnien der mittleren Wolga und des Nordens handelte. Der Anteil der Russen durfte somit bei etwa 90 Prozent gelegen haben. Im folgenden Jahrhundert kamen Ukrainer, Weißrussen und die Ethnien Sibiriens hinzu. Der Anteil der Nichtrussen stieg auf knapp 30 Prozent im Jahre 1718/19. Bereits Ende des 18. Jahrhunderts stellten die Russen nur noch etwa 53 Prozent der auf 37 Millionen angewachsenen Gesamtbevölkerung. Weitere Gebietsveränderungen der nächsten Jahre verminderte die Zahl der Russen auf weniger als 50 Prozent im Jahre 1848.[39] Ähnliche Vielfalt zeigte sich bei der Konfession, jedoch überwog hier der Anteil der Christen mit etwa 91 Prozent der Gesamtbevölkerung im Jahre 1719 und 94 Prozent im Jahre 1815, innerhalb derer die Orthodoxie zahlenmäßig den größten Anteil stellte. Neben dem Judentum, dem Islam und dem Buddhismus befanden sich auch Angehörige von Naturreligionen im Reiche der Zaren.[40] Die Konfession war wichtiger als die Ethnie:

> "Seit dem Mittelalter diente die Abgrenzung von den ungläubigen Muslimen, Lateinern und Animisten als Faktor russischer Identität. Das Moskauer Reich war nach dem Fall Konstantinopels einziger Hort der Orthodoxie, und auch das verwestlichte Rußland des 18. Jahrhunderts konnte nicht auf die Orthodoxie als Integrationsideologie verzichten."[41]

Russland war somit eine Variante der Vielvölkerreiche Europas der Vormoderne, geprägt von einer strukturellen Heterogenität, in der ethnische Minderheiten das Staatsvolk zahlenmäßig dominierten, und einer Ambivalenz zwischen den alten asiatischen und neuen europäischen Traditionen.

Die Modernisierungen des 19. Jahrhunderts, insbesondere die Bauernbefreiung und die Industrialisierung, aber auch die soziale und nationale Mobilisierung veränderten den Charakter des Vielvölkerreiches. Hinzu kam die Expansion in den Kaukasus und nach Mittelasien, wodurch die Heterogenität des Reiches zusätzlich verstärkt wurde. Die ethnische Zusammensetzung des Russischen Reiches veränderte sich zu Ungunsten der Russen und Ostslawen.

---

[39] Vgl.: Ebd., S. 100ff.
[40] Vgl.: Ebd., S. 121f.
[41] Ebd., S. 135.

So sank der Anteil der Russen von etwa 53 Prozent im Jahre 1795 auf 44,3 Prozent im Jahre 1897, der Anteil der Ostslawen von 83 auf 66,8 Prozent. Mehr als die Hälfte der 125 Millionen waren somit nicht russisch.[42]

Die Orthodoxie, der 71 Prozent der Bevölkerung angehörten, blieb weiterhin einigende Kraft des Reiches. Die zweitgrößte Glaubensgemeinschaft waren von nun an nicht mehr die Römisch-Katholiken, sondern Muslime mit einem Anteil von 11 Prozent an der Gesamtbevölkerung, gefolgt von den Katholiken (9%), den Juden (5,4%), den Lutheranern (2,7%), den Angehörigen der Armenisch-Gregorianischen Kirche (0,9%), den buddhistischen Lamaisten (0,4%) und weiteren kleineren Religionsgemeinschaften.[43]

T 1: Ethnische Gruppen des Russischen Reiches (in den jeweiligen Grenzen)[44]

	1719		1897	
	in 1000	%	in 1000	%
Total	15 764,8	100,00	125 640,0	100,00
Russen	11 127,5	70,58	55 667,5	44,31
Ukrainer	2 025,8	12,85	22 380,6	17,81
Weißrussen	382,7	2,43	5 885,6	4,68
Ostslawen	**13 356,0**	**85,86**	**83 933,7**	**66,80**
Karelier	80,9	0,51	208,1	0,17
Ischoren	14,6	0,09	13,8	0,01
Wepsen	8,3	0,05	25,8	0,02
Lappen	1,5	0,01	1,8	0,00
Syrjänen	50,6	0,32	258,3	0,20
Samojeden	6,0	0,04	15,9	0,01
Norden	**161,9**	**1,03**	**523,7**	**0,42**
Wolgatataren	293,1	1,86	1 834,2	1,46
Tschuwaschen	217,9	1,38	843,8	0,67
Mordwinen	107,4	0,68	1 023,8	0,81
Tscheremissen	61,9	0,39	375,4	0,30
Wotjaken	48,1	0,31	420,8	0,33
Baschkiren	171,9	1,09	1 321,4	1,05
Teptjaren	22,6	0,14	117,8	0,09
Wolga/Ural	**922,9**	**5,85**	**5 937,2**	**4,73**

---

[42] Vgl.: Ebd, S. 233ff.
[43] Vgl.: Ebd., S. 234f.
[44] Aus: Ebd., S. 342ff.

Sibirische Tataren	15,3	0,10	50,0	0,04
Ostjaken	16,7	0,11	19,7	0,02
Wogulen	2,0	0,01	7,7	0,01
Chakassen u.a.	13,1	0,08	37,7	0,03
Schorzen			12,0	0,01
Altaier			40,0	0,03
Burjäten	47,8	0,30	288,7	0,23
Tungusen	17,7	0,11	65,5	0,05
Jakuten	35,2	0,22	227,4	0,18
Tschuktschen			11,8	0,01
Übrige	7,9	0,05	21,6	0,02
Sibirien	**155,7**	**0,99**	**782,1**	**0,62**
Kalmücken	200,0	1,27	190,6	0,15
Nogaier	113,6	0,72	64,1	0,05
Krimtataren			220,0	0,18
Steppe	**313,6**	**1,99**	**474,7**	**0,38**
Esten	309,2	1,96	1 002,7	0,80
Letten	162,2	1,03	1 435,3	1,14
Finnen	164,2	1,04	143,1	0,11
Schweden	8,0	0,05	14,2	0,01
Polen			7 931,3	6,31
Litauer			1 659,1	1,32
Juden			5 063,2	4,03
Rumänen (Moldauer)			1 121,7	0,89
Bulgaren			172,5	0,14
Gagausen			55,8	0,04
Westen	**643,6**	**4,08**	**18 598,9**	**14,81**
Georgier			1 352,5	1,08
Armenier			1 173,1	0,93
Aserbaidschaner			1 440	1,15
Kurden			99,9	0,08
Abchasen			72,1	0,06
Übrige			302,2	0,24
Transkaukasien			**4 439,8**	**3,53**

Tschetschenen			226,5	0,18
Awaren			212,7	0,17
Osseten			171,7	0,14
Lesgier			159,2	0,13
Kabardiner			98,6	0,08
Darginer			130,2	0,10
Kumyken			83,4	0,07
Inguschen			47,4	0,04
Laken + Tabasaranen			90,8	0,07
Tscherkessen			44,7	0,04
Karatschaier			27,2	0,02
Balkaren			27,1	0,02
Übrige			1,6	0,00
Kaukasus			**1 321,1**	**1,05**
Kasachen			3 881,8	3,09
Kirgisen			634,8	0,51
Usbeken			1 800	1,43
Tadschiken			350,4	0,28
Turkmenen			281,4	0,22
Karakalpaken			104,3	0,08
Uiguren			100	0,08
Übrige				
Mittelasien			**7 152,8**	**5,69**
Deutsche	31,1	0,20	1 790,5	1,43
Griechen			186,9	0,15
[Roma.DOT]			44,5	0,04
Koreaner			26,0	0,02
Übrige			334	0,27
Diaspora-Gruppen			**2 470,9**	**1,91**

3.1.2. Die Habsburger Monarchie Österreich-Ungarn

Aufgrund des Verlustes der Vorherrschaft in Deutschland sah sich die habsburgische Monarchie gezwungen, ab ca. 1850 ein Bündnis mit den Magyaren einzugehen. Dieser Österreichisch-Ungarische Ausgleich war das Werk des österreichischen Außenministers Graf Friedrich Ferdinand von Beust und der ungarischen Verhandler Ferenc Deák und Graf Gyula Andrássy. Der Ausgleich des Jahres 1867 machte aus der absolutistisch-zentralistischen Habsburgermonarchie einen Staat mit zwei weitgehend selbstständig regierten Teilen. Aus Transleithanien (Ungarn mit seinen Nebenländern) und Zisleithanien (die deutsch-slawischen Kronländer) entstand die Doppelmonarchie Österreich-Ungarn. Die neu geschaffene Ordnung des Dualismus sah vor, dass beide Monarchien selbstständig regierten und verwalteten, mit Ausnahme der gemeinsamen Angelegenheiten, die in die Zuständigkeit der drei gemeinsamen Ministerien Außenpolitik, Heerwesen und Finanzen fielen.

> "Die Einheit des dualistischen Reiches wurde durch den Herrscher gesichert, der in seiner Person 'zwei staatsrechtlich getrennte Funktionen – Kaiser von Österreich und König von Ungarn' – vereinigte."[45]

Die Habsburger Monarchie Österreich-Ungarn nahm den Südosten Mitteleuropas ein mit einer Nord-Süd-Ausdehnung von 1.050 km und einer West-Ost-Ausdehnung von 1.267 km.

> "Die Monarchie war nach Russland der zweigrößte Staat Europas [und stand hinsichtlich der Bevölkerungszahl. DOT] an dritter Stelle nach Russland und dem Deutschen Reich."[46]

Die Bevölkerung der Doppelmonarchie gliederte sich in die größeren Gruppen der Germanen, Magyaren, Nordslawen (Tschechen, Polen, Rutheken und Slowaken), Südslawen (Serben, Kroaten, Slowenen), Westromanen (Italiener, Ladiner und Friauler) und Ostromanen (Rumänen und Walachen). Die Doppelmonarchie war somit ein Vielvölkerstaat. Konfessionell war sie einheitlicher, da sich drei Viertel der Bevölkerung zur katholischen Kirche bekannte. Daneben waren vor allem Griechisch-Orthodoxe, Protestanten, Israeliten und Muslime in der Monarchie vertreten.[47]

Auf dem Berliner Kongress von 1878 erlangte Österreich-Ungarn die Zustimmung zur Besetzung und Verwaltung der türkischen Provinz Bosnien und Herzegowina und des Sandžaks Novipazar, welche 1908 schließlich komplett annektiert wurden. Die Serben empfanden dies als große Demütigung, die Europa noch teuer zu stehen kommen sollte: Den Auslöser des Ersten Weltkrieges lieferte die Reaktion auf diese Demütigung.

---

[45] Pesendorfer, Franz: Ungarn und Österreich – Tausend Jahre Partner oder Gegner, Wien, 1998, S. 190.
[46] Basch-Ritter, Renate: Österreich-Ungarn in Wort und Bild. Menschen und Länder, Graz, 1989, S. 336.
[47] Vgl.: Ebd., S. 338.

3.1.3. Das Osmanische Reich

Die Eroberung Konstantinopels 1453 durch die Truppen des Osmanischen Reiches führte zu einschneidenden Veränderungen in Südosteuropa. Dieses Reich, das ab dem 14. Jahrhundert immer größere Teile Südosteuropas eroberte und zeitweise den größten Teil der Halbinsel kontrollierte, brachte eine neue Religion und neue ethnische Gruppen mit sich. Die Großmacht, die über den Vorderen Orient bis nach Nordafrika reichte, machte Wanderungsbewegungen aus Asien und Afrika möglich, der keine Grenzen gesetzt waren. Für Michael Weithmann ist dies neben dem Wechsel eines beträchtlichen Anteils der einheimischen Balkanbevölkerung zur Religion der Eroberermacht mit ein Grund für das heutige "problematische Durcheinandersiedeln verschiedener Ethnien auf kleinem Raum"[48].

Eine wichtige Ethnie, die mit der Ausbreitung der osmanischen Herrschaft in Südosteuropa nach Europa kam, waren die Türken. Der Begriff *Türke* wird fälschlicherweise sehr gerne als Synonym für *Osmane* gebraucht und sollte daher klar differenziert werden. Türken sind Teil der Turkvölker Zentralasiens, wie Usbeken, Turkmenen, Kirgisen, Bachkiren oder Tataren. Bei den *Osmanen* handelt es sich vielmehr um eine Führungselite, die sich aus türkischen und nicht türkischen Angehörigen zusammensetzte[49]. Ursprünglich entstammen diese Völker dem östlichen Zentralasien. So gilt das Gebiet um den Baikalsee als die Urheimat der Turkvölker.[50] Erstmals erwähnt werden die T'u-küe, die Türken, in chinesischen Annalen des Jahres 552 nach unserer Zeitrechnung, als das vermutlich erste Staatswesen dieses Volkes in Form eines Verbandes von Nomadenstämmen gegründet wurde.[51] Das Reich zerfiel jedoch sehr schnell wieder. In den folgenden Jahrhunderten wanderten türkische Stammesverbände in verschiedenste Richtungen ab. Zu den westwärts wandernden Stammesverbänden gehörten die Oghusen. Von diesen spaltete sich im 10. Jahrhundert ein Stamm unter der Führung Selçuks ab

---

[48] Weithmann, Michael W.: Der Balkan zwischen Ost und West, in: Weithmann, Michael W. [Hrsg.]: Der ruhelose Balkan. Die Konfliktregionen Südosteuropas, München, 1993, S. 12.
[49] Vgl.: Kaser, Karl: Raum und Besiedlung, in: Hatschikjan, Magarditsch/Troebst, Stefan [Hrsg.]: Südosteuropa. Gesellschaft, Politik, Wirtschaft, Kultur. Ein Handbuch, München, 1999, S. 64.
[50] Vgl.: Ebd., S. 64.
[51] Vgl.: Matuz, Josef: Das Osmanische Reich. Grundlinien seiner Geschichte, 2. Aufl., Darmstadt, 1990, S. 9.

und trat dem Islam bei. Bereits in der Mitte des 11. Jahrhunderts gelang es ihnen, ihre Truppen soweit zu stärken, dass sie der byzantinischen Armee im Jahre 1071 in Malazgirt eine herbe Niederlage verpassen konnten und anschließend die Besiedlung Anatoliens einleiteten. Es folgte eine Zeit des Aufstiegs und Zerfalls mehrerer Großreiche. Einem Stammesfürstentum unter dem Anführer Osman, nach dem das Reich später benannt werden sollte, gelang es um 1300 jedoch, sich im Nordwesten Kleinasiens, vor den Toren des Byzantinischen Reiches, zu formieren und seine Grenzen rasch zu erweitern. Innerhalb weniger Jahrzehnte erlangte dieses Fürstentum die Kontrolle über weite Teile Anatoliens. Nach der Eroberung Konstantinopels erreichte das Osmanische Reich schließlich eine Großmachtstellung in Europa und stand erstmals vor den Toren der habsburgischen Residenzstadt Wien. Bis zu seinem Zerfall in den ersten beiden Jahrzehnten des 20. Jahrhunderts hinterließ es ethnisch unterschiedliche als auch muslimische Bevölkerungsteile in weiten Teilen Südosteuropas.

Die Osmanen legten keinen Wert auf erzwungene Konvertierung der nicht muslimischen, insbesondere der christlichen Bevölkerungsgruppen. Die administrative Gliederung des Osmanischen Reiches sah das sogenannte Millet-System vor:

> "[E]in System von Selbstverwaltungskörperschaften auf religiös-ethnischer Grundlage [...]. Christen, Armenier, Juden und Muslime waren in diesem System organisiert. Dies hatte im Wesentlichen zweierlei Auswirkungen. Einerseits blieben auf diese Weise die ethnischen und religiösen Identitäten erhalten – eine Grundlage für die nationalen Befreiungsbewegungen im 19. und 20. Jahrhundert. Andererseits waren die nicht-muslimischen Millets benachteiligt; die wesentlichen ökonomischen und finanziellen Ressourcen blieben somit auf die muslimische Elite konzentriert."[52]

Somit konnten Nichtmuslime im Allgemeinen kein Land erwerben, ebenso war ein Aufstieg im Staatsdienst nicht möglich. Auch wenn die nicht muslimische Bevölkerung nicht verfolgt wurde, war sie bis zu den Reformgesetzen des 19. Jahrhunderts benachteiligt. Ein Wechsel der Religion konnte daher zwar sinnvoll sein, war jedoch nicht zwingend notwendig. Die überwiegende

---

[52] Kaser, Karl: Raum und Besiedlung, in: Hatschikjan, Magarditsch/Troebst, Stefan [Hrsg.]: Südosteuropa. Gesellschaft, Politik, Wirtschaft, Kultur. Ein Handbuch, München, 1999, S. 65.

Mehrheit der einheimischen Bevölkerung blieb bei ihrer Religion. Eine Ausnahme bildete die bosnische und albanische Bevölkerung, deren Islamisierungsgrad relativ hoch war. Schlüssige Argumente gibt es hierfür nicht[53].

Die *Knabenlese*, das heißt, die Rekrutierung und Zwangskonvertierung nicht muslimischer Kinder für die Armee und Administration, bildete eine Ausnahme in der Konvertierungspolitik der Osmanen. Nach Kaser kann "von einer geplanten Bevölkerungspolitik im Sinne einer organisierten Ansiedlung von türkischen Familien in Südosteuropa kaum die Rede sein. Dennoch kam es sowohl zu türkischen Ansiedlungen wie auch zu Glaubensübertritten."[54] Allerdings sind diese Aussagen mit Vorsicht zu genießen. Auch wenn eine große Mehrheit der Forscher mit Kasers Argumentationen übereinstimmt, gibt es auch kritische Stimmen, die nicht weniger schlüssig argumentieren und das System des Osmanischen Reiches auf das Heftigste kritisieren. Zu ihnen gehören Ivan Pǎrvev, der für die Balkanchristen während der Osmanenherrschaft eine negative Bilanz zieht[55], oder Gustav Edmund von Grunebaum, der eine Zweitrangigkeit der Minoritäten konstatiert, die "ihre Sicherheit um den Preis der Geschichtslosigkeit"[56] erworben hätten. Das Millet-System mag zwar verhältnismäßig gerecht erscheinen, jedoch darf nicht vergessen werden, dass diese Gerechtigkeit auf einer Ungerechtigkeit aufgebaut war, schließlich wurden diese religiösen und ethnischen Gruppen von einer fremden Macht beherrscht. So kann das Millet-System insgesamt als *Unabhängigkeit in einer Abhängigkeit* beschrieben werden. Selbst die Einteilung in die Millets, die bis in das 19. Jahrhundert nur die jüdische, armenische und griechische Glaubensgemeinschaft anerkannte, gestaltete sich problematisch; Sprachen, religiöse Inhalte oder Theologien spielten im Millet-System keine Rolle, was dazu beitrug, dass Unterscheidungen zwischen Ethnien und Konfessionen nach dem Zerfall des Reiches unklar waren. Folge waren blutige Konflikte bei den Nationalisierungsprozessen.

---

[53] Vgl.: Ebd., S. 65f.
[54] Ebd., S. 65.
[55] Vgl.: Pǎrvev, Ivan: Osmanische Traditionen auf dem Balkan vom 14. bis zum 19. Jahrhundert, in: Heuberger, Valeria/Suppan, Arnold/Vyslonzil, Elisabeth [Hrsg.]: Der Balkan. Friedenszone oder Pulverfaß?, Frankfurt am Main, 1998, S. 45-62.
[56] Von Grunebaum, Gustav Edmund: Der Islam im Mittelalter, Zürich, 1963, S. 231.

In Südosteuropa leben heute türkisch-muslimische Bevölkerungsanteile vor allem in Bulgarien, wo sie neun Prozent der Gesamtbevölkerung ausmachen. Kleine Gruppen leben im Kosovo, in Makedonien und in Thrakien in Westgriechenland. Daneben gibt es auch christlich-türkische Minderheiten – die Gagausen, die vorwiegend in der Republik Moldau (153 000), in der Ukraine (32 000) und in kleineren Gruppen im Nordosten Bulgariens um Varna sowie in Griechenland leben.

Die Juden waren in das Osmanische Reich eingewandert, nachdem sie aus katholischen Ländern vertrieben wurden, insbesondere die Juden der iberischen Halbinsel – die Sepharden. Als diese gegen Ende des 15. Jahrhunderts Spanien verlassen mussten, bot ihnen das Osmanische Reich Zuflucht an. Bevorzugte Ziele waren Istanbul und andere größere Städte wie Saloniki. Im nicht osmanischen Südosteuropa hingegen dominierten die aschkenasischen Juden aus den deutschen Gebieten, deren Zuzug seit dem 14. Jahrhundert anstieg. Heute leben in Folge der Verfolgung und Vernichtung während des Zweiten Weltkrieges kaum noch Juden in Südosteuropa. Die Sepharden wurden fast vollständig in den Vernichtungslagern des faschistischen Deutschlands ermordet. Einzig die Juden Bulgariens bildeten eine Ausnahme. Die wenigen Überlebenden flohen in den neu gegründeten Staat Palästina.

Unter osmanischer Herrschaft gelangten auch Roma nach Südosteuropa, deren Vorfahren Indien vermutlich zwischen dem 9. und 11. Jahrhundert verlassen hatten. Über Nordafrika kamen sie nach Spanien und über Kleinasien nach Südosteuropa. Aber auch Armenier kamen mit den Osmanen nach Südosteuropa, die sich in erster Linie aufgrund ihrer Berufe in den Städten niederließen. Viele armenische Wanderungswellen waren Folge der Massaker der Osmanen an den Armeniern. Insbesondere im 19. Jahrhundert und vor allem 1915 wurde die armenische Bevölkerung auf grausamste Art vertrieben und vernichtet.

Das Turkvolk der Tataren wanderte in Folge des Krimkrieges von 1853-1856 von der Krim auf die Halbinsel, speziell in die Dobrudscha, ein. Heute leben noch über 20 000 Tataren in Rumänien, einige Tausend in Bulgarien.[57]

---

[57] Vgl.: Kaser, Karl: Raum und Besiedlung, in: Hatschikjan, Magarditsch/Troebst, Stefan [Hrsg.]: Südosteuropa. Gesellschaft, Politik, Wirtschaft, Kultur. Ein Handbuch, München, 1999, S. 66f.

T 2: Die osmanische Bevölkerung in Europa (1872) und Asien (1874)[58]

Region	Oberfläche (in km²)	Bevölkerung		
		Muslime	Nichtmuslime	Summe
Europa	20 240,9	3 841 174	10 991 646	14 752 820
Asien	95 611,7	11 426 057	2 854 234	14 280 291
Afrika mit Ägypten	140 639,6	11 308 550	170 450	11 479 000
Summe	256 492,2	26 575 781	13 936 330	40 512 111

3.2. Vom Berliner Kongress nach Sèvres

3.2.1. Südosteuropa bis zur Jahrhundertwende

Ab dem 16. Jahrhundert teilten sich das Osmanische Reich und die Habsburger Monarchie sowie die Venezianische Republik die Herrschaft über Südosteuropa. Es existierten somit bis zur Gründung des neuen Staates Griechenland im Jahre 1830 nur die Grenzen zwischen den Habsburgern und den Osmanen und jene zwischen diesen und Venedig. Die größte Feindschaft entwickelte sich entlang der Grenzen des Osmanischen und Habsburger Reiches. In erster Linie ging es diesen beiden Mächten um die Erhaltung des Status quo durch Stabilisierung der Grenze, die in der Mitte des 16. Jahrhunderts quer durch Kroatien verlief und nach der Niederlage der Osmanen vor Wien im Jahre 1683 um das Grenzstück entlang der Save und durch Abschnitte im Banat und Siebenbürgen verlängert wurde. Dieser "Raum, der beiderseits dieser historischen Grenze teilweise viele Kilometer in das Hinterland reichte, ist einer der wohl interessantesten und wichtigsten in der neuzeitlichen Geschichte Europas. Er bildete eine Grenze zwischen Islam und Christentum, mit Abstrichen auch eine zwischen Orthodoxie und Katholizismus. Hinsichtlich dieser Grenze und der Verbreitung der Religionen hat sich bis heute nicht viel geändert [...]. Diese Grenze wird in vielen historischen Werken als abendländisches Bollwerk gegen den Islam dargestellt – eine im nachhinein erdachte, ideologisch gefärbte Konstruktion [...]. In der Grenz- und Gefahrenzone [...] wurde der Verbreitung des Islam und vorderasiati-

---

[58] Aus: Kreiser, Klaus: Der Osmanische Staat 1300-1922, München, 2011, S. 224f.

scher Kulturelemente eine Schranke gesetzt. Die Grenze verhinderte aber auch für Jahrhunderte den wirtschaftlichen und kulturellen Austausch zwischen den Völkern unter osmanischer und habsburgischer Herrschaft. Damit trug sie zur Differenzierung zwischen den südosteuropäischen Nationen und Ethnien im Allgemeinen und zwischen den südslawischen im Besonderen bei."[59] Diese Grenze hatte selbstverständlich Auswirkungen auf Mentalität und Lebenshaltung der Völker.

Dass Südosteuropa nur von zwei Grenzen durchzogen war, hatte tiefgreifende Folgen auf die Binnenmigration innerhalb der einzelnen Reiche – nicht nur negative: Die Weidewirtschaft profitierte hiervon, da je nach Jahreszeit zwischen Sommer- und Winterweiden ohne Grenzunterbrechung gewechselt werden konnte. Aber nicht nur Menschen profitierten aufgrund der ununterbrochenen Handels- und Transportwege, sondern auch Städte, wie Istanbul, Saloniki oder Sarajevo, die sich zu multikulturellen Zentren entwickelten.[60]

Die osmanische Herrschaft begann ab dem 16. Jahrhundert zu bröckeln. Die Phase der inneren Reformen, der *Tanzimat* (Neuordnung), die eine Gleichberechtigung der christlichen Untertanen (1856), die Einführung einer Verfassung (1876) und die Einberufung eines Parlamentes (1877) vorsah, konnte den Tod des Kranken Mannes am Bosporus nicht verhindern. Den Sultanen gelang es nicht, die kollabierende Wirtschaft zu sanieren, weshalb die Pforte schließlich ihre Zinsen nicht mehr bezahlen konnte und 1875 den Staatsbankrott erklärte[61]. Eine internationale Verwaltung übernahm 1881 die Kontrolle der Staatsfinanzen.[62] Der Halbmond verblasste in Südosteuropa zudem aufgrund des Reiches der Romanovs im Osten, das als neue Großmacht auf der Balkanhalbinsel in Erscheinung trat.

"Seiner Staatsdoktrin nach ist das russische Zarenreich das 'Dritte Rom' [...]. Das 'Heilige Rußland', Wahrer der Orthodoxie, tritt auf als Nachfolger der byzantinischen Weltherrschaft. Es fühlt sich geschichtlich berufen, Konstantinopel zu er-

---

[59] Ebd., S. 68f.
[60] Vgl.: Ebd., S. 69.
[61] Hierzu vgl.: Zusammenfassung von Manzenreiter, Johann: Der Staatsbankrott des Osmanischen Reiches (1875/76), in: Materialia Turcica, 1 (1975). S. 90-104.
[62] Vgl.: Boeckh, Katrin: Von den ersten Balkankriegen zum Ersten Weltkrieg. Kleinstaatpolitik und ethnische Selbstbestimmung auf dem Balkan, München, 1996, S. 19.

obern und alle 'Rechtgläubigen' in einem Reich zu vereinigen, dafür den Balkan vom Islam zu befreien und die Balkanchristen vor den 'Lateinern' zu schützen."[63]

Gleichzeitig wuchs der Druck der nationalen Kräfte, insbesondere der Völker des Balkans, gegen die osmanische Herrschaft.

Nach dem ersten erfolglosen Aufstand von 1804-1813 gelang es den Serben im zweiten Aufstand von 1815 ein autonomes Gebiet zu erschaffen. Der Sultan musste mehrere Zugeständnisse machen. 1817 noch ein autonomes Fürstentum, wurde Serbien 1833 faktisch unabhängig, auch wenn es formal bis zum Berliner Kongress 1878 dem Sultan unterstellt war. 1882 proklamierte Fürst Milan IV./I. Obrenović das Königtum Serbien.[64]

Die Griechen wurden 1832 nach den Aufständen von 1821-1827 auf den Peloponnes souverän. Gründe für den Sieg des griechischen Freiheitskampfes waren einerseits die Konzentration der osmanischen Truppen im Osten gegen Persien, die 1821 die Schwierigkeiten des Nachbarstaates ausnutzen wollten und angriffen, andererseits die Unterstützung der griechischen Befreiungsbewegung durch Freiwillige der *philhellenischen* Bewegung in Europa.[65] Die Vereinbarungen des Berliner Kongresses resultierten in erheblichen Gebietsgewinnen Griechenlands und gleichzeitig Verlusten für das Osmanische Reich, unter anderem Thessalien sowie Teile des Epiros.

Die zwei tributpflichtigen Vasallen der Pforte, die Donaufürstentümer Moldau und Walachei, vereinigten sich 1861 und erklärten sich 1877 für unabhängig. 1881 wurde Rumänien schließlich Königreich und Karl von Hohenzollern-Sigmaringen zum König ausgerufen. Nachdem die Unabhängigkeit im Rahmen des Berliner Kongresses anerkannt wurde, ging Rumänien nach dem Verlust Südwest-Bessarabiens an Russland auf antirussischen Kurs und verbündete sich in einem Geheimabkommen mit Österreich-Ungarn und Deutschland.

Das jüngste Königreich Montenegro, das aufgrund seiner gebirgigen und undurchlässigen Geografie niemals komplett von der Hohen Pforte be-

---

[63] Weithmann, Michael W.: Der Balkan zwischen Ost und West, in: Weithmann, Michael W. [Hrsg.]: Der ruhelose Balkan. Die Konfliktregionen Südosteuropas, München, 1993, S. 13.
[64] Vgl.: Boeckh, Katrin: Von den ersten Balkankriegen zum Ersten Weltkrieg. Kleinstaatpolitik und ethnische Selbstbestimmung auf dem Balkan, München, 1996, S. 20.
[65] Vgl.: Matuz, Josef: Das Osmanische Reich. Grundlinien seiner Geschichte, 2. Aufl., Darmstadt, 1990, S. 218.

herrscht werden konnte, war seit 1852 ein unabhängiges Fürstentum geworden und durch den Berliner Kongress bestätigt. Neben den anderen südslawischen Staaten Bulgarien und Serbien war Montenegro außenpolitisch im Einflussbereich des russischen Reiches.

Nachdem der Berliner Kongress die Unabhängigkeit Serbiens, Montenegros und Rumäniens offiziell anerkannte, sahen sich die Bulgaren ebenfalls ermutigt sich aus dem Osmanischen Reich loszulösen. Dies gelang den Bulgaren endgültig 1908, als wiedermals ein Herrscher aus dem Ausland, Ferdinand aus dem Hause der Sachsen-Coburg, den Titel des Zaren annahm und das Land für unabhängig erklärte. Den Osmanen blieb nichts anderes übrig, als auch diesen Verlust hinzunehmen.

Der Berliner Kongress, nach den Verträgen von Karlowitz und Küçük Kaynarca der dritte große Schritt zur Entmachtung der Osmanen, die inzwischen zum *Kranken Mann am Bosporus* geworden waren[66], verstärkte nationalistische Tendenzen in allen Regionen Südosteuropas und wurde zur vereinigenden und mobilisierenden Macht.

> "Alle Serben, Griechen, Bulgaren und Rumänen sollten vom 'Türkenjoch' befreit und in jeweils ihrem Nationalstaat, in 'Großgriechenland', 'Großserbien', 'Großbulgarien' [...] und 'Großrumänien' vereinigt werden. Zu diesem Zweck führten die Länder jedoch [...] keinen formellen Krieg mehr gegen das Osmanische Reich. Nun trat eine andere Kampfmethode in den Vordergrund [...], [die.DOT] zum Sinnbild dessen wurde, was das übrige Europa für die Verhältnisse am Balkan als typisch empfand: die Guerilla."[67]

Bewaffnete Banden erhielten Unterstützung der jeweiligen Regierung und führten einen blutigen Feldzug im osmanischen Reststaat auf dem Balkan, insbesondere in Epiros, Makedonien, Thrakien und Albanien. Die Gewalt richtete sich nicht nur gegen die Besatzertruppen des Sultans, sondern auch gegen die Zivilbevölkerung. So sollten christliche Minderheiten der jeweils anderen Staaten zum nationalen Bekenntnis gezwungen werden. Auf der Gegenseite formierten sich ebenfalls Nationalbewegungen, wie die nationalistische Organisation der Jungtürken, deren Ziel die Gründung eines türki-

---

[66] Vgl.: Ebd., S. 240.
[67] Boeckh, Katrin: Von den ersten Balkankriegen zum Ersten Weltkrieg. Kleinstaatpolitik und ethnische Selbstbestimmung auf dem Balkan, München, 1996, S. 21.

schen Nationalstaates war. Von Saloniki aus verbreitete sich dieses Gedankengut bis in das anatolische Kernland. Letztendlich leiteten diese Bandenkämpfe, angetrieben von überhöhtem Nationalismus, das letzte Kapitel des *Orientalischen Geschwüres* ein – das der Balkankriege.[68] Die Anstrengungen des Sultans mit der Ideologie des *Osmanismus* das Zusammengehörigkeitsgefühl aller osmanischen Staatsbürger gegenüber den einzelnen Nationalismen der Völker zu fördern, konnte die Auflösungserscheinungen des Reiches nicht verhindern.[69]

T 3: Statistische Bevölkerungsübersicht um 1900[70]

(Betrifft die heutigen Länder und Regionen: Slowakei, Ungarn, Karpatenukraine, Rumänien, Republik Moldau, Slowenien, Kroatien, Bosnien, Serbien (mit Montenegro), Kosovo, Makedonien, Albanien, Bulgarien).

Volk	1900
Albaner	1 000 000
Bulgaren	3 017 700
Deutsche	1 704 900
Juden	1 347 500
Kroaten	2 568 200
Makedonier	600 000
Muslime	600 000
Rumänen	9 678 000
Serben	4 375 900
Slowaken	1 937 000
Slowenen	1 000 000
Türken	610 100
Ungarn	8 126 300

Volk = Staatsvolk plus connationale ethn. Gruppen in den betreffenden Ländern.

---

[68] Vgl.: Ebd., S. 21f.
[69] Vgl.: Matuz, Josef: Das Osmanische Reich. Grundlinien seiner Geschichte, 2. Aufl., Darmstadt, 1990, S. 241.
[70] Aus: Seewann, Gerhard: Zwangsmigration von Minderheiten in Südosteuropa im 20. Jahrhundert, in: Solomon, Flavius/Rubel, Alexander/Zub Alexandru [Hrsg.]: Südosteuropa im 20. Jahrhundert. Ethnostrukturen, Identitäten, Konflikte, Konstanz, 2004, S. 54.

3.2.2. Der Erste Balkankrieg

Der Versuch, die Landkarte Südosteuropas mit den Vereinbarungen des Berliner Kongresses neu zu ordnen und die Machthaber zu befrieden, misslang. Zwar wurden die neuen Balkanstaaten Serbien, Rumänien, Montenegro und Bulgarien völkerrechtlich unabhängig, jedoch konnte von echter Souveränität nicht die Rede sein. Angesichts des in Chauvinismus mündenden Nationalismus gerieten sogar christliche Völker in Zwist.[71]

> "Es entsteht ein Nebeneinander von Puffer-, Vasallen-, Trabanten- und Satellitenstaaten, die durch tradierte Feindschaften fest ineinander verzahnt sind. [...] Die von Petersburg, Wien, London, Paris, Berlin und Rom abhängige halbkoloniale Kleinstaatenwelt Südosteuropas [...]. Bismarcks außenpolitische Maxime ist es, dieses 'Orientalische Geschwür offenzuhalten und dadurch die Einigkeit der anderen Großmächte zu vereiteln'. Die *orientalischen Geschwüre* haben sich seit dem Berliner Kongress [...] nicht geschlossen: Territorialstreitigkeiten und Minderheitenprobleme in Makedonien, im Kosovo, in Bosnien, in Bessarabien, in Siebenbürgen, in der Dobrudscha, in Thrakien. Ein paar weitere kommen in der Folgezeit noch hinzu."[72]

Eine große Rolle spielte Russland, dem es in den kommenden Jahrzehnten als neue Konzeption der Außenpolitik gelang, ein Bündnissystem im Balkan aufzubauen, um seine Vormachtstellung und ein Gegengewicht zur Habsburger Monarchie herzustellen. So gelang es Russland, einen Balkanbund zu bilden, dem Serbien, Bulgarien, Griechenland und Montenegro angehörten. Ziel war es, die restlichen Gebiete der Osmanen auf europäischem Boden zu befreien – Makedonien, Thrakien, Albanien, den Epiros und den Sandżak. Auf der anderen Seite übernahm in Folge der *jungtürkischen Revolution* von 1908 das *Komitee für Einheit und Fortschritt* (İttihat ve Terakki Cemiyeti) die Macht in Konstantinopel, dessen "Vorstellung einer Türkisierung des Osmanischen Reiches [...] keineswegs den Interessen der christlichen Balkanländer [entsprach.DOT], siedelten doch noch griechische, serbische und bulgarische Bevölkerungsteile auf dem osmanischen Staatsgebiet, vor allem in Makedo-

---

[71] Vgl.: Ebd., S. 243.
[72] Weithmann, Michael W.: Der Balkan zwischen Ost und West, in: Weithmann, Michael W. [Hrsg.]: Der ruhelose Balkan. Die Konfliktregionen Südosteuropas, München, 1993, S. 15ff.

nien, auf das sich die territorialen Interessen der Balkanstaaten konzentrierten"[73].

Die Strategie Russlands ging auf, auch wenn die weiteren Etappen der Bildung des Balkanbundes nicht mehr auf russische Initiative hin entstanden. Mit der Ratifikation des Bündnisses zwischen Serbien und Montenegro am 15. Oktober 1912 war der Balkanbund komplett – eine Allianz zwischen Bulgarien und Serbien, Bulgarien und Griechenland, Serbien und Montenegro sowie einer mündlichen Vereinbarung zwischen Bulgarien und Montenegro. Griechenland war zwar mit Montenegro und Serbien nicht offiziell verbündet, es bestand jedoch eine Übereinkunft über eine gemeinsame Verteidigung.[74] Mit dem Balkanbund von 1912 entstand ein großes und komplexes Bündnissystem im Balkan, dessen Ziel die Vertreibung der Osmanen aus Südosteuropa war. Jedoch wurde bis zu diesem Zeitpunkt noch wenig über die Zeit nach dem Krieg gesprochen, so dass territoriale Veränderungen sehr unklar formuliert waren, vermutlich deshalb, weil sich alle Staaten größere Anteile der 'befreiten' Gebiete erhofften.[75] Das Osmanische Reich befand sich zu dieser Zeit im Tripolis-Krieg gegen Italien, in dem es die Herrschaft über Tripolitanien und die Cyrenaika verlor. Des Weiteren wurde die Insel der Dodekanes an der Südwestküste Anatoliens von den Italienern besetzt. Die Bedingungen schienen für einen Angriff ideal zu sein, es fehlte jedoch der Auslöser.

Es war die Bombe eines makedonisch-bulgarischen Freischärlers, die im August 1912 auf dem Markt von Kocani zehn Menschen, darunter auch Muslime, tötete und die Fronten zwischen den Parteien verhärtete. Die Hohe Pforte reagierte mit einer Vergeltungsaktion, bei der 38 Slawen und Westeuropäer ums Leben kamen und 180 verletzt wurden. Es folgten weitere Attentate auf beiden Seiten. Die Grenzen des Osmanischen Reiches zu Griechenland, Serbien, Bulgarien und besonders Montenegro wurden Schauplatz heftiger Gefechte. Neben einer allgemeinen Mobilmachung aller beteiligten Staaten verlangten die Staaten des Balkanbundes unverzügliche Reformen zur Verbesserung der Situation der christlichen Minderheiten im Osmani-

---

[73] Boeck, Katrin: Von den ersten Balkankriegen zum Ersten Weltkrieg. Kleinstaatpolitik und ethnische Selbstbestimmung auf dem Balkan, München, 1996, S. 24.
[74] Vgl.: Ebd., S. 29.
[75] Vgl.: Ebd., S. 29.

schen Reich. König Nikola von Montenegro forderte die europäischen Mächte zu militärischem Eingreifen auf. Am 6. Oktober 1912 brach das Land die diplomatischen Beziehungen zur Pforte ab und erklärte ihr kurzerhand den Krieg. Als Ziel gab sie die Befreiung der serbischen Bevölkerung aus dem 'Türkenjoch' an. "Weshalb ausgerechnet Nikola von Montenegro als erster in den Kampf gegen die Türken zog, war den Zeitgenossen lange Zeit nicht klar."[76] Vermutlich versprach sich das kleinste Land des Bundes maximalen Landgewinn. Zudem befand es sich bereits seit längerem faktisch im Krieg mit den Osmanen und konnte sich nun sicher sein, dass die anderen Balkanstaaten nachziehen würden. Diese legten Konstantinopel am 13. Oktober 1912 eine Kollektivnote vor, in der sie Reformen forderten. Dazu gehörten unter anderem die Autonomie der christlichen Völker, ihre Vertretung im Parlament, die Gleichstellung ihrer Schulen mit muslimischen und die Rekrutierung von Christen für den Heeresdienst, jedoch unter christlichem Kader. Nachdem der Außenminister des Osmanischen Reiches, Gabriel Naradungian, ablehnte, riefen die Bündnispartner am 17. Oktober ihre Botschafter aus Konstantinopel zurück und folgten noch am selben Tag dem Beispiel Montenegros.

"Mit dem Überschreiten der serbischen Grenze durch die Truppen des Landes trat eine 'jahrhundertealte geschichtliche Abrechnung zwischen den Serben und Türken in die letzte Phase', wie es die serbische Hofgeschichtsschreibung der Zwischenkriegszeit formulierte."[77]

T 4: Die territorialen Verhältnisse der Balkanstaaten vor dem Ersten Balkankrieg[78]

Land	Fläche in km²	Einwohnerzahl
Türkei (europ. Gebiet)	169 300	6 130 200
Bulgarien	96 345	4 337 513
Serbien	48 303	2 957 087
Rumänien	131 353	7 086 796
Griechenland	64 657	2 631 952
Montenegro	9 080	285 000

Auf dem Schlachtfeld ergab sich ein ungleiches Bild. Während dem Osmanischen Reich etwa 290 000 Soldaten zur Verfügung standen, kommandierten

---
[76] Ebd., S. 33.
[77] Ebd., S. 34.
[78] Aus: Ebd., S. 70.

die Balkanstaaten gemeinsam über 474 000 Soldaten (Bulgarien 233 000, Serbien 130 000, Griechenland 80 000, Montenegro 31 000)[79]. Ohne eine gemeinsam abgestimmte Koordinierung griffen die Staaten des Balkanbundes an. Die Bulgaren konzentrierten sich auf Thrakien und Adrianopel (Edirne), die Serben auf Üsküb (Skopje) und Monastir (Bitola), während die Griechen nach Makedonien und auf den Epirus vordrangen und die Montenegriner die Gebiete des Sandžak und Novipazars einnahmen. Thrakien war besonders umkämpft. Den Bulgaren gelang es schon knapp einen Monat nach Kriegsausbruch, bis auf die letzte Sicherungslinie der Osmanen vor Konstantinopel vorzustoßen – Çatalca. Die Pforte war mit wenigen Ausnahmen fast komplett vom europäischen Kontinent vertrieben worden.

Angesichts der Niederlagen sah sich die Hohe Pforte gezwungen, die Waffenstillstandsabkommen zu unterzeichnen, die durch einen Putsch der sogenannten *Jungtürken* für kurze Zeit unterbrochen wurden.

Kriegshistorisch hatte der Balkankrieg eine Besonderheit: Zum ersten Mal wurden schnurlose Telegraphenverbindungen und Flugzeuge in Kriegen eingesetzt.[80]

Der Vertrag von London, der den Ersten Balkankrieg beendete, konnte am 30. Mai 1913 von den Staaten des Balkanbundes auf der einen und vom Osmanischen Reich auf der anderen Seite unterzeichnet werden. Das Kriegsziel war erreicht: Bis auf ein Fetzen Land in Thrakien waren die Osmanen komplett aus Europa verdrängt worden. Sogar Adrianopel, als Edirne 600 Jahre lang eine osmanische Stadt mit der größten Moschee auf dem Balkan, mussten die Osmanen abtreten. Für die Siegermächte kam es jedoch erst nach ihrem Sieg zu einer Zerreißprobe. Wem sollte Makedonien gehören, wem Albanien? Trotz eines Kompromisses auf der Londoner Konferenz im Mai 1913 gingen "in der von der Balkan-Liga eroberten Ländermasse [...] die Forderungen, Grenz- und Demarkationslinien völlig wirr durcheinander! [...] die

---

[79] Vgl.: Soyupak, Kemal/Kabasakal, Huseyin: The Turkish army in the First Balkan War, in: Kiraly, Bela K./Djordjevic, Dimitrije [Hrsg.]: East Central European Society and the Balkan War, New York, 1987, S. 159 und Yonov, Momchil: Bulgarian Military Operations in the Balkan Wars, in: Kiraly, Bela K./Djordjevic, Dimitrije [Hrsg.]: East Central European Society and the Balkan War, New York, 1987, S. 372.

[80] Vgl.: Boeckh, Katrin: Von den ersten Balkankriegen zum Ersten Weltkrieg. Kleinstaatpolitik und ethnische Selbstbestimmung auf dem Balkan, München, 1996, S. 37.

russische Diplomatie [versagt.DOT]. Die Nationalismen und gegenseitigen Animositäten der Balkanvölker erweisen sich stärker als der Appell des Zaren an die gemeinsame Orthodoxie. Die Bulgaren verlassen ihre Waffenstillstandstellungen. Das Bündnis entgleitet den russischen Drahtziehern und zerbricht schließlich."[81]

Welche Rolle hatte Deutschland während der Balkankriege gespielt?

"Deutschlands Südosteuropapolitik sah [...] kein aktives Eingreifen in die Kämpfe vor, ansonsten strebte man die Aufrechterhaltung des gegenwärtigen Zustandes an. Österreich-Ungarns Großmachtstellung sollte nicht gefährdet werden, auch nicht der Bestand der asiatischen Türkei, schon wegen der dortigen wirtschaftlichen Interessen des Reiches – deshalb hatte man sich auch für die Bagdad-Bahn engagiert."[82]

Eine weitere Perspektive bietet Matuz: Nach der Niederlage des Osmanischen Reiches im Krieg gegen die Russen 1877-1878 "gelang es der deutschen Industrie, den osmanischen Rüstungsmarkt unter anderem auf Betreiben der deutschen Militärberater, unter ihnen der Preuße von der Goltz, zu erobern. Die von der deutschen Schwerindustrie aus geschäftlichen Gründen forcierte Aufrüstung des osmanischen Heeres [...], die besonders die Verteidigungs- und Wirtschaftsinteressen Rußlands und Großbritanniens tangierten [...] trugen zu einer verstärkten Aufrüstung der Großmächte, aber auch der kleineren Balkanländer bei. Auch unter dieser Perspektive müssen die Balkankriege, [...] und nicht zuletzt der Erste Weltkrieg gesehen werden."[83]

Da hierbei die Wirtschaftsinteressen der europäischen Mächte im Vordergrund standen, weniger die Bedürfnisse des Osmanischen Reiches, war eine ungleichmäßige Entwicklung der Wirtschaft des Reiches unumgänglich. Die kapitalistische Produktionsweise begann sich allmählich durchzusetzen und die feudalen Strukturen – wenn dieser Prozess auch heute noch nicht abgeschlossen ist – aufzulösen.[84]

---

[81] Weithmann, Michael W.: Balkan-Chronik. 2000 Jahre zwischen Orient und Okzident, Regensburg, 2000, S. 317.
[82] Boeckh, Katrin: Von den ersten Balkankriegen zum Ersten Weltkrieg. Kleinstaatpolitik und ethnische Selbstbestimmung auf dem Balkan, München, 1996, S. 41.
[83] Vgl.: Matuz, Josef: Das Osmanische Reich. Grundlinien seiner Geschichte, 2. Aufl., Darmstadt, 1990, S. 247f.
[84] Vgl.: Ebd., S. 248.

3.2.3. Der Fall Kosovo

Während des ersten Balkankrieges drangen serbische, montenegrinische und griechische Truppen in Albanien ein und besetzten es. Um eine Aufteilung zu verhindern, erklärte der *Albanische Nationalkongress* die Unabhängigkeit und bildete die erste Regierung unter dem muslimischen Ismail Qemali Bey, dessen Stellvertreter ein katholischer Priester war. Ohne Unterstützung aus Wien und Rom wären die Überlebenschancen eines unabhängigen Albaniens sehr gering gewesen. Für Wien war Albanien ein Sperrriegel gegenüber dem Anspruch der Serben, Zugang zum Mittelmeer zu erhalten. Rom erhoffte sich währenddessen ein neues Kolonialgebiet. Beide Staaten wollten eine Aufteilung Albaniens unter Serbien und Griechenland um jeden Preis verhindern.

> "Auf der Botschafter-Konferenz in London 1913 wird der neue Staat mit der Hauptstadt Durrës (Durazzo) anerkannt. Doch seine Grenzen sind noch völlig unklar. Montenegro verlangt Skodra (Shkodër, Skutari), Griechenland beansprucht den ganzen Südteil mit Korça, die Serben fordern den gesamten Kosovo, sowie Durrës als Hafen. Schließlich setzt sich 1913 im Londoner Friedensvertrag nur Serbien – im Hintergrund steht Rußland! – durch: Zwar nicht mit dem Adria-Hafen, aber mit dem Kosovo!"[85]

Das überwiegend von Albanern bewohnte Kosovo wurde somit Serbien zugesprochen. Ein Drittel der vor allem islamisch geprägten Albaner befanden sich nun außerhalb des albanischen Staatsgebietes. Mit dem Kosovo entstand die gefährlichste Brandregion Südosteuropas, um die fast 90 Jahre später noch ein Krieg geführt werden sollte. Über die albanische Bevölkerung im Kosovo soll sich der damalige serbische Ministerpräsident Nikola Pašić folgendermaßen geäußert haben: "Wir werden sie serbisieren, und wenn sie sich nicht serbisieren lassen, werden wir sie vertreiben, und wenn sie sich nicht vertreiben lassen, werden wir sie umbringen!"[86] Die Ereignisse in den Jahren nach der bosnischen Annexionskrise hatten somit auch den Albanern als letztem Volk des Balkans den Weg zu einem eigenen souveränen Staat geebnet.

---

[85] Weithmann, Michael W.: Balkan-Chronik. 2000 Jahre zwischen Orient und Okzident, Regensburg, 2000, S. 323.
[86] Ebd., S. 323.

3.2.4. Der Zweite Balkankrieg

Die Aufteilung Albaniens war durch den Einspruch Italiens und Österreich-Ungarns verhindert worden. Als Beute des ersten Balkankrieges blieb somit nur noch Makedonien übrig, über dessen Aufteilung sich die Griechen, Bulgaren und Serben nicht einigen konnten. Bulgarien besetzte kurzerhand Makedonien, griff Serbien an und marschierte Richtung Thessaloniki. Erst Entlastungsangriffe der Griechen aus dem Süden und der Rumänen aus dem Norden brachten den bulgarischen Vormarsch zum Erliegen. Rumänien, der größte und völkerreichste selbstständige Staat Südosteuropas, hatte sich bislang neutral verhalten. Allerdings hatten die Rumänen noch eine Rechnung mit den Bulgaren offen[87] und sahen jetzt die Gelegenheit, diese zu begleichen. Rumänische Truppen marschierten in bulgarische Gebiete ein und überschritten die Donau. Unerwartet setzte auch das Osmanische Reich seine Truppen in Bewegung, um verloren gegangene Gebiete in Bulgarien wieder zurückzuerobern.

Der zweite Balkankrieg, welcher durch eine Selbstüberschätzung der Bulgaren ausgelöst wurde, war nur von kurzer Dauer. Bereits im August 1913 wurden in Bukarest Friedensverhandlungen geführt. Makedonien wurde letztendlich unter Griechenland und Serbien aufgeteilt. Serbien hatte sein Staatsgebiet fast verdoppelt, während Griechenland ein Gebietszuwachs von einem Drittel vermelden konnte. Bulgarien hatte zwar im Westen Makedonien verloren, gewann aber dafür das Rhodosgebirge und das thrakische Küstengebiet um Dedeağaç (Alexandroupolis) und Gümülcüne (Komotini) und war somit eine ägäische und mittelmeerische Macht geworden. Rumänien gab sich mit dem Südteil der Dobrudscha zufrieden. Sogar die Osmanen, welche nach dem ersten Balkankrieg fast komplett aus Europa verbannt wurden, gingen nicht leer aus. Ihnen wurde Adrianopel (Edirne) und Ostthrakien zugesprochen. "Natürlich sind die Balkanstaaten auch jetzt nur Randfiguren. Beim Friedenschluss sitzen die Großmächte im Hintergrund und ziehen die Fäden."[88]

---

[87] Die Bulgaren hatten den Zuschlag der Dobrudscha zu Rumänien während des Berliner Kongresses 1878 immer in Zweifel gezogen.
[88] Weithmann, Michael W.: Balkan-Chronik. 2000 Jahre zwischen Orient und Okzident, Regensburg, 2000, S. 327.

K 1: Die territorialen Veränderungen Südosteuropas nach den Balkankriegen[89]

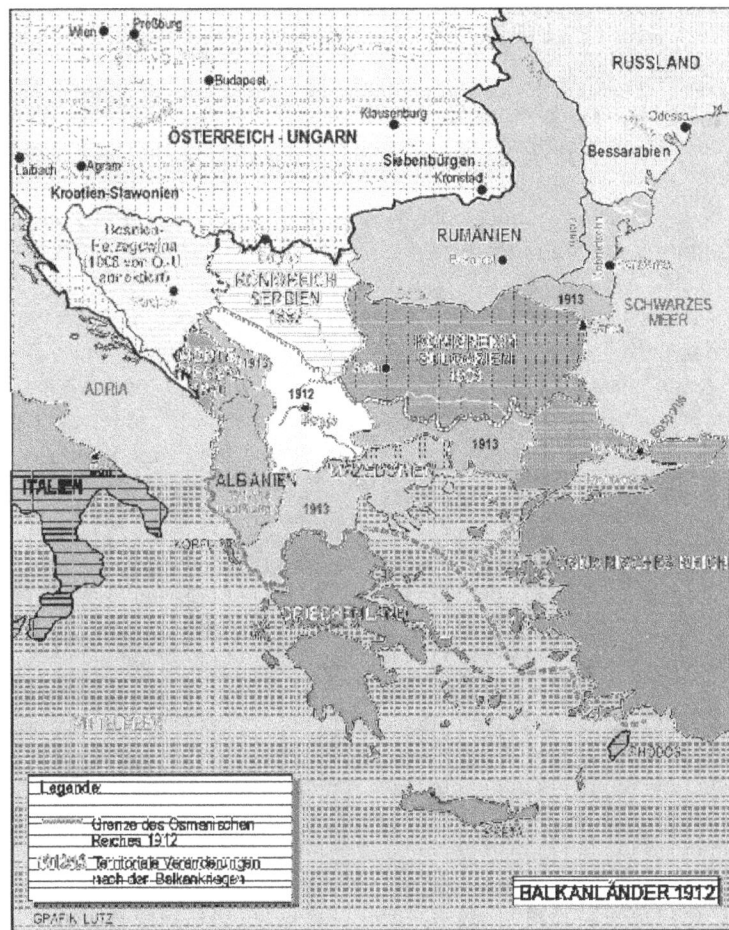

Weithmann zieht für den südosteuropäischen Raum nach den Balkankriegen das gleiche Fazit wie nach dem Berliner Kongress:

"Die Balkanstaaten sind Objekte, nicht Subjekte der großen Politik. Kein einziges nationales Problem ist gelöst. Die Grenzziehung bewirkt ein System gegenseitiger Feindschaften, das von den Großmächten je nach Situation in Schach gehalten oder zum Ausbruch verändert werden kann. Das 'orientalische Geschwür' ist für

---

[89] Aus: Österreichische Militärische Zeitschrift/Grafikarchiv: http://www.bmlv.gv.at/omz/grafiken/vollbild/brill2500.png (Zuletzt eingesehen am 18.05.2012).

die Zukunft offengehalten! Ein Blick auf die neue Landkarte des Balkans verrät, dass unhaltbare Grenzregelungen getroffen und geopolitisch unhaltbare Staatengebilde geschaffen worden sind. Aus eigener Kraft wird diese 'balkanisierte' Kleinstaatenwelt zu keinem übergreifenden Ordnungsgedanken gelangen. Deutlich zeichnet sich das Bündnissystem der zwei großen weltpolitischen Machkonstellationen der 'Mittelmächte' und der 'Tripel-Allianz' auf dem Balkan ab. [... Der Balkan entwickelt sich. DOT] zu einem Konfliktherd von gewaltiger Sprengkraft."[90]

Ganz besonders in Serbien, "das sich durch das Dazwischentreten Österreich-Ungarns um die Früchte seines glanzvollen Sieges vom Jahre 1913 betrogen sah"[91], wuchs die Aversion gegen den Vielvölkerstaat: Österreich-Ungarn hatte immer noch Bosnien-Herzegowina in seinem Herrschaftsbereich, das Serbien stets für sich beanspruchte. Eine Versöhnung des serbischen Nationalismus unter diesen Umständen war unmöglich. Überall in Südosteuropa brodelte es. Streitereien um Grenzverläufe standen ganz oben auf der Tagesordnung. Europa stand am Vorabend des Ersten Weltkrieges.

T 5: Die territorialen Veränderungen nach den Balkankriegen[92]

Land	1 (in km²)	2 (in km²)	3	4
Türkei (europ. Gebiet)	26 100	-143 200	1 891 100	-4 239 000
Bulgarien	114 105	17 760	4 766 906	429 393
Serbien	87 300	38 997	4 160 000	1 202 913
Rumänien	139 690	8 337	7 601 660	280 000
Griechenland	115 975	51 318	4 256 000	1 624 048
Montenegro	15 180	5 100	443 000	150 000
Albanien	28 000	(28 000)	(800 000)	(800 000)

1= Staatsterritorium nach Bukarester Frieden.
2= Gewinn/Verlust gegenüber Vorkriegsstand.
3= Neuer Bevölkerungsstand.
4= Gewinn/Verlust gegenüber Vorkriegsstand.

---

[90] Weithmann, Michael W.: Balkan-Chronik. 2000 Jahre zwischen Orient und Okzident, Regensburg, 2000, S. 327f.
[91] Hösch, Edgar: Geschichte der Balkanländer. Von der Frühzeit bis zur Gegenwart, 5. Aufl., München, 2008, S. 186.
[92] Aus: Boeckh, Katrin: Von den ersten Balkankriegen zum Ersten Weltkrieg. Kleinstaatpolitik und ethnische Selbstbestimmung auf dem Balkan, München, 1996, S. 70.

3.2.5. Der Erste Weltkrieg

K 2: Europa vor dem Ersten Weltkrieg[93]

---

[93] Aus: Haus der Heimat des Landes Baden-Württemberg [Hrsg.]: Umsiedlung, Flucht und Vertreibung der Deutschen als internationales Problem. Zur Geschichte eines europäischen Irrwegs, Stuttgart, 2005, S. 41.

Anfang Juni 1914 teilte der deutsche Kaiser Wilhelm dem Reichskanzler Theobald von Betmann-Hollweg mit: "Es kommt bald das dritte Kapitel des Balkankrieges, an dem wir alle beteiligt werden. Daher die kolossalen russischen und französischen Kriegsvorbereitungen."[94] Deutschland bereitete sich ebenfalls auf den Krieg vor.

Der österreichische Generalstab hatte für Ende Juni 1914 ein Manöver in Bosnien vorbereitet, um seine Stärke demonstrieren zu können.

> "Als besondere Attraktion wird der Besuch des Thronfolger-Paares für den 28. Juni in Sarajevo angekündigt. [...Der 28. Juni.DOT], der Vidovdan, der Veitstag! Der nationale Trauer- und Gedenktag aller Serben! Der 525. Jahrestag ihrer unglücklichen Schlacht auf dem Kosovo-Polje, dem Amselfeld [...]. Und auch der Tag, an dem vor 36 Jahren auf dem Berliner Kongreß Bosnien und Herzegowina Österreich anheimgestellt worden waren!"[95]

Der Zeitpunkt war die reinste Provokation. Die Situation in Europa, vor allem auf dem Balkan, glich bereits seit der Annexion Bosniens und Herzegowinas 1908 einem Pulverfass, dessen Lunte nur noch angezündet werden musste. Diese Aufgabe übernahm die studentische Gruppe mit dem Namen *Mlada Bosa*. Der serbische Nationalist Gavrilo Princip ermordete am 28. Juni 1914 in Sarajevo den österreichischen Thronfolger Erzherzog Franz Ferdinand und dessen Gemahlin Sophie. Österreich-Ungarn stellte daraufhin Serbien ein so gut wie unerfüllbares Ultimatum. Von den 10 Forderungen lieferten vor allem Punkt 5 und 6 Zündstoff. Von den Serben wurde gefordert, "5. einzuwilligen, daß in Serbien Organe der k. u. k. Regierung bei der Unterdrückung der gegen die territoriale Integrität der Monarchie gerichteten subversiven Bewegung mitwirken; 6. eine gerichtliche Untersuchung gegen jene Teilnehmer des Komplottes vom 28. Juni einzuleiten, die sich auf serbischem Territorium befinden; von der k. u. k. Regierung hierzu delegierte Organe werden an den diesbezüglichen Erhebungen teilnehmen"[96]. Deutschland unterstützte Österreich-Ungarn in seiner harten Haltung gegenüber Serbien, das wiederum von Russland unterstützt wurde. Alle Mächte wollten regelrecht einen Krieg. Am

---

[94] Weithmann, Michael W.: Balkan-Chronik. 2000 Jahre zwischen Orient und Okzident, Regensburg, 2000, S. 329.
[95] Ebd., S. 333ff.
[96] Österreichisch-ungarisches Rotbuch. Diplomatische Aktenstücke zur Vorgeschichte des Krieges 1914, Wien, 1915.

28. Juli 1914 erklärte Österreich-Ungarn schließlich Serbien den Krieg. Der Erste Weltkrieg, welcher für Südosteuropa eigentlich bereits einige Jahre zuvor mit den Balkankriegen begonnen hatte, war jetzt offiziell.

"Das Räderwerk der gegenseitigen Bündnisverpflichtungen läuft an und läßt sich nicht mehr aufhalten [...] Vom 1. bis zum 12. August 1914 erklären sich die Bündnispartner der Mittelmächte Österreich-Ungarn und Deutschland und der Triple-Entente Frankreich, Russland und England wechselseitig den Krieg."[97]

Ohne zu zögern überschritten die Truppen der Mittelmächte die Grenze zu Serbien. Anfangs konnten die serbischen Truppen die österreichisch-ungarische Offensive abwehren. Als aber im November 1914 das Osmanische Reich, ein wichtiger und treuer Bündnispartner Deutschlands[98], und Bulgarien im September 1915 auf Seiten der Mittelmächte in den Krieg eintraten, brach Serbien militärisch zusammen. Später erklärten Italien und Rumänien den Mittelmächten den Krieg und 1917 traten auch noch die Vereinigten Staaten von Amerika auf Seiten der Alliierten in den Krieg ein.

Die Mittelmächte waren dieser Übermacht nicht mehr gewachsen[99] und verloren 1918 den Krieg.

Der Vielvölkerstaat Österreich-Ungarn stand vor dem Zusammenbruch. Als die verschiedenen Nationalitäten im Habsburger Reich schließlich den Austritt aus dem Staatenbund proklamierten, war Österreich-Ungarn somit als Großmacht von der Landkarte Südosteuropas verschwunden.[100]

"Erstmals seit über einem Jahrtausend bot sich den Völkern Südosteuropas die Gelegenheit, ihr weiteres politisches Schicksal selbst in die Hand zu nehmen, nachdem auch das zaristische Russland durch die Oktoberrevolution von 1917 und die Türkei als Kriegsverlierer bei der Neugestaltung der Balkangeschichte ausgeschieden waren."[101]

Der Pariser Frieden setzte sich aus den Verträgen von Versailles (mit Deutschland), von St. Germain (mit Österreich), von Trianon (mit Ungarn),

---

[97] Ebd., S. 339.
[98] Vgl.: Ebd., S. 340.
[99] Österreich-Ungarn hatte auch mit innenpolitischen Problemen zu kämpfen.
[100] Vgl.: Görlich, Ernst Joseph: Grundzüge der Geschichte der Habsburgermonarchie und Österreichs, 3. Aufl., Darmstadt, 1988, S. 267ff.
[101] Hösch, Edgar: Geschichte der Balkanländer. Von der Frühzeit bis zur Gegenwart, 5. Aufl., München, 2008, S. 188.

von Neuilly (mit Bulgarien) und von Sèvres[102] (mit dem Osmanischen Reich) zusammen. Zu den größten Veränderungen der Landkarte Südosteuropas nach den Pariser Verträgen zählten die völlige Zerschlagung des Habsburger Reiches Österreich-Ungarns sowie die Schaffung einer jugoslawischen Staatenföderation und eines großrumänischen Reiches. Ähnlich wie bei Österreich, das weite Teile seines Staatsgebietes an die neue Tschechoslowakei verlor, "verhielt es sich auch bei dem ungarischen Staat, der aus dem Trianon-Vertrag [...] hervorging; er war nur noch ein Überbleibsel des Vorkriegskönigreiches. Ungarn verblieb das, was übrig geblieben war, nachdem die meisten Forderungen der Tschechoslowakei, Rumäniens und Jugoslawiens erfüllt worden waren. Ein kleiner und in der Mehrheit deutschsprachiger Teil kam zu Österreich. [...] außerdem musste es einige Gebietsteile mit einheitlich magyarischer Bevölkerung abtreten. Die Slowakei erhielt magyarische Gebiete aus wirtschaftlichen Gründen – um der Tschechoslowakei einen Zugang zur Donau zu ermöglichen"[103] und da der Norden insgesamt als wirtschaftlicher galt. Weiterhin trat Ungarn große Teile Kroatiens und Sloweniens an das neu entstandene Jugoslawien ab.

> "Die meisten dieser Gebiete hatten unbestreitbar einen nicht magyarischen Charakter und genossen schon vor dem Kriege eine gewisse Autonomie, ebenso der größte Teil des Territoriums zwischen Szeged und Belgrad, in dem teilweise geschlossene magyarische Bevölkerungsgruppen lebten und das Jugoslawien offensichtlich zu dem zugeschlagen wurde, um für die Hauptstadt Belgrad einen größeren Brückenkopf nördlich der Donau zu schaffen."[104]

Somit hatte Ungarn nur noch knapp ein Drittel seines ehemaligen Staatsgebietes und verlor 60 Prozent seiner Bevölkerung.[105] Eine Million Magyaren, eine halbe Million Ruthenen, eine Viertelmillion Deutsche und fast zwei Millionen Slowaken wurden in die Tschechoslowakei einverleibt.[106]

---

[102] Die Bestimmungen von Sèvres wurden jedoch nach dem Sieg des nationalen Widerstands unter Mustafa Kemal mit dem Vertrag von Lausanne revidiert.
[103] Parker, R. A. C. [Hrsg.]: Fischer Weltgeschichte. Band 34: Das Zwanzigste Jahrhundert I, Frankfurt/Main, 1985, S. 42.
[104] Ebd., S. 43.
[105] Vgl.: Scheuch, Manfred: Das größere Europa – Polen, Ungarn, Tschechien, Slowakei, Slowenien und die Baltischen Staaten in Geschichte und Gegenwart, Wien, 2002, S. 62.
[106] Vgl.: Parker, R. A. C. [Hrsg.]: Fischer Weltgeschichte. Band 34: Das Zwanzigste Jahrhundert I, Frankfurt/Main, 1985, S. 42.

Rumänien hatte sein Staatsgebiet mehr als verdoppelt. Das umstrittene Siebenbürgen, die Bukowina und der Banat von Timișoara fielen an Rumänien. Außerdem musste auch das ehemalige Russische Reich Bessarabien an Rumänien abtreten.

Für Bulgarien brachte der Friedensvertrag von Neuilly keine größeren Veränderungen mit sich.

> "Zwei kleine Bezirke [...Süd-.DOT] Bulgariens wurden an Jugoslawien abgetreten. Die Begründung war strategischer Natur: zwischen der Eisenbahnlinie durch Jugoslawien nach Saloniki und der bulgarischen Grenze sollte ein größerer Abstand geschaffen werden. [...] und dies bedeute, dass Bulgarien den Zugang zum Ägäischen Meer verlor. Hätte die Volkstumszugehörigkeit bei der Abtretung West-Thraziens eine Rolle gespielt, so hätte der größte Teil des Gebietes an die Türkei fallen müssen, doch den Türken sprach man die Eignung für die Herrschaftsübernahme ab."[107]

Wieder einmal waren die Grenzziehungen weder exakt noch für alle Parteien akzeptabel. Wirtschaftliche und strategische Faktoren, wie zum Beispiel Zugänge zu Meeren oder Flüssen, bei der Festlegung der neuen Staaten führten zu willkürlichen Grenzziehungen. Der Erste Weltkrieg hatte ein neues Europa entstehen lassen.

> "Ein großer Teil der Bevölkerung Europas fand sich als Ergebnis des Ersten Weltkrieges, ohne dass er seinen Heimatort verlassen hatte, in einem neuen Staat wieder. Für etwa 80 Millionen Menschen änderten die vorgenommenen Grenzziehungen die Staatsbürgerschaft."[108]

Staaten, in denen eine Ethnie mehr als 90 Prozent der Bevölkerung stellte, blieben die Ausnahme. Zahlreicher waren die Staaten, in denen eine oder mehrere Nationalitäten eine beträchtliche Minderheit bildeten.

---

[107] Ebd., S. 44.
[108] Haus der Heimat des Landes Baden-Württemberg [Hrsg.]: Umsiedlung, Flucht und Vertreibung der Deutschen als internationales Problem. Zur Geschichte eines europäischen Irrwegs, Stuttgart, 2005, S. 7.

K 3: Veränderungen der Staatsgrenzen in Europa nach dem Ersten Weltkrieg[109]

Alliierte und assoziierte Hauptmächte und Mächte

Polen nach 1921

Besiegte Mächte und deren Verbündete

Von Deutschland durch den Friedensvertrag von Versailles abgetretene Gebiete (28.06.1919)

Von Deutsch-Österreich durch den Friedensvertrag von Saint-Germain-en-Laye abgetretene Gebiete (19.09.1919)

Von Bulgarien durch den Friedensvertrag von Neuilly abgetretene Gebiete (27.11.1919)

Von Ungarn durch den Friedensvertrag von Trianon abgetretene Gebiete (04.06.1920)

Von der Russischen Sozialistischen Föderativen Sowjetrepublik abgetretene Gebiete (27.11.1919)

■ Vertragsorte

---

[109] Aus: Haus der Heimat des Landes Baden-Württemberg [Hrsg.]: Umsiedlung, Flucht und Vertreibung der Deutschen als internationales Problem. Zur Geschichte eines europäischen Irrwegs, Stuttgart, 2005, S. 43.

K 4: Veränderungen der Staatsgrenzen in Südosteuropa nach den Friedensverträgen[110]

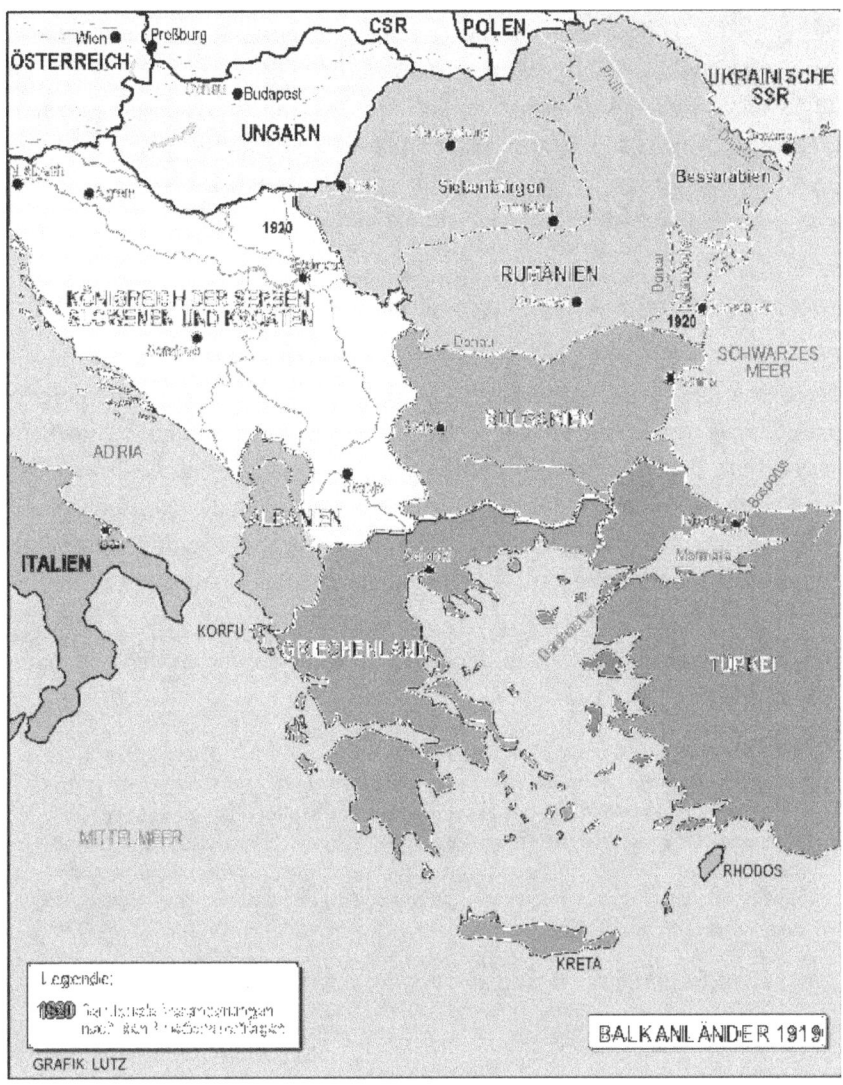

---

[110] Aus: Österreichische Militärische Zeitschrift/Grafikarchiv: http://www.bmlv.gv.at/omz/grafiken/vollbild/brill3500.png.

3.2.6. Der Vertrag von Sèvres (1920)

Der Erste Weltkrieg endete für das Osmanische Reich mit einer bedingungslosen Kapitulation. Am 31. Oktober 1918 wurde in Mudros an der ägäischen Küste ein Waffenstillstandsabkommen abgeschlossen. Knapp zwei Jahre später, am 10. August 1920, musste der Sultan den Friedensvertrag von Sèvres unterschreiben. Dieser Vertrag ging über die anderen Pariser Verträge hinaus. Jacques Benoist-Méchin bewertet die Vertragsbedingungen:

> "C'était uni condamnation á mort. L'empire était anéanti; l'Anatolie, démembrée; le peuple turc, colonisé et voué à la servitude."[111]

Die Staatshoheit wurde den Osmanen fast komplett entrissen – so war sogar der Besitz der Hauptstadt Istanbul widerrufbar. Des Weiteren schrumpfte das ehemals riesige Reich auf ein relativ kleines Gebiet zusammen: Griechenland erhielt den größten Teil Ostthrakiens, die ägäische Inselwelt und das reiche Hinterland um Smyrna.[112] Artikel 88 und 89 sahen die vollständige und teilweise Abtretung der "vilayets of Erzerum, Trebizond, Van and Bitlis"[113] an das auf russischem Boden am 8. Mai 1919 gegründete unabhängige Armenien vor.

Die Artikel 62 bis 64 gestanden dem kurdischen Volk zwar lokale Autonomie zu, jedoch waren die Zusagen unpräzise:

> "If within one year from the coming into force of the present Treaty the Kurdish peoples within the areas defined in Article 62 shall address themselves to the Council of the League of Nations in such manner as to show that a majority of the population of these areas desire independence from Turkey, and if the Council then considers that these peoples are capable of such independence and recommends that it should be granted to them, Turkey hereby agrees to execute such a recommendation, and to renounce all rights and title over these areas."[114]

Dies galt nicht für Südkurdistan, das im Irak aufgehen sollte.

---

[111] Benoist-Méchin, Jacques: Le Loup et le Leopard. Mustafa Kèmal ou la mort d'un empire, Paris, 1954, S. 239.
[112] Vgl.: Matuz, Josef: Das Osmanische Reich. Grundlinien seiner Geschichte, 2. Aufl., Darmstadt, 1990, S. 273.
[113] Martin, Lawrence: The Treaties of Peace, 1919-1923, Vol. II, New York, 1924, S. 815.
[114] Ebd., S. 807f.

"Es versteht sich, dass den armenischen und kurdischen Vertretern in Paris bewusst war, dass sich ihre Ansprüche vielfach überschnitten. Auch ist hervorzuheben, dass der neue Staat Armenien in Sèvres gleichberechtigt neben den europäischen Kleinstaaten von Belgien bis zur Tschechoslowakei am Verhandlungstisch saß, während der kurdischen Delegation unter dem ehemaligen osmanischen Diplomaten Serif Pascha nicht einmal ein Katzentisch eingeräumt war. Da es den Kurden an mächtigen Fürsprechern fehlte, begnügte sich ihr Wortführer mit dem Autonomiegebiet, das nur ein Drittel der ehemals osmanischen Kurdenbevölkerung erfasste."[115]

Große Teile Anatoliens gingen an Italien (von Adana bis nach Bursa und Afyonkarahisar), Frankreich (von Kilikien bis nach Norden weit über Sivas hinaus) und Großbritannien. Die Flotte des Sultans wurde auf wenige Schiffe beschränkt[116], ebenso die Armee, die auf 50 700 Mann, einschließlich der 35 000 Mann starken Gendarmerie, reduziert wurde (Artikel 152-164).[117]

Artikel 140 bis 151 regelten die Minoritätenpolitik, wonach alle Minderheiten in Wahlen proportional zu ihrer Größe vertreten sein sollten. Ebenso wurden allen ethnischen, religiösen und sprachlichen Gruppen die gleichen bürgerlichen und kulturellen Rechte eingeräumt[118]. Die Meerengen wurden entmilitarisiert und unter Kontrolle einer internationalen Kommission gestellt.[119] Die Artikel 231-260 legten fest, dass das Reich den Alliierten sämtliche Einnahmen als Entschädigung zu bezahlen habe.[120]

Dieser Friedensvertrag, der das Osmanische Reich auf knapp die Hälfte des Staatsgebietes der heutigen Türkei schrumpfen ließ und ihr keine eigentliche Souveränität einräumte, hatte weite Teile Anatoliens den europäischen Westmächten zur wirtschaftlichen Ausbeutung übertragen.[121]

"Seul restait à la Turquie un territoire de 120.000 kilomètres carrés, couvert en majeure partie de terres incultes et de broussailles, privé de toute possibilité de développement et même d'existence économique, ligoté non seulement par les anciennes Capitulations, mais par un nouveau système de 'garanties' qui ve-

---

[115] Kreiser, Klaus/Neumann, Christoph K.: Kleine Geschichte der Türkei, Bonn, 2005, S. 379.
[116] Vgl.: Matuz, Josef: Das Osmanische Reich. Grundlinien seiner Geschichte, 2. Aufl., Darmstadt, 1990, S. 274.
[117] Vgl.: Martin, Lawrence: The Treaties of Peace, 1919-1923, Vol. II, New York, 1924, S. 834ff.
[118] Vgl.: Ebd. S. 828ff.
[119] Vgl.: Ebd., S. 799ff.
[120] Vgl.: Ebd., S. 854ff.
[121] Vgl.: Kreiser, Klaus/Neumann, Christoph K.: Kleine Geschichte der Türkei, Bonn, 2005, S. 379.

naient se superposer à elles. En un mot, la Turquie n'était plus qu'un petit Etat mutilé, émasculé, n'ayant qu'une indépendance nominale et contraint d'obéir en tout aux Puissances victorieuses. Car chaque détail de la vie de Turcs devait être soumis à une réglementation sévère."[122]

3.3. Von Sèvres nach Lausanne

3.3.1. Der nationale Widerstand Mustafa Kemals und die *Megali Idea*

Die zum Sultan oppositionelle Gegenregierung in Ankara erkannte den Vertrag von Sèvres nicht an. Zur selben Zeit trafen die Briten eine Entscheidung mit weitreichenden Folgen: Sie stimmten der Entsendung Mustafa Kemals nach Anatolien zu, der die versprengten Truppen des Osmanischen Reiches zusammensammeln und entwaffnen sollte. Statt die Truppen zu entwaffnen, organisierte dieser einen nationalen Widerstand der Türken gegen die Besatzer.

> "Schon im September 1919 hatte der türkische Widerstand gegen die französischen Truppen begonnen. Im Mai 1920 zogen sich die Franzosen zurück und konzentrierten sich fortan auf Syrien und den Libanon. Zwei Monate zuvor hatte Italien nach nur wenigen Scharmützeln Konya und Antalya geräumt und gleichzeitig auf alle Ansprüche in der Türkei verzichtet. Ende September wehrten die Türken einen Angriff der armenischen Daschnaken ab und überschritten die Grenze zu Armenien."[123]

Die Armenier, die keine Unterstützung erhielten, stimmten der Revision der Bedingungen von Sèvres im Frieden von Gümrü (Leninakan) am 3. Dezember 1920 zu.[124] Die Union der Sozialistischen Sowjetrepubliken unter Lenin hatte die Regierung in Ankara bereits im Juni, als Revanche für die antirevolutionären Angriffe der Alliierten auf die Oktoberrevolution, anerkannt. Die Ostflanke war somit abgesichert. Während sich die Türken, ausgerüstet mit Waffen und Kriegsmaterialien der Bolschewiki, nun auf die Front im Westen gegen

---

[122] Benoist-Méchin, Jacques: Le Loup et le Leopard. Mustafa Kèmal ou la mort d'un empire, Paris, 1954, S. 240.
[123] Seufert, Günter/Kubaseck, Christopher: Die Türkei. Politik, Geschichte, Kultur, 2. Aufl., München, 2006, S. 83.
[124] Vgl.: Matuz, Josef: Das Osmanische Reich. Grundlinien seiner Geschichte, 2. Aufl., Darmstadt, 1990, S. 274.

die Griechen konzentrierten, stellte Großbritannien die Hilfslieferungen an die Griechen ein.[125] Diese waren im Mai 1919 in Izmir gelandet, hielten sich jedoch nicht an die Abmachungen von Sèvres, sondern marschierten in Westanatolien und Ostthrakien ein mit dem Ziel der Verwirklichung der nationalistischen *Megali Idea*, der Großen Idee, alle griechischen Siedlungsgebiete in einem Staat zu vereinen und Konstantinopel zurückzugewinnen. Der Marsch in Richtung Ankara konnte jedoch von den Truppen Ismet Paschas am Fluss Sakarya nördlich von Eskişehir aufgehalten werden.

"Griechenland, das sich von allen Seiten im Stich gelassen fühlte, schritt zu einer Verzweiflungstat: Ende Juli 1922 verkündete es, es werde Konstantinopel besetzen. Gleichzeitig wurde die Unabhängigkeit 'Ioniens', d.h. der Umgegend von Smyrna (Izmir) proklamiert. Eine griechische Besetzung der osmanischen Hauptstadt paßte allerdings nicht in die Pläne der Entente-Mächte [...]. So konnte Ankara Ende August einen Generalangriff auf die griechischen Stellungen riskieren, bei dem die Griechen in wenigen Tagen eine vernichtende Niederlage erlitten"[126] und die Westküste Kleinasiens schließlich verließen. Am 9. September 1922 marschierten türkische Truppen in Smyrna ein. Es wiederholte sich dieselbe Tragik wie beim Einmarsch der Griechen vor drei Jahren: *Çetes* begannen ein Massaker an der griechischen und armenischen Zivilbevölkerung, das ausländischen Berichterstattern zufolge etwa 100 000 Menschenleben forderte. Ein Brand, über dessen Urheberschaft heftig diskutiert wird[127], Augenzeugenberichten zufolge aber von der türkischen Armee initiiert wurde[128], zerstörte die Stadt fast vollständig. 300 000 Überlebende wurden evakuiert. Am 11. Oktober 1922 einigten sich die Entente-Mächte und die Kemalisten, deren Truppen gegenüber sich die

---

[125] Vgl.: Pitsoulis, Athanassios: Vertreibung und Diplomatie: Hintergründe und Umdeutungen des griechisch-türkischen 'Bevölkerungsaustausch' von 1923, in: IMIS-Beiträge, (36) 2010, S. 45f.

[126] Matuz, Josef: Das Osmanische Reich. Grundlinien seiner Geschichte, 2. Aufl., Darmstadt, 1990, S. 276f.

[127] In ersten Berichten wird die türkische Armee verantwortlich gemacht. Das französische Außenministerium veröffentlichte jedoch einen Bericht, wonach Armenier bzw. Griechen das Feuer gelegt hätten. Bis heute schieben sich Griechen und Türken gegenseitig die Verantwortung für den Brand zu (vgl.: Pitsoulis, Athanassios: Vertreibung und Diplomatie: Hintergründe und Umdeutungen des griechisch-türkischen 'Bevölkerungsaustausch' von 1923, in: IMIS-Beiträge, (36) 2010, S. 48, Anmerkung Nr. 40).

[128] Vgl.: Milton, Giles: Paradise Lost. Smyrna 1922: The Destruction of a Christian City in the Islamic World, New York, 2008, S. 307.

Entente-Mächte erstaunlich passiv verhalten hatten, in Mudanya darauf, neue Friedensverhandlungen zu beginnen. Voraussetzung für den Sieg Mustafa Kemals waren nach Klaus Kreiser und Christoph K. Neumann "die militärischen Siege gegen Griechenland und der Prestigeverlust der Istanbuler Regierung in der Bevölkerung. Die türkische Geschichte wäre ohne die (aus griechischer Sicht) 'kleinasiatische Katastrophe' und ohne den Sultan-Kalifen, der mehr als die Hälfte Anatoliens zu opfern bereit war, um die Stellung seines Hauses zu retten, anders verlaufen. Darüber hinaus verbesserte sich die Lage der Nationalisten durch die Zusammenarbeit mit Moskau und die abnehmende Bereitschaft von Italien und Frankreich, hinter die Interessen Großbritanniens zurückzutreten."[129]

Nach Athanassios Pitsoulis fasste der US-Botschafter in Athen, Henry S. Morgenthau, die diplomatische Konstellation treffend zusammen:

> "Frankreich und Italien standen dem Vertrag von Sèvres kritisch gegenüber, akzeptierten ihn aber, um ihr Verhältnis zu Großbritannien nicht zu gefährden; als besonders problematisch galten ihnen aber die großen Territorialkonzessionen an Griechenland und die darauf erwachsene Bedeutung des Landes als Seemacht im Mittelmeer. Die französische und italienische Regierung betrachteten Griechenland als Agent eines britischen Plans zur Beherrschung des Osmanischen Reiches."[130]

3.3.2. Der Vertrag von Lausanne (1923)

Dem Sieg der türkischen Nationalisten folgten erneut Friedensverhandlungen. Diese begannen im November 1922 im schweizerischen Lausanne. Am Verhandlungstisch saßen Vertreter Großbritanniens, Frankreichs, Italiens, Japans, Griechenlands, Rumäniens, des Serbo-Kroatisch-Slowenischen Königreiches und der Türkei. Zur wichtigsten Aufgabe des türkischen Abgesandten zählte die Revision der Bedingungen des Diktatfriedens von Sèvres. Atatürk wählte die Delegierten selbst aus und setzte Ismet Pascha an ihre Spitze.

> "On s'étonne qu'il ait choisi un militaire, pur mener à bien une mission diplomatique aussi délicate. Mais plusieurs raisons lui avaient dicté ce choix. D'abord, le

---

[129] Kreiser, Klaus/Neumann, Christoph K.: Kleine Geschichte der Türkei, Bonn, 2005, S. 385.
[130] Pitsoulis, Athanassios: Vertreibung und Diplomatie: Hintergründe und Umdeutungen des griechisch-türkischen 'Bevölkerungsaustausch' von 1923, in: IMIS-Beiträge, (36) 2010, S. 45, Anmerkung Nr. 33.

Ghazi avait une confiance absolue en son ancien chef d'état-major. Il savait qu'il lui était entièrement dévoué et suivrait ses directives à la lettre."[131]

Ähnliche Gründe werden in der türkischen Literatur aufgeführt: "Zudem war er [gemeint: Ismet Pascha. DOT] auch ein Soldat, der die Befehle Mustafa Kemal Paschas ohne Kommentare durchführte."[132] In Lausanne saßen die Türken, anders als in Sèvres, nicht mehr als Verlierer am Verhandlungstisch. Der türkischen Delegation ging es neben der Revision auch um den Übergang von der osmanischen Herrschaft zur nationalen Souveränität und die Verankerung der Türkei in Europa. Nach intensiven Verhandlungen und einer Unterbrechung unterzeichneten die Parteien am 24. Juli 1923 schließlich den Friedensvertrag von Lausanne. Josef Matuz bezeichnet diesen Vertrag nicht als Diktatfrieden, sondern eher als Kompromissfrieden, da die neue Türkei nicht mehr als Verlierer galt und andererseits die Front der Gegner sich schon länger gelockert hatte.[133]

Der Lausanner Vertrag akzeptierte die Teilung Thrakiens und markierte die Grenze zu Griechenland größtenteils entlang des Flusses Maritza. Edirne unterlag somit wieder türkischer Herrschaft. Izmir (Smyrna) und sein Hinterland wurden der Türkei ohne Einschränkung der Souveränität zugesprochen.[134] Die Inseln Tenedos und Imbros und die Küsten der Dardanellen und des Bosporus wurden wieder türkisches Hoheitsgebiet.[135] Auf die arabischen Länder erhoben die Türken keinen Anspruch, lediglich an Mosul zeigten sie Interesse, jedoch gelang es ihnen nicht, die überwiegend kurdische Stadt einzuverleiben. Die Grenze zu Syrien wurde bereits am 20. Oktober 1921 in einem französisch-türkischen Abkommen festgelegt, während sich über die Grenze zum Irak die Türkei und Großbritannien innerhalb von neun Monaten einigen sollten (Artikel 3).[136] Im Gegensatz zu den anderen Verlierernationen des Ersten Weltkrieges, Deutschland, Österreich-Ungarn und Bulgarien,

---

[131] Benoist-Méchin, Jacques: Le Loup et le Leopard. Mustafa Kèmal ou la mort d'un empire, Paris, 1954, S. 303.
[132] Çavdaroğlu, Hüseyin Avni: Önce ve Sonrası ile Lozan (Vor und nach Lausanne), İstanbul, 2011, S. 67 (Hem de Mustafa Kemal Paşa'nin emirlerini yorumsuz uygulayan bir asker; Übersetzung des Verfassers).
[133] Vgl.: Matuz, Josef: Das Osmanische Reich. Grundlinien seiner Geschichte, 2. Aufl., Darmstadt, 1990, S. 277.
[134] Vgl.: Martin, Lawrence: The Treaties of Peace, 1919-1923, Vol. II, New York, 1924, S. 961f.
[135] Vgl.: Ebd., S. 965.
[136] Vgl.: Ebd., S. 962.

musste die neue Türkei keine Reparationszahlungen an die Alliierten leisten.[137] Ein kritischer Punkt waren jedoch die Minderheiten, deren Schutz in den Artikeln 30-45 festgelegt wurde.[138] Bedauerlicherweise unterschied der Vertrag von Lausanne lediglich zwischen Muslimen und Nichtmuslimen, so dass die Türkei immer wieder mit dem Vertragswerk argumentierte, um muslimische Minderheiten, wie zum Beispiel die Kurden, von diesen Vereinbarungen de facto auszuklammern.

Das Schicksal der griechischen und türkischen Minderheiten wurde in einem bilateralen Abkommen in Form eines Bevölkerungsaustausches geregelt.[139]

> "Zwei weitere Völker – untereinander verfeindet – hatten in anderer Weise ebenfalls sehr zu leiden: Die Forderungen der Armenier und der Kurden wurden bei der Konferenz schlicht übergangen. Von einem unabhängigen Armenien war nicht mehr die Rede, und von einem autonomen Kurdistan ebensowenig. Es wurden noch Vorschläge zur Schaffung einer armenischen 'nationalen Heimstatt' gemacht, aber die Türken weigerten sich, darüber zu diskutieren, und die Franzosen und die Briten beharrten nicht darauf. So blieben die Armenier ein geteiltes Volk[...]. Die Kurden dagegen wurden zum 'Nicht-Volk' in Kemals Nationalstaat; man erklärte sie kurzerhand zu 'Bergtürken'."[140]

Mehrere Rebellionen der Kurden in den Folgejahren wurden brutal unterdrückt. "Das Minderheitenproblem war also ganz im Sinne der türkischen Nationalisten geregelt."[141] Mit der Vernichtung und Deportation der beiden christlichen Minderheiten, der Armenier in den Jahrzehnten zuvor und der Griechen während und nach dem *nationalen Widerstand*, war das Minderheitenproblem aus türkischer Sicht sowieso erledigt. "Malgré sa situation difficile, Ismet avait réussi à faire triompher ses revendications dans une mesure rarement atteinte au cours de négociations de ce genre"[142], urteilt Benoist-Méchin.

---

[137] Vgl.: Palmer, Alan: Verfall und Untergang des Osmanischen Reiches, München, 1992, S. 378.
[138] Vgl.: Martin, Lawrence: The Treaties of Peace, 1919-1923, Vol. II, New York, 1924, S. 969ff.
[139] Vgl.: Ebd., S. 1036ff.
[140] Palmer, Alan: Verfall und Untergang des Osmanischen Reiches, München, 1992, S. 379.
[141] Matuz, Josef: Das Osmanische Reich. Grundlinien seiner Geschichte, 2. Aufl., Darmstadt, 1990, S. 277.
[142] Benoist-Méchin, Jacques: Le Loup et le Leopard. Mustafa Kèmal ou la mort d'un empire, Paris, 1954, S. 306.

4. Sieg oder Niederlage? – Die Verträge von Sèvres und Lausanne aus türkischer Perspektive

Wie werden die Verträge von Lausanne und Sèvres in der Türkei bzw. von türkischer Seite bewertet? Ali Naci Karacan, der während der Verhandlungen in Lausanne persönlich anwesend war und von Ismet Pascha als auch anderen führenden Kemalisten gelobt wird[143] und zu einem Vertreter der offiziellen Staatsideologie gehört, sieht im Vertrag von Lausanne das "historische Ereignis, das den neuen türkischen Staat geschaffen hat"[144]. Dieses "große türkische Wunder"[145] begann, so Karacan, mit dem Einzug Mustafa Kemals und seiner Truppen in Izmir und ermöglichte letztendlich, dass "seit Jahrhunderten zum ersten Mal ein junger türkischer General nach Europa zog, nicht wegen der Vergehen seines Volkes, sondern um die Lorbeeren des Sieges einzusammeln"[146] Für ihn steht ohne Zweifel fest, dass die Errungenschaften der Lausanner Friedensverhandlungen mit ein Grund waren, dass 20 Jahre später "die Türkei dem schlimmsten Feuer der Welt"[147], dem Zweiten Weltkrieg, fernbleiben konnte. Er schreibt, dass der *nationale Befreiungskrieg* die Großmächte zwang, einen Frieden abzuschließen, um den Vormarsch der türkischen Truppen zu beenden. Das Ergebnis war die Anerkennung des neuen Staates.[148] Karacan geht auf die Situation im Vorfeld der Verhandlungen ein, wonach die "Minderheiten sich um ihr Leben sorgten, während die Staaten hingegen [...] in Hast waren, um so viel wie möglich aus dem Feuer zu holen"[149]. In einem Telegramm von Ismet Pascha sieht Karacan

---

[143] Vgl.: Karacan, Ali Naci: Lozan (Lausanne), 2. Aufl. Istanbul, 1971, S. 7f.
[144] Ebd., S. 15 (Yeni Türk Devletini kuran tarihi olayın; Übersetzung des Verfassers).
[145] Ebd., S. 16 (Büyük Türk mucizesini; Übersetzung des Verfassers).
[146] Ebd., S. 16 (Yüzyıllardan beri ilk defa olarak genç bir Türk Generali, Avrupa'nın karşısına, milletinin kabahatlerini ödemeye değil, fakat zaferinin sonuçlarını toplamaya gelmiştir; Übersetzung des Verfassers).
[147] Ebd., S. 17 (Türkiye'yi, dünyanın en korkunç yangınının ortasında; Übersetzung des Verfassers).
[148] Vgl.: Ebd., S. 75.
[149] Ebd., S. 77 (Azınlıklar can korkusunda iken devletler de [...] yangından ne koparabilecekleri telaşında idiler; Übersetzung des Verfassers).

den Vorstoß der Türkei, zum ersten Mal in Augenhöhe mit den großen Staaten zu sprechen. Das Telegramm beinhaltete gleichzeitig eine Drohung: "Ein Hinauszögern der Konferenz könnte Folgen nach sich ziehen, die von uns nicht mehr zu beherrschen sind."[150] Worauf lässt sich dieses Selbstbewusstsein, das schließlich zur Selbstüberschätzung führen sollte, zurückführen? Karacan erklärt hierzu:

> "Die türkischen Armeen hatten in enormer Geschwindigkeit Anatolien vom Feind gesäubert und gelangten bis an die Tore von Istanbul und Çanakkale und gingen nicht noch weiter, weil sie dem Vertrag von Mudanya und den Worten der Alliierten vertrauten."[151]

Die Türkei war nicht mehr das Osmanische Reich, das "verstorben"[152] war, weil es als Gegner der Alliierten in den Krieg eintrat, sondern, "wie es Ismet Pascha [...] sagte, ein Nationalstaat. Ihre Nationalität hatte sie während des Kampfes gegen die Griechen gezeigt, indem sie siegte [...]. Die Alliierten haben das Osmanische Reich besiegt. Indem sie aus diesem Reich arabischsprechende Gebiete abtrennten, sonderten sie insbesondere eine türkische Masse ab."[153]

Ganz zentral scheint für Karacan das frühzeitige Erscheinen Ismet Paschas in Lausanne zu sein, worauf er immer wieder eingeht. Diese Pünktlichkeit brachte demnach die Verhandlungspartner in Schwierigkeiten.[154] Daneben waren es, nach Karacan, in erster Linie die Fähigkeiten des Ismet Pascha, mit denen die Sympathien der Reporter und Anwesenden gewonnen wurden.

> "Er wog jedes Wort ab [...] und sprach in einem perfekten Französisch. Dass dieser türkische Kommandant, der die riesige Armee der Griechen zerschlagen hat-

---

[150] Ebd., S. 80 (Eğer konferans gecikirse, öyle sonuçlar doğurabilir ki önüne geçemeyiz; Übersetzung des Verfassers).
[151] Ebd., S. 80 (Türk orduları müthiş bir hızla Anadolu'yu düşmandan temizlemişler, İstanbul'un kapılarına ve Çanakkale önlerine gelmişler, ancak Mudanya antlaşmasıyla ve müttefiklerin sözlerine inanarak daha ileri gitmemişlerdi; Übersetzung des Verfassers).
[152] Ebd., S. 81 (vefat eden; Übersetzung des Verfassers).
[153] Ebd., S. 81f. (Türkiye, İsmet Paşa'nın [...] dediği gibi, Millî bir devlettir. Milliyetini, Yunanlılara karşı yaptığı mücadelede düşmanlarını yenerek göstermiştir[...]. Müttefikler Osmanlı İmparatorluğunu mağlûbettiler. Bu İmparatorluktan Arapça konuşan memleketleri ayırmakla özellikle Türk bir kitleyi ayırmış oldular; Übersetzung des Verfassers).
[154] Vgl.: Ebd., S. 78ff. und S. 86.

te, so aufrichtig sprach [...] hatten sie nicht erwartet [...]. Er gebrauchte kein einziges Mal ein 'Ich' oder 'mh'."[155]

Eine ähnliche Bewertung finden wir bei dem Franzosen Benoist-Méchin:

"Dans chacune des mille questions que soulevaient la liquidation de l'empire ottoman et la rédaction du traité, il chercha et sut trouver des alliés dans les rangs des diplomates de l'Entente. Dès qu'une question était réglée et que la suivante venait en discussion, il abandonnait aussitôt ses alliés pour d'autres, qui lui semblaient plus utiles en l'occurrence. 'Opérant sur la ligne intérieure, changeant ses batteries avec uni opiniâtreté inébranlable à ses reendications fondementales, le général turc surclassa les diplomates européens, dans toutes les phases de la négociation'."[156]

Mustafa Kemal dankt persönlich in einem Telegramm, kurz nach Unterzeichnung des Vertrages, Ismet Pascha für seine Verdienste.[157] Auch andere Autoren loben Ismet Paschas Verhandlungstalente und sehen ihn als den "erfolgreichsten Diplomaten in der Diplomatiegeschichte der modernen Türkei"[158]. Jedoch sollte erwähnt werden, dass Ismet Pascha von M. Tschitscherin, einem sowjetischen Delegierten, unterstützt wurde.[159] Des Weiteren findet sich bei Hüseyin Avni Çavdaroğlus Bewertung Ismet Paschas ein Widerspruch zu Karacans Ausführungen bezüglich der Französischkenntnisse des Delegierten: "Ismet Pascha sprach bis auf wenige Worte Französisch keine weitere Fremdsprache. Die Gespräche wurden ihm übersetzt."[160]

---

[155] Ebd., S. 86f. (o kelimeleri tartarak, [...] tertemiz fransızca söylemeye başladığında [...]. Koca Yunan ordusunu darmadağınık eden bu Türk Kumandanının bu derece samimî konuşması [...] hiç beklemedikleri bir olaydı [...]. hiçbir defa <ben>li ve <m>li siga kullanmadı; Übersetzung des Verfassers).

[156] Benoist-Méchin, Jacques: Le Loup et le Leopard. Mustafa Kèmal ou la mort d'un empire, Paris, 1954, S. 305.

[157] Vgl.: Kökütürk, Yalın İştenç: Lozan Konferansı. Gazi Mustafa Kemal (Die Lausanner Konferenz. Gazi Mustafa Kemal), İstanbul, 2011, S. 126f.

[158] Sonyel, Salâhi R.: Türk Kurtuluş Savaşı [sic!] ve Dış Politika II. Büyük Millet Meclisi'nin Açılışından Lozan Anlaşmasına Kadar (Der türkische Befreiungskrieg und die Außenpolitik II. Von der Parlamentseröffnung bis zum Lausanner Vertrag), Ankara, 1986, S. 356 (Türkiye'de modern diplomasinin en başarılı bir diplomatı olarak; Übersetzung des Verfassers).

[159] Vgl.: de Bischoff, Norbert: La Turquie dans le monde. Paris, 1936, S. 124.

[160] Çavdaroğlu, Hüseyin Avni: Önce ve Sonrası ile Lozan (Vor und nach Lausanne), İstanbul, 2011, S. 67 (İsmet Paşa az miktarda Fransızca'dan başka yabancı dil bilmiyordu. [...] Konuşmalar kendisine tercüme ediliyordu; Übersetzung des Verfassers).

Den Europäern wirft Karacan vor, bei den Verhandlungen das alte Osmanische Reich erwartet zu haben, obwohl mit dem Betreten anatolischen Bodens durch Mustafa Kemal ein neuer Staat entstanden sei.[161] So hätten sich alle Staaten vereint, um die neue Türkei wie das alte Osmanische Reich zu behandeln.[162] Nach zähen Verhandlungen habe sich Ismet Pascha schließlich durchsetzen können. Zu den wichtigsten Punkten gehörten Freiheit, Unabhängigkeit und Souveränität. Im Anschluss erwähnt er die Minderheiten der Türkei, insbesondere die Armenier, deren Pläne eines unabhängigen Staates vom Sèvres-Vertrag zunichte gemacht worden seien[163], und fügt eine interessante Bemerkung hinzu:

> "Die neuen Türken wollen nicht nur Soldaten und Staatsdiener werden, sondern auch Bankiers, Ärzte, Ingenieure, Gelehrte [...]. Vieles was bisher die nicht türkischen Nationen machten, wollen die Türken jetzt selbst leisten."[164]

In dieser Aussage lässt sich eine mögliche Erklärung für den Hass der Türken gegenüber den Griechen und Armeniern finden. Mit ethnischen Säuberungen, sei es während der Deportation der Armenier oder dem griechisch-türkischen Bevölkerungsaustausch, versuchte die türkische Elite, die bisherige Bourgeoisie durch ihre eigene nationale Bourgeoisie zu ersetzen – so lag dieser Status bisher in den Händen der Armenier und Griechen.

Ein rigider Ethno-Nationalismus, der durch ständige Wiederholungen verstärkt wird, kommt in Karacans Ausführungen zum Ausdruck. Es scheint, als ob um jeden Preis eine neue Nation erschaffen werden müsse.

Im Schlussteil seiner Ausführungen geht Karacan auf den Vertrag von Sèvres ein, fasst ihn zusammen und bewertet ihn:

> "Thrakien sollte Griechenland gehören, Istanbul wäre zwischenstaatlich geworden, Westanatolien eine griechische Kolonie, Ostanatolien Armenien, Adana eine französische Kolonie, Antalya eine italienische Kolonie, wir hätten keine Armee, keine Kriegsflotte besessen. Der Palast wäre von allen Staaten, ob klein oder groß, kontrolliert worden und hätte nur Macht über ein-zwei Provinzen in Zent-

---

[161] Vgl.: Karacan, Ali Naci: Lozan (Lausanne), 2. Aufl., Istanbul, 1971, S. 93f.
[162] Vgl.: Ebd., S. 622.
[163] Vgl.: Ebd., S. 627.
[164] Ebd., S. 627f. (Yeni Türkler yanlız asker ver memur olmakla kalmak istemiyorlar. Bankacı, doktor, mühendis, âlim olmak istiyorlar [...]. Türk olmıyan milletlerin şimdiye kadar yaptıkları pek çok işleri artık Türkler kendileri başarmak istiyorlar; Übersetzung des Verfassers).

ralanatolien ausüben können. Unser Finanzwesen, unsere Justiz [...], unsere Militärakademie, unser Schifffahrtswesen, unsere Landesgrenzen, unsere Meerengen [...] und all unsere anderen Institutionen [...] sollten unter fremder Kontrolle stehen. Die türkische Nation wäre versklavt worden. Die Herren der türkischen Nation wären Fremde und Christen geworden. Die Türken [...denen wirtschaftliche Freiheiten entzogen werden sollten.DOT], wären aus großen Städten und Küsten zerstreut worden, die unsterbliche türkische Nation sollte, wie sie es wollten, sterben [...] und die türkische Flagge sollte im Mittel-und Marmarameer nie wieder zu sehen sein. Das wollten sie, dies war die Bedeutung von 'Sèvres'."[165]

Als Grund führt er auf, dass die türkische Nation damals keine Soldaten und Waffen besaß. Anschließend erläutert der Autor die Folgen von Sèvres und fasst die Ergebnisse zusammen:

"Was geschehen ist, wissen wir alle. Die heilige Revolution hat sich in den Bergen Izmirs den Griechen, vor den Toren Anteps den Besatzungsmächten Adanas, an der Ostgrenze den armenischen Streitkräften entgegen gestellt. [...] Wir haben gesiegt. Die Besatzer Antalyas haben sich zurückgezogen. Glück ihnen, da sie ihr Leben gerettet haben. Diejenigen, die geblieben sind, liegen nun unter der Erde Anatoliens. Heute gehören Westanatolien, Ostanatolien, Adana, Thrakien, Antalya, Hatay, die Meerengen und Istanbul uns; wir haben eine Armee, eine Kriegsflotte, keinen Palast; unser Finanzwesen, unsere Justiz, [...] unsere Militärakademie, unser Schifffahrtswesen sind frei. Wir sind die Herren. Wir haben eine geographische und nationale Einheit geschaffen. Der privilegierteste Mensch in der Türkei ist wieder der Türke [...]. Dies war Ziel des Unabhängigkeitskrieges, dies ist die Bedeutung des Lausanner Vertrages."[166]

---

[165] Ebd., S. 643f. (Trakya Yunanistan'ın olacaktı; İstanbul beynelminel olacaktı; Batı Anadolu Yunan sömürgesi olacaktı; Doğu Anadolu Ermenistan olacaktı; Adana Fransız sömürgesi olacaktı; Antalya, İtalyan sömürgesi olacaktı; ordumuz olmıyacaktı; donanmamız omıyacaktı; saray, büyük küçük bütün devletlerin denetiminde ve Orta Anadolu'da bir iki vilâyet bu sarayın [...] hükmünde kalacaktı. Maliyemiz, adliyemiz, [...] harbiyemiz, denizciliğimiz, kara sınırlarımız, boğazlarımız [...] ve bütün diğer müesseselerimiz [...] yabancı kontrolu altında bulunacaktı. Türk milleti köle, yabancı ve hristiyanlar Türk milletinin efendisi olacaktı. [...] ekonomi ve ticaret te kazanç hakkını kaldırarak büyük şehirlerde ve sahillerde yaşıyan Türkler dağıtılacak, öyle istiyorlardı ki ölmez Türk Milleti ölecek, [...] Akdeniz ve Marmara sularında bir daha Türk Bayrağı görünmeyecekti. İstedikleri bu idi, 'Sèvres' antlaşmasının anlamı budur; Übersetzung des Verfassers).
[166] Ebd., S. 644 (Neler olduğunu hepimiz biliyoruz. Kutsal ihtilal İzmir dağlarında Yunanlılara, Antep kapılarında Adana istilâ kuvvetine, doğu sınırında Ermenistan kuvvetine karşı koydu. [...] yendik. Antalya istilâsı çekilip gitti. Gidenlere ne mutlu, çünkü canlarını kurtardılar. Kalanlar ise Anadolu topraklarının altında yatıyorlar. Bugün Batı Anadolu, Doğu Anadolu, Adana, Trakya, Antalya, Hatay, boğazlar ve İstanbul bizimdir; ordumuz vardır, donanmamız vardır, saray yoktur, maliyemiz, adliyemiz, [...] harbiyemiz, denizciliğimiz serbesttir. Efendiyiz.

Der Ethno-Nationalismus wird stets gelobt. Dass in der Türkei, mit ihren unzähligen Minderheiten in Anatolien, später ein Minderheitenproblem entstehen sollte, ist sicherlich auch dem Lausanner Vertrag zu verdanken. Eine ähnliche Sichtweise wie Karacan hat M. Cemil Bilsel, der den Vertrag von Sèvres mit dem Begriff *Tod* betitelt[167] und ähnlich heroisiert wie Karacan:

> "Die Alliierten hatten die Türkei bedingungslos beherrscht. Der Sultan mochte ihre Herrschaft vielleicht stützen. Aber die türkischen Herzen konnten sie nicht beherrschen. Die Unterdrückung verwandelte die tiefen Schmerzen in allen Herzen zu Hass. Es entstanden Hass-, Rache- und Aufstandsgefühle."[168]

Bilsel geht ähnlich vor wie Karacan und vergleicht die Verträge von Lausanne und Sèvres miteinander:

> "Auf der einen Seite beinhaltete der Vertrag von Sèvres die gnadenlos harten Bedingungen, die von den Siegermächten des Weltkrieges den Verlierernationen auferlegt wurden, auf der anderen Seite die Aufteilung und Vernichtung des Osmanischen Reiches gemeinsam mit der türkischen Nation durch jene Staaten, die das Osmanische Reich untereinander aufteilen wollten."[169]

Gleichzeitig fragt er, ob es möglich gewesen wäre, den Vertrag nicht zu unterschreiben, sieht darin jedoch keinen Ausweg aus dem Vertrag. Der einzige Ausweg habe in den Händen der Nation gelegen, die zur gleichen Zeit in Anatolien mit der Mobilisierung begonnen hatte.[170] In Lausanne hatten "die Türken die Ehre, Europa auf den richtigen Weg zu bringen". Überall in Europa herrschte, nach Bilsel, die Meinung vor, dass dieser Friedensvertrag ein Sieg

---

Coğrafî birlik, millî birlik gerçekleşmiştir. Türkiye'de en imtiyazlı insan yine Türk'tür. [...] İstiklâl savaşının gayesi bu idi, Lozan Antlaşmasının anlamı budur; Übersetzung des Verfassers).

[167] Vgl.: Bilsel, Cemil M.: Lozan (Lausanne), Bd. 1, Istanbul, 1933, S. 194.

[168] Ebd., S. 211 (Müttefikler Türkiyeye kayıtsız şartsız hâkim olmuşlardı. Padişah ta onların bu hâkimiyetine istinat edebilirdi. Ancak, Türk yüreğine hâkim olamamışlardı. [...]. Zulüm bütün yüreklerde hicranları kine çeviriyor; kin, intikam ve kıyam fikri doğuyordu; Übersetzung des Verfassers).

[169] Ebd., S. 305 (Sevr Muahedesi, bir yandan, dünya harbinde yenen devletlerin yenilen devletlere kıyarcasına tatbik ettikleri ağır şartları havidir. Öbür yandan, Osmanlı İmparatorluğunu paylaşmak istiyen devletlerin bu İmparatorluğu Türk milleti ile beraber parçalayış ve yok edişleridir; Übersetzung des Verfassers).

[170] Vgl.: Ebd., S. 574.

der Türken war. In den letzten Abschnitten fasst der Autor zusammen: Mit Lausanne habe die türkische Nation nach 400 Jahren ihre Souveränität wieder zurückerhalten. Für die Unabhängigkeit sei sie bereit gewesen, ihr Leben zu opfern, da man "Unabhängigkeit nicht erhält, sondern erlangt. [...] Die türkische Nation hat die Unabhängigkeit selbst erlangt."[171] Eine große Rolle habe hierbei Ismet Pascha gespielt, der in Lausanne seine Heimat würdevoll vertreten habe. "Die gesamte Befreiung, Lausanne mit eingeschlossen, war ein Werk des Gazi Mustafa Kemal"[172], sind die letzten Worte in Cemals Buch.

Die Bewertungen der kemalistischen Autoren in der Zeitgeschichte fallen ähnlich aus, so schreibt Bilal N. Şimşir:

> "Lausanne ist ein großes Ereignis. Es hat die türkische Nation nach einer 11-jährigen Kriegsphase in den Frieden geführt. Von den Wohltaten dieses Friedens profitieren wir immer noch [...]. Des Weiteren hat Lausanne die Zeit des Osmanischen Reiches beendet. Den von Europa bis nach Asien und Afrika reichenden alten Staat begrub es in der Geschichte [...]. Dem gegenüber hat Lausanne den neuen türkischen Staat auf die Bühne der Geschichte emporgehoben."[173]

Im Gegensatz zu den Pariser Friedensverträgen nach dem Ersten Weltkrieg, die keine 20 Jahre später mit dem Zweiten Weltkrieg an Bedeutung verloren hätten und verschwunden seien, hielte der Lausanner Frieden diesem Krieg stand und lebte bis heute fort, wie sonst selten ein Friedensvertrag[174]. Noch heute nähme er einen wichtigen Platz in der türkischen Außenpolitik ein.[175] Dieselbe Einschätzung – Lausanne als Friedensstifter – findet sich auch in an-

---

[171] Bilsel, Cemil M.: Lozan (Lausanne), Bd. 2, Istanbul, 1933, S. 583 (Hürriyet verilmez alınır [...] Türk milleti istiklâlini kendi aldı; Übersetzung des Verfassers).
[172] Ebd., S. 583 (Lozan da dahil olarak bütün kurtuluş, Gazi Mustafa Kemalin abidesi olduğu gibi; Übersetzung des Verfassers).
[173] Şimşir, Bilâl N.: Lozan Telgrafları. Türk Diplomatik Belgelerinde Lozan Barış Konferansı (Die Lausanner Telegramme. Der Friedensvertrag von Lausanne in türkisch-diplomatischen Dokumenten), Bd. 1, Ankara, 1990, S. IX (Lozan, büyük bir olaydır. Türk ulusunu onbir yıl süren savaş döneminden çıkarıp barışa kavuşturmuştur. O barışın nimetlerinden hala yararlanıyoruz. Bunun ötesinde Lozan, Osmalı İmparatorluğunu sona erdirmiştir. Avrupa'dan Asya'ya ve Afrika'ya uzanan o eski devleti tarihe gömmüştür [...] Buna karşılık Lozan, yeni Türk devletine tarih sahnesi çıkarmıştır; Übersetzung des Verfassers).
[174] Vgl.: T.C. Kültür Bakanlığı [Redakteur: Özel, Mehmet]: 70. Yıldönümünde Lozan (Lausanne zum 70. Jahrestag), 1993, S. 93.
[175] Vgl.: Şimşir, Bilâl N.: Lozan Telgrafları. Türk Diplomatik Belgelerinde Lozan Barış Konferansı (Die Lausanner Telegramme. Der Friedensvertrag von Lausanne in türkisch-diplomatischen Dokumenten), Bd. 1, Ankara, 1990, S. IXf.

deren staatlich herausgegebenen Werken.[176] Şimşir geht in seinem Buch besonders auf das Thema Armenien ein. Ismet Pascha hatte demnach die Anweisung erhalten, die Gespräche abzubrechen, sofern ein unabhängiges Armenien in Erwägung gezogen werden sollte. Ein weiteres heikles Thema war die Kapitulation, die von Ismet Pascha nicht zu akzeptieren war und im äußersten Fall zu einem Abbruch der Gespräche führen sollte. Von den insgesamt 14 Anweisungen, die von neuen Grenzen bis hin zu Reparationszahlungen reichten, war nur ein Punkt mit einem 'sofortigen Abbruch der Gespräche' verknüpft – Armenien. Hier war die türkische Regierung unnachgiebig und bereit, einen Krieg zu riskieren.[177] Derselbe Autor wirft den Armeniern in einem weiteren Werk vor, die Verhandlungen in Lausanne manipuliert zu haben.[178]

Anlässlich der Jahrestage des Lausanner Friedensvertrages bringt die türkische Regierung regelmäßig Publikationen heraus. Zum 70. Jahrestag zum Beispiel eine Rede von Ismet Inönü, der in bekannten Tönen den Lausanner Frieden als großes Werk und die "Republik, als Ergebnis des Unabhängigkeitskrieges und nicht des Ersten Weltkrieges"[179] darstellt. Ebenfalls zum 70. Jahrestag erschien ein umfangreiches Werk, das bereits optisch die Bedeutung Lausannes hervorhebt und ebenfalls die Geburt eines neuen Staates und einer neuen Nation betont.[180] Hier geht man sogar weiter und bezeichnet "Lausanne nicht nur als Wendepunkt in der Geschichte der modernen Türkei, sondern auch in der Menschheits- und Diplomatiegeschichte"[181].

---

[176] Vgl.: T.C. Kültür Bakanlığı [Redakteur: Özel, Mehmet]: 70. Yıldönümünde Lozan (Lausanne zum 70. Jahrestag), 1993, S. 93. Oder Sakınmaz, Şenol Koray: Lozan. Bir Milletin Yeniden Dirilişi (Lausanne. Die Wiederauferstehung einer Nation), İstanbul, 2008, S. 15f.

[177] Vgl.: Şimşir, Bilâl N.: Lozan Telgrafları. Türk Diplomatik Belgelerinde Lozan Barış Konferansı (Die Lausanner Telegramme. Der Friedensvertrag von Lausanne in türkisch-diplomatischen Dokumenten), Bd. 1, Ankara, 1990, S. XIV.

[178] Vgl.: Şimşir, Bilâl N.: Ermeni Meselesi (Die Armenierproblematik). 1774-2005, 2. Aufl., Ankara, 2005, S. 143ff.

[179] İnönü, İsmet: Lozan Barış Antlaşması'nın 70. Yıldönümü. İstiklâl Savaşı ve Lozan (Der 70. Jahrestag des Lausanner Friedensvertrages. Der Unabhängigkeitskrieg und Lausanne), Ankara, 1993, S. 1 (Cumhuriyet, istiklâl savaşının neticesidir; Birinci Cihan savaşının değildir; Übersetzung des Verfassers).

[180] Vgl.: T.C. Kültür Bakanlığı [Redakteur: Özel, Mehmet]: 70. Yıldönümünde Lozan (Lausanne zum 70. Jahrestag), 1993, S. 6.

[181] Ebd., S. 7 (Lozan, yanlızca çağdaş Türkiye'nin tarihinde değil, insanlığın ve diplomasinin tarihinde de bir dönüm noktasıdır; Übersetzung des Verfassers).

Mustafa Kemal selbst bezeichnete den Lausanner Frieden ebenfalls als Wendepunkt der türkischen Geschichte und sah darin einen politischen Sieg der türkischen Nation.[182] Er schreibt über den Vertrag von Lausanne: "Dieser Vertrag ist ein Dokument für das Scheitern des seit Jahrhunderten vorbereiteten Versuches, die türkische Nation zu vernichten, der mit dem Vertrag von Sèvres zu gelingen schien. In der osmanischen Geschichte ist ein politischer Sieg seinesgleichen nicht zu finden"[183]. Kemal listet sämtliche Unterschiede zwischen dem Vertrag von Sèvres und Lausanne auf.[184]

In dieser Tradition steht auch Taner Baytok, der einen Zusammenhang zwischen dem EU-Beitritt der Türkei und den Verträgen von Sèvres und Lausanne sieht:

"Die Themen, die der Türkei als Hindernisse für einen EU-Beitritt in den Weg gestellt werden, waren leider bereits in Sèvres und Lausanne an der Tagesordnung. Die türkisch-griechischen Verhältnisse, die Armenienfrage, Kurdistan, der Pontosgriechen-Staat, die Ägäischen Inseln, die Minderheitenrechte, wirtschaftliche Probleme [...] . Aus diesem Grund stellt sich die Frage, was sich denn an den Prinzipien der Politik des Westens gegenüber der Türkei, von gestern bis heute verändert hat?"[185]

Dass sich scheinbar nichts verändert hat, findet Baytok besorgniserregend.

In nationalistisch-islamischen Kreisen wird der Vertrag von Lausanne als Niederlage bewertet. Kadir Mısıroğlu fragt in seinem Buch 'Ist Lausanne ein Sieg oder eine Niederlage?', wie der Friedensvertrag von Lausanne zu bewerten sei, und kommt zu dem Ergebnis, dass mit Lausanne ein gewaltiges Großim-

---

[182] Vgl.: Ebd., S. 101.
[183] Pehlivanoğlu, A. Öner: Sevr, Lozan Antlaşmaları ve Avrupa Birliği (Die Verträge von Sèvres und Lausanne und die Europäische Union), Istanbul, 2005, S. 111 (Bu anlaşma, Türk ulusuna karşı, yüzyıllardan beri hazırlanmış ve Sevr Antlaşmasıyla tamamlandığı sanılmış büyük bir yok etme girişiminin yıkılışını ifade eden bir belgedir. Osmanlı tarihinde benzeri görülmemiş bir siyasi zaferdir; Übersetzung des Verfassers).
[184] Vgl.: Karacan, Ali Naci: Lozan (Lausanne), 2. Aufl., Istanbul, 1971, S. 622ff.
[185] Baytok, Taner: İngiliz Belgeleriyle Sevr'den Lozan'a. Dünden Bugüne Değişen Ne Var? (Von Lausanne nach Sèvres in englischen Dokumenten. Was hat sich von gestern auf heute verändert?), Istanbul, 2007, S. 370 (Avrupa Birliği'ne katılmak isteyen Türkiye'nin karşısına bugün çıkarılan engeller maalesef, Sevr ve Lozan'ın da gündemindeki konulardır. Türk-Yunan ilişkileri, Ermeni meselesi, Kürdistan, Rum Pontus Devleti, Ege adaları, azınlıkların hakları, ekonomik [...] sorunlar. [...] O zaman akla gelen soru şu oluyor: Batı'nın Türkiye'ye karşı uyguladığı politikaların esas ve ana ilkerinde dünden bugüne değişen ne var ki?; Übersetzung des Verfassers).

perium ausverkauft worden sei. Unter dem Vorwand, die Türken zu bekämpfen, sei Rache am Islam ausgeübt und die gesamte islamische Welt ohne Führung gelassen worden. Ismet Inönü bezeichnet er in diesem Rahmen als "gefälschten 'Lausanner Helden'"[186]. Die Türkei sei um Zypern, Westthrakien, Kirkuk betrogen und mit den Minderheitenrechten sei ihr eine schwere Last aufgebürdet worden. Yücel Hacaloğlu bewertet den Vertrag ähnlich: "Wir feiern zwar Lausanne [...], aber unsere Enkelkinder werden den Lausanner Vertrag ablehnen und ganz gewiss verändern."[187] Dieselbe Meinung findet man bei Muzaffer Taşyürek vor. Er zitiert Ali Şükrü Bey, der im Parlament Mustafa Kemal zugerufen haben soll, dass der glorreiche Sieg der türkischen Soldaten in Lausanne verspielt worden sei[188], und sieht den Beginn der Probleme in Kurdistan, der Ägäis, Westthrakien, Zypern und somit aller "Themen, die der Türkei heute in der Außenpolitik Kopfschmerzen bereiten"[189] in Lausanne. Er kritisiert die Haltung der "Staatshistoriker, die Lausanne ständig als *Sieg ohne Krone* loben, mit Sèvres vergleichen und als Unabhängigkeitserklärung der türkischen Nation darstellen"[190]. Dies würde, wie auch die kemalistischen Prinzipien, bereits in der Schule den Schülern dogmatisch vermittelt, so Taşyürek. Er erwähnt ebenfalls die Fehler des Vertrages, zu denen unter anderem das Abtreten Zyperns an Großbritannien und der Verlust der arabischen Staaten und Westthrakiens zählen würden. Weitere Kritikpunkte sind, dass den Griechen keine Reparationszahlungen auferlegt worden wären, dass Mosul, Kirkuk und Suleymaniye nicht haben einverleibt werden können, ebenso Hatay und die Inseln in der Ägäis, und dass das orthodoxe Patriarchat nicht aus dem Land habe verbannt werden können. Daneben lis-

---

[186] Vgl.: Mısıroğlu, Kadir: Lozan Zafer Mi, Hezimet Mi? (Ist Lausanne ein Sieg oder eine Niederlage?), Istanbul, 1992, S. 19.

[187] Vgl.: Hacaloğlu Yücel: Lozan, Zafer mi, Hezimet mi? (Ist Lausanne ein Sieg oder eine Niederlage), in: Yeni İstanbul Gazetesi, 1.12.1965 (Biz Lozan'ı kutlarız [...] Evlatlarımız Lozan anlaşmasını istemiyecekler ve bunu mutlaka değiştireceklerdir; Übersetzung des Verfassers).

[188] Vgl.: Taşyürek, Muzaffer: Lozan'a Hayır Diyenler (Jene, die Nein zu Lausanne sagten), Istanbul, 1995, S. 7

[189] Ebd., S. 8 (Bügün Türkiye'nin başını ağrıtan dış politika konularının mukaddimesiydi; Übersetzung des Verfassers).

[190] Ebd., S. 8 (Lozan Türkiye'nin Resmi Tarihçileri tarafından hep göklere çıkarıldı 'taçsız bir zafer' Sevr Antlaşması'yla kıyas edilerek 'Türk milletinin bağımsızlık bildirisi' gibi lanse edildi; Übersetzung des Verfassers).

tet Taşyürek weitere kleinere Themenbereiche auf.[191] Den Verlust Mosuls bezeichnet er als wirtschaftliches Desaster und sieht darin den Ursprung des PKK-Konfliktes.[192]

Den nationalistisch-islamischen Kreisen geht es vor allem um den Verlust des islamischen Osmanischen Reiches, den sie nicht akzeptieren wollen. Jedoch wird in diesen Ausführungen deutlich, dass diese Kritiker nach einem Ideal streben, das den tatsächlich vorherrschenden Bedingungen kaum entspricht. Es geht dementsprechend nicht um die Herstellung eines Friedens, sondern um die Schaffung eines Groß-Osmanischen Reiches wie zu dessen Blütezeiten. Dass die Osmanen das Reich heruntergewirtschaftet haben und der praktizierte Islam die gesamte Gesellschaft versteinerte, wird (bewusst?) übersehen.

Kritische Stimmen werden auch aus dem linken politischen Spektrum laut. Ataol Behramoğlu, ein sozialistischer Schriftsteller und Lehrender an der Istanbuler Universität, schreibt im Vorwort seines Theaterstückes mit dem Titel 'Lausanne':

> "Bereits bei meinen ersten Arbeiten stellte ich fest, dass wenn man sich Gedanken über Lausanne macht, im Grunde genommen man sich Gedanken über den Imperialismus machen muss. Ich bin der Meinung, dass es auch heute viel wichtiger ist, sich damit auseinanderzusetzen, was der Imperialismus ist, statt über Sieg oder Niederlage in Lausanne zu diskutieren."[193]

Tolga Ersoy geht in dieselbe Richtung und fragt, wieso kemalistische Autoren als auch Mustafa Kemal selbst die Verträge von Sèvres und Lausanne miteinander vergleichen, um die Bedeutung des letztgenannten hervorzuheben. Er bezieht sich auf das bereits erwähnte Zitat von Mustafa Kemal: "Dieser Vertrag ist ein Dokument für das Scheitern des seit Jahrhunderten vorbereiteten Versuches, die türkische Nation zu vernichten, der mit dem Vertrag von Sèvres zu gelingen schien. In der osmanischen Geschichte ist ein politi-

---

[191] Vgl.: Ebd., S. 379ff.
[192] Vgl.: Taşyürek, Muzaffer: Lozan'a Hayır Diyenler (Jene, die Nein zu Lausanne sagten), Istanbul, 1995, S. 377.
[193] Behramoğlu, Ataol: Lozan. İyi Bir Yurttaş Aranıyor (Lausanne. Ein guter Staatsbürger wird gesucht), Istanbul, 1993, S. 9 (Daha ilk çalışmalarım sırasında Lozan konusunda düşünmenin aslında emperyalizm üzerine düşünmek olduğunu anlamıştım. Bugün de Lozan'ın bir 'zafer'mi, yoksa bir 'hezimet' mi olduğunu tartışmaktan çok, emperyalizmin ne olduğunu tartışmamız gerektiğine inanıyorum; Übersetzung des Verfassers).

scher Sieg seinesgleichen nicht zu finden"[194], und kritisiert die Vorgehensweise. Anstatt "Lausanne an und für sich mit seinen möglichen Folgen zu bewerten, wird es mit einem Vertrag verglichen, den die halb-koloniale und untergehende osmanische Regierung abschloss oder abschließen musste"[195]. Ersoy geht mit seiner Kritik weiter und fragt nach der Mentalität Mustafa Kemals und seiner Anhänger, die auf der einen Seite ihren *Unabhängigkeitskrieg* als antiimperialistisch deklarierten, auf der anderen Seite jedoch von denselben imperialistischen Mächten anerkannt werden wollten.[196] Zudem propagiert die kemalistische Staatsideologie, so Ersoy, dass sämtliche Grenzen gefestigt oder wiederhergestellt werden konnten. Die Realität sehe jedoch anders aus. Einzig die Grenze zu Griechenland habe gefestigt werden können. Die Grenzen zu Syrien und dem Irak, und somit die Kontrolle über das Erdöl Mosuls, seien zugunsten der Kolonien Frankreichs und Großbritanniens korrigiert worden.[197]

Der Kommunist Ibrahim Kaypakkaya, der in seinen Analysen in den frühen 1970er Jahren schlussfolgert, dass der Kemalismus eine faschistische Staatsideologie sei, kritisiert ebenfalls den Vertrag von Lausanne und sieht in ihm einen niederträchtigen Akt der Kemalisten und Imperialisten gegen das Selbstbestimmungsrecht der Völker. Ohne Rücksicht auf die Interessen des kurdischen Volkes sei um die Gebiete Kurdistans gefeilscht worden. Die kemalistische Diktatur, so Kaypakkaya, sei schließlich so weit gegangen und habe die Menschheitsgeschichte von Neuem geschrieben. Sie "strich die Geschichte der anderen Minderheiten aus den Büchern komplett heraus"[198]

---

[194] Pehlivanoğlu, A. Öner: Sevr, Lozan Antlaşmaları ve Avrupa Birliği (Die Verträge von Sèvres und Lausanne und die Europäische Union), İstanbul, 2005, S. 111 (Bu anlaşma, Türk ulusuna karşı, yüzyıllardan beri hazırlanmış ve Sevr Antlaşmasıyla tamamlandığı sanılmış büyük bir yok etme girişiminin yıkılışını ifade eden bir belgedir. Osmanlı tarihinde benzeri görülmemiş bir siyasi zaferdir; Übersetzung des Verfassers).

[195] Ersoy, Tolga: Lozan. Bir Antiemperyalizm Masalı Nasıl Yazıldı? (Lausanne. Wie wurde ein antiimperialistisches Märchen geschrieben?), 2. Aufl., İstanbul, 2005, S. 13 (Lozan kendi başına ve olası sonuçlarıyla değerlendirmek yerine, yarı-sömürge ve çöküntü halindeki Osmanlı yönetiminin yaptığı ya da yapmak zorunda kaldığı anlaşmalarla karşılaştırılmakdır; Übersetzung des Verfassers).

[196] Vgl.: Ebd., S. 14.

[197] Vgl.: Ebd., S. 15.

[198] Kaypakkaya, İbrahim: Seçme Yazılar (Ausgewählte Werke), Altınçağ Yayımcılık, İstanbul, 1999, S. 119 (Diğer azınlık milliyetlerin tarihini, kitaplardan tamamen sildi; Übersetzung des Verfassers).

und entwickelte rassistische und faschistische Theorien, wie die *Güneş Dil Theorie* ('Sonnensprachtheorie'), wonach alle anderen Nationen als auch Sprachen der Welt den Türken bzw. dem Türkischen entstammten: "Die Linie, der die kemalistische Diktatur in der nationalen Frage folgt, ist ganz und gar türkisch-chauvinistisch."[199] Des Weiteren geht Kaypakkaya auf Ismet Inönü ein, der sich während der Verhandlungen in Lausanne auch als Vertreter der Kurden sah, und bezeichnet dies als niederträchtige Handlung gegen das Selbstbestimmungsrecht der kurdischen Nation, das im marxistisch-leninistischen Sinne auch das Recht auf Lostrennung und Bildung eines unabhängigen Staates beinhalte[200]. Einzig das kurdische Volk habe über seine Zukunft zu entscheiden. Der Nationalismus des Mustafa Kemal müsse bekämpft werden[201], da er eine gewalttätige Türkisierung der Minderheiten vorantreibe und diese bei Aufständen hinschlachte, wie zum Beispiel im Jahre 1938 in Dersim, wo über 60 000 Menschen ermordet wurden[202]. In der Tat waren nach Artikel 88 der Verfassung der Türkei aus dem Jahre 1924 alle Einwohner der Türkei "ohne Ansehung der Religion und Rasse"[203] 'Türken'. Der Gebrauch von Begriffen wie "Kurde, Lase, Tscherkesse bzw. Kurdistân und Lâzistân [...] wurde zwar nicht per Gesetz, aber durch einen Runderlass des Erziehungsministeriums schon 1925 verboten"[204].

---

[199] Vgl.: Ebd., S. 120 (Kemalist diktatörlüğün milli meselede izlediği çizgi, tam anlamıyla Türk şovenizmidir; Übersetzung des Verfassers).
[200] Vgl.: Ebd., S. 202f.
[201] Vgl.: Ebd., S. 213.
[202] Vgl.: Ebd., S. 119.
[203] Verfassung der Türkei, 1924.
[204] Kreiser, Klaus/Neumann Christoph K.: Kleine Geschichte der Türkei, Bonn, 2005, S. 387.

5. Flucht, Vertreibung, Zwangsumsiedlungen und der Vertrag von Lausanne

Die heutige Gliederung des südosteuropäischen Raumes nach Nationen und Nationalitäten ist relativ jung und ein Ergebnis des 'langen 19. Jahrhunderts', der Epoche vom Ende des 19. Jahrhunderts bis zur Zwischenkriegszeit. Einige Nationen sind sogar noch jünger. Der Prozess der Nationsbildung ist in manchen Fällen bis heute nicht abgeschlossen. Dieses lange 19. Jahrhundert ist gekennzeichnet vom Übergang von der traditionellen Interethnizität, d.h. des jahrhundertelangen Zusammenlebens, des wechselseitigen Beeinflussens und der physischen Durchmischung der ethnischen Gruppen, zur modernen nationalen Exklusivität in Südosteuropa.[205]

Dieses Kapitel beschäftigt sich mit den definitorischen Grundlagen der Nationen, Ethnien und Minderheiten, geht anschließend auf zwei Beispiele der ethnischen Säuberung ein und zieht eine Bilanz für Südosteuropa.

5.1. Nationen, Ethnien, Minderheiten – Definitorische Grundlagen

"Jeder Mensch ist Glied einer Nation, und jede Nation soll einen Staat bilden, den Nationalstaat. Diese im 18. Jahrhundert entstandene Vorstellung war Ausdruck der schöpferischen Kraft des Nationalismus."[206] Seitdem wurden der Nationalstaat und die Nation zum Leitbild des politischen und gesellschaftlichen Handelns. Heute noch fasziniert die Idee des Nationalstaates und wird als selbstverständliche Organisationsform gesehen. Was jedoch ist der Nationalstaat oder die Nation?

---

[205] Vgl.: Sundhaussen, Holm: Nationsbildung und Nationalismus im Donau-Balkan-Raum, in: Torke, Hans-Joachim [Hrsg.]: Forschungen zur osteuropäischen Geschichte, Berlin, 1993, S. 238.

[206] Beer, Mathias: Auf dem Weg zum ethnisch reinen Nationalstaat. Einführung, in: Beer, Mathias [Hrsg.]: Auf dem Weg zum ethnisch reinen Nationalstaat, 2. Aufl., Tübingen, 2007, S. 8.

Der von Benedict Anderson geprägte Begriff *imagined community*[207] bringt den Begriff *Nation* auf den Punkt. Hierbei handelt es sich um eine vorgestellte Gemeinschaft[208] und somit um nichts überzeitlich Gültiges. Diese "imaginäre Gemeinschaft, erdacht von Menschen"[209] ist ein historisches Phänomen, mit einem Anfang und vermutlich einem Ende, das in ferner Zukunft liegt. Nach Anderson sind Nation und Nationalstaat keine Ewigkeitswerte, sondern "kulturelle Produkte"[210], die von Menschen gestaltet werden und vergänglich sind. Einige Forscher gehen sogar weiter und identifizieren die Nation als *gemeinsamen Irrtum* einer Gruppe von Menschen und sprechen ihr jeglichen substantiellen Charakter ab. Damit jedoch keine Missverständnisse auftreten, stellt Holm Sundhaussen klar, dass "Nationen und Nationalismus [...keine. DOT] Fiktionen [...sind. DOT]. Ganz im Gegenteil: Sie sind Realitäten, sehr wirksame und oft genug gefährliche Realitäten. Aber die Nation ist eben nicht durch *allgemeingültige*, objektive Kriterien definierbar. Nationen existieren, weil Menschen an sie *glauben* (bzw. man hat sie gelehrt, daran zu glauben), weil Menschen sich mit ihnen identifizieren."[211] Selbstzuschreibung und Fremdzuschreibung sowie der Glaube – keine Fakten – verbinden Menschen zu einer 'gemeinsamen Abstammung und Gemeinschaft' und sind wichtiger als faktisch nachweisbare Abstammung. Nationen sind somit das Ergebnis eines gruppendynamischen Prozesses.[212] 1956 zeigte Theodor Schieder die beiden unzertrennlich miteinander verbundenen Seiten des Nationalismus und der Nationalstaatsidee auf, wonach der Nationalismus "der Inbegriff der Erwartungen und Hoffnungen ganzer Generationen [war.DOT], die im Nationalstaat die Vollendung ihres Persönlichkeitsideals sahen, und er wurde der Schrecken ganzer Völker, die durch nationalisti-

---

[207] Vgl.: Anderson, Benedict: Imagined Communities. Reflections on the Origin and Spread of Nationalism, London, 1983.
[208] Langewiesche, Dieter: Was heißt "Erfindung der Nation"?, in: Beer, Mathias [Hrsg.]: Auf dem Weg zum ethnisch reinen Nationalstaat, 2. Aufl., Tübingen, 2007, S. 19.
[209] Ebd., S. 19
[210] Ebd., S. 29.
[211] Sundhaussen, Holm: Nationsbildung und Nationalismus im Donau-Balkan-Raum, in: Torke, Hans-Joachim [Hrsg.]: Forschungen zur osteuropäischen Geschichte, Berlin, 1993, S. 235.
[212] Vgl.: Ebd., S. 235.

schen Fanatismus ihre Freiheit oder ihre Heimat verloren."[213] Der Nationalstaat versprach Partizipation, eine Verfassung, die Grund- und Menschenrechte für alle garantiert, und Integration, womit das friedliche Zusammenleben der Nationsmitglieder gemeint war. Im Gegensatz zu den vorherigen Modellen überrascht die Anziehungskraft des Nationalstaates nicht. Jedoch brachte der Partizipationsgedanke auch eine Gewaltbereitschaft mit sich, wie Dieter Langewiesche formulierte: "Ein spezifisches Gemisch von Partizipation und Aggression kennzeichnet die Berufung auf die Nation als Letztwert gesellschaftlicher Legitimität zu allen Zeiten."[214]

Der Prozess der Nationalstaatsbildung war, wie es Mathias Beer treffend formuliert, "von Anfang an gewalt- und blutdurchtränkt"[215]. Alles, was aus Sicht des Staatsvolkes nicht dazugehörte, war fremd. Beer fasst zusammen:

> "Mit bis in die graue Vorzeit der Geschichte zurückreichenden Mythen, die zu angeblich abgesicherten 'historischen Argumenten' funktionalisiert werden, wird der Anspruch und die Rechtmäßigkeit des Einklanges von einem bestimmten Territorium und seinem Volk immer wieder zu untermauern versucht. Eine postulierte Abstammungsgemeinschaft, gemeinsame Herkunftsmythen und Erinnerungen dienen dazu, ein Bewusstsein zu verfestigen, eine Nation zu sein, die anders ist als die anderen."[216]

Waren der Nationalismus und Nationalstaat in ihren Anfängen Hoffnungsträger der Völker, verwandelten sie sich besonders in Südosteuropa zu einer völkerverachtenden Ideologie. Die Fehlinterpretation des Nationalismus als Ethno-Nationalismus, das heißt der zunehmenden Ethnisierung der Nation, führte seit dem Ende des 19. Jahrhunderts zu einem breiten Spektrum an Homogenisierungsmaßnahmen. Zu diesen gehörte eine sprachliche und kulturelle Angleichungspolitik, wie sie zum Beispiel die Türkei unerbittlich gegen

---

[213] Schieder, Theodor: Das Problem des Nationalismus in Osteuropa, in: Theodor Schieder (Dann, Otto/Wehler Hans-Ulrich [Hrsg.]): Nationalismus und Nationalstaat. Studien zum nationalen Problem im modernen Europa, Göttingen, 1991, S. 347.

[214] Langewiesche, Dieter: Nationalismus im 19. und 20. Jahrhundert. Zwischen Partizipation und Aggression, in: Langewiesche, Dieter [Hrsg.]: Nation, Nationalismus. Nationalstaat in Deutschland und Europa, München, 2000, S. 41.

[215] Beer, Mathias: Auf dem Weg zum ethnisch reinen Nationalstaat. Einführung, in: Beer, Mathias [Hrsg.]: Auf dem Weg zum ethnisch reinen Nationalstaat, 2. Aufl., Tübingen, 2007, S. 10.

[216] Ebd., S. 8f.

ihre Minderheiten, wie die Kurden, Zaza und Aleviten oder die kaum noch verbliebenen christlichen Minderheiten, noch heute praktiziert, "mit dem Ziel des Aufgehens der Minderheiten in der Titularnation innerhalb einzelner Staaten, bis hin zum Anpassen der Grenzen an das Ethnikum bzw. des Ethnikums an die Grenzen. Abgrenzung, Ausgrenzung, Assimilierung, Umsiedlung, Vertreibung und [...] die planmäßige und zielgerichtete Vernichtung der einmal hinausdefinierten religiösen, sprachlichen, ethnischen und nationalen Minderheiten waren das Ergebnis des Zeitalters des Totalen, wie das 20. Jahrhundert auch bezeichnet wurde."[217]

Das Südosteuropa des 19. Jahrhunderts bietet hierfür etliche Beispiele, die noch bis in die Gegenwart reichen. Der türkisch-bulgarische Bevölkerungsaustausch von 1913, die Grenzveränderungen in Folge der Pariser Vorortverträge nach dem Ersten Weltkrieg und die damit einhergehenden Umsiedlungen und Vertreibungen, der türkisch-griechische Bevölkerungsaustausch in Folge der Lausanner Konvention, die Vertreibungs- und Vernichtungspolitik des NS-Regimes sowie alle Zwangsumsiedlungen nach 1945 haben trotz ungleichmäßiger Entwicklung ein gemeinsames Merkmal – den Krieg. In einem Krieg bedarf es auch keiner besonderen Rechtfertigung mehr.

Der Begriff *ethnische Säuberung* wird in der Bevölkerung sehr gerne mit dem Balkan in Verbindung gebracht. Bei ethnischen Säuberungen ist "nicht die Ermordung und Vernichtung einer Gruppe das vorrangige Ziel, sondern deren gewaltsame Entfernung aus einem bestimmten Gebiet"[218]. Nach Definition des internationalen Gerichtshofes in Den Haag und der UNO handelt es sich bei ethnischen Säuberungen um eine systematisch organisierte, mit Gewalt verbundene und dauerhafte Zwangsumsiedlung einer Gruppe.[219] Philipp Ther unterscheidet zwischen den vier Varianten *Flucht*, *Vertreibung*, *Deportation* und *Zwangsaussiedlung*. Termini wie *Bevölkerungsaustausch* oder *Umsiedlung* hält er für verharmlosende Quellenbegriffe.[220] Jede ethnische

---

[217] Ebd., S. 10f.
[218] Ther, Philipp: Die dunkle Seite der Nationalstaaten. 'Ethnische Säuberungen' im modernen Europa, Göttingen, 2011, S. 7.
[219] Hierzu: Carmichael, Cathie: Ethnic Cleansing in the Balkans. Nationalism and the Destruction of Tradition, London, 2002, S. 2.
[220] Vgl.: Ther, Philipp: Die dunkle Seite der Nationalstaaten. 'Ethnische Säuberungen' im modernen Europa, Göttingen, 2011, S. 7f.

Säuberung hat ihren eigenen Charakter, Ursprung und Ausgang, auch wenn sie vieles gemeinsam haben. Norman M. Naimark charakterisiert den Begriff folgendermaßen:

> "Ethnic cleansing is always accompanied by extreme violence, directed at women as well as men. The violence is organized by political leadership of states and is not primarily the result of spontaneous pogroms or massacres. It is totalistic in its goals; it allows for few exceptions to the rule that all 'other' must go. It usually takes place in the context of war or the transition from war to peace. Terrible depredations take place to populations under the cover of war. Not only are ethnic populations driven from home territories, but their cultural and architectural heritage is also destroyed."[221]

Obwohl heute geächtet, waren ethnische Säuberungen in der ersten Hälfte des 20. Jahrhunderts eine gängige Methode, an der die internationale Staatengemeinschaft sogar mitwirkte.

Ethnische Säuberungen unterscheiden sich von *Genoziden*, auch wenn beide Begriffe Überlappungen besitzen. Hauptunterschiede sind ihre Zielsetzung, die Resultate und ihre räumliche Dimensionen. So ist das Ziel eines Genozides, die Vernichtung einer Bevölkerungsgruppe, laut UN-Konvention *destruction*, wofür jedoch im Völkerrecht ein Vorsatz, *dolus specialis*, vorausgesetzt wird, wohingegen ethnische Säuberungen eine systematische Entfernung einer bestimmten Gruppe aus einem Gebiet sich zum Ziel setzen. Der Unterschied im Resultat wird deutlich im "quantitativen Verhältnis von Todesopfern und Überlebenden, das bei ethnischen Säuberungen selten 10 Prozent überschreitet, beim Genozid hingegen 100% erreichen kann"[222]. Die räumliche Differenzierung ist insoweit wichtig, da ethnische Säuberungen grenzüberschreitend sind, das heißt die Vertreibung ist verbunden mit einem Zielgebiet und somit raumübergreifend, während Genozide an Ort und Stelle durchgeführt werden. Eric Hobsbawm sieht einen direkten Zusammenhang zwischen ethnischen Säuberungen und Nationalstaaten:

> "The logical implication of trying to create a continent neatly divided into coherent territorial states each inhabited by a separate ethnically und linguistically

---

[221] Naimark, Norman M.: Das Problem der ethnischen Säuberung im modernen Europa, in: Zeitschrift für Ostmitteleuropaforschung, 48 (3), 1991, S. 349.
[222] Ther, Philipp: Die dunkle Seite der Nationalstaaten. 'Ethnische Säuberungen' im modernen Europa, Göttingen, 2011, S. 8.

homogenous population, was the mass expulsion or extermination of minorities."[223]

Für Ther sind ethnische Säuberungen sogar ein "Kind des Nationalstaates und damit ein zentraler Bestandteil der europäischen Moderne."[224]

In diesem Zusammenhang gewinnt ein weiterer Begriff an Bedeutung – die *Ethnie*. Sie wird als Organisationsform gesehen, aus der in vielen Fällen die Nation entstanden ist. Quellen zeigen, dass der Begriff Ethnie wenige Jahrhunderte alt und äußerst schwer zu definieren ist. So werden Ethnien oft von dominierenden Gruppen bestimmt, die den Fremden, den Anderen schaffen wollen. Neben der Fremdzuschreibung und Eigenbezeichnung, wer einbezogen und wer ausgeschlossen ist, gibt es keine objektivierbaren Kriterien. Kriterien wie Kultur, Religion, Hautfarbe sind sozial konstruiert und sind einem ständigen Wandel unterworfen. Selbst 'messbare' Kriterien wie die Sprache können Ethnien nicht definieren. Man denke an US-Amerikaner und Briten, die niemand als eine Ethnie bezeichnen würde, trotz ihrer gemeinsamen Sprache.

"Ethnie (ethnic communities) may [...] be defined as names human populations with shared ancestry myths, histories and cultures, having an association with a specific territory and a sense of solidarity."[225] Hieraus ergibt sich, dass Ethnien imaginäre Gemeinschaften sind, jedoch trotzdem existieren. "Mit anderen Worten, Ethnizität ist spezifisch für Zeit, Ort und Kultur und sogar die Individuen, die ihre Bedeutung festlegen."[226] Sie unterscheiden sich von Nationen unter anderem dadurch, dass sie einen geringeren gesellschaftlichen und politischen Organisationsgrad besitzen und ihnen das Streben nach einem souveränen Staat und das Nationalbewusstsein fehlen. Viel wichtiger sind hingegen Stamm, Sippe und Dorfgemeinschaft.[227]

---

[223] Hobsbawm, Eric: Nations and Nationalism since 1780, Cambridge, 1990, S. 133.
[224] Ther, Philipp: Die dunkle Seite der Nationalstaaten. 'Ethnische Säuberungen' im modernen Europa, Göttingen, 2011, S. 7.
[225] Smith, A. D.: The Ethnic Origins of Nations. Oxford, 1989, S. 32.
[226] Naimark, Norman M.: Flammender Haß. Ethnische Säuberungen im 20. Jahrhundert, München, 2004, S. 14.
[227] Vgl.: Sundhaussen, Holm: Nationsbildung und Nationalismus im Donau-Balkan-Raum, in: Torke, Hans-Joachim [Hrsg.]: Forschungen zur osteuropäischen Geschichte, Berlin, 1993, S. 236.

Wie Nationen und Ethnien sind auch Minderheiten keine Ewigkeitswerte.

"Die Einteilung in ethnische bzw. nationale Minderheiten und Mehrheiten ist ein Produkt der modernen Staatsbildung. Die Vorstellung, daß die heutigen Minderheiten das Resultat von Migrationen sind, ist ebenso weit verbreitet wie falsch oder irreführend. Der Begriff 'Minderheit' bezieht sich immer auf eine 'Mehrheit'. Und diese wird zumindest mit der jeweiligen 'staatstragenden' Nation gleichgesetzt. Infolge zahlreicher Veränderungen der Staatsgrenzen hat sich das Verhältnis von Mehrheiten zu Minderheiten wiederholt verschoben [zum Beispiel während der Balkankriege innerhalb kürzester Zeit.DOT]. Der Verschiebung staatlicher Grenzen folgte oft – aber nicht immer – die Wanderung von Menschen, die entweder zur Minderheit geworden waren und abwanderten (beziehungsweise vertrieben wurden) oder die aus einem Nachbargebiet zuwanderten, da sie sich als Teil der neuen Mehrheitsnation verstanden."[228]

---

[228] Sundhaussen Holm: Südosteuropa, in: Bade, Klaus J./Emmer, Pieter C., Lucassen, Leo/Oltmer Jochen [Hrsg.]: Enzyklopädie Migration in Europa. Vom 17. Jahrhundert bis zur Gegenwart, 2. Aufl., Paderborn, 2008, S. 291.

5.2. Südosteuropa – Eine Bilanz

K 5: Verteilung der Sprachen in Mittel- und Südeuropa 1910[229]

---

[229] Aus: Haus der Heimat des Landes Baden-Württemberg [Hrsg.]: Umsiedlung, Flucht und Vertreibung der Deutschen als internationales Problem. Zur Geschichte eines europäischen Irrwegs, Stuttgart, 2005, S. 39.

Betrachtet man den südosteuropäischen Raum zur Jahrhundertwende ergibt sich folgendes Mosaik: Bei einer Volkszählung im Jahre 1910 wurden in Österreich-Ungarn 12 Millionen Deutsche, 10 Millionen Magyaren, 6,5 Millionen Tschechen, 5 Millionen Polen, 4 Millionen Ukrainer, 3,2 Millionen Rumänen, 2,9 Millionen Kroaten, 2,3 Millionen Slowenen und 800 000 Italiener gezählt. Die Zusammensetzung des Osmanischen Reiches sah ähnlich aus: Um 1900 zählte man 14 Millionen Muslime (Türken, Kurden und Araber), 2,57 Millionen Griechen, mehr als eine Million Armenier, 830 000 Bulgaren, 215 000 Juden, 120 000 Katholiken, 32 000 Maroniten sowie eine Reihe weiterer Minderheitsgruppen.[230]

Was für ein ethnisches Durcheinander nach dem Zusammenfall dieser beiden Reiche in Europa entstanden war, lässt sich erahnen.

Die erste Hälfte des 20. Jahrhunderts war in Südosteuropa, wie bereits in den vorherigen Kapiteln erläutert, geprägt von Flucht, Umsiedlung und Vertreibung ethnischer Völker. Die Staaten der Region betrieben eine Homogenisierungspolitik mit dem Ziel einer ethnisch-sprachlichen Uniformität, welche die westeuropäischen Staaten als Vorbild hatte. Die Grenzen der neuen Nationalstaaten wurden nicht nach ethnischen, sondern oft nach wirtschaftlich-strategischen Aspekten errichtet. Deshalb waren auch die Nationalstaaten Osteuropas darauf aus, ihr Territorium ethnisch zu homogenisieren. Dieser Gedanke eines einheitlichen, möglichst nur von einer ethnischen Gruppe bewohnten Nationalstaates gewann seit Beginn des 20. Jahrhunderts an Bedeutung. Danach waren Minderheiten an und für sich ein Problem, störten dieser Auffassung zufolge alleine durch ihre bloße Existenz sowohl den inneren Frieden der Staaten als auch die internationalen Beziehungen.

Eine ganze Reihe von Anthropologen und Völkerkundlern erhofften sich durch national homogenisierte Staaten den Abbau von Konfliktpotential in und zwischen den Staaten.

---

[230] Vgl.: Suppan, Arnold/Heuberger, Valeria: Nationen und Minderheiten in Mittel-, Ost- und Südosteuropa seit 1918, in: Heuberger, Valeria/Kolar, Othmar u.a. [Hrsg.]: Nationen, Nationalitäten, Minderheiten – Probleme des Nationalismus in Jugoslawien, Ungarn, Rumänien, der Tschechoslowakei, Bulgarien, Polen, der Ukraine, Italien und Österreich 1945-1990, Wien, 1994, S. 15f.

"Ethnisch (und im Falle der Muslime auch religiös) unterschiedliche Minderheiten wurden deshalb ausgegrenzt und als irredentistische Bedrohung [...] der territorialen Integrität angesehen. Deshalb trachteten die Staaten [...] danach, ihr Territorium ethnisch zu homogenisieren. [...] Die langfristig wirksamen Resultate solcher [...Prozesse.DOT] sind:

- Assimilation, das heißt aus dem Blickwinkel der Minderheit Angleichung an die Mehrheit und Aufgabe der eigenen Gruppenidentität;
- Vertreibung und Abwanderung im passiven Fall oder Separation und Sezession im aktiven Fall;
- Geno- oder Ethnozid."[231]

Bereits in den Jahren 1875-1878, als die Osmanen aus Südosteuropa verdrängt wurden, mussten schätzungsweise zwei Millionen Menschen ihre Wohnorte verlassen, darunter eine Million Muslime. Bis 1912 wanderten noch einmal etwa 350 000 Osmanen aus Bulgarien aus.

In der zweiten Migrationswelle, welche mit den Balkankriegen ansetzte, wurden unter anderem "in der türkisch-bulgarischen Konvention von 1913 die Umsiedlung von etwa 48.500 Türken und 46.500 Bulgaren aus einem 15 Kilometer breiten Grenzstreifen der beiden Staaten vereinbart. Wie bei späteren Vorgängen handelte es sich hier auch lediglich um die formale Bestätigung von bereits durchgeführten Vertreibungen."[232] In Folge des Vertrages von Lausanne vom 30.01.1923 zwischen Griechenland und der Türkei wurden nochmals ca. 1,3 Millionen Griechen und ca. 400 000 Bürger des ehemaligen Osmanischen Reiches umgesiedelt.[233] Jahrhunderte alte Wohngebiete mussten aufgegeben werden.

Der Gedanke eines Bevölkerungstransfers war nicht neu. Bereits 1898 machte Siegfried Lichtenstädter unter dem Pseudonym Dr. Mehmet Emin Efendi den Vorschlag eines Bevölkerungsaustausch in der Türkei:

---

[231] Seewann, Gerhard: Minderheiten und Nationalitätenpolitik, in: Hatschikjan, Magarditsch/Troebst Stefan [Hrsg.]: Südosteuropa. Gesellschaft, Politik, Wirtschaft, Kultur. Ein Handbuch, München, 1999, S. 170.

[232] Haus der Heimat des Landes Baden-Württemberg [Hrsg.]: Umsiedlung, Flucht und Vertreibung der Deutschen als internationales Problem. Zur Geschichte eines europäischen Irrwegs, Stuttgart, 2005, S. 10.

[233] Vgl.: Sundhausen, Holm: Von "Lausanne" nach "Dayton". Ein Paradigmenwechsel bei der Lösung ethnonationaler Konflikte, in: Hohls, Rüdiger/Schröder, Iris/Siegrist Hannes [Hrsg.]: Europa und die Europäer. Quellen und Essays zur modernen europäischen Geschichte, München, 2005, S. 410.

"Wenn in einem Organismus Fremdkörper sich befinden und krankhafte Störungen verursachen, so giebt es je nach Lage des Falles verschiedene Heilmittel. Das gründlichste Mittel ist, den Fremdkörper zu beseitigen, ihn aus dem Organismus zu entfernen. [...] Dies ist aber nicht immer durchführbar. Ein milderes Mittel wendet die Natur oft an, indem sie den Fremdkörper einzukapseln und dadurch für den Organismus unschädlich zu machen sucht [...]. Solange die christlichen Völkerschaften in der bisherigen Zahl und Größe im Gebiete des türkischen Reiches existiren, ist eine dauernde Gesundung desselben nicht möglich. Folglich müssen die ersteren, soweit möglich, vom Gebiete des türkischen Reiches verschwinden. Dies ist die allererste und wichtigste Bedingung für die Gesundung des türkischen Staatswesens. Um dieses Ziel zu erreichen, giebt es verschiedene Methoden. Das brutalste, rücksichtsloseste Mittel wäre die Tödtung der Christen. [...] Das Beste wäre es offenbar, die Christen zur freiwilligen Auswanderung zu bewegen; bis zu einem gewissen Grade wird sich dies wohl ohne große Härte bewirken lassen [...].

Der Gedanke eines derartigen Bevölkerungsaustausches mag wohl Manchem befremdlich erscheinen und widerstreben. Ich verkenne auch nicht, dass ein solches Unternehmen eine gewaltige Summe von Geschick, Organisationstalent, Thatkraft und Ausdauer erfordern wird. Allein dem Ziele, das jede zugleich verständige und ehrliche Orientpolitik verfolgen muß – Beseitigung der religiösen Gegensätze und Schaffung von Friede und Ordnung – würde man wenigstens in einem Theile des Orients dadurch um eine Strecke näher kommen."[234]

Zu einer weiteren Reihe von Migrationen kam es auch nach dem Ersten Weltkrieg in den neu gezogenen Grenzen des zusammengebrochenen Habsburger Reiches: in der Tschechoslowakei, in Ungarn, Jugoslawien und Rumänien. 350 000 Magyaren, von denen 197 000 aus Rumänien und 47 000 aus Jugoslawien stammten, flüchteten in das verkleinerte Mutterland Ungarn. Umgekehrt flüchteten 50 000 Südslawen aus ungarischen Siedlungsgebieten in Richtung Jugoslawien.[235]

Die Grenzveränderungen in Folge der Wiener Schiedssprüche führten ebenfalls zu einem Bevölkerungsaustausch. 320 000 Rumänen flüchteten aus Nord-Siebenbürgen, das zwischen 1941 und 1944 zu Ungarn gehörte, und aus der bulgarisch gewordenen Süd-Dobrudscha, 273 000 Serben aus den

---

[234] Efendi, Mehemed Emin (Pseudonym): Die Zukunft der Türkei. Ein Beitrag zur Lösung der orientalischen Frage. Berlin und Leipzig, 1898, S. 13f.
[235] Vgl.: Seewann, Gerhard: Minderheiten und Nationalitätenpolitik, in: Hatschikjan, Magarditsch/Troebst Stefan [Hrsg.]: Südosteuropa. Gesellschaft, Politik, Wirtschaft, Kultur. Ein Handbuch, München, 1999, S. 171.

Nachbarländern nach Serbien. Gleichzeitig übersiedelten 142 000 Magyaren nach Rumänien und 122 000 Bulgaren aus Bulgarien nach Makedonien und Westthrakien, das von bulgarischen Truppen besetzt war. Nach Ende des Zweiten Weltkrieges mussten beide Gruppen ihre neu besiedelten Gebiete wieder verlassen.[236] Die dritte und größte Migrationswelle setzte mit dem Zweiten Weltkrieg ein, vor allem als das faschistische Deutschland weite Teile Südosteuropas besetzt hatte. Fast 2,5 Millionen Menschen waren von dieser Migrationswelle und den Massakern betroffen, an erster Stelle die Juden. Aus Ungarn und ungarisch besetzten Gebieten wurden 500 000 Juden, aus Rumänien 200 000, aus Griechenland 70 000, aus Jugoslawien 60 000 und aus Albanien 600 in die deutschen Vernichtungslager deportiert und ermordet.[237] Sehr viele Juden flohen aber auch nach Palästina. "Unter ihnen befanden sich über 90% der 44 000 Juden Bulgariens, deren von deutscher Seite geplante Deportation 1943 von Zar und Parlament verhindert worden war."[238] Über die Deutschen hingegen äußerte sich der Exil-Staatspräsident der Tschechoslowakei, Dr. Edvard Beneš, vor tschechischen Offizieren am 22. Januar 1942:

> "Ein weiteres und brennendes Problem ist, wie wir die Deutschen loswerden sollen. Selbst glaube ich, dass es möglich sein wird, sich etwa zwei Millionen Deutscher zu entledigen. Das Problem wird sehr schwer sein. Am besten wird es sein, es via facti zu erledigen, sonst durch Übereinkommen. Alle jungen Deutschen bis zu einem bestimmen Alter müssen weg."[239]

Diese wenigen Beispiele verdeutlichen:

> "Jede Vertreibung, jede Umsiedlungsaktion zog wieder neue nach sich, um plötzlich entstandene, oft riesige demographische Lücken neu aufzufüllen[240] [...]. Zieht

---

[236] Vgl.: Ebd., S. 172.
[237] Vgl.: Ebd., S. 171.
[238] Ebd., S. 171.
[239] Laštovička, Bohuslav: V Londýně za valky [In London während des Krieges], Prag, 1961, Faksimile. Zit. Nach Dokumente zur Vertreibung der Sudetendeutschen. [Hrsg.]: Sudetendeutscher Rat, München, 1992, S. 48.
[240] Wie zum Beispiel die Binnenmigration innerhalb Jugoslawiens nach der Vertreibung der Deutschen. In Vojvodana wurden anstelle der bis 1945 ansässigen 350 000 Deutschen eine Viertel Million Serben und Montenegriner angesiedelt (vgl.: Seewann, Gerhard: Minderheiten und Nationalitätenpolitik, in: Hatschikjan, Magarditsch/Troebst Stefan [Hrsg.]: Südosteuropa. Gesellschaft, Politik, Wirtschaft, Kultur. Ein Handbuch, München, 1999, S. 172).

man eine Bilanz der mehr als 30 Millionen Menschen umfassenden Ost-West-Migration von 1918 bis 1998, so ist festzuhalten, dass diese zu 75% aus ethnischen Gründen und nur zu 10% aus politischen Gründen erfolgt ist, während 15% als Arbeitsemigranten nach Westeuropa zogen."[241]

K 6: Bevölkerungsverschiebungen 1917-1938[242]

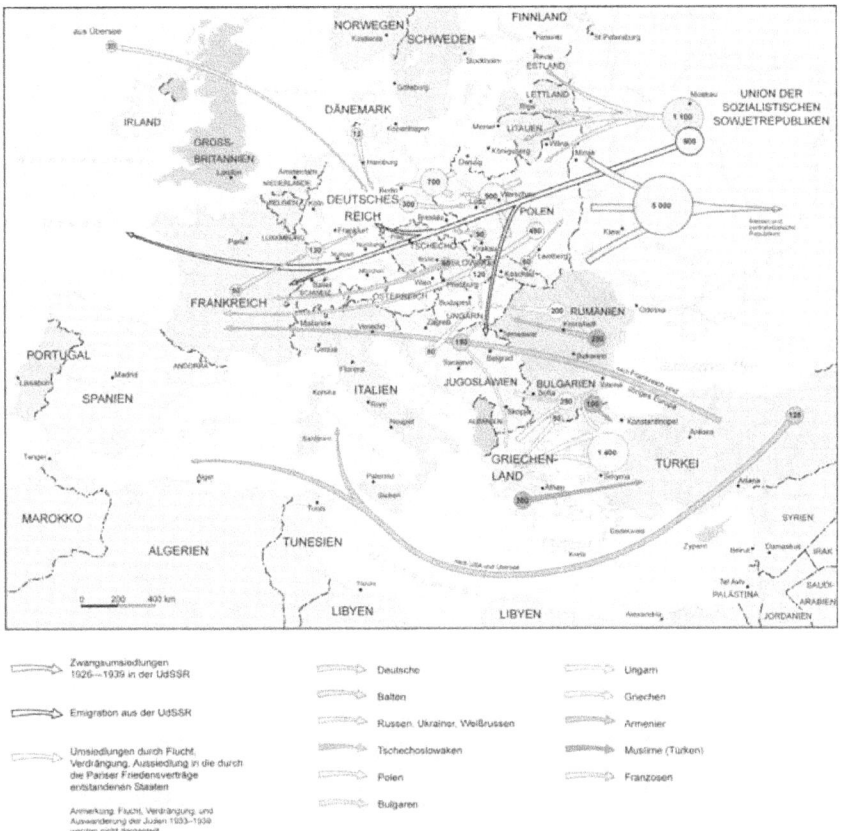

[241] Seewann, Gerhard: Minderheiten und Nationalitätenpolitik, in: Hatschikjan, Magarditsch/Troebst Stefan [Hrsg.]: Südosteuropa. Gesellschaft, Politik, Wirtschaft, Kultur. Ein Handbuch, München, 1999, S. 172f.
[242] Aus: Haus der Heimat des Landes Baden-Württemberg [Hrsg.]: Umsiedlung, Flucht und Vertreibung der Deutschen als internationales Problem. Zur Geschichte eines europäischen Irrwegs, Stuttgart, 2005, S. 53.

Eine historische Zäsur stellt die Vernichtung und Vertreibung des jahrhundertelang in Anatolien beheimateten armenischen Volkes aus ihrer Heimat in Folge der in den vorherigen Kapiteln aufgeführten Vorstellung von Nation und Nationalstaat dar. Dieses Ereignis steht in engem Zusammenhang mit dem griechisch-türkischen Bevölkerungsaustausch und bedarf einer näheren Betrachtung.

5.3. Die armenische Tragödie: *Meds Yeghern*[243]

> "Das Wort 'Genozid' ist für mich nicht entscheidend. Wenn wir uns der Geschichte mit juristischen Begriffen nähern, die international eine spezifische Bedeutung haben, verhindern wir, dass wir begreifen, was damals passiert ist. Wir brauchen eine ethische Annäherung an die Geschichte."[244] (Hrant Dink)

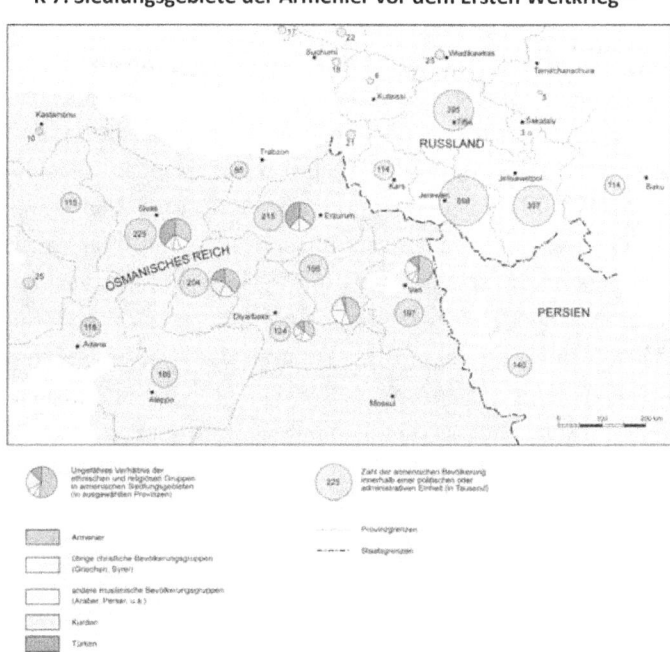

K 7: Siedlungsgebiete der Armenier vor dem Ersten Weltkrieg[245]

---

[243] Armenisch: 'Großes Verbrechen'.
[244] "Das Wort 'Genozid' ist nicht entscheidend": http://jungle-world.com/artikel/2005/17/15123.html (Zuletzt eingesehen am 18.05.2012).
[245] Aus: Haus der Heimat des Landes Baden-Württemberg [Hrsg.]: Umsiedlung, Flucht und Vertreibung der Deutschen als internationales Problem. Zur Geschichte eines europäischen Irrwegs, Stuttgart, 2005, S. 50.

'Wer redet heute denn noch von der Vernichtung der Armenier?' soll Hitler am 22. August 1939 kurz vor dem Einmarsch in Polen vor Wehrmachtsgenerälen und hohen NS-Funktionären gesagt haben.[246] Entgegen weitläufiger Meinung bezog er sich hier aber nicht auf die Genozidpläne an den Juden, sondern auf die Vernichtung einer großen Anzahl der polnischen Intelligenz.[247] Ob er sich dabei tatsächlich auf den Völkermord an den Armenier von 1915 bezogen hat, ist zudem ungewiss.[248] Nichtsdestotrotz existieren genug Quellen, die belegen, dass der Völkermord an den Armeniern der europäischen Politik bekannt war. Viele Angehörige des Deutschen Reiches leisteten während des Ersten Weltkrieges Dienst in den osmanischen Streitkräften, so auch der deutsche Offizier Johannes Albert Theodor Hochbaum, der ein Tagebuch führte. Während einer Reise durch ehemals armenisch besiedelte Regionen am 14. Mai 1918 machte sich Hochbaum "seine eigenen Gedanken: 'Von Armeniern nichts mehr zu sein [sinngemäß: sehen]. In dem Greuljahr [sic!] 1916 [korrekt 1915] alles ermordet oder weggeführt. Mit dem Besitz haben sich die Türken bereichert. Für teures Geld kann man Decken, Geschirr usw. aus den Armenierhäusern auf dem Bazar von Adabazar von Türken kaufen. Ein schönes Dorf mit fleißiger Bevölkerung wurde hier vernichtet. Der Nomade treibt den höheren Kulturträger aus Hof und Haus und kann ihn doch nie ersetzen. – Es ist mir nie klargewesen, welches eigentlich die letzten Gründe dieser Armenierbewegung sind. Der Türke hatte wohl Angst um sein Land, seine Nation. Armenier, Griechen und andere dachten ihn durch ihre höhere Kultur allmählich zu verdrängen'. Bei einem Besuch der griechischen, römischen und byzantinischen Bauten bei Pergamon meinte Hochbaum: '...verdrängen sie [die Türken]...die was schaffen und lassen selbst alles verkommen. So sieht man überall Schmutz und Verfall und doch ists unendlich malerisch!'"[249] Über das deutsch-türkische Verhältnis macht er

---

[246] Vgl.: Naimark, Norman M.: Flammender Haß. Ethnische Säuberungen im 20. Jahrhundert, München, 2004, S. 77.

[247] Vgl.: Akten zur deutschen auswärtigen Politik, 1918-1945, Serie D (1937-1945), Bd. 7, Baden-Baden, 1956, S. 171f.

[248] Vgl.: Kevork B. Bardakijan: Hitler and the Armenian Genocide, Cambridge, 1985, S. 1-36.

[249] Bihl, Wolfdieter: Das Osmanische Reich aus der Sicht eines deutschen Offiziers im Ersten Weltkrieg, in: Lukan, Walter/Suppan, Arnold [Hrsg.]: Nationalitäten und Identitäten in Ostmitteleuropa. Festschrift aus Anlaß des 70. Geburtstages von Richard Georg Plaschka, Wien, 1995, S. 34f.

am 14. Oktober 1918 Notizen und bezeichnet die Türken als gute Verbündete Deutschlands, selbst "wenn es ihnen auch schlecht genug geht".[250] Am 18. Oktober 1918 notiert er die Aussagen des letzten Großwesirs Izzet Pascha, der statt eines Vertrauensbruches an den Deutschen den Totschlag bevorzuge.[251] Welchen Einfluss die deutschen Offiziere auf die Deportationspläne der Osmanen hatten, ist noch ungeklärt und bedarf einer gründlichen Untersuchung.

Daneben dokumentieren andere Quellen, dass der Völkermord an den Armeniern zur Entwicklung der Vernichtungspläne Adolf Hitlers beigetragen habe. In *Heimatland*, dem *vaterländischen Wochenblatt für das Bayerische Volk*, das dem 'Führer' Treue verspricht und daher vermutlich ein Presseorgan der Nationalsozialisten war, findet sich 1923 ein Artikel mit dem Titel 'Mustapha Kemal Pascha und sein Werk'. Darin wird die Politik der Türkei gelobt und Lehren aus ihr gezogen: "Uns Deutsche interessiert naturgemäß neben dem geschichtlichen Verlauf der kleinasiatischen Ereignisse vor allen Dingen das 'Wie' und 'Auf welche Weise' dieses Gelingens."[252] Als erster wichtiger Punkt wird die Schaffung einer inneren Einheitsfront aufgeführt und ergänzt:

> "Hand in Hand mit der Schaffung der Einheitsfront muß die völkische Reinigung gehen. In dieser Beziehung waren die Verhältnisse in Kleinasien gleich wie bei uns. Die Blutsauger und Parasiten am türkischen Volkskörper waren die Griechen und Armenier. Sie mußten beseitigt und unschädlich gemacht werden, oder aber der ganze Freiheitskampf war in Frage gestellt. Mit sanften Mitteln – das hat die Geschichte immer bewiesen – ist dabei nicht auszukommen [...], weil dabei wieder ein Kompromiss herauskommen würde, und Kompromisse sind der Anfang vom Ende [...]. Die im Kampfgebiet wohnenden Fremdstämmigen mußten fast ausnahmslos über die Klinge springen, ihre Zahl ist mit 500 000 nicht zu gering angegeben."[253]

Die Handlungsweise der Türken wird als "absolut berechtigt und notwendig"[254] betrachtet. Eine Erklärung hierfür lautet: "Der Armenier und Grieche

---

[250] Ebd., S. 35.
[251] Vgl.: Ebd., S. 37.
[252] Tröbst, Hans: Mustapha Kemal Pascha und sein Werk, Teil VI, in: Heimatland: vaterländisches Wochenblatt für das Bayerische Volk, 42, 1923, S. 7.
[253] Ebd.
[254] Ebd.

vermehrte sich im Gegensatz zum Türken sehr schnell, Handel und Wandel lag ausschließlich in seinen Händen und er verstand sich in der perfidesten Weise auf die Auspowerung der ihm immer mehr und mehr wehrlos ausgelieferten Bevölkerung."[255] Paradoxerweise werden Armenier und Griechen als Gäste der Türken bezeichnet. "Der Türke [...habe.DOT] den Beweis geliefert, daß die Reinigung eines Volkes im größten Stile von Fremdkörpern jeder Art sehr wohl möglich"[256] sei.

Das Fazit des nationalsozialistischen Propagandablattes lautet: "Einheitsfront, völkische Reinigung und eine wahre Freiwilligenarmee, das sind heute die Grundlagen für die nationale Wiedergeburt. Das ist in kurzen Worten die große Lehre, die wir aus dem türkischen Freiheitskampf zu ziehen haben."[257]

In diesem Zusammenhang steht auch Folgendes: Falih Rıfkı Atay, ein enger Freund Mustafa Kemals, gibt in seinem Buch 'Çankaya' die Aussage Adolf Hitlers wieder, die dieser während eines Besuches gemacht haben soll: "Mustafa Kemal hat bewiesen, dass ein Volk, das selbst sämtlicher Mittel beraubt wurde, erneut Mittel zur eigenen Befreiung schaffen kann. Sein erster Schüler ist Mussolini, der zweite bin ich."[258] In der Tat könnte also der Völkermord an den Armeniern, aber auch die ethnische Säuberung im türkisch-griechischen Bevölkerungsaustausch einen Einfluss auf den Holocaust und die Vertreibungen während der NS-Diktatur gehabt haben – wenn auch in anderen Dimensionen. Talat Pascha, ein Drahtzieher des Völkermordes an den Armeniern, wurde am 15. März 1921 in Deutschland von einem Armenier ermordet. Ein deutsches Gericht sprach diesen kurze Zeit später frei.[259]

Was war in jenem Jahr 1915 geschehen?

Der Völkermord an den Armeniern ist ohne die Balkankriege 1912/13 nicht zu verstehen. Der größte Teil der christlichen Bevölkerung des Balkans lehnte sich in den Balkankriegen gegen die osmanische Herrschaft auf. Dies war ein Grund für den wachsenden Nationalismus der Ittihadisten. Hinzu kam die

---

[255] Ebd.
[256] Ebd.
[257] Ebd.
[258] Atay, Falih Rıfkı: Çankaya, Istanbul, 2010, S. 369 (Mustafa Kemal, bir millet bütün vasıtalarından mahrum edilse dahi, kendini kurtaracak vasıtaları yaratabileceğini ispat eden adamdır. Onun ilk talebesi Mussolini'dir, ikinci talebesi benim!; Übersetzung des Verfassers).
[259] Vgl.: Dadrian, Vahakn N.: Einleitung, in: Gust, Wolfgang [Hrsg.]: Der Völkermord an den Armeniern 1915/16. Dokumente aus dem Politischen Archiv des deutschen Amts, Leck, 2005, S. 7.

Vertreibung Hunderttausender Muslime ins Osmanische Reich, was bei den Jungtürken Hass und Zorn erzeugte. Von nun an galten christliche Völker als potentielle Verräter und Abtrünnige. Talat Pascha erklärte auf einem "ittihadistischen Parteikongreß: 'Es wurde als notwendig erachtet, die Armenier von allen Kriegsschauplätzen und aus der Nähe von Eisenbahnlinien zu entfernen, damit unsere Armee nicht zwischen zwei Feuer geriet'."[260] Eine der größten Tragödien der Weltgeschichte nahm seinen Lauf. Ende Februar 1915 begannen die Morde an der armenischen Bevölkerung und ihre Deportation, noch vor dem formellen Befehl zur Deportation vom 27. Mai 1915.[261] Männer in wehrfähigem Alter wurden in Arbeitsbataillone gesteckt, später ermordet, Alte, Frauen und Kinder ins Exil nach Aleppo in Nordsyrien geschickt. Sie mussten durch die Wüste und Wildnis marschieren, ohne Nahrungsmittel und Schutz vor Banditen und türkischen Soldaten.[262] Viele Armenier wurden bereits vor Ort gefoltert und ermordet oder starben vor Erschöpfung während der Deportation. Paradoxerweise waren die eigentlichen 'Schlächter' der Armenier eine weitere Minderheit in der Türkei – die Kurden.

Abb. 1: Transport von Armeniern in sogenannten Hammelwagen der Anatolischen Bahn (1915)[263]

---

[260] Naimark, Norman M.: Flammender Haß. Ethnische Säuberungen im 20. Jahrhundert, München, 2004, S. 42f.
[261] Vgl.: Ebd., S. 43.
[262] Vgl.: Melson, Robert: Revolution and Genocide. On the Origins of the Armenian Genocide and the Holocaust, Chicago, London, 1992, S. 143-145.
[263] Aus: Wikimedia Commons, unter: http://commons.wikimedia.org/wiki/File:Armenian_genocide3.jpg

Neben der ethnischen Säuberung ging eine kulturelle Säuberung einher. Sämtliche Erinnerungen an die Armenier – Monumente, Kirchen, Friedhöfe – wurden zerstört, armenische Stadtviertel regelrecht ausradiert.[264]

Die Zahlen, die für die Opfer des Völkermordes an den Armeniern berichtet werden, gehen weit auseinander. Steven Katz spricht von 550 000 bis 800 000 Toten[265], Ronald G. Suny schätzt die Zahl auf zwischen 200 000 und etwa 1,5 Millionen[266], was der offiziellen armenischen Schätzung (1,6 Mio.) entsprechen würde. Das armenische Patriarchat kommt auf 2,1 Millionen. Arnold Toynbee schätzt die Zahl der Opfer auf 600 000, wobei die gleiche Anzahl der Deportation entkommen sein soll.[267] Türkische Historiker, die nicht der offiziellen Staatsideologie angehören, geben eine wahrscheinliche Zahl von 800 000 an, die plausibel erscheint, angesichts einer Bevölkerungszahl von 1,3 Millionen Armeniern im Osmanischen Reich vor dem Völkermord.[268] Eine beachtliche Anzahl von Armeniern schaffte es, den Massakern zu entkommen – einige, indem sie mit ihren Kindern zum Islam übertraten. Die genaue Zahl der Opfer, so Hrant Dink, der am 19. Januar 2007 in Istanbul von einem türkischen Nationalisten ermordet wurde, ist weniger wichtig als das Ergebnis des Völkermordes – die Auslöschung der armenischen Minderheit in Anatolien.

---

[264] Vgl.: Naimark, Norman M.: Flammender Haß. Ethnische Säuberungen im 20. Jahrhundert, München, 2004, S. 57.

[265] Vgl.: Katz, Steven T.: The Holocaust in Historical Context, Bd. 1: The Holocaust and Mass Death before the Modern Age, New York, 1994, S. 87.

[266] Suny, Ronald Grigor: Looking Toward Ararat. Armenia in Modern History, Bloomington, 1993, S. 114.

[267] Vgl.: Melson, Robert: Provocation or Nationalism: A Critical Inquiry into the Armenian Genocide of 1915, in: Hovannisian Richard G. [Hrsg.]: The Armenian Genocide in Perspective, New Brunswick, 1986, S. 64ff.

[268] Vgl.: Akçam, Taner: Armenien und der Völkermord. Die Istanbuler Prozesse und die türkische Nationalbewegung, Hamburg, 1996, S. 76; Dadrian, Vahakn N.: The History of the Armenian Genocide: Ethnic Conflict from the Balkans to Anatolia and to the Caucasus, Providence, 1995, S. 225.

Abb. 2: Massenmord an Armeniern aus dem Jahre 1915[269]

Die Genozidfrage entzweit die Wissenschaftler. Naimark, der sich mit fünf ethnischen Säuberungen beschäftigte, erwähnt, "dass das armenische Beispiel das umstrittenste und schwierigste historiographische Problem"[270] seiner Studien ist. In der Tat fällt auf, dass viele europäische Forscher die Bezeichnung *Genozid* für die armenische Tragödie verwenden, während viele US-amerikanische Forscher hingegen die staatlich organisierte Gewalt infrage stellen und somit zu dem Schluss kommen, dass es sich um keinen Genozid gehandelt habe.[271] Eine abschließende Bewertung darüber, welcher Begriff die Ereignisse am besten beschreibt, kann und soll im Rahmen dieser Studie nicht erfolgen[272], jedoch gewinnt man bei näherer Betrachtung der

---

[269] Aus: Wikimedia Commons, unter: http://commons.wikimedia.org/wiki/File:Morgenthau336.jpg
[270] Naimark, Norman M.: Das Problem der ethnischen Säuberung im modernen Europa, in: Zeitschrift für Ostmitteleuropaforschung, 48 (3), 1991, S. 320.
[271] Hierzu: Öke, Kemal: The Armenien Question 1914-1923, Oxford, 1988, S. 126-136; Lowry, Heath W.: The Story behind Ambassador Morgenthau's Story, Istanbul, 1990; Shaw, Stanford Jay: History of Ottoman Empire and Modern Turkey, Bd. 2, Cambridge, 1977, S. 30.
[272] Für den aktuellen Forschungsstand: Thelen, Sibylle: Die Armenierfrage in der Türkei, Berlin, 2010; Weiterführende Literatur: Akçam, Taner: Armenien und der Völkermord. Die Istanbuler Prozesse und die türkische Nationalbewegung, Hamburg, 1996; Gust, Wolfgang [Hrsg.]:

Problematik den Eindruck, dass die Opfer des Völkermordes hinter der Diskussion zurückbleiben, was nicht Sinn und Zweck solch eines Diskurses sein darf.

In der Türkei ist das Thema nach wie vor ein Tabu. Es wird nur im Rahmen der Diskussion nach der *Genozidfrage* behandelt, wobei das Ergebnis einer solchen Debatte immer ist, dass es sich um eine kriegerische Auseinandersetzung gehandelt habe. Die Opfer werden dabei als Kollateralschaden abgetan. Dies ist der Grund, weshalb ein Umdenken in der Bewertung des Völkermordes stattfinden muss. Bei aller Bedeutung der Frage, ob es sich um Genozid oder ethnische Säuberung handelte, dürfen die Opfer nicht in Vergessenheit geraten. Dink erklärt in einem Interview: "Das Wort 'Genozid' ist für mich nicht entscheidend. Wenn wir uns der Geschichte mit juristischen Begriffen nähern, die international eine spezifische Bedeutung haben, verhindern wir, dass wir begreifen, was damals passiert ist. Wir brauchen eine ethische Annäherung an die Geschichte"[273] – daher muss sich die Öffentlichkeit in der Türkei dieser Verantwortung stellen und sich mit ihrer Geschichte auseinandersetzen, um eine Vergangenheitsbewältigung und Versöhnung mit dem armenischen Volk voranzutreiben – unabhängig von der Diskussion um Opferzahlen oder Begriffsklassifizierung.

Die türkische Regierung, Wissenschaft und öffentliche Meinung leugnet den von der *İttihat ve Terakki Cemiyeti* durchgeführten Massenmord nach wie vor. Es seien einige Hunderttausend Armenier während der Deportation und Niederschlagung armenischer Aufstände ums Leben gekommen.

> "Insgesamt seien weit mehr Moslems (Türken, Kurden und andere) von den verbündeten Russen und Armeniern umgebracht worden als Armenier von den Türken und Kurden. Die wechselseitigen Massaker [...] seien durch die armenischen

---

Der Völkermord an den Armeniern 1915/16. Dokumente aus dem Politischen Archiv des deutschen Amts, Leck, 2005.

[273] "Das Wort 'Genozid' ist nicht entscheidend": http://jungle-world.com/artikel/2005/17/15123.html (Zuletzt eingesehen am 18.05.2012).

Nationalrevolutionäre, die von Rußland, Großbritannien, Frankreich und den USA angestachelt und finanziert worden seien, ausgelöst worden."[274]

Die Massaker seien im Rahmen eines Bürgerkrieges zu verstehen, in dem, so Bilal Şimşir, die Armenier die "Armenische Megali idea"[275] zu verwirklichen suchten, wie später die Griechen im Westen.

Nichtsdestotrotz gibt es eine wachsende Zahl von Menschen in der Türkei, die sich, trotz der staatlichen Repressalien, aufrichtig für den Völkermord an den Armeniern entschuldigen und für eine Versöhnung der beteiligten Völker einsetzen.

Wie sehr die Armenier von den Ereignissen der Jahre um 1915 geprägt sind, zeigt das Foto von einer Gedenkveranstaltung für den ermordeten Hrant Dink. Die Demonstrantin sieht einen engen Zusammenhang zwischen der Ermordung Dinks und den Ereignissen von 1915.

Abb. 3: Ein Plakat von einer Gedenkveranstaltung für den ermordeten Hrant Dink[276]

---

[274] Jahn, Egbert: Erinnerung an Völkermord als politische Waffe in der Gegenwart. Das Beispiel des osmanischen Genozids an den Armeniern, in: Jahn, Egbert: Politische Streitfragen, Wiesbaden, 2008, S. 83.
[275] Şimşir, Bilâl N.: Ermeni Meselesi (Die Armenierproblematik). 1774-2005, 2. Aufl., Ankara, 2005, (Ermeni Megali Ideası).
[276] Aus: http://www.turnusol.biz/UserFiles/Image/2010/erivanteyze.gif

Nach diesen katastrophalen Erfahrungen mit den Armeniern führten die Befürworter von ethnischer Homogenisierung den türkisch-griechischen Bevölkerungsaustausch als Beispiel für eine legale und gelungene Umsiedlung von Ethnien auf. Inwieweit dieses Vorgehen erfolgsversprechend war, wird im folgenden Kapitel erläutert.

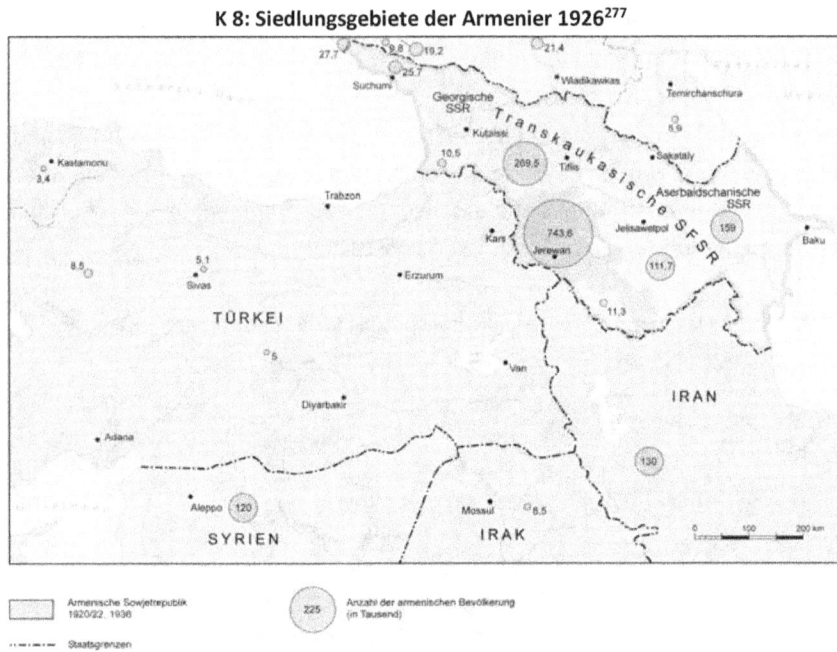

K 8: Siedlungsgebiete der Armenier 1926[277]

---

[277] Aus: Haus der Heimat des Landes Baden-Württemberg [Hrsg.]: Umsiedlung, Flucht und Vertreibung der Deutschen als internationales Problem. Zur Geschichte eines europäischen Irrwegs, Stuttgart, 2005, S. 51.

5.4. Lehrstück Lausanne? Die vertragliche Regelung des Bevölkerungsaustausches

> "When the formula of political nationality is applied to mixed populations where nationality is hard to disentangle from profession or class, an irreducible residuum of minorities is bound to be left on the wrong side of the definitive frontier lines, and this residuum is a fruitful cause of estrangement. Each nation fears that its own hostages in the other's territory may be ill-treated, and that the other's hostages in the own territory may undermine is sovereignty, and such expectations have a fatal tendency to realize themselves."[278]

Wanderungsbewegungen stehen für viele Staaten sehr oft in Zusammenhang mit Machtkonsolidierung, Schaffung von ethnischer, religiöser und kultureller Homogenität, Evakuierung strategisch wichtiger Gebiete, aber auch als Instrument für außenpolitische Ziele, wie zum Beispiel als Druckmittel gegen andere Regierungen. Das folgende Beispiel verdeutlicht dies besonders eindrucksvoll.

"Sind Zwangsumsiedlungen ein geeignetes Mittel zur Lösung von Minderheitenkonflikten"[279], fragt Pitsoulis und bezieht sich auf den Vertrag von Lausanne, der als erster prominenter Fall gilt, in dem ein obligatorischer Bevölkerungsaustausch durch eine völkerrechtliche Konvention legalisiert wurde. Der Vertrag, mit dem Ziel einer "ethnonationale[n.DOT] Homogenisierung der jeweiligen Bevölkerung in der Türkei respektive Griechenland [...], [war.DOT] das Ergebnis von Friedensverhandlungen und kam unter Mitwirkung der internationalen Gemeinschaft – des Völkerbundes [...] zustande"[280]. Der griechisch-türkische Bevölkerungsaustausch von 1923 wurde zum völkerrechtlichen und politischen Präzedenzfall als ultima ratio zur Lösung ethnischer Konflikte zwischen Nachbarstaaten. Unterschiedlichste Akteure wie

---

[278] Toynbee, Arnold Jay: The Western Question in Greece and Turkey. A Study in the Contact of Civilizations, London, 2010, S. 322f.
[279] Pitsoulis, Athanassios: Legitimierte Vertreibung. Minderheitenpolitik im Vertrag von Lausanne, in: WeltTrends. Zeitschrift für internationale Politik, 19, (76)2001, S. 97.
[280] Sundhausen, Holm: Von "Lausanne" nach "Dayton". Ein Paradigmenwechsel bei der Lösung ethnonationaler Konflikte, in: Hohls, Rüdiger/Schröder, Iris/Siegrist Hannes [Hrsg.]: Europa und die Europäer. Quellen und Essays zur modernen europäischen Geschichte, München, 2005, S. 409.

Adolf Hitler oder Winston Churchill haben sich später auf das *Lausanner Modell* berufen. Letzterer erklärte:

> "The disentanglement of populations which took place between Greece and Turkey after the last war [...] was in many ways a success, and has produced friendly relations between Greece and Turkey ever since."[281]

Dass Churchills Bewertung alles andere als treffend war, zeigen die zum Teil kriegerischen Auseinandersetzungen zwischen beiden Staaten.

Was war geschehen? Nach der griechischen *kleinasiatischen Katastrophe* Ende des Jahres 1922 gelang es Mustafa Kemal und seinen Truppen, den Vertrag von Sèvres vom 10. August 1920 durch den Lausanner Vertrag vom 24. Juli 1923 zu ersetzen, dem die türkisch-griechische Konvention vom 30. Januar 1923 vorausgegangen war. Diese Konvention beinhaltete einen Bevölkerungsaustausch, der nicht nur jene Personen betraf, die nach Vertragsschluss zwangsumgesiedelt werden sollten, sondern auch diejenigen, die bereits zu Hunderttausenden geflohen waren.

In den beiden betroffenen Staaten heben frühe Arbeiten "in der Regel im Einklang mit den nationalen Geschichtsbildern Griechenlands und der Türkei die Vorteile der Schaffung von Homogenität hervor, sind aber apologetisch in Bezug auf die negativen Folgewirkungen. In der offiziellen Geschichtsleseart wird die Erinnerung an den Austausch in den Vordergrund gestellt. Die Leiden der Flüchtlinge und die immensen Herausforderungen für die Griechen und ihren Staat sollten nicht in Vergessenheit geraten."[282] Die offizielle Geschichtsschreibung der Türkei hingegen sieht in Lausanne, wie im 4. Kapitel dargestellt wurde, einzig das Geburtsepos der Türkei. Das Leid der Menschen ist auch hier kaum ein Thema – wenn, dann nur das Leid der Türken vor der Unterzeichnung des Lausanner Vertrages.

Lausanne stellt daneben eine wichtige historische Zäsur in der Geschichte dar. Die fast dreitausendjährige Existenz der Griechen in Kleinasien ging zu

---

[281] Rede Winston Churchills vom 15.12.1944:
http://hansard.millbanksystems.com/commons/1944/dec/15/poland#S5CV0406P0_19441215_HOC_44.

[282] Pitsoulis, Athanassios: Vertreibung und Diplomatie: Hintergründe und Umdeutungen des griechisch-türkischen 'Bevölkerungsaustausch' von 1923, in: IMIS-Beiträge, (36) 2010, S. 38.

Ende.[283] Nachdem sich Ende des 19. Jahrhunderts ein ethnisch definiertes Verständnis von Nation durchgesetzt hatte, begannen selbsternannte Titularnationen, trotz der ethnischen Vielfalt in Südosteuropa, Bevölkerungsgruppen auszuschließen, die nicht in ihre ethnonationale Definition passten. Zur Homogenisierung kamen verschiedene Mittel zum Einsatz – von der Assimilierung über Vertreibung und Umsiedlung bis hin zum Völkermord. Die ersten groß angelegten ethnischen Säuberungen der jüngsten Geschichte fanden während der beiden Balkankriege von 1912 und 1913 statt.[284] Diese Vertreibungs- und Abwanderungswellen zielten vor allem auf muslimische Bevölkerungsgruppen in Südosteuropa ab. Im Anschluss an die Balkankriege schlossen Bulgarien und das Osmanische Reich am 15. November 1913 im Vertrag von Neuilly den ersten internationalen Vertrag über einen Bevölkerungsaustausch ab, jedoch beschränkte sich dieser auf die Umsiedlung von Bulgaren und Muslimen auf eine 15 km breite Zone entlang der Grenze zwischen beiden Staaten. Es handelte sich aber bei dieser Umsiedlung um eine Legitimierung von bereits stattgefundenen Umsiedlungen.[285] Der eigentliche Unterschied zum türkisch-griechischen Bevölkerungsaustusch lag in der geographischen Reichweite der Abkommen. Während Neuilly nur auf die Grenzregion beschränkt blieb, galt das Lausanner Abkommen für zwei komplette Staaten – mit den regionalen Ausnahmen Istanbuls und Westthrakiens[286]. Weitere ethnische 'Flurbereinigungen' ließen nicht lange auf sich warten. Während des Pogroms von Istanbul im Jahre 1955 verließ der größte Teil der knapp 125 000 Griechen die Stadt. Heute leben in Istanbul nur noch etwa 1.650 Griechen.[287] In Westthrakien wiederum betrieb Griechenland eine Dis-

---

[283] Vgl.: Ebd., S. 38.
[284] Vgl.: Sundhausen, Holm: Von "Lausanne" nach "Dayton". Ein Paradigmenwechsel bei der Lösung ethnonationaler Konflikte, in: Hohls, Rüdiger/Schröder, Iris/Siegrist Hannes [Hrsg.]: Europa und die Europäer. Quellen und Essays zur modernen europäischen Geschichte, München, 2005, S. 409.
[285] Vgl.: Pitsoulis, Athanassios: Vertreibung und Diplomatie: Hintergründe und Umdeutungen des griechisch-türkischen 'Bevölkerungsaustausch' von 1923, in: IMIS-Beiträge, (36) 2010, S. 40.
[286] Vgl.: Martin, Lawrence: The Treaties of Peace, 1919-1923, Vol. II, New York, 1924, S. 1036ff.
[287] Vgl.: Seufert, Günter/Kubaseck, Christopher: Die Türkei. Politik, Geschichte, Kultur, 2. Aufl., München, 2006, S. 162.

kriminierungspolitik gegen die türkische Minderheit, deren Zahl sich in Folge dieses Vorgehens dezimierte.

Das Time Magazine schrieb: "In effect, the Lausanne Settlement turned Europe bag and baggage out of Turkey instead of turning Turkey bag and baggage out of Europe. It signified the complete shipwreck of Lloyd George's five years nursing of Greek ambitions."[288]

---

[288] Time Magazine, 14.04.1924, S. 2.

K 9: Der griechisch-türkische Bevölkerungsaustausch aufgrund des Vertrages von Lausanne 1923 und seine Folgen[289]

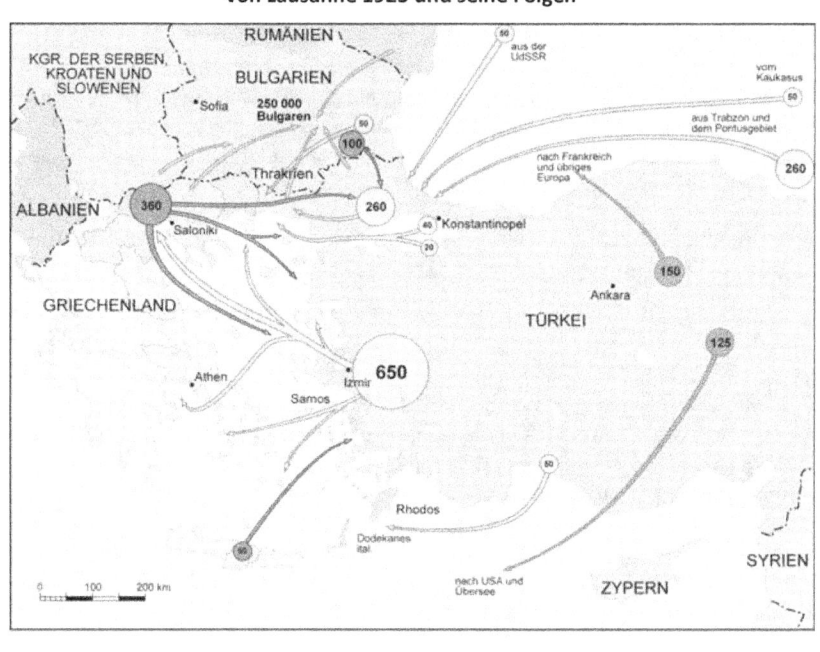

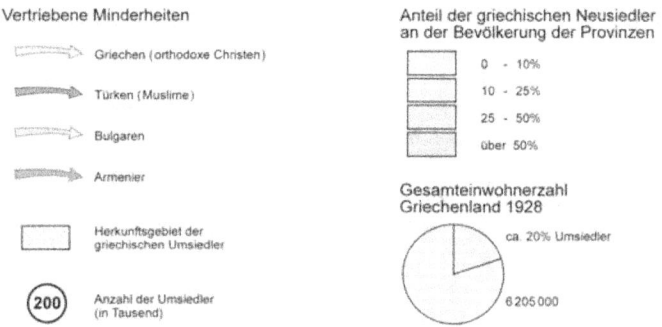

---

[289] Aus: Haus der Heimat des Landes Baden-Württemberg [Hrsg.]: Umsiedlung, Flucht und Vertreibung der Deutschen als internationales Problem. Zur Geschichte eines europäischen Irrwegs, Stuttgart, 2005, S. 52.

Die umzusiedelnde Bevölkerungsgruppe wurde nicht nach ethnischem Selbstverständnis oder ihrer Sprache bestimmt, sondern nach der Religionszugehörigkeit.

> "Rund 1,3 Millionen 'Griechen', von denen einige die griechische Sprache nicht beherrschten, sowie annährend 400 000 Muslime (mit unterschiedlichen Sprachen und unterschiedlicher ethnischer Zuordnung) verloren ihre angestammte Heimat und ihre bisherige Staatsbürgerschaft."[290]

Dieser Bevölkerungsaustausch wurde von Fridtjof Nansen, dem Flüchtlingskommissar des Völkerbundes, vorgeschlagen[291]. Ein Statement von ihm macht deutlich, auf wessen Initiative der Bevölkerungsaustausch zustande kam:

> "It was while I was engaged on this task that I was invited by the representatives of the four Great Powers in Constantinople to endeavour to initiate negotiations between the Turkish and Greek Governments with a view to the conclusion of a treaty for the exchange of minority populations. In view of the fact that the Governments of the four Great Powers all believed such an exchange to be desirable, and as I shared their view that such an exchange, if it were made, should be made at once and without waiting for the conclusion of the final Treaty of Peace, I immediately entered into negotiations with the two Governments with a view to arranging an immediate agreement."[292]

Nansen erwähnt auch die Gründe, weshalb die Großmächte einen Bevölkerungsaustausch bevorzugten:

> "[...] because they believe that to unmix the populations of the Near East will tend to secure the true pacification of the Near East and because they believe an exchange of populations is the quickest and most efficacious way of dealing with the grave movements of populations which has already occurred."[293]

---

[290] Sundhausen, Holm: Von "Lausanne" nach "Dayton". Ein Paradigmenwechsel bei der Lösung ethnonationaler Konflikte, in: Hohls, Rüdiger/Schröder, Iris/Siegrist Hannes [Hrsg.]: Europa und die Europäer. Quellen und Essays zur modernen europäischen Geschichte, München, 2005, S. 410.

[291] Vgl.: Ladas, Stephen P.: The Exchange of Minorities. Bulgaria, Greece and Turkey, New York, 1932, S. 338.

[292] Lausanne Conference on Near Eastern Affairs 1922-1923: Records of Proceedings and Draft Terms of Peace (Dokument Cmd. 1813), London, 1923, S. 114.

[293] Ebd., S. 114.

Paradoxerweise arbeiteten die verfeindeten Staaten bei der Durchführung eng zusammen, konnten doch die umgesiedelten Bevölkerungsgruppen als "Manövriermasse"[294] genutzt werden, um die ethnisch-religiöse Balance in strategisch wichtigen Punkten zu beeinflussen. So siedelte Griechenland die Flüchtlinge vor allem in grenznahe und heterogene Gebiete wie Makedonien an, während die Türkei ebenfalls in Rahmen der Homogenisierungspolitik handelte.

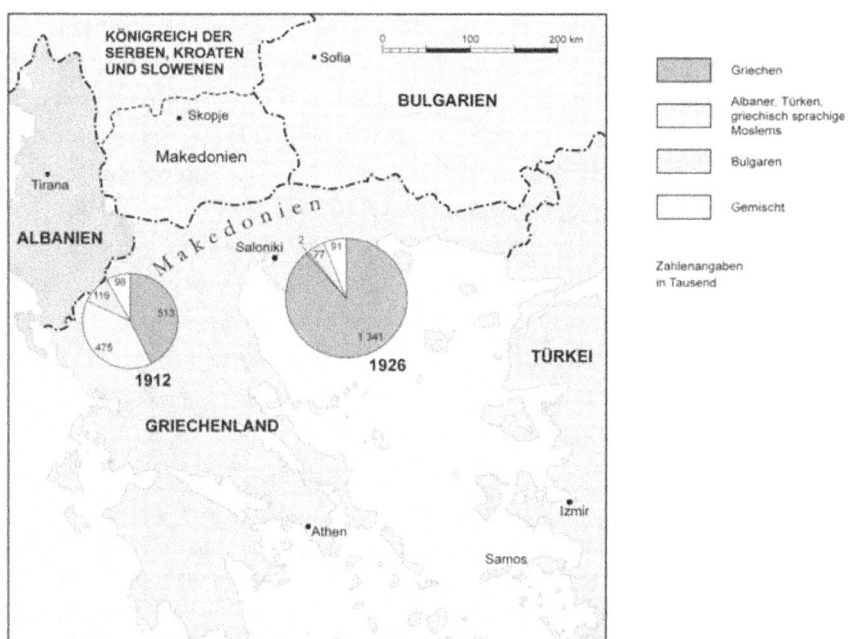

K 10: Ethnische Verhältnisse im griechischen Makedonien 1912 und 1926[295]

---

[294] Pitsoulis, Athanassios: Legitimierte Vertreibung. Minderheitenpolitik im Vertrag von Lausanne, in: WeltTrends. Zeitschrift für internationale Politik, 19, (76)2001, S. 99.
[295] Aus: Haus der Heimat des Landes Baden-Württemberg [Hrsg.]: Umsiedlung, Flucht und Vertreibung der Deutschen als internationales Problem. Zur Geschichte eines europäischen Irrwegs, Stuttgart, 2005, S. 51.

Ein weiteres Ziel der Türkei war die "'Turkifizierung der Wirtschaft' [...]: Die ehemals armenisch, griechisch und jüdisch dominierte Händlerschicht sollte mittel- und langfristig durch eine türkische ersetzt werden."[296]

Wie ist der Lausanner Bevölkerungsaustausch zu bewerten? *Lausanne* ging davon aus, dass die ethnische und religiöse Heterogenität Anatoliens Ursache des türkisch-griechischen Krieges war. Durch Entmischung sollte genau diese Ursache beseitigt werden. Der Vertrag hat beide Staaten tatsächlich einer Homogenität nähergebracht: In Makedonien stieg der Anteil der Griechen zwischen 1912 und 1926 von 42,6% auf 88,8%.[297] Es darf jedoch nicht vergessen werden, dass es sich bei diesem Bevölkerungsaustausch um keine freiwillige Transaktion handelte, auch wenn alle betroffenen Parteien nur die positiven Seiten zu betonen versuchten, die es, wie wir inzwischen eindeutig sagen können, nicht gab. Letztendlich hat sich diese *positive Umdeutung* der Vertreibung, nachhaltig negativ auf andere Minderheitenprobleme ausgewirkt, da es nicht nur möglich war, ungewollte Menschen umzusiedeln, sondern auch ethnische Säuberungen nachträglich in legale Bevölkerungstransfers zu verwandeln. Ein Beispiel hierfür ist der Vorschlag der Peel-Kommission vom 30. November 1937 an die britische Regierung, die einen Austausch zwischen Juden und Arabern vorsah. In diesem Zusammenhang wurden Griechenland und Türkei für die vermeintlich beispielhafte Lösung des Minderheitenproblems in hohen Tönen gelobt:

> "A precedent is afforded by the exchange effected between the Greek and Turkish populations on the morrow of the Greco-Turkish War of 1922. A convention was signed by the Greek and Turkish Governments, providing that, under the supervision of the League of Nations, Greek nationals of the Orthodox religion living in Turkey should be compulsorily removed to Greece, and Turkish nationals of the Moslem religion living in Greece to Turkey. The numbers involved were high—no less than some 1,300,000 Greeks and some 400,000 Turks. But so vigorously and effectively was the task accomplished that within about eighteen months from the spring of 1923 the whole exchange was completed. The cour-

---

[296] Ebd., S. 99. (Mehr hierzu: Aktar, Ayhan: Homogenising the Nation, Turkifying the Economy. The Turkish Experience of Population Exchange Reconsidered, in: Hirschon, Renee [Hrsg.]: Crossing the Aegean. An Appraisal of the 1923 Compulsory Population Exchange between Greece and Turkey, New York, S. 79-95).

[297] Ladas, Stephen P.: The Exchange of Minorities. Bulgaria, Greece and Turkey, New York, 1932, S. 700.

age of the Greek and Turkish statesmen concerned has been justified by the result. Before the operation the Greek and Turkish minorities had been a constant irritant. Now Greco-Turkish relations are friendlier than they have ever been before."[298]

Die Kommission ignorierte hierbei, dass die meisten Betroffenen bereits vor der Unterzeichnung des Lausanner Vertrages aus ihrer Heimat vertrieben worden waren und viele dabei den Tod fanden. Churchill führte den Lausanner Austausch sogar explizit auf, als es um die Vertreibung der deutschen Bevölkerung Osteuropas ging.[299] Weitere bekannte Bevölkerungstransfers, denen Lausanne als Vorbild diente, waren das deutsch-italienische Abkommen vom 23. Juni 1939 und die indisch-pakistanische Separation von 1947.[300] Lange Zeit wurde nicht hinterfragt, "ob der gesellschaftliche Wohlfahrtszuwachs durch größere Homogenität nicht weit geringer ausfiel als die gesellschaftlichen Wohlfahrtsverluste der Vertreibungen und Umsiedlungen"[301] – nicht nur für die Betroffenen, sondern für die Gesamtgesellschaft.

Um das Risiko eines nachträglich legalisierten Bevölkerungsaustausches zu verhindern, fordert Pitsoulis von der internationalen Gemeinschaft "eine klare Abwendung vom Prinzip der nachträglich anerkannten Vertreibungen [...]. Anreize, Minderheiten zu vertreiben, verringern sich, wenn nicht damit zu rechnen ist, dass sie sich *ex post* legalisieren lassen. Um dies zu erreichen, könnte ein Rückkehrrecht vertriebener Minderheiten in der UN-Charta festgeschrieben werden."[302] Holm Sundhausen sieht im Dayton-Abkommen für Bosnien und Herzegowina von 1995 eine Abkehr vom Lausanner Prinzip. Im Gegensatz zum Lausanner Abkommen sieht das Dayton-Abkommen nämlich eine Rückkehr der während des Krieges geflohenen oder vertriebenen Men-

---

[298] Mandate for Palestine – UK summary of the Palestine Royal Commission (Peel Commission) report Cmd. 5479 – League of Nations/Non-UN document: http://unispal.un.org/UNISPAL.NSF/0/08E38A718201458B052565700072B358.

[299] Vgl.: De Zayas, Alfred M.: Nemesis at Potsdam: The Anglo-Americans and the Expulsion of the Germans, London, 1979, S. 11.

[300] Vgl.: Pitsoulis, Athanassios: Vertreibung und Diplomatie: Hintergründe und Umdeutungen des griechisch-türkischen 'Bevölkerungsaustausch' von 1923, in: IMIS-Beiträge, (36) 2010, S. 65.

[301] Ebd., S. 63.

[302] Pitsoulis, Athanassios: Legitimierte Vertreibung. Minderheitenpolitik im Vertrag von Lausanne, in: WeltTrends. Zeitschrift für internationale Politik, 19, (76)2001, S. 101.

schen in ihre Heimat vor. Es ging somit um eine "Rückgängigmachung bzw. um die Wiederherstellung von Multiethnizität [...in Bosnien-Herzegowina. DOT]. Erst mit dem 'Dayton-Abkommen – 72 Jahre nach 'Lausanne' – vollzog die internationale Gemeinschaft eine grundsätzliche Kehrtwende."[303]
Das Lausanner Abkommen mit seinen katastrophalen Folgen für die betroffenen Menschen und Staaten brachte mit der Aufnahme und Eingliederung der Vertriebenen auch große wirtschaftliche und soziale Probleme mit sich. Insbesondere aus stadtgeographischer Perspektive, denn der Bevölkerungsaustausch brachte Griechenland eine Nettozuwanderung von knapp einer Million Neubürgern. Ein großer Teil fand dabei Zuflucht in Athen. So entstanden um die Stadtkerne von Athen und Piräus wild gebaute Siedlungen, die teilweise noch heute Namen mit der Vorsilbe Néa- (Neu-) tragen, wie zum Beispiel Néa Smýrni oder Néa Ionía, deren Namen an die Heimatstädte in Kleinasien erinnern sollten. Die Folge war ein zu schnelles und ungeplantes Wachstum Athens, wodurch der Charme der kleinen Residenzstadt dahin war.[304] Aus stadtplanerischer Sicht war der Zuzug dieser Massen grundsätzlich nicht zu bewältigen.
Die nationale Geschichtsschreibung der beiden beteiligten Staaten erwähnte lange Zeit nur die Vorteile des Bevölkerungsaustausches. Die negativen Folgen, die stark überwogen, wurden ignoriert. Die Frage der Restitution zurückgelassenen Besitzes wurde am 30. Oktober 1930 gelöst. Venizelos und Mustafa Kemal einigten sich in der Ankara-Konvention auf einen gegenseitigen Verzicht auf die Restitution von Eigentum der Flüchtlinge.

> "Im Nachhinein mutet daher der Bevölkerungsaustausch von Lausanne als 'fait accompli' zweier Regierungen auf Kosten einer gewaltsam zwischen beiden aufgeteilten heterogenen Population an."[305]

---

[303] Sundhausen, Holm: Von "Lausanne" nach "Dayton". Ein Paradigmenwechsel bei der Lösung ethnonationaler Konflikte, in: Hohls, Rüdiger/Schröder, Iris/Siegrist, Hannes [Hrsg.]: Europa und die Europäer. Quellen und Essays zur modernen europäischen Geschichte, München, 2005, S. 409.
[304] Rondholz, Eberhard: Griechenland. Ein Länderporträt, Bonn, 2011, S. 164f.
[305] Pitsoulis, Athanassios: Vertreibung und Diplomatie: Hintergründe und Umdeutungen des griechisch-türkischen 'Bevölkerungsaustausch' von 1923, in: IMIS-Beiträge, (36) 2010, S. 62.

6. Zusammenfassung:
Brüche und Kontinuitäten in einem Raum

Der Berliner Kongress von 1878, die Balkenkriege der Jahre 1912/13 und das Attentat von Sarajevo 1914 hatten ihre Ursachen in ungelösten Territorialproblemen. Die Grenzziehungen waren schon im ausgehenden 19. Jahrhundert willkürlich vorgenommen worden. Es wurde kaum Rücksicht genommen auf die ethnische Zusammensetzung und die nationalen Wünsche der betroffenen Staaten. Wirtschaftliche und strategische Faktoren, wie Zugänge zu Meeren oder Flüssen, wurden als weitaus wichtiger eingestuft. Die neuen Grenzen wurden in der Regel ohne Beteiligung der Betroffenen festgelegt. Eine Folge war latenter Ethno-Nationalismus, der grundsätzlich alle Grenzregelungen infrage und maximale Territorialforderungen stellte. Die Griechen träumten von der Großen Idee, der *Megali Idea*, die Serben von Großserbien mit seinen Grenzen des Dušan-Reiches im 14. Jahrhundert und die Türken von einem pantürkischen Reich. Die anderen Nationen hatten ähnliche entartete Vorstellungen. Alle knüpften dabei an die "Kontinuität mittelalterlicher Reichsbildung an wie der Dakismus der Rumänen oder der Rückbezug der Albaner auf die Illyrer oder der Bulgaren auf die Thraker und die turksprachigen Protobulgaren. Derartige Kontinuitätstheorien implizierten völlig überzogene Raumvorstellungen der jeweiligen Titularnation."[306] Die Formierung von Nationalstaaten in einer Region, die keine klaren ethnischen Abgrenzungen besaß, gleichzeitig ein Mosaik an Kulturen, Sprachen und Ethnien bot, war eine teure Hypothek. Bevölkerungsgruppen, die noch zur Mehrheit gehörten, wurden in kürzester Zeit zu Minderheiten, genauso umgekehrt. Die neue Elite des neuen Staates versuchte anschließend, die neuen Grenzen und Machtverhältnisse durch nationale Homogenisierung zu legitimieren. Verstärkt wurden diese Tendenzen von der Vorstellung des Gottesgnadentums.

---

[306] Hösch, Edgar: Die Konfliktregion Südosteuropa in historischer Perspektive, in: Konfliktregion Südosteuropa. Vergangenheit und Perspektiven, München, 1997, S. 7.

Die Folgen dieser Homogenisierungspolitik waren gestörte Nachbarschaftsverhältnisse und interethnische Konflikte. Ethnische Minderheiten galten den Nationalstaaten als potentielle Bedrohung.

Die Nation war vielen von Anfang an heilig und unantastbar. Für die Menschen war es unvorstellbar, dass Nationen und der Nationalstaat historische Produkte waren, dazu noch relativ jung, und deshalb Veränderungen unterworfen sind.

> "Denn Geschichte ist Veränderung und steht im Gegensatz zur Essenz, zu dem, was während der Veränderung unverändert bleibt. Für viele ist Nation Essenz und nicht Produkt der Geschichte – ein 'Gegenstand', der schon immer 'da' war, auch wenn er von den Zeitgenossen nicht bemerkt wurde."[307]

Holm Sundhausen bezeichnet dies sogar als einen der größten Irrtümer der letzten zwei Jahrhunderte. Diese Verabsolutierung der Nation verhindere eine tolerante und offene Gesellschaft.

> "Eine zwangsläufige Folge waren die schon zu Ende des 19. Jahrhunderts im Streit um Mazedonien erbitterte Volkstumskämpfe, gezielter Bandenterror, gewaltsame ethnische Säuberungen, Zwangsassimilierung, Mord und Totschlag. Sie haben die Bewohner der südöstlichen Peripherie des europäischen Kontinents schon lange vor den schrecklichen Ereignissen der letzten Jahre in der sog. zivilisierten Welt in Verruf gebracht."[308]

Als deutlich wurde, dass ethnische Säuberungen nicht nur die ethnische Zusammensetzung eines Raumes veränderten, sondern mit einer physischen Liquidierung ganzer Völker einhergingen, wie ihn die Armenier in den Jahren um 1915 erlebt hatten, griff man zu neuen Methoden: Es kam zur Anwendung vertraglich geregelter Bevölkerungstransfers, wie beim griechisch-türkischen Bevölkerungsaustausch im Anschluss an den Lausanner Vertrag. Etwa 1,7 Millionen Menschen mussten ihre Heimat verlassen. Das Lausanner Modell wurde schnell zum Präzedenzfall zur Lösung von Minderheitenproblemen, der den Zwangsumsiedlungen auch noch eine Legitimität gab. Dies war in keiner Weise ein rational durchdachtes Verhandlungsergebnis. Es

---

[307] Sundhaussen, Holm: Nationsbildung und Nationalismus im Donau-Balkan-Raum, in: Torke, Hans-Joachim [Hrsg.]: Forschungen zur osteuropäischen Geschichte, Berlin, 1993, S. 253.
[308] Hösch, Edgar: Die Konfliktregion Südosteuropa in historischer Perspektive, in: Konfliktregion Südosteuropa. Vergangenheit und Perspektiven, München, 1997, S. 9.

wurde übersehen, dass der Bevölkerungsaustausch zwischen der Türkei und Griechenland gar keiner war, weil der Großteil der umzusiedelnden Menschen bereits vor dem Abschluss der Vertrages vertrieben worden war, was nicht selten in blutigen Exzessen endete. Es handelte sich lediglich um eine nachträgliche Legitimierung bereits erfolgter Vertreibungen. Die vertragliche Regelung führte vielmehr zu einer Ausweitung dieser menschenverachtenden Methode.

Die ungelösten Territorialfragen der Vergangenheit sind heute noch eine teure Hypothek für den südosteuropäischen Raum. Ob die Völker die Chance nutzen und aus der Vergangenheit lernen werden, um die Missstände der Verträge, die unter dem Diktat der Großmächte entstanden waren, und der Politik in der Zwischen- und Nachkriegszeit zu beseitigen, ist nicht absehbar. Eins ist jedoch sicher: Die Balkanhalbinsel ist keine klassische Konfliktregion in Europa und ihre Bewohner haben kein Interesse an Kriegen. Ethnische Säuberungen und Kriege gehören nicht zu einer bestimmten Kultur. Falsch wäre der Glaube, die Bevölkerung Südosteuropas sei konfliktbereiter oder grausamer als Menschen anderer Regionen. Es sind nicht so sehr die räumlichen Gegebenheiten, sondern die Handlungen der Menschen selbst, die angesiedelt in konkreten gesellschaftlichen, politischen und wirtschaftlichen Ordnungen zu untersuchen sind, statt der scheinbar bösen Vergangenheit der Serben, Türken, Deutschen, Russen oder anderer Völker. Heterogenität darf niemals Grund für kriegerische Auseinandersetzungen sein. Weder Kulturen noch Sprachen bringen Kriegsgründe hervor.

> "Der Krieg ist [vielmehr. DOT] die Ausgeburt des überzogenen Machtstrebens einer kleinen Clique, die eine manipulierte öffentliche Meinung und inszenierte Aufmärsche einer indoktrinierten Bevölkerung für ihre eigenen egoistischen Zwecke mißbraucht."[309]

---

[309] Ebd., S. 10.

7. Quellen- und Literaturverzeichnis

Akçam, Taner: Armenien und der Völkermord. Die Istanbuler Prozesse und die türkische Nationalbewegung, Hamburg, 1996.

Aktar, Ayhan: Homogenising the Nation, Turkifying the Economy. The Turkish Experience of Population Exchange Reconsidered, in: Hirschon, Renee [Hrsg.]: Crossing the Aegean. An Appraisal of the 1923 Compulsory Population Exchange between Greece and Turkey, New York, 2003, S. 79-95.

Akten zur deutschen auswärtigen Politik, 1918-1945, Serie D (1937-1945), Bd. 7, Baden-Baden, 1956.

Anderson, Benedict: Imagined Communities. Reflections on the Origin and Spread of Nationalism, London, 1983.

Atay, Falih Rıfkı: Çankaya, Istanbul, 2010.

Bardakijan, Kevork B.: Hitler and the Armenian Genocide, Cambridge, 1985.

Basch-Ritter, Renate: Österreich-Ungarn in Wort und Bild. Menschen und Länder, Graz, 1989.

Baytok, Taner: İngiliz Belgeleriyle Sevr'den Lozan'a. Dünden Bugüne Değişen Ne Var? (Von Lausanne nach Sèvres in englischen Dokumenten. Was hat sich von gestern auf heute verändert?), Istanbul, 2007.

Beer Mathias: Auf dem Weg zum ethnisch reinen Nationalstaat. Einführung, in: Beer, Mathias [Hrsg.]: Auf dem Weg zum ethnisch reinen Nationalstaat, 2. Aufl., Tübingen, 2007, S. 7-18.

Beer, Mathias: Flucht und Vertreibung der Deutschen. Voraussetzungen, Verlauf, Folgen, München, 2011.

Behramoğlu, Ataol: Lozan. İyi Bir Yurttaş Aranıyor (Lausanne. Ein guter Staatsbürger wird gesucht), Istanbul, 1993.

Bihl, Wolfdieter: Das Osmanische Reich aus der Sicht eines deutschen Offiziers im Ersten Weltkrieg. In: Lukan, Walter/Suppan, Arnold [Hrsg.]: Nationalitäten und Identitäten in Ostmitteleuropa. Festschrift aus Anlaß des 70. Geburtstages von Richard Georg Plaschka, Wien, 1995, S. 25-41.

Bilsel, Cemil M.: Lozan (Lausanne), Bd. 1, Istanbul, 1933.

Bilsel, Cemil M.: Lozan (Lausanne), Bd. 2, Istanbul, 1933.

Carmichael, Cathie: Ethnic Cleansing in the Balkans. Nationalism and the Destruction of Tradition, London, 2002.

Dadrian, Vahakn N.: Einleitung, in: Gust, Wolfgang [Hrsg.]: Der Völkermord an den Armeniern 1915/16. Dokumente aus dem Politischen Archiv des deutschen Amts, Leck, 2005.

Dadrian, Vahakn N.: The History of the Armenian Genocide: Ethnic Conflict from the Balkans to Anatolia and to the Caucasus, Providence, 1995.

De Bischoff, Norbert: La Turquie dans le monde, Paris, 1936.

De Zayas, Alfred M.: Nemesis at Potsdam: The Anglo-Americans and the Expulsion of the Germans, London, 1979.

Boden, Martina: Nationalitäten, Minderheiten und ethnische Konflikte in Europa. Ursprünge, Entwicklungen, Krisenherde, Augsburg, 1993.

Boeckh, Katrin: Von den ersten Balkankriegen zum Ersten Weltkrieg. Kleinstaatpolitik und ethnische Selbstbestimmung auf dem Balkan, München, 1996.

Çavdaroğlu, Hüseyin Avni: Önce ve Sonrası ile Lozan (Vor und nach Lausanne), Istanbul, 2011.

Clewing, Konrad: Nationsbildung und Nationalismus in Südosteuropa, in: Clewing, Konrad/Schmitt, Oliver Jens [Hrsg.]: Geschichte Südosteuropas. Vom frühen Mittelalter bis zur Gegenwart, Regensburg, 2011, S. 708-731.

Clewing, Konrad: Staatensystem und innerstaatliches Agieren im multiethnischen Raum: Südosteuropa im langen 19. Jahrhundert, in: Clewing, Konrad/Schmitt, Oliver Jens [Hrsg.]: Geschichte Südosteuropas. Vom frühen Mittelalter bis zur Gegenwart, Regensburg, 2011, S. 432-553.

Clewing, Konrad/Schmitt, Oliver Jens: Südosteuropa: Raum und Geschichte, in: Clewing, Konrad/Schmitt, Oliver Jens [Hrsg.]: Geschichte Südosteuropas. Vom frühen Mittelalter bis zur Gegenwart, Regensburg, 2011, S. 1-16.

Efendi, Mehemed Emin (Pseudonym): Die Zukunft der Türkei. Ein Beitrag zur Lösung der orientalischen Frage. Berlin und Leipzig, 1898.

Ersoy, Tolga: Lozan. Bir Antiemperyalizm Masalı Nasıl Yazıldı? (Lausanne. Wie wurde ein antiimperialistisches Märchen geschrieben?), 2. Aufl., Istanbul, 2005.

Görlich, Ernst Joseph: Grundzüge der Geschichte der Habsburgermonarchie und Österreichs, 3. Aufl., Darmstadt, 1988.

Gust, Wolfgang [Hrsg.]: Der Völkermord an den Armeniern 1915/16. Dokumente aus dem Politischen Archiv des deutschen Amts, Leck, 2005, S. 7-16.

Haus der Heimat des Landes Baden-Württemberg [Hrsg.]: Umsiedlung, Flucht und Vertreibung der Deutschen als internationales Problem. Zur Geschichte eines europäischen Irrwegs, Stuttgart, 2005.

Hobsbawm, Eric: Nations and Nationalism since 1780, Cambridge, 1990.

Hoerder, Dirk/Lucassen, Jan/Lucassen, Leo: Terminologien und Konzepte in der Migrationsforschung, in: Bade, Klaus J./Emmer, Pieter C./ Lucassen, Leo/Oltmer Jochen [Hrsg.]: Enzyklopädie Migration in Europa. Vom 17. Jahrhundert bis zur Gegenwart, 2. Aufl., Paderborn, 2008, S. 29-53.

Höffe, Otfried: Nationalstaaten im Zeitalter der Globalisierung, in: Beer, Mathias [Hrsg.]: Auf dem Weg zum ethnisch reinen Nationalstaat, 2. Aufl., Tübingen, 2007, S. 197-210.

Hösch, Edgar: Die Konfliktregion Südosteuropa in historischer Perspektive, in: Konfliktregion Südosteuropa. Vergangenheit und Perspektiven, München, 1997, S. 1-10.

Hösch, Edgar: Geschichte der Balkanländer. Von der Frühzeit bis zur Gegenwart, 5. Aufl., München, 2008.

Huntington, Samuel Phillips: The Clash of Civilizations and the Remaking of World Order, New York, 1998.

İnönü, İsmet: Lozan Barış Antlaşması'nın 70. Yıldönümü. İstiklâl Savaşı ve Lozan (Der 70. Jahrestag des Lausanner Friedensvertrages. Der Unabhängigkeitskrieg und Lausanne), Ankara, 1993.

Jahn, Egbert: Erinnerung an Völkermord als politische Waffe in der Gegenwart. Das Beispiel des osmanischen Genozids an den Armeniern. in: Jahn, Egbert: Politische Streitfragen, Wiesbaden, 2008. S. 81-97.

Kappeler, Andreas: Rußland als Vielvölkerreich. Entstehung – Geschichte - Zerfall, 2. Aufl., München, 2008.

Karacan, Ali Naci: Lozan (Lausanne), 2. Aufl., Istanbul, 1971.

Kaser, Karl: Raum und Besiedlung, in: Hatschikjan, Magarditsch/Troebst, Stefan [Hrsg.]: Südosteuropa. Gesellschaft, Politik, Wirtschaft, Kultur. Ein Handbuch, München, 1999, S. 53-72.

Kaser, Karl: Südosteuropäische Geschichte und Geschichtswissenschaft, 2. Aufl., Wien, 2002.

Katz, Steven T.: The Holocaust in Historical Context, Bd. 1: The Holocaust and Mass Death before the Modern Age, New York, 1994.

Kaypakkaya, İbrahim: Seçme Yazılar (Ausgewählte Werke), Altınçağ Yayımcılık, Istanbul, 1999.

Kayra, Cahit: Sevr Dosyası (Die Akte Sèvres), Istanbul, 2011.

Kökütürk, Yalın İştenç: Lozan Konferansı. Gazi Mustafa Kemal (Die Lausanner Konferenz. Gazi Mustafa Kemal), Istanbul, 2011.

Kreiser, Klaus: Der Osmanische Staat 1300-1922, München, 2011.

Kreiser, Klaus/Neumann, Christoph K.: Kleine Geschichte der Türkei, Bonn, 2005.

Ladas, Stephen P.: The Exchange of Minorities. Bulgaria, Greece and Turkey, New York, 1932.

Langewiesche, Dieter: Nationalismus im 19. und 20. Jahrhundert. Zwischen Partizipation und Aggression, in: Langewiesche, Dieter [Hrsg.]: Nation, Nationalismus. Nationalstaat in Deutschland und Europa, München, 2000, S. 35-54.

Langewiesche, Dieter: Was heißt "Erfindung der Nation"? in: Beer, Mathias [Hrsg.]: Auf dem Weg zum ethnisch reinen Nationalstaat, 2. Aufl., Tübingen, 2007, S. 19-40.

Laštovička, Bohuslav: V Londýně za valky [In London während des Krieges], Prag, 1961, Faksimile. Zit. Nach Dokumente zur Vertreibung der Sudetendeutschen. [Hrsg.]: Sudetendeutscher Rat, München, 1992.

Lausanne Conference on Near Eastern Affairs 1922-1923: Records of Proceedings and Draft Terms of Peace (Dokument Cmd. 1813), London, 1923.

Lemberg, Hans: "Ethnische Säuberungen": Ein Mittel zur Lösung von Nationalitätenproblemen?, in: Aus Politik und Zeitgeschichte, B 46/1992, S. 27-38.

Lowry, Heath W.: The Story behind Ambassador Morgenthau's Story, Istanbul, 1990.

Manzenreiter, Johann: Der Staatsbankrott des Osmanischen Reiches (1875/76), in: Materialia Turcica, 1 (1975). S. 90-104.

Martin, Lawrence: The Treaties of Peace, 1919-1923, Vol. II, New York, 1924.

Matuz, Josef: Das Osmanische Reich. Grundlinien seiner Geschichte, 2. Aufl., Darmstadt, 1990.

Mechin-Benoist, Jacques: Le Loup et le Leopard. Mustafa Kèmal ou la mort d'un empire, Paris, 1954.

Melson, Robert: Provocation or Nationalism: A Critical Inquiry into the Armenian Genocide of 1915, in: Hovannisian, Richard G. [Hrsg.]: The Armenian Genocide in Perspective, New Brunswick, 1986, S. 61-84.

Melson, Robert: Revolution and Genocide. On the Origins of the Armenian Genocide and the Holocaust, Chicago, London, 1992.

Milton, Giles: Paradise Lost. Smyrna 1922: The Destruction of a Christian City in the Islamic World, New York, 2008.

Mısıroğlu, Kadir: Lozan Zafer Mi, Hezimet Mi? (Ist Lausanne ein Sieg oder eine Niederlage?), Istanbul, 1992.

Naimark, Norman M.: Das Problem der ethnischen Säuberung im modernen Europa. In: Zeitschrift für Ostmitteleuropaforschung, 48 (3), 1991, S. 317-349.

Naimark, Norman M.: Flammender Haß. Ethnische Säuberungen im 20. Jahrhundert, München, 2004.

Öke, Kemal: The Armenien Question 1914-1923, Oxford, 1988, S. 126-136.

Palmer, Alan: Verfall und Untergang des Osmanischen Reiches, München, 1992.

Österreichisch-ungarisches Rotbuch. Diplomatische Aktenstücke zur Vorgeschichte des Krieges 1914, Wien, 1915.

Parker, R. A. C. [Hrsg.]: Fischer Weltgeschichte. Band 34: Das Zwanzigste Jahrhundert I., Frankfurt/Main, 1985.

Părvev, Ivan: Osmanische Traditionen auf dem Balkan vom 14. bis zum 19. Jahrhundert, in: Heuberger, Valeria/Suppan, Arnold/Vyslonzil, Elisabeth [Hrsg.]: Der Balkan. Friedenszone oder Pulverfaß?, Frankfurt am Main, 1998, S. 45-62.

Von Grunebaum, Gustav Edmund: Der Islam im Mittelalter, Zürich, 1963,

Pehlivanoğlu, A. Öner: Sevr, Lozan Antlaşmaları ve Avrupa Birliği (Die Verträge von Sèvres und Lausanne und die Europäische Union), Istanbul, 2005.

Pesendorfer, Franz: Ungarn und Österreich – Tausend Jahre Partner oder Gegner, Wien, 1998.

Pitsoulis, Athanassios: Legitimierte Vertreibung. Minderheitenpolitik im Vertrag von Lausanne. In: WeltTrends. Zeitschrift für internationale Politik, 19, (76)2001, S. 97-101.

Pitsoulis, Athanassios: Vertreibung und Diplomatie: Hintergründe und Umdeutungen des griechisch-türkischen 'Bevölkerungsaustausch' von 1923, in: IMIS-Beiträge, (36) 2010, S. 37-66.

Portmann, Michael: Politische Geschichte Südosteuropas von 1918-1945, in: Clewing, Konrad/Schmitt, Oliver Jens [Hrsg.]: Geschichte Südosteuropas. Vom frühen Mittelalter bis zur Gegenwart, Regensburg, 2011, S. 554-596.

Riedel, Sabine: Die Erfindung der Balkanvölker. Identitätspolitik zwischen Konflikt und Integration, Wiesbaden, 2005.

Rondholz, Eberhard: Griechenland. Ein Länderporträt, Bonn, 2011.

Sakınmaz, Şenol Koray: Lozan. Bir Milletin Yeniden Dirilişi (Lausanne. Die Wiederauferstehung einer Nation), Istanbul, 2008.

Scheuch, Manfred: Das größere Europa – Polen, Ungarn, Tschechien, Slowakei, Slowenien und die Baltischen Staaten in Geschichte und Gegenwart, Wien, 2002.

Schieder, Theodor: Das Problem des Nationalismus in Osteuropa, in: Theodor Schieder (Dann, Otto/Wehler Hans-Ulrich [Hrsg.]): Nationalismus und Nationalstaat. Studien zum nationalen Problem im modernen Europa, Göttingen, 1991, S. 347-359.

Seewann, Gerhard: Minderheiten und Nationalitätenpolitik, in: Hatschikjan, Magarditsch/Troebst, Stefan [Hrsg.]: Südosteuropa. Gesellschaft, Politik, Wirtschaft, Kultur. Ein Handbuch, München, 1999, S. 169-196.

Seewann, Gerhard: Zwangsmigration von Minderheiten in Südosteuropa im 20. Jahrhundert, in: Solomon, Flavius/Rubel, Alexander/Zub Alexandru [Hrsg.]: Südosteuropa im 20. Jahrhundert. Ethnostrukturen, Identitäten, Konflikte, Konstanz, 2004, S. 47-54.

Seufert, Günter/Kubaseck, Christopher: Die Türkei. Politik, Geschichte, Kultur, 2. Aufl., München, 2006.

Shaw, Stanford Jay: History of Ottoman Empire and Modern Turkey, Bd. 2, Cambridge, 1977.

Şimşir, Bilâl N.: Ermeni Meselesi (Die Armenierproblematik). 1774-2005, 2. Aufl., Ankara, 2005.

Şimşir, Bilâl N.: Lozan Telgrafları. Türk Diplomatik Belgelerinde Lozan Barış Konferansı (Die Lausanner Telegramme. Der Friedensvertrag von Lausanne in türkisch-diplomatischen Dokumenten), Bd. 1, Ankara, 1990.

Şimşir, Bilâl N.: Lozan Telgrafları. Türk Diplomatik Belgelerinde Lozan Barış Konferansı (Die Lausanner Telegramme. Der Friedensvertrag von Lausanne in türkisch-diplomatischen Dokumenten), Bd. 2, Ankara, 1994.

Smith, A. D.: The Ethnic Origins of Nations. Oxford, 1989.

Sonyel, Salâhi R.: Türk Kurtuluş Şavaşı [sic!] ve Dış Politika II. Büyük Millet Meclisi'nin Açılışından Lozan Anlaşmasına Kadar (Der türkische Befreiungskrieg und die Außenpolitik II. Von der Parlamentseröffnung bis zum Lausanner Vertrag), Ankara, 1986.

Soyupak, Kemal/Kabasakal, Huseyin: The Turkish army in the First Balkan War, in: Kiraly, Bela K./Djordjevic, Dimitrije [Hrsg.]: East Central European Society and the Balkan War, New York, 1987.

Sundhaussen, Holm: Bevölkerungsstruktur und Sozialstruktur, in: Hatschikjan, Magarditsch/Troebst, Stefan [Hrsg.]: Südosteuropa. Gesellschaft, Politik, Wirtschaft, Kultur. Ein Handbuch, München, 1999, S. 136-150.

Sundhaussen Holm: Die Ethnisierung von Staat, Nation und Gerechtigkeit. Zu den Anfängen nationaler "Homogenisierung" im Balkanraum, in: Beer, Mathias [Hrsg.]: Auf dem Weg zum ethnisch reinen Nationalstaat, 2. Aufl., Tübingen, 2007, S. 69-90.

Sundhaussen, Holm: Die Wiederentdeckung des Raums, in: Südosteuropa. Von moderner Vielfalt und nationalstaatlicher Vereinheitlichung, München, 2005, S. 13-33.

Sundhaussen, Holm: Nationsbildung und Nationalismus im Donau-Balkan-Raum, in: Torke, Hans-Joachim [Hrsg.]: Forschungen zur osteuropäischen Geschichte, Berlin, 1993, S. 233-258.

Sundhaussen Holm: Südosteuropa. In: Bade, Klaus J./Emmer, Pieter C., Lucassen, Leo/Oltmer Jochen [Hrsg.]: Enzyklopädie Migration in Europa. Vom 17. Jahrhundert bis zur Gegenwart, 2. Aufl., Paderborn, 2008, S. 288-313.

Sundhaussen, Holm: Südosteuropäische Gesellschaft und Kultur vom Beginn des 19 bis zur Mitte des 20. Jahrhunderts, in: Clewing, Konrad/Schmitt, Oliver Jens [Hrsg.]: Geschichte Südosteuropas. Vom frühen Mittelalter bis zur Gegenwart, Regensburg, 2011, S. 345-425.

Sundhausen, Holm: Von "Lausanne" nach "Dayton". Ein Paradigmenwechsel bei der Lösung ethnonationaler Konflikte. In: Hohls, Rüdiger/Schröder, Iris/Siegrist, Hannes [Hrsg.]: Europa und die Europäer. Quellen und Essays zur modernen europäischen Geschichte, München, 2005, S. 409-414.

Suny, Ronald Grigor: Looking Toward Ararat. Armenia in Modern History, Bloomington, 1993.

Suppan, Arnold: Nationalstaaten und nationale Minderheiten, in: Heuberger, Valeria/Suppan, Arnold/Vyslonzil, Elisabeth [Hrsg.]: Brennpunkt Osteuropa. Minderheiten im Kreuzfeuer des Nationalismus, Wien, 1996, S. 9-17.

Taşyürek, Muzaffer: Lozan'a Hayır Diyenler (Jene, die Nein zu Lausanne sagten), Istanbul, 1995.

T.C. Kültür Bakanlığı [Hazırlayan (Redakteur): Özel, Mehmet]: 70. Yıldönümünde Lozan (Lausanne zum 70. Jahrestag), 1993.

Thelen, Sibylle: Die Armenierfrage in der Türkei, Berlin, 2010.

Ther, Philipp: Die dunkle Seite der Nationalstaaten. 'Ethnische Säuberungen' im modernen Europa, Göttingen, 2011.

Toynbee, Arnold Jay: The Western Question in Greece and Turkey. A Study in the Contact of Civilizations, London, 2010.

Troebst, Stefan: Politische Entwicklung in der Neuzeit, in: Hatschikjan, Magarditsch/Troebst, Stefan [Hrsg.]: Südosteuropa. Gesellschaft, Politik, Wirtschaft, Kultur. Ein Handbuch, München, 1999, S. 73-102.

Tröbst, Hans: Mustapha Kemal Pascha und sein Werk, Teil VI. In: Heimatland: vaterländisches Wochenblatt für das Bayerische Volk, 42, 1923, S. 7-8.

Yonov, Momchil: Bulgarian Military Operations in the Balkan Wars, in: Kiraly, Bela K./Djordjevic, Dimitrije [Hrsg.]: East Central European Society and the Balkan War, New York, 1987. S. 63-84.

Weichlein, Siegfried: Nationalbewegungen und Nationalismus in Europa, Darmstadt, 2006.

Weithmann, Michael W.: Balkan-Chronik. 2000 Jahre zwischen Orient und Okzident, 3. Aufl., Regensburg, 2000.

Weithmann, Michael W.: Der Balkan zwischen Ost und West, in: Weithmann, Michael W. [Hrsg.]: Der ruhelose Balkan. Die Konfliktregionen Südosteuropas, München, 1993, S. 7-43.

Internetquellen (Zuletzt eingesehen am 18.05.2012):

"Das Word 'Genozid' ist nicht entscheidend": http://jungle-world.com/artikel/2005/17/15123.html

Mandate for Palestine - UK summary of the Palestine Royal Commission (Peel Commission) report Cmd. 5479 - League of Nations/Non-UN document: http://unispal.un.org/UNISPAL.NSF/0/08E38A718201458B052565700072B358

Rede Winston Churchills vom 15.12.1944: http://hansard.millbanksystems.com/commons/1944/dec/15/poland#S5CV0406P0_19441215_HOC_44.

8. Anhang

8.1. Zeittafel

1.-3. Jh.	Südosteuropa im Herrschaftsbereich des Römischen Imperiums (Provinzen: Pannonien, Illyrien, Mösien, Thrakien, Makedonien, Dakien)
330	Gründung Konstantinopels
395	Reichsteilung in lateinisch-katholischen Westteil und griechisch-byzantinischen Ostteil (Byzantinisches Reich)
6./7. Jh.	Eindringen der Slawen in den Balkanraum
Ab Mitte 9. Jh.	Christianisierung der Balkanslawen
1054	Schisma: Spaltung der Kirche in katholische West- und orthodoxe Ostkirche
1071	Sieg der Türken in Malazgirt; Einleitung der Besiedlung Anatoliens
Mitte 12. Jh.	Einwanderung Deutscher nach Siebenbürgen
1346	Großserbisches Reich unter Stefan Dušans
Ab Mitte 14. Jh.	Erstes Vordringen der Osmanen nach Europa
1389	Sieg der Osmanen auf dem Amselfeld (Kosovo polje) gegen die Serben. Serbien wird nach und nach osmanisch
1393	Bulgarien wird osmanisch
1453	Eroberung Konstantinopels durch die Osmanen. Untergang des Byzantinischen Reiches. Konstantinopel neue osmanische Hauptstadt
1463	Bosnien wird osmanisch
1468	Albanien wird osmanisch
1479	Griechenland wird osmanisch

1526-1541	Ungarn wird osmanische Provinz
1529	Erste Wienbelagerung der Osmanen
1683	Zweite Wienbelagerung der Osmanen: Erster habsburgisch-osmanischer Krieg
1718	Zweiter habsburgischer-osmanischer Krieg
1739	Dritter Krieg der Habsburger (im Bündnis mit Russland) gegen die Osmanen: Friede von Belgrad
1774	Russisch-osmanischer Friede von Küçük Kaynarca (Bulgarien): Russisches Protektorat über die orthodoxen Völker des Osmanischen Reiches
1804-1815	Nach serbischem Aufstand Erlangung von Autonomie innerhalb des Osmanischen Reiches
1812	Russisch-Osmanischer Frieden von Bukarest: Bessarabien wird russisch
1830	Unabhängigkeit Griechenlands nach Freiheitskrieg
1830	Fürstentum Serbien
1852	Fürstentum Montenegro
1856	Gleichberechtigung von Christen mit Muslimen im Osmanischen Reich
1859/1861	Fürstentum Rumänien (aus Donaufürstentümer Moldau und Walachei)
1867	Österreichisch-Ungarische Doppelmonarchie; Unabhängigkeit Serbiens
1876	Antiosmanischer Aufstand in Bulgarien
1877/1878	Russisch-osmanischer Balkankrieg
März 1878	Vorfriede von San Stefano
Juni/Juli 1878	Neuordnung des Balkans im Berliner Kongress: Rumänien und Montenegro werden unabhängig, Serbiens Unabhängigkeit wird bestätigt, Bulgarien wird autonomes Fürstentum, Make-

	donien bleibt unter osmanischer Herrschaft. Habsburger Monarchie erhält Recht auf Okkupation Bosnien-Herzegowinas
1903	Antiosmanischer Aufstand in Makedonien
1908	Jungtürkische Revolution
Okt. 1908	Bosnische Annexionskrise nach förmlichem Anschluss des seit 1878 besetzten Bosniens und der Herzegowina an Österreich-Ungarn
1912	Erster Balkankrieg
1913	Zweiter Balkankrieg
1913	Unabhängigkeit Albaniens
1914-1918	Erster Weltkrieg
1915	Deportation der Armenier
1917	Oktoberrevolution unter der Führung Lenins
16. Okt. 1918	Ende der Doppelmonarchie Österreich-Ungarn
1919-1920	Pariser Vorortverträge der Siegermächte mit Deutschland (Versailles), Österreich (St. Germain), Ungarn (Trianon), Bulgarien (Neuilly) und dem Osmanischen Reich (Sèvres)
1922	Niederlage der Griechen im griechisch-türkischen Krieg
1922	Gründung der Sowjetunion
1923	Friedensvertrag von Lausanne; Gründung der Republik Türkei; griechisch-türkischer Bevölkerungsaustausch
1937-38	Niederschlagung des Aufstandes in Dersim

Zusammengestellt nach:

- Kreiser, Klaus: Der Osmanische Staat 1300-1922, München, 2011, S. 207ff.
- Weithmann, Michael W. [Hrsg.]: Der ruhelose Balkan. Die Konfliktregionen Südosteuropas, München, 1993, S. 305ff.
- Hösch, Edgar: Geschichte der Balkanländer. Von der Frühzeit bis zur Gegenwart, 5. Aufl., München, 2008, S. 387ff.

8.2. Der Vertrag von Sèvres vom 19. August 1920

TREATY OF PEACE BETWEEN THE ALLIED AND ASSOCIATED POWERS AND TURKEY - SIGNED AT SÈVRES - AUGUST 10, 1920

THE BRITISH EMPIRE, FRANCE, ITALY AND JAPAN,

These Powers being described in the present Treaty as the Principal Allied Powers;

ARMENIA, BELGIUM, GREECE, THE HEDJAZ, POLAND, PORTUGAL, ROUMANIA, THE SERB-CROAT-SLOVENE STATE AND CZECHO-SLOVAKIA,

These Powers constituting, with the Principal Powers mentioned above, the Allied Powers, of the one part;

AND TURKEY, of the other part;

Whereas on the request of the Imperial Ottoman Government an Armistice was granted to Turkey on October 30, 1918, by the Principal Allied Powers in order that a Treaty of Peace might be concluded, and

Whereas the Allied Powers are equally desirous that the war in which certain among them were successively involved, directly or indirectly, against Turkey, and which originated in the declaration of war against Serbia on July 28, 1914, by the former Imperial and Royal Austro-Hungarian Government, and in the hostilities opened by Turkey against the Allied Powers on October 29, 1914, and conducted by Germany in alliance with Turkey, should be replaced by a firm, just and durable Peace,

For this purpose the HIGH CONTRACTING PARTIES have appointed as their Plenipotentiaries:

HIS MAJESTY THE KING OF THE UNITED KINGDOM OF GREAT BRITAIN AND IRELAND AND OF THE BRITISH DOMINIONS BEYOND THE SEAS, EMPEROR OF INDIA:
    Sir George Dixon GRAHAME, K. C. V. O., Minister Plenipotentiary of His Britannic Majesty at Paris;

And

for the DOMINION of CANADA:
    The Honourable Sir George Halsey PERLEY, K.C. M. G
    High Commissioner for Canada in the United Kingdom;

for the COMMONWEALTH of AUSTRALIA:
    The Right Honourable Andrew FISHER, High Commissioner for Australia in the United Kingdom;

for the DOMINION of NEW ZEALAND:
    Sir George Dixon GRAHAME, K. C. V. O., Minister Plenipotentiary of His Britannic Majesty at Paris;

for the UNION of SOUTH AFRICA:
    Mr. Reginald Andrew BLANKENBERG, O. B. E., Acting High Commissioner for the Union of South Africa in the United Kingdom;

for INDIA:
    Sir Arthur HIRTZEL, K. C. B., Assistant Under Secretary of State for India;

THE PRESIDENT OF THE FRENCH REPUBLIC:
    Mr. Alexandre MILLERAND, President of the Council, Minister for Foreign Affairs
    Mr. Frederic FRANÇOIS-MARSAL, Minister of Finance
    Mr. Auguste Paul-Louis ISAAC, Minister of Commerce and Industry;
    Mr. Jules CAMBON, Ambassador of France
    Mr. Georges Maurice PALÉOLOGUE, Ambassador of France, Secretary-General of the Ministry of Foreign Affairs;

HIS MAJESTY THE KING OF ITALY:
    Count LELIO BONIN LONGARE, Senator of the Kingdom
    Ambassador Extraordinary and Plenipotentiary of H. M. the King of Italy at Paris
    General Giovanni MARIETTI, Italian Military Representative on the Supreme War Council;

HIS MAJESTY THE EMPEROR OF JAPAN:
    Viscount CHINDA, Ambassador Extraordinary and Plenipotentiary of H. M. the Emperor of Japan at London;

Mr. K. MATSUI, Ambassador Extraordinary and Plenipotentiary of H. M. the Emperor of Japan at Paris;

ARMENIA:
Mr. Avetis AHARONIAN, President of the Delegation of the Armenian Republic;

HIS MAJESTY THE KING OF THE BELGIANS:
Mr. Jules VAN DEN HEUVEL, Envoy Extraordinary and Minister Plenipotentiary, Minister of State;
Mr. ROLIN JAEQUEMYNS, Member of the Institute of Private International Law, Secretary-General of the Belgian Delegation;

HIS MAJESTY THE KING OF THE HELLENES:
Mr. Eleftherios K. VENIZELOS, President of the Council of Ministers;
Mr. Athos ROMANOS, Envoy Extraordinary and Minister Plenipotentiary of H. M. the King of the Hellenes at Paris;

HIS MAJESTY THE KING OF THE HEDJAZ:

THE PRESIDENT OF THE POLISH REPUBLIC:
Count Maurice ZAMOYSKI, Envoy Extraordinary and Minister Plenipotentiary of the Polish Republic at Paris;
Mr. Erasme PILTZ;

THE PRESIDENT OF THE PORTUGUESE REPUBLIC:
Dr. Affonso da COSTA, formerly President of the Council of Ministers;

HIS MAJESTY THE KING OF ROUMANIA:
Mr. Nicolae TITULESCU, Minister of Finance;
Prince DIMITRIE GHIKA, Envoy Extraordinary and Minister Plenipotentiary of H. M. the King of Roumania at Paris;

HIS MAJESTY THE KING OF THE SERBS, THE CROATS AND THE SLOVENES:
Mr. Nicolas P. PACHITCH, formerly President of the Council of Ministers;
Mr. Ante TRUMBIC, Minister for Foreign Affairs;

THE PRESIDENT OF THE CZECHO-SLOVAK REPUBLIC:
Mr. Edward BENES, Minister for Foreign Affairs;
Mr. Stephen OSUSKY, Envoy Extraordinary and Minister Plenipotentiary of the Czecho-Slovak Republic at London;

TURKEY:
General HAADI Pasha, Senator;
RIZA TEVFIK Bey, Senator;
RECHAD HALISS Bey, Envoy Extraordinary and Minister Plenipotentiary of Turkey at Berne;

WHO, having communicated their full powers, found in good and due form, have AGREED AS FOLLOWS:
From the coming into force of the present Treaty the state of war will terminate.
From that moment and subject to the provisions of the present Treaty, official relations will exist between the Allied Powers and Turkey.

PART I.
THE COVENANT OF THE LEAGUE OF NATIONS.
ARTICLES 1 TO 26 AND ANNEX
See Part I, Treaty of Versailles.

PART II.
FRONTIERS OF TURKEY.

ARTICLE 27.

I. In Europe, the frontiers of Turkey will be laid down as follows:

1. *The Black Sea*:
from the entrance of the Bosphorus to the point described below.

2. *With Greece*:
From a point to be chosen on the Black Sea near the mouth of the Biyuk Dere, situated about 7 kilometres north-west of Podima, south-westwards to the most north-westerly point of the limit of the basin of the Istranja Dere (about 8 kilometres northwest of Istranja), a line to be fixed on the ground passing through Kapilja Dagh and Uchbunar Tepe;

thence south-south-eastwards to a point to be chosen on the railway from Chorlu to Chatalja about 1 kilometre west of the railway station of Sinekli, a line following as far as possible the western limit of the basin of the Istranja Dere;

thence south-eastwards to a point to be chosen between Fener and Kurfali on the watershed between the basins of those rivers which flow into Biyuk Chekmeje Geul, on the north-east, and the basin of those rivers which flow direct into the Sea of Marmora on the south-west, a line to be fixed on the ground passing south of Sinekli;

thence south-eastwards to a point to be chosen on the Sea of Marmora about 1 kilometre south-west of Kalikratia, a line following as far as possible this watershed.

3. *The Sea of Marmora*:
from the point defined above to the entrance of the Bosphorus.

II. In Asia, the frontiers of Turkey will be laid down as follows:

1. *On the West and South*:
From the entrance of the Bosphorus into the Sea of Marmora to a point described below, situated in the eastern Mediterranean Sea in the neighbourhood of the Gulf of Alexandretta near Karatash Burun the Sea of Marmora, the Dardanelles, and the Eastern Mediterranean Sea; the islands of the Sea of Marmora, and those which are situated within a distance of 3 miles from the coast, remaining Turkish, subject to the provisions of Section IV and Articles 84 and 122, Part III (Political Clauses).

2. *With Syria*:
From a point to be chosen on the eastern bank of the outlet of the Hassan Dede, about 3 kilometres north-west of Karatash Bu- run, north-eastwards to a point to be chosen on the Djaihun Irmak about 1 kilometre north of Babeli, a line to be fixed on the ground passing north of Karatash; thence to Kesik Kale, the course of the Djaihun Irmak upstream;

thence north-eastwards to a point to be chosen on the Djaihun Irmak about 15 kilometres east-southeast of Karsbazar, a line to be fixed on the ground passing north of Kara Tepe;

thence to the bend in the Djaihun Irmak situated west of Duldul Dagh, the course of the Djaihun Irmak upstream;

thence in a general south-easterly direction to a point to be chosen on Emir Musi Dagh about 15 kilometres south-south-west of Giaour Geul a line to be fixed on the ground at a distance of about 18 kilometres from the railway, and leaving Duldul Dagh to Syria;

thence eastwards to a point to be chosen about 5 kilometres north of Urfa a generally straight line from west to east to be hxed on the ground passing north of the roads connecting the towns of Bagh- che, Aintab, Biridjik, and Urfa and leaving the last three named towns to Syria;

thence eastwards to the south-western extremity of the bend in the Tigris about 6 kilometres north of Azekh (27 kilometres west of Djezire-ibn-Omar), a generally straight line from west to east to be fixed on the ground leaving the town of Mardin to Syria;

thence to a point to be chosen on the Tigris between the point of confluence of the Khabur Su with the Tigris and the bend in the Tigris situated about 10 kilometres north of this point,
the course of the Tigris downstream, leaving the island on which is situated the town of Djezire-ibn-Omar to Syria.

3. *With Mesopotamia*:
Thence in a general easterly direction to a point to be chosen on the northern boundary of the vilayet of Mosul,

a line to be fixed on the ground;
thence eastwards to the point where it meets the frontier between Turkey and Persia, the northern boundary of the vilayet of Mosul, modified, however, so as to pass south of Amadia.

4. *On the East and the North East*:

From the point above defined to the Black Sea, the existing frontier between Turkey and Persia, then the former frontier between Turkey and Russia, subject to the provisions of Article 89.

5. *The Black Sea.*

ARTICLE 28.

The frontiers described by the present Treaty are traced on the one in a million maps attached to the present Treaty. In case of differences between the text and the map, the text will prevail. [See Introduction.]

ARTICLE 29.

Boundary Commissions, whose composition is or will be fixed in the present Treaty or in Treaties supplementary thereto, will have to trace these frontiers on the ground.

They shall have the power, not only of fixing those portions which are defined as "a line to be fixed on the ground," but also, if the Commission considers it necessary, of revising in matters of detail portions defined by administrative boundaries or otherwise. They shall endeavour in all cases to follow as nearly as possible the descriptions given in the Treaties, taking into account, as far as possible, administrative boundaries and local economic interests.

The decisions of the Commissions will be taken by a majority, and shall be binding on the parties concerned.

The expenses of the Boundary Commissions will be borne in equal shares by the parties concerned.

ARTICLE 30.

In so far as frontiers defined by a waterway are concerned, the phrases "course" or "channel" used in the descriptions of the present Treaty signify, as regards non-navigable rivers, the median line of the waterway or of its principal branch, and, as regards navigable rivers, the median line of the principal channel of navigation. It will rest with the Boundary Commissions provided for by the present Treaty to specify whether the frontier line shall follow any changes of the course or channel which may take place, or whether it shall be definitely fixed by the position of the course or channel at the time when the present Treaty comes into force.

In the absence of provisions to the contrary in the present Treaty, islands and islets lying within three miles of the coast are included within the frontier of the coastal State.

ARTICLE 31.

The various States concerned undertake to furnish to the Commissions all documents necessary for their tasks, especially authentic copies of agreements fixing existing or old frontiers, all large scale maps in existence, geodetic data, surveys completed but unpublished, and information concerning the changes of frontier watercourses. The maps, geodetic data, and surveys, even if unpublished, which are in the possession of the Turkish authorities must be delivered at Constantinople, within thirty days from the coming into force of the present Treaty, to such representative of the Commissions concerned as may be appointed by the principal Allied Powers.

The States concerned also undertake to instruct the local authorities to communicate to the Commissions all documents, especially plans, cadastral and land books, and to furnish on demand all details regarding property, existing economic conditions, and other necessary information.

ARTICLE 32.

The various States interested undertake to give every assistance to the Boundary Commissions, whether directly or through local authorities, in everything that concerns transport, accommodation, labour, materials (signposts, boundary pillars) necessary for the accomplishment of their mission.

In particular the Turkish Government undertakes to furnish to the Principal Allied Powers such technical personnel as they may consider necessary to assist the Boundary Commissions in the accomplishment of their mission.

ARTICLE 33.

The various States interested undertake to safeguard the trigonometrical points, signals, posts or frontier marks erected by the Commissions.

ARTICLE 34

The pillars will be placed so as to be intervisible; they will be numbered, and their position and their number will be noted on a cartographic document.

ARTICLE 35.

The protocols defining the boundary and the maps and documents attached thereto will be made out in triplicate, of which two copies will be forwarded to the Governments of the limitrophe States, and the third to the

Government of the French Republic, which will deliver authentic copies to the Powers who sign the present Treaty.

PART III.
POLITICAL CLAUSES.
SECTION I.
CONSTANTINOPLE.

ARTICLE 36.

Subject to the provisions of the present Treaty, the High Contracting Parties agree that the rights and title of the Turkish Government over Constantinople shall not be affected, and that the said Government and His Majesty the Sultan shall be entitled to reside there and to maintain there the capital of the Turkish State. Nevertheless, in the event of Turkey failing to observe faithfully the provisions of the present Treaty, or of any treaties or conventions supplementary thereto, particularly as regards the protection of the rights of racial, religious or linguistic minorities, the Allied Powers expressly reserve the right to modify the above provisions, and Turkey hereby agrees to accept any dispositions which may be taken in this connection.

SECTION II.
STRAITS.

ARTICLE 37.

The navigation of the Straits, including the Dardanelles, the Sea of Marmora and the Bosphorus, shall in future be open, both in peace and war, to every vessel of commerce or of war and to military and commercial aircraft, without distinction of flag.

These waters shall not be subject to blockade, nor shall any belligerent right be exercised nor any act of hostility be committed within them, unless in pursuance of a decision of the Council of the League of Nations.

ARTICLE 38.

The Turkish Government recognises that it is necessary to take further measures to ensure the freedom of navigation provided for in Article 37, and accordingly delegates, so far as it is concerned, to a Commission to be called the "Commission of the Straits," and hereinafter referred to as 'the Commission," the control of the waters specified in Article 39.

The Greek Government, so far as it is concerned, delegates to the Commission the same powers and undertakes to give it in all respects the same facilities.

Such control shall be exercised in the name of the Turkish and Greek Governments respectively, and in the manner provided in this Section.

ARTICLE 39.

The authority of the Commission will extend to all the waters between the Mediterranean mouth of the Dardanelles and the Black Sea mouth of the Bosphorus, and to the waters within three miles of each of these mouths. This authority may be exercised on shore to such extent as may be necessary for the execution of the provisions of this Section.

ARTICLE 40.

The Commission shall be composed of representatives appointed respectively by the United States of America (if and when that Government is willing to participate), the British Empire, France, Italy, Japan, Russia (if and when Russia becomes a member of the League of Nations), Greece, Roumania, and Bulgaria and Turkey (if and when the two latter States become members of the League of Nations). Each Power shall appoint one representative. The representatives of the United States of America, the British Empire, France, Italy, Japan and Russia shall each have two votes. The representatives of Greece, Roumania, and Bulgaria and Turkey shall each have one vote. Each Commissioner shall be removable only by the Government which appointed him.

[...ARTICLE 41.-61...]

[...ANNEX...]

SECTION III.
KURDISTAN.

ARTICLE 62.

A Commission sitting at Constantinople and composed of three members appointed by the British, French and Italian Governments respectively shall draft within six months from the coming into force of the present Treaty a scheme of local autonomy for the predominantly Kurdish areas lying east of the Euphrates, south of the southern boundary of Armenia as it may be hereafter determined, and north of the frontier of Turkey with Syria and Mesopotamia, as defined in Article 27, II (2) and (3). If unanimity cannot be secured on any question, it will be referred by the members of the Commission to their respective Governments. The scheme shall contain full safeguards for the protection of the Assyro-Chaldeans and other racial or religious minorities within these areas, and with this object a Commission composed of British, French, Italian, Persian and Kurdish representatives shall visit the spot to examine and decide what rectifications, if any, should be made in the Turkish frontier where, under the provisions of the present Treaty, that frontier coincides with that of Persia.

ARTICLE 63.
The Turkish Government hereby agrees to accept and execute the decisions of both the Commissions mentioned in Article 62 within three months from their communication to the said Government.

ARTICLE 64.
If within one year from the coming into force of the present Treaty the Kurdish peoples within the areas defined in Article 62 shall address themselves to the Council of the League of Nations in such a manner as to show that a majority of the population of these areas desires independence from Turkey, and if the Council then considers that these peoples are capable of such independence and recommends that it should be granted to them, Turkey hereby agrees to execute such a recommendation, and to renounce all rights and title over these areas.

The detailed provisions for such renunciation will form the subject of a separate agreement between the Principal Allied Powers and Turkey.

If and when such renunciation takes place, no objection will be raised by the Principal Allied Powers to the voluntary adhesion to such an independent Kurdish State of the Kurds inhabiting that part of Kurdistan which has hitherto been included in the Mosul vilayet.

SECTION IV.
SMYRNA.

ARTICLE 65.
The provisions of this Section will apply to the city of Smyrna and the adjacent territory defined in Article 66, until the determination of their final status in accordance with Article 83.

ARTICLE 66.
The geographical limits of the territory adjacent to the city of Smyrna will be laid down as follows:
From the mouth of the river which flows into the Aegean Sea about 5 kilometres north of Skalanova, eastwards,
the course of this river upstream;
then south-eastwards, the course of the southern branch of this river;
then south-eastwards, to the western point of the crest of the Gumush Dagh;
A line to be fixed on the ground passing west of Chinar K, and east of Akche Ova;
thence north-eastwards, this crest line;
thence northwards to a point to be chosen on the railway from Ayasoluk to Deirmendik about 1 kilometre west of Balachik station,
a line to be fixed on the ground leaving the road and railway from Sokia to Balachik station entirely in Turkish territory;
thence northwards to a point to be chosen on the southern boundary of the Sandjak of Smyrna,
a line to be fixed on the ground;
thence to a point to be chosen in the neighbourhood of Bos Dagh situated about 15 kilometres north-east of Odemish,
the southern and eastern boundary of the Sandjak of Smyrna;
thence northwards to a point to be chosen on the railway from Manisa to Alashehr about 6 kilometres west of Salihli,
a line to be fixed on the ground;
thence northwards to Geurenez Dagh,
a line to be fixed on the ground passing east of Mermer Geul west of Kemer, crossing the Kum Chai approximately south of Akshalan, and then following the watershed west of Kavakalan;
thence north-westwards to a point to be chosen on the boundary between the Cazas of Kirkagach and Ak Hissar about 18 kilometres east of Kirkagach and 20 kilometres north of Ak Hissar,
a line to be fixed on the ground;
thence westwards to its junction with the boundary of the Caza of Soma,
the southern boundary of the Caza of Kirkagach,
thence westwards to its junction with the boundary of the Sandjak of Smyrna,
the southern boundary of the Caza of Soma;
thence northwards to its junction with the boundary of the vilayet of Smyrna,

the north-eastern boundary of the Sandjak of Smyrna;
thence westwards to a point to be chosen in the neighbourhood of Charpajik (Tepe).
the northern boundary of the vilayet of Smyrna;
thence northwards to a point to be chosen on the ground about 4 kilometres southwest of Keuiluje,
a line to be fixed on the ground;
thence westwards to a point to be selected on the ground between Cape Dahlina and Kemer Iskele,
a line to be fixed on the ground passing south of Kemer and Kemer Iskele together with the road joining these places.

ARTICLE 67.

A Commission shall be constituted within fifteen days from the coming into force of the present Treaty to trace on the spot the boundaries of the territories described in Article 66. This Commission shall be composed of three members nominated by the British, French and Italian Governments respectively, one member nominated by the Greek Government, and one nominated by the Turkish Government.

ARTICLE 68.

Subject to the provisions of this Section, the city of Smyrna and the territory defined in Article 66 will be assimilated, in the application of the present Treaty, to territory detached from Turkey.

ARTICLE 69.

The city of Smyrna and the territory defined in Article 66 remain under Turkish sovereignty. Turkey, however, transfers to the Greek Government the exercise of her rights of sovereignty over the city of Smyrna and the said territory. In witness of such sovereignty the Turkish flag shall remain permanently hoisted over an outer fort in the town of Smyrna. The fort will be designated by the Principal Allied Powers.

ARTICLE 70.

The Greek Government will be responsible for the administration of the city of Smyrna and the territory defined in Article 66, and will effect this administration by means of a body of officials which it will appoint specially for the purpose.

ARTICLE 71.

The Greek Government shall be entitled to maintain in the city of Smyrna and the territory defined in Article 66 the military forces required for the maintenance of order and public security.

ARTICLE 72.

A local parliament shall be set up with an electoral system calculated to ensure proportional representation of all sections of the population, including racial, linguistic and religious minorities. Within six months from the coming into force of the present Treaty the Greek Government shall submit to the Council of the League of Nations a scheme for an electoral system complying with the above requirements; this scheme shall not come into force until approved by a majority of the Council.

The Greek Government shall be entitled to postpone the elections for so long as may be required for the return of the inhabitants who have been banished or deported by the Turkish authorities, but such postponement shall not exceed a period of one year from the coming into force of the present Treaty.

ARTICLE 73.

The relations between the Greek administration and the local parliament shall be determined by the said administration in accordance with the principles of the Greek Constitution.

ARTICLE 74.

Compulsory military service shall not be enforced in the city of Smyrna and the territory defined in Article 66 pending the final determination of their status in accordance with Article 83.

ARTICLE 75.

The provisions of the separate Treaty referred to in Article 86 relating to the protection of racial, linguistic and religious minorities, and to freedom of commerce and transit, shall be applicable to the city of Smyrna and the territory defined in Article 66.

ARTICLE 76.

The Greek Government may establish a Customs boundary along the frontier line defined in Article 66, and may incorporate the city of Smyrna and the territory defined in the said Article in the Greek customs system.

ARTICLE 77.

The Greek Government engages to take no measures which would have the effect of depreciating the existing Turkish currency, which shall retain its character as legal tender pending the determination, in accordance with the provisions of Article 83, of the final status of the territory.

ARTICLE 78.
The provisions of Part XI (Ports, Waterways and Railways) relating to the regime of ports of international interest, free ports and transit shall be applicable to the city of Smyrna and the territory defined in Article 66.

ARTICLE 79.
As regards nationality, such inhabitants of the city of Smyrna and the territory defined in Article 66 as are of Turkish nationality and cannot claim any other nationality under the terms of the present Treaty shall be treated on exactly the same footing as Greek nationals. Greece shall provide for their diplomatic and consular protection abroad.

ARTICLE 80.
The provisions of Article 241, Part VIII (Financial Clauses) will apply in the case of the city of Smyrna and the territory defined in Article 66.
The provisions of Article 293, Part IX (Economic Clauses) will not be applicable in the case of the said city and territory.

ARTICLE 81.
Until the determination, in accordance with the provisions of Article 83, of the final status of Smyrna and the territory defined in Article 66, the rights to exploit the salt marshes of Phocea belonging to the Administration of the Ottoman Public Debt, including all plant and machinery and materials for transport by land or sea, shall not be altered or interfered with. No tax or charge shall be imposed during this period on the manufacture, exportation or transport of salt produced from these marshes. The Greek administration will have the right to regulate and tax the consumption of salt at Symrna and within the territory defined in Article 66.
If after the expiration of the period referred to in the preceding paragraph Greece considers it opportune to effect changes in the provisions above set forth, the salt marshes of Phocea will be treated as a concession and the guarantees provided by Article 312, Part IX (Economic Clauses) will apply, subject, however, to the provisions of Article 246, Part VIII (Financial Clauses) of the present Treaty.

ARTICLE 82.
Subsequent agreements will decide all questions which are not decided by the present Treaty and which may arise from the execution of the provisions of this Section.

ARTICLE 83.
When a period of five years shall have elapsed after the coming into force of the present Treaty the local parliament referred to in Article 72 may, by a majority of votes, ask the Council of the League of Nations for the definitive incorporation in the Kingdom of Greece of the city of Smyrna and the territory defined in Article 66. The Council may require, as a preliminary, a plebiscite under conditions which it will lay down. In the event of such incorporation as a result of the application of the foregoing paragraph, the Turkish sovereignty referred to in Article 69 shall cease. Turkey hereby renounces in that event in favour of Greece all rights and title over the city of Smyrna and the territory defined in Article 66.

SECTION V.
GREECE.

ARTICLE 84.
Without prejudice to the frontiers of Bulgaria laid down by the Treaty of Peace signed at Neuilly-sur-Seine on November 27, 1919, Turkey renounces in favour of Greece all rights and title over the territories of the former Turkish Empire in Europe situated outside the frontiers of Turkey as laid down by the present Treaty.
The islands of the Sea of Marmora are not included in the transfer of sovereignty effected by the above paragraph.
Turkey further renounces in favour of Greece all her rights and title over the islands of Imbros and Tenedos. The decision taken by the Conference of Ambassadors at London in execution of Articles 5 of the Treaty of London of May 17-30, 1913, and 15 of the Treaty of Athens of November 1-14, 1913, and notified to the Greek Government on February 13, 1914, relating to the sovereignty of Greece over the other islands of the Eastern Mediterranean, particularly Lemnos, Samothrace, Mytilene, Chios, Samos and Nikaria, is confirmed, without prejudice to the provisions of the present Treaty relating to the islands placed under the sovereignty of Italy and referred to in Article 122, and to the islands lying less than three miles from the coast of Asia.
Nevertheless, in the portion of the zone of the Straits and the islands, referred to in Article 178, which under the present Treaty are placed under Greek sovereignty, Greece accepts and undertakes to observe, failing any contrary stipulation in the present Treaty, all the obligations which, in order to assure the freedom of the Straits, are imposed by the present Treaty on Turkey in that portion of the said zone, including the islands of the Sea of Marmora, which remains under Turkish sovereignty.

ARTICLE 85.
A Commission shall be constituted within fifteen days from the coming into force of the present Treaty to trace on the spot the frontier line described in Article 27, 1 (2). This Commission shall be composed of four members nominated by the Principal Allied Powers, one member nominated by Greece, and one member nominated by Turkey.

ARTICLE 86.
Greece accepts and agrees to embody in a separate Treaty such provisions as may be deemed necessary, particularly as regards Adrianople, to protect the interests of inhabitants of that State who differ from the majority of the population in race, language or religion.

Greece further accepts and agrees to embody in a separate Treaty such provisions as may be deemed necessary to protect freedom of transit and equitable treatment for the commerce of other nations.

ARTICLE 87.
The proportion and nature of the financial obligations of Turkey which Greece will have to assume on account of the territory placed under her sovereignty will be determined in accordance with Articles 241 to 244, Part VIII (Financial Clauses) of the present Treaty.

Subsequent agreements will decide all questions which are not decided by the present Treaty and which may arise in consequence of the transfer of the said territories.

SECTION VI.
ARMENIA.

ARTICLE 88.
Turkey, in accordance with the action already taken by the Allied Powers, hereby recognises Armenia as a free and independent State.

ARTICLE 89.
Turkey and Armenia as well as the other High Contracting Parties agree to submit to the arbitration of the President of the United States of America the question of the frontier to be fixed between Turkey and Armenia in the vilayets of Erzerum, Trebizond, Van and Bitlis, and to accept his decision thereupon, as well as any stipulations he may prescribe as to access for Armenia to the sea, and as to the demilitarisation of any portion of Turkish territory adjacent to the said frontier.

ARTICLE 90.
In the event of the determination of the frontier under Article 89 involving the transfer of the whole or any part of the territory of the said Vilayets to Armenia, Turkey hereby renounces as from the date of such decision all rights and title over the territory so transferred. The provisions of the present Treaty applicable to territory detached from Turkey shall thereupon become applicable to the said territory.

The proportion and nature of the financial obligations of Turkey which Armenia will have to assume, or of the rights which will pass to her, on account of the transfer of the said territory will be determined in accordance with Articles 241 to 244, Part VIII (Financial Clauses) of the present Treaty.

Subsequent agreements will, if necessary, decide all questions which are not decided by the present Treaty and which may arise in consequence of the transfer of the said territory.

ARTICLE 91.
In the event of any portion of the territory referred to in Article 89 being transferred to Armenia, a Boundary Commission, whose composition will be determined subsequently, will be constituted within three months from the delivery of the decision referred to in the said Article to trace on the spot the frontier between Armenia and Turkey as established by such decision.

ARTICLE 92.
The frontiers between Armenia and Azerbaijan and Georgia respectively will be determined by direct agreement between the States concerned.

If in either case the States concerned have failed to determine the frontier by agreement at the date of the decision referred to in Article 89, the frontier line in question will be determined by the Pricipal Allied Powers, who will also provide for its being traced on the spot.

ARTICLE 93.
Armenia accepts and agrees to embody in a Treaty with the Principal Allied Powers such provisions as may be deemed necessary by these Powers to protect the interests of inhabitants of that State who differ from the majority of the population in race, language, or religion.

Armenia further accepts and agrees to embody in a Treaty with the Principal Allied Powers such provisions as these Powers may deem necessary to protect freedom of transit and equitable treatment for the commerce of other nations.

SECTION VII.
SYRIA, MESOPOTAMIA, PALESTINE.
ARTICLE 94.
The High Contracting Parties agree that Syria and Mesopotamia shall, in accordance with the fourth paragraph of Article 22, Part I (Covenant of the League of Nations), be provisionally recognised as independent States subject to the rendering of administrative advice and assistance by a Mandatory until such time as they are able to stand alone.

A Commission shall be constituted within fifteen days from the coming into force of the present Treaty to trace on the spot the frontier line described in Article 27, II (2) and (3). This Commission will be composed of three members nominated by France, Great Britain and Italy respectively, and one member nominated by Turkey; it will be assisted by a representative of Syria for the Syrian frontier, and by a representative of Mesopotamia for the Mesopotamian frontier.

The determination of the other frontiers of the said States, and the selection of the Mandatories, will be made by the Principal Allied Powers.

ARTICLE 95.
The High Contracting Parties agree to entrust, by application of the provisions of Article 22, the administration of Palestine, within such boundaries as may be determined by the Principal Allied Powers, to a Mandatory to be selected by the said Powers. The Mandatory will be responsible for putting into effect the declaration originally made on November 2, 1917, by the British Government, and adopted by the other Allied Powers, in favour of the establishment in Palestine of a national home for the Jewish people, it being clearly understood that nothing shall be done which may prejudice the civil and religious rights of existing non-Jewish communities in Palestine, or the rights and political status enjoyed by Jews in any other country.

The Mandatory undertakes to appoint as soon as possible a special Commission to study and regulate all questions and claims relating to the different religious communities. In the composition of this Commission the religious interests concerned will be taken into account. The Chairman of the Commission will be appointed by the Council of the League of Nations.

ARTICLE 96.
The terms of the mandates in respect of the above territories will be formulated by the Principal Allied Powers and submitted to the Council of the League of Nations for approval.

ARTICLE 97.
Turkey hereby undertakes, in accordance with the provisions of Article 132, to accept any decisions which may be taken in relation to the questions dealt with in this Section.

SECTION VIII.
HEDJAZ.
ARTICLE 98.
Turkey, in accordance with the action already taken by the Allied Powers, hereby recognises the Hedjaz as a free and indepedent State, and renounces in favour of the Hedjaz all rights and titles over the territories of the former Turkish Empire situated outside the frontiers of Turkey as laid down by the present Treaty, and comprised within the boundaries which may ultimately be fixed.

ARTICLE 99.
In view of the sacred character attributed by Moslems of all countries to the cities and the Holy Places of Mecca and Medina His Majesty the King of the Hedjaz undertakes to assure free and easy access thereto to Moslems of every country who desire to go there on pilgrimage or for any other religious object, and to respect and ensure respect for the pious foundations which are or may be established there by Moslems of any countries in accordance with the precepts of the law of the Koran.

ARTICLE 100.
His Majesty the King of the Hedjaz undertakes that in commercial matters the most complete equality of treatment shall be assured in the territory of the Hedjaz to the persons, ships and goods of nationals of any of the Allied Powers, or of any of the new States set up in the territories of the former Turkish Empire, as well as to the persons, ships and goods of nationals of States, Members of the League of Nations.

SECTION IX.
EGYPT, SOUDAN, CYPRUS.
1. EGYPT.

ARTICLE 101.

Turkey renounces all rights and title in or over Egypt. This renunciation shall take effect as from November 5, 1914. Turkey declares that in conformity with the action taken by the Allied Powers she recognises the Protectorate proclaimed over Egypt by Great Britain on December 18, 1914.

ARTICLE 102.

Turkish subjects habitually resident in Egypt on December 18, 1914, will acquire Egyptian nationality ipso facto and will lose their Turkish nationality, except that if at that date such persons were temporarily absent from, and have not since returned to, Egypt they will not acquire Egyptian nationality without a special authorisation from the Egyptian Government.

ARTICLE 103.

Turkish subjects who became resident in Egypt after December 18, 1914, and are habitually resident there at the date of the coming into force of the present Treaty may, subject to the conditions prescribed in Article 105 for the right of option, claim Egyptian nationality, but such claim may in individual cases be refused by the competent Egyptian authority.

ARTICLE 104.

For all purposes connected with the present Treaty, Egypt and Egyptian nationals, their goods and vessels, shall be treated on the same footing, as from August 1, 1914, as the Allied Powers, their nationals, goods and vessels, and provisions in respect of territory under Turkish sovereignty, or of territory detached from Turkey in accordance with the present Treaty, shall not apply to Egypt.

ARTICLE 105.

Within a period of one year after the coming into force of the present Treaty persons over eighteen years of age acquiring Egyptian nationality under the provisions of Article 102 will be entitled to opt for Turkish nationality. In case such persons, or those who under Article 103 are entitled to claim Egyptian nationality, differ in race from the majority of the population of Egypt, they will within the same period be entitled to opt for the nationality of any State in favour of which territory is detached from Turkey, if the majority of the population of that State is of the same race as the person exercising the right to opt.

Option by a husband covers a wife and option by parents covers their children under eighteen years of age. Persons who have exercised the above right to opt must, except where authorised to continue to reside in Egypt, transfer within the ensuing twelve months their place of residence to the State for which they have opted. They will be entitled to retain their immovable property in Egypt, and may carry with them their movable property of every description. No export or import duties or charges may be imposed upon them in connection with the removal of such property.

ARTICLE 106.

The Egyptian Government shall have complete liberty of action in regulating the status of Turkish subjects in Egypt and the conditions under which they may establish themselves in the territory.

ARTICLE 107.

Egyptian nationals shall be entitled, when abroad, to British diplomatic and consular protection.

ARTICLE 108.

Egyptian goods entering Turkey shall enjoy the treatment accorded to British goods.

ARTICLE 109.

Turkey renounces in favour of Great Britain the powers conferred upon His Imperial Majesty the Sultan by the Convention signed at Constantinople on October 29, 1888, relating to the free navigation of the Suez Canal.

ARTICLE 110.

All property and possessions in Egypt belonging to the Turkish Government pass to the Egyptian Government without payment.

ARTICLE 111.

All movable and immovable property in Egypt belonging to Turkish nationals (who do not acquire Egyptian nationality) shall be dealt with in accordance with the provisions of Part IX (Economic Clauses) of the present Treaty.

ARTICLE 112.

Turkey renounces all claim to the tribute formerly paid by Egypt.

Great Britain undertakes to relieve Turkey of all liability in respect of the Turkish loans secured on the Egyptian tribute.

These loans are:

The guaranteed loan of 1855;

The loan of 1894 representing the converted loans of 1854 and 1871;

The loan of 1891 representing the converted loan of 1877.

The sums which the Khedives of Egypt have from time to time undertaken to pay over to the houses by which these loans were issued will be applied as heretofore to the interest and the sinking funds of the loans of 1894 and 1891 until the final extinction of those loans. The Government of Egypt will also continue to apply the sum hitherto paid towards the interest on the guaranteed loan of 1855.

Upon the extinction of these loans of 1894, 1891 and 1855, all liability on the part of the Egyptian Government arising out of the tribute formerly paid by Egypt to Turkey will cease.

2. SOUDAN.

ARTICLE 113.

The High Contracting Parties declare and place on record that they have taken note of the Convention between the British Government and the Egyptian Government defining the status and regulating the administration of the Soudan, signed on January 19, 1899, as amended by the supplementary Convention relating to the town of Suakin signed on July 10, 1899.

ARTICLE 114.

Soudanese shall be entitled when in foreign countries to British diplomatic and consular protection.

3. CYPRUS

ARTICLE 115.

The High Contracting Parties recognise the annexation of Cyprus proclaimed by the British Government on November 5, 1914.

ARTICLE 116.

Turkey renounces all rights and title over or relating to Cyprus, including the right to the tribute formerly paid by that island to the Sultan.

ARTICLE 117.

Turkish nationals born or habitually resident in Cyprus will acquire British nationality and lose their Turkish nationality, subject to the conditions laid down in the local law.

SECTION X.
MOROCCO, TUNIS.

ARTICLE 118.

Turkey recognises the French Protectorate in Morocco, and accepts all the consequences thereof. This recognition shall take effect as from March 30, 1912.

ARTICLE 119.

Moroccan goods entering Turkey shall be subject to the same treatment as French goods.

ARTICLE 120.

Turkey recognises the French Protectorate over Tunis and accepts all the consequences thereof. This recognition shall take effect as from May 12, 1881.

Tunisian goods entering Turkey shall be subject to the same treatment as French goods.

SECTION XI.
LIBYA, AEGEAN ISLANDS.

ARTICLE 121.

Turkey definitely renounces all rights and privileges which under the Treaty of Lausanne of October 18, 1912, were left to the Sultan in Libya.

ARTICLE 122.

Turkey renounces in favour of Italy all rights and title over the following islands of the Aegean Sea; Stampalia (Astropalia), Rhodes (Rhodos), Calki (Kharki), Scarpanto, Casos (Casso) Pscopis (Tilos), Misiros (Nisyros),

Calymnos (Kalymnos) Leros, Patmos, Lipsos (Lipso), Sini (Symi), and Cos (Kos), which are now occupied by Italy, and the islets dependent thereon, and also over the island of Castellorizzo.

SECTION XII.
NATIONALITY.

ARTICLE 123.

Turkish subjects habitually resident in territory which in accordance with the provisions of the present Treaty is detached from Turkey will become ipso facto, in the conditions laid down by the local law, nationals of the State to which such territory is transferred.

ARTICLE 124.

Persons over eighteen years of age losing their Turkish nationality and obtaining ipso facto a new nationality under Article 123 shall be entitled within a period of one year from the coming into force of the present Treaty to opt for Turkish nationality.

ARTICLE 125.

Persons over eighteen years of age habitually resident in territory detached from Turkey in accordance with the present Treaty and differing in race from the majority of the population of such territory shall within one year from the coming into force of the present Treaty be entitled to opt for Armenia, Azerbaijan, Georgia, Greece, the Hedjaz, Mesopotamia, Syria, Bulgaria or Turkey, if the majority of the population of the State selected is of the same race as the person exercising the right to opt.

ARTICLE 126.

Persons who have exercised the right to opt in accordance with the provisions of Articles 124 or 125 must within the succeeding twelve months transfer their place of residence to the State for which they have opted.

They will be entitled to retain their immovable property in the territory of the other State where they had their place of residence before exercising their right to opt.

They may carry with them their movable property of every description. No export or import duties may be imposed upon them in connection with the removal of such property.

ARTICLE 127.

The High Contracting Parties undertake to put no hindrance in the way of the exercise of the right which the persons concerned have under the present Treaty, or under the Treaties of Peace concluded with Germany, Austria, Bulgaria or Hungary or under any treaty concluded by the Allied Powers, or any of them, with Russia, or between any of the Allied Powers themselves, to choose any other nationality which may be open to them.

In particular, Turkey undertakes to facilitate by every means in her power the voluntary emigration of persons desiring to avail themselves of the right to opt provided by Article 125, and to carry out any measures which may be prescribed with this object by the Council of the League of Nations.

ARTICLE 128.

Turkey undertakes to recognise any new nationality which has been or may be acquired by her nationals under the laws of the Allied Powers or new States and in accordance with the decisions of the competent authorities of these Powers pursuant to naturalisation laws or under Treaty stipulations, and to regard such persons as having, in consequence of the acquisition of such new nationality, in all respects severed their allegiance to their country of origin.

In particular, persons who before the coming into force of the present Treaty have acquired the nationality of one of the Allied Powers in accordance with the law of such Power shall be recognised by the Turkish Government as nationals of such Power and as having lost their Turkish nationality, notwithstanding any provisions of Turkish law to the contrary. No confiscation of property or other penalty provided by Turkish law shall be incurred on account of the acquisition of any such nationality.

ARTICLE 129.

Jews of other than Turkish nationality who are habitually resident, on the coming into force of the present Treaty, within the boundaries of Palestine, as determined in accordance with Article 95 will ipso facto become citizens of Palestine to the exclusion of any other nationality.

ARTICLE 130.

For the purposes of the provisions of this Section, the status of a married woman will be governed by that of her husband and the status of children under eighteen years of age by that of their parents.

ARTICLE 131.

The provisions of this Section will apply to the city of Smyrna and the territory defined in Article 66 as from the establishment of the final status of the territory in accordance with Article 83.

SECTION XIII.
GENERAL PROVISIONS.
[...ARTICLE 132.-139...]

PART IV.
PROTECTION OF MINORITIES.

ARTICLE 140.
Turkey undertakes that the stipulations contained in Articles 141, 145 and 147 shall be recognised as fundamental laws, and that no civil or military law or regulation, no Imperial Iradeh nor official action shall conflict or interfere with these stipulations, nor shall any law, regulation, Imperial Iradeh nor official action prevail over them.

ARTICLE 141.
Turkey undertakes to assure full and complete protection of life and liberty to all inhabitants of Turkey without distinction of birth, nationality, language, race or religion. All inhabitants of Turkey shall be entitled to the free exercise, whether public or private, of any creed, religion or belief.

The penalties for any interference with the free exercise of the right referred to in the preceding paragraph shall be the same whatever may be the creed concerned.

ARTICLE 142.
Whereas, in view of the terrorist regime which has existed in Turkey since November 1, 1914, conversions to Islam could not take place under normal conditions, no conversions since that date are recognised and all persons who were non-Moslems before November 1, 1914, will be considered as still remaining such, unless, after regaining their liberty, they voluntarily perform the necessary formalities for embracing the Islamic faith. In order to repair so far as possible the wrongs inflicted on individuals in the course of the massacres perpetrated in Turkey during the war, the Turkish Government undertakes to afford all the assistance in its power or in that of the Turkish authorities in the search for and deliverance of all persons, of whatever race or religion, who have disappeared, been carried off, interned or placed in captivity since November 1, 1914.

The Turkish Government undertakes to facilitate the operations of mixed commissions appointed by the Council of the League of Nations to receive the complaints of the victims themselves, their families or their relations, to make the necessary enquiries, and to order the liberation of the persons in question.

The Turkish Government undertakes to ensure the execution of the decisions of these commissions, and to assure the security and the liberty of the persons thus restored to the full enjoyment of their rights.

ARTICLE 143.
Turkey undertakes to recognise such provisions as the Allied Powers may consider opportune with respect to the reciprocal and voluntary emigration of persons belonging to racial minorities.

Turkey renounces any right to avail herself of the provisions of Article 16 of the Convention between Greece and Bulgaria relating to reciprocal emigration, signed at Neuilly-sur-Seine on November 27, 1919. Within six months from the coming into force of the present Treaty, Greece and Turkey will enter into a special arrangement relating to the reciprocal and voluntary emigration of the populations of Turkish and Greek race in the territories transferred to Greece and remaining Turkish respectively.

In case agreement cannot be reached as to such arrangement, Greece and Turkey will be entitled to apply to the Council of the League of Nations, which will fix the terms of such arrangement.

ARTICLE 144.
The Turkish Government recognises the injustice of the law of 1915 relating to Abandoned Properties *(Emval-i-Metroukeh)*, and of the supplementary provisions thereof, and declares them to be null and void, in the past as in the future.

The Turkish Government solemnly undertakes to facilitate to the greatest possible extent the return to their homes and re-establishment in their businesses of the Turkish subjects of non-Turkish race who have been forcibly driven from their homes by fear of massacre or any other form of pressure since January 1, 1914. It recognises that any immovable or movable property of the said Turkish subjects or of the communities to which they belong, which can be recovered, must be restored to them as soon as possible, in whatever hands it may be found. Such property shall be restored free of all charges or servitudes with which it may have been burdened and without compensation of any kind to the present owners or occupiers, subject to any action which they may be able to bring against the persons from whom they derived title.

The Turkish Government agrees that arbitral commissions shall be appointed by the Council of the League of Nations wherever found necessary. These commissions shall each be composed of one representative of the Turkish Government, one representative of the community which claims that it or one of its members has been injured, and a chairman appointed by the Council of the League of Nations. These arbitral commissions shall

hear all claims covered by this Article and decide them by summary procedure.
The arbitral commissions will have power to order:
(1) The provision by the Turkish Government of labour for any work of reconstruction or restoration deemed necessary. This labour shall be recruited from the races inhabiting the territory where the arbitral commission considers the execution of the said works to be necessary
(2) The removal of any person who, after enquiry, shall be recognised as having taken an active part in massacres or deportations or as having provoked them; the measures to be taken with regard to such person's possessions will be indicated by the commission;
(3) The disposal of property belonging to members of a community who have died or disappeared since January 1, 1914, without leaving heirs; such property may be handed over to the community instead of to the State

(4) The cancellation of all acts of sale or any acts creating rights over immovable property concluded after January 1, 1914. The indemnification of the holders will be a charge upon the Turkish Government, but must not serve as a pretext for delaying the restitution. The arbitral commission will, however have the power to impose equitable arrangements between the interested parties, if any sum has been paid by the present holder of such property.
The Turkish Government undertakes to facilitate in the fullest possible measure the work of the commissions and to ensure the execution of their decisions, which will be final. No decision of the Turkish judicial or administrative authorities shall prevail over such decisions.

ARTICLE 145.

All Turkish nationals shall be equal before the law and shall enjoy the same civil and political rights without distinction as to race, language or religion.
Difference of religion, creed or confession shall not prejudice any Turkish national in matters relating to the enjoyment of civil or political rights, as for instance admission to public employments, functions and honours, or the exercise of professions and industries.
Within a period of two years from the coming into force of the present Treaty the Turkish Government will submit to the Allied Powers a scheme for the organisation of an electoral system based on the principle of proportional representation of racial minorities.
No restriction shall be imposed on the free use by any Turkish national of any language in private intercourse, in commerce, religion, in the press or in publications of any kind, or at public meetings. Adequate facilities shall be given to Turkish nationals of non-Turkish speech for the use of their language, either orally or in writing, before the courts.

ARTICLE 146.

The Turkish Government undertakes to recognize the validity of diplomas granted by recognised foreign universities and schools, and to admit the holders thereof to the free exercise of the professions and industries for which such diplomas qualify.
This provision will apply equally to nationals of Allied powers who are resident in Turkey.

ARTICLE 147.

Turkish nationals who belong to racial, religious or linguistic minorities shall enjoy the ame treatment and security in law and in fact as other Turkish nationals. In particular they shall have an equal right to establish, manage and control at their own expense, and independently of and without interference by the Turkish authorities, any charitable, religious and social institutions, schools for primary, secondary and higher instruction and other educational establishments, with the right to use their own language and to exercise their own religion freely therein.

ARTICLE 148.

In towns and districts where there is a considerable proportion of Turkish nationals belonging to racial, linguistic or religious minorities, these minorities shall be assured an equitable share in the enjoyment and application of the sums which may be provided out of public funds under the State, municipal or other budgets for educational or charitable purposes.
The sums in question shall be paid to the qualified representatives of the communities concerned.

ARTICLE 149.

The Turkish Government undertakes to recognise and respect the ecclesiastical and scholastic autonomy of all racial minorities in Turkey. For this purpose, and subject to any provisions to the contrary in the present Treaty, the Turkish Government confirms and will uphold in their entirety the prerogatives and immunities of an ecclesiastical, scholastic or judicial nature granted by the Sultans to non-Moslem races in virtue of special orders or imperial decrees (firmans, hattis, berats, etc.) as well as by ministerial orders or orders of the Grand Vizier.
All laws, decrees, regulations and circulars issued by the Turkish Government and containing abrogations,

restrictions or amendments of such prerogatives and immunities shall be considered to such extent null and void.
Any modification of the Turkish judical system which may be introduced in accordance with the provisions of the present Treaty shall be held to override this Article, in so far as such modification may affect individuals belonging to racial minorities.

ARTICLE 150.
In towns and districts where there is resident a considerable proportion of Turkish nationals of the Christian or Jewish religions the Turkish Government undertakes that such Turkish nationals shall not be compelled to perform any act which constitutes a violation of their faith or religious observances, and shall not be placed under any disability by reason of their refusal to attend courts of law or to perform any legal business on their weekly day of rest. This provision, however, shall not exempt such Turkish nationals (Christians or Jews) from such obligations as shall be imposed upon all other Turkish nationals for the preservation of public order.

ARTICLE 151.
The Principal Allied Powers, in consultation with the Council of the League of Nations, will decide what measures are necessary to guarantee the execution of the provisions of this Part. The Turkish Government hereby accepts all decisions which may be taken on this subject.

PART V.
MILITARY, NAVAL AND AIR CLAUSES.

In order to render possible the initiation of a general limitation of the armaments of all nations, Turkey undertakes strictly to observe the military, naval and air clauses which follow.

SECTION I.
MILITARY CLAUSES.
CHAPTER I.
GENERAL CLAUSES.

ARTICLE 152.
The armed force at the disposal of Turkey shall only consist of:
(1) The Sultan's bodyguard;
(2) Troops of gendarmerie, intended to maintain order and security in the interior and to ensure the protection of minorities
(3) Special elements intended for the reinforcement of the troops of gendarmerie in case of serious trouble, and eventually to ensure the control of the frontiers.

ARTICLE 153.
Within six months from the coming into force of the present Treaty, the military forces other than that provided for in Article 152 shall be demobilised and disbanded.

CHAPTER II.
EFFECTIVES, ORGANISATION AND CADRES OF THE TURKISH ARMED FORCE.

ARTICLE 154.
The Sultan's bodyguard shall consist of a staff and infantry and cavalry units, the strength of which shall not exceed 700 officers and men. This strength is not included in the total force provided for in Article 155. The composition of this guard is given in Table 1 annexed to this Section.

ARTICLE 155.
The total strength of the forces enumerated in paragraphs (2) and (3) of Article 152 shall not exceed 50,000 men, including staffs, officers, training personnel and depot troops.

ARTICLE 156.
The troops of gendarmerie shall be distributed over the territory of Turkey, which for this purpose will be divided into territorial areas to be delimited as provided in Article 200.
A legion of gendarmerie, composed of mounted and unmounted troops, provided with machine guns and with administrative and medical services will be organised in each territorial region, it will supply in the vilayets, sandjaks, cazas, etc., the detachments necessary for the organisation of a fixed protective service, mobile reserves being at its disposal at one or more points within the region.
On account of their special duties, the legions shall not include either artillery or technical services. The total strength of the legions shall not exceed 35,000 men, to be included in the total strength of the armed force provided for in Article 155.

The maximum strength of any one legion shall not exceed one quarter of the total strength of the legions. The elements of any one legion shall not be employed outside the territory of their region, except by special authorisation from the Inter-Allied Commission provided for in Article 200.

ARTICLE 157.

The special elements for reinforcements may include details of infantry, cavalry, mountain artillery, pioneers and the corresponding technical and general services; their total strength shall not exceed 15,000 men, to be included in the total strength provided for in Article 155.

The number of such reinforcements for any one legion shall not exceed one third of the whole strength of these elements without the special authority of the Inter-Allied Commission provided for in Article 200. The proportion of the various arms and services entering into the composition of these special elements is laid down in Table II annexed to this Section.

Their quartering will be fixed as provided in Article 200.

ARTICLE 158.

In the formations referred to in Articles 156 and 157, the proportion of officers, including the personnel of staffs and special services, shall not exceed one twentieth of the total effectives with the colours, and that of non-commissioned officers shall not exceed one twelfth of the total effectives with the colours.

ARTICLE 159.

Officers supplied by the various Allied or neutral Powers shall collaborate, under the direction of the Turkish Government, in the command, the organisation and the training of the gendarmerie officers authorised by Article 158, but their number shall not exceed fifteen per cent. of that strength. Special agreements to be drawn up by the Inter-Allied Commission mentioned in Article 200 shall fix the proportion of these officers according to nationality, and shall determine the conditions of their participation in the various missions assigned to them by this Article.

ARTICLE 160.

In any one territorial region all officers placed at the disposal of the Turkish Government under the conditions laid down in Article 159 shall in principle be of the same nationality.

ARTICLE 161.

In the zone of the Straits and islands referred to in Article 178, excluding the islands of Lemnos, Imbros, Samothrace Tenedos and Mitylene, the forces of gendarmerie, Greek and Turkish, will be under the Inter-Allied Command of the forces in occupation of that zone.

ARTICLE 162.

All measures of mobilisation, or appertaining to mobilisation or tending to an increase of the strength or of the means of transport of any of the forces provided for in this Chapter are forbidden.

The various formations, staffs and administrative services shall not, in any case, include supplementary cadres.

ARTICLE 163.

Within the period fixed by Article 153, all existing forces of gendarmerie shall be amalgamated with the legions provided for in Article 156.

ARTICLE 164.

The formation of any body of troops not provided for in this Section is forbidden.

The suppression of existing formations which are in excess of the authorised strength of 50,000 men (not including the Sultan's bodyguard) shall be effected progressively from the date of the signature of the present Treaty, in such manner as to be completed within six months at the latest after the coming into force of the Treaty, in accordance with the provisions of Article 158.

The number of officers, or persons in the position of officers, in the War Ministry and the Turkish General Staff, as well as in the administrations attached to them, shall, within the same period, be reduced to the establishment considered by the Commission referred to in Article 200 as strictly necessary for the good working of the general services of the armed Turkish force, this establishment being included in the maximum figure laid down in Article 158.

CHAPTER III.
RECRUITING.

ARTICLE 165.

The Turkish armed force shall in future be constituted and recruited by voluntary enlistment only. Enlistment shall be open to all subjects of the Turkish State equally, without distinction of race or religion. As regards the legions referred to in Article 156, their system of recruiting shall be in principle regional, and so regulated that the Moslem and non-Moslem elements of the population of each region may be, so far as possi-

ble, represented on the strength of the corresponding legion.
The provisions of the preceding paragraphs apply to officers as well as to men.

ARTICLE 166.
The length of engagement of non-commissioned officers and men shall be twelve consecutive years. The annual replacement of men released from service for any reason whatever before the expiration of their term of engagement shall not exceed five per cent. of the total effectives fixed by Article 155.

ARTICLE 167.
All officers must be regulars (officers *de carrière*).
Officers at present serving in the army or the gendarmerie who are retained in the new armed force must undertake to serve at least up to the age of forty-five.
Officers at present serving in the army or the gendarmerie who are not admitted to the new armed force shall be definitely released from all military obligations, and must not take part in any military exercises, theoretical or practical.
Officers newly-appointed must undertake to serve on the active list for at least twenty-five consecutive years. The annual replacement of officers leaving the service for any cause before the expiration of their term of engagement shall not exceed five per cent. of the total effectives of officers provided by Article 158.

CHAPTER IV.
SCHOOLS, EDUCATIONAL ESTABLISHMENTS, MILITARY CLASS AND SOCIETIES
[…ARTICLE 168.-169…]

CHAPTER V.
CUSTOMS OFFICIALS, LOCAL URBAN AND RURAL POLICE, FOREST GUARDS.

ARTICLE 170.
Without prejudice to the provisions of Article 48, Part III (Political Clauses), the number of customs officials, local urban or rural police, forest guards or other like officials shall not exceed the number of men employed in a similar capacity in 1913 within the territorial limits of Turkey as fixed by the present Treaty.

The number of these officials may only be increased in the future in proportion to the increase of population in the localities or municipalities which employ them.

These employees and officials, as well as those employed in the railway service, must not be assembled for the purpose of taking part in any military exercises.

In each administrative district the local urban and rural police and forest guards shall be recruited and officered according to the principles laid down in the case of the gendarmerie by Article 165.

In the Turkish police, which, as forming part of the civil administration of Turkey, will remain distinct from the Turkish armed force, officers or officials supplied by the various Allied or neutral Powers shall collaborate, under the direction of the Turkish Government, in the organisation the command and the training of the said police. The number of these officers or officials shall not exceed fifteen per cent. of the strength of similar Turkish officers or officials.

CHAPTER VI.
ARMAMENT, MUNITIONS AND MATERIAL

ARTICLE 171.
On the expiration of six months from the coming into force of the present Treaty, the armament which may be in use or held in reserve for replacement in the various formations of the Turkish armed force shall not exceed the figures fixed per thousand men in Table III annexed to this Section.

ARTICLE 172.
The stock of munitions at the disposal of Turkey shall not exceed the amounts fixed in Table III annexed to this Section.

ARTICLE 173.
Within six months from the coming into force of the present Treaty all existing arms, munitions of the various categories and war material in excess of the quantities authorised shall be handed over to the Military Inter-Allied Commission of Control provided for in Article 200 in such places as shall be appointed by this Commission.
The Principal Allied Powers will decide what is to be done with this material.

ARTICLE 174.

The manufacture of arms, munitions and war material, including aircraft and parts of aircraft of every description, shall take place only in the factories or establishments authorised by the Inter-Allied Commission referred to in Article 200.

Within six months from the coming into force of the present Treaty all other establishments for the manufacture, preparation, storage or design of arms, munitions or any war material shall be abolished or converted to purely commercial uses.

The same will apply to all arsenals other than those utilised as depots for the authorised stocks of munitions.

The plant of establishments or arsenals in excess of that required for the authorised manufacture shall be rendered useless or converted to purely commercial uses, in accordance with the decisions of the Military Inter-Allied Commission of Control referred to in Article 200.

ARTICLE 175

The importation into Turkey of arms, munitions and war materials, including aircraft and parts of aircraft of every description, is strictly forbidden, except with the special authority of the Inter-Allied Commission referred to in Article 200.

The manufacture for foreign countries and the exportation of arms, munitions and war material of any description is also forbidden.

ARTICLE 176.

The use of flame-throwers, asphyxiating, poisonous or other gases and all similar liquids, materials or processes being forbidden, their manufacture and importation are strictly forbidden in Turkey.

Material specially intended for the manufacture, storage or use of the said products or processes is equally forbidden.

The manufacture and importation into Turkey of armoured cars, tanks or any other similar machines suitable for use in war are equally forbidden.

CHAPTER VII.
FORTIFICATIONS

ARTICLE 177.

In the zone of the Straits and islands referred to in Article 178 the fortifications will be disarmed and demolished as provided in that Article.

Outside this zone, and subject to the provisions of Article 89, the existing fortified works may be preserved in their present condition, but will be disarmed within the same period of three months.

CHAPTER VIII.
MAINTENANCE OF THE FREEDOM OF THE STRAITS

ARTICLE 178.

For the purpose of guaranteeing the freedom of the Straits, the High Contracting Parties agree to the following provisions:

(1) Within three months from the coming into force of the present Treaty, all works, fortifications and batteries within the zone defined in Article 179 and comprising the coast and islands of the Sea of Marmora and the coast of the Straits, also those in the Islands of Lemnos, Imbros, Samothrace, Tenedos and Mitylene, shall be disarmed and demolished.

The reconstruction of these works and the construction of similar works are forbidden in the above zone and islands. France, Great Britain and Italy shall have the right to prepare for demolition any existing roads and railways in the said zone and in the islands of Lemnos, Imbros, Samothrace, and Tenedos which allow of the rapid transport of mobile batteries, the construction there of such roads and railways remaining forbidden.

In the islands of Lemnos, Imbros, Samothrace and Tenedos the construction of new roads or railways must not be undertaken except with the authority of the three Powers mentioned above.

(2) The measures prescribed in the first paragraph of (I) shall be executed by and at the expense of Greece and Turkey as regards their respective territories, and under control as provided in Article 203.

(3) The territories of the zone and the islands of Lemnos, Imbros, Samothrace, Tenedos, and Mitylene shall not be used for military purposes, except by the three Allied Powers referred to above, acting in concert. This provision does not exclude the employment in the said zone and islands of forces of Greek and Turkish gendarmerie, who will be under the Inter-Allied command of the forces of occupation, in accordance with the provisions of Article 161, nor the maintenance of a garrison of Greek troops in the island of Mitylene, nor the presence of the Sultan's bodyguard referred to in Article 152.

(4) The said Powers, acting in concert, shall have the right to maintain in the said territories and islands such military and air forces as they may consider necessary to prevent any action being taken or prepared which might directly or indirectly prejudice the freedom of the Straits.
This supervision will be carried out in naval matters by a guard-ship belonging to each of the said Allied Powers.
The forces of occupation referred to above may, in case of necessity, exercise on land the right of requisition, subject to the same conditions as those laid down in the Regulations annexed to the Fourth Hague Convention, 1907, or any other Convention replacing it to which all the said Powers are parties. Requisitions shall, however, only be made against payment on the spot.

ARTICLE 179.

The zone referred to in Article 178 is defined as follows:
(1) In Europe:
From Karachali on the Gulf of Xeros north-eastwards,
a line reaching and then following the southern boundary of the basin of the Beylik Dere to the crest of the Kuru Dagh;
then following that crest line,
then a straight line passing north of Emerli, and south of Derelar,
then curving north-north-eastwards and cutting the road from Rodosto to Malgara 3 kilometres west of Ainarjik and then passing 6 kilometres south-east of Ortaja Keui,
then curving north-eastwards and cutting the road from Rodosto to Hairobolu 18 kilometres northwest of Rodosto,
then to a point on the road from Muradli to Rodosto about kilometre south of Muradli,
a straight line;
thence east-north-eastwards to.Yeni Keui,
a straight line, modified, however, so as to pass at a minimum distance of 2 kilometres north of the railway from Chorlu to Chatalja;
thence north-north-eastwards to a point west of Istranja,
situated on the frontier of Turkey in Europe as defined in Article 27, 1 (2),
a straight line leaving the village of Yeni Keui within the zone; thence to the Black Sea,
the frontier of Turkey in Europe as defined in Article 27, 1 (2).
(2) In Asia:
From a point to be determined by the Principal Allied Powers between Cape Dahlina and Kemer Iskele on the gulf of Adramid east-north-eastwards,
a line passing south of Kemer Iskele and Kemer together with the road joining these places;
then to a point immediately south of the point where the Decauville railway from Osmanlar to Urchanlar crosses the Diermen Dere,
a straight line;
thence north-eastwards to Manias Geul,
a line following the right bank of the Diermen Dere, and Kara Dere Suyu;
thence eastwards, the southern shore of Manias Geul;
then to the point where it is crossed by the railway from Panderma to Susighirli, the course of the Kara Dere upstream;
thence eastwards to a point on the Adranos Chai about kilometres from its mouth near Kara Oghlan,
a straight line;
thence eastwards, the course of this river downstream then the southern shore of Abulliont Geul;
then to the point where the railway from Mudania to Brusa crosses the Ulfer Chai, about 5 kilometres northwest of Brusa,
a straight line;
thence north-eastwards to the confluence of the rivers about 6 kilometres north of Brusa,
the course of the Ulfer Chai downstream;
thence eastwards to the southernmost point of Iznik Geul,
a straight line;
thence to a point 2 kilometres north of Iznik,
the southern and eastern shores of this lake;
thence north-eastwards to the westernmost point of Sbanaja Geul,
a line following the crest line Chirchir Chesme, Sira Dagh,
Elmali Dagh, Kalpak Dagh, Ayu Tepe, Hekim Tepe; thence northwards to a point on the road from Ismid to Armasha, 8 kilometres southwest of Armasha,
a line following as far as possible the eastern boundary of the basin of the Chojali Dere;

thence to a point on the Black Sea, 2 kilometres east of the mouth of the Akabad R,
a straight line.

ARTICLE 180.

A Commission shall be constituted within fifteen days from the coming into force of the present Treaty to trace on the spot the boundaries of the zone referred to in Article 178, except in so far as these boundaries coincide with the frontier line described in Article 27,1(2). This Commission shall be composed of three members nominated by the military authorities of France, Great Britain and Italy respectively, with, for the portion of the zone placed under Greek sovereignty, one member nominated by the Greek Government, and, for the portion of the zone remaining under Turkish sovereignty, one member nominated by the Turkish Government. The decisions of the Commission, which will be taken by a majority, shall be binding on the parties concerned. The expenses of this Commission will be included in the expenses of the occupation of the said zone.

[...TABLE I: COMPOSITION OF THE SULTAN'S BODYGUARDS...]

[...TABLE II: STRENGTH OF THE VARIOUS ARMS AND SERVICES ENTERING INTO THE COMPOSITION OF THE SPECIAL ELEMENTS FOR REINFORCEMENT...]

[...TABLE III: MAXIMUM AUTHORISED ARMAMENTS AND MUNITION SUPPLIES...]

SECTION II.
NAVAL CLAUSES.

ARTICLE 181.

From the coming into force of the present Treaty all warships interned in Turkish ports in accordance with the Armistice of October 30, 1918, are declared to be finally surrendered to the Principal Allied Powers.

Turkey will, however, retain the right to maintain along her coasts for police and fishery duties a number of vessels which shall not exceed:

7 sloops,
6 torpedo boats.

These vessels will constitute the Turkish Marine, and will be chosen by the Naval Inter-Allied Commission of Control referred to in Article 201 from amongst the following vessels:

SLOOPS

Aidan Reis. *Hizir Reis.*
Burock Reis. *Kemal Reis.*
Sakiz. *Issa Reis.*
Prevesah.

TORPEDO-BOATS

Sivri Hissar. *Moussoul.*
Sultan Hissar. *Ack Hissar.*
Drach. *Younnous.*

The authority established for the control of customs will be entitled to appeal to the three Allied Powers referred to in Article 178 in order to obtain a more considerable force, if such an increase is considered indispensable for the satisfactory working of the services concerned.

Sloops may carry a light armament of two guns inferior to 77 m /m. and two machine guns. Torpedo-boats (or patrol launches) may carry a light armament of one gun inferior to 77 m/m.

All the torpedoes and torpedo-tubes on board will be removed.

ARTICLE 182.

Turkey is forbidden to construct or acquire any warships other than those intended to replace the units referred to in Article 181. Torpedo-boats shall be replaced by patrol launches.

The vessels intended for replacement purposes shall not exceed:

600 tons in the case of sloops;
100 tons in the case of patrol launches.

Except where a ship has been lost, sloops and torpedo-boats shall only be replaced after a period of twenty years, counting from the launching of the ship.

ARTICLE 183.

The Turkish armed transports and fleet auxiliaries enumerated below shall be disarmed and treated as merchant ships:

Rechid Pasha (late *Port Antonio*).
Tir-i-Mujghian (late *Pembroke Castle*).
Kiresund (late *Warwick Castle*).
Millet (late *Seagull*).

Akdeniz.
Bosphorus ferry-boats Nos. 60, 61, 63 and 70.

ARTICLE 184.
All warships, including submarines, now under construction in Turkey shall be broken up, with the exception of such surface vessels as can be completed for commercial purposes.
The work of breaking up these vessels shall be commenced on the coming into force of the present Treaty.

ARTICLE 185.
Articles, machinery and material arising from the breaking up of Turkish warships of all kinds, whether surface vessels or submarines, may not be used except for purely industrial or commercial purposes. They may not be sold or disposed of to foreign countries.

ARTICLE 186.
The construction or acquisition of any submarine, even for commercial purposes, shall be forbidden in Turkey.

ARTICLE 187.
The vessels of the Turkish Marine enumerated in Article 181 must have on board or in reserve only the allowance of war material and armaments fixed by the Naval Inter-Allied Commission of Control referred to in Article 201. Within a month from the time when the above quantities are fixed all armaments, munitions or other naval war material including mines and torpedoes, belonging to Turkey at the time of the signing of the Armistice of October 30, 1918, must definitely be surrendered to the Principal Allied Powers.
The manufacture of these articles in Turkish territory for, and their export to, foreign countries shall be forbidden.
All other stocks, depots or reserves of arms, munitions or naval war material of all kinds are forbidden.

ARTICLE 188.
The Naval Inter-Allied Commission of Control will fix the number of officers and men of all grades and corps to be admitted in accordance with the provisions of Article 189, into the Turkish Marine. This number will include the personnel for manning the ships left to Turkey in accordance with Article 181, and the administrative personnel of the police and fisheries protection services and of the semaphore stations.
Within two months from the time when the above number is fixed, the personnel of the former Turkish Navy in excess of this number shall be demobilised.
No naval or military corps or reserve force in connection with the Turkish Marine may be organised in Turkey without being included in the above strength.

ARTICLE 189.
The personnel of the Turkish Marine shall be recuited entirely by voluntary engagements entered into for a minimum period of twenty-five consecutive years for officers, and twelve consecutive years for petty officers and men.
The number engaged to replace those discharged for any reason other than the expiration of their term of service must not exceed five per cent. per annum of the total personnel fixed by the Naval Inter-Allied Commission of Control.
The personnel discharged from the former Turkish Navy must not receive any kind of naval or military training.
Officers belonging to the former Turkish Navy and not demobilised must undertake to serve till the age of forty-five, unless discharged for sufficient reason.
Officers and men belonging to the Turkish mercantile marine must not receive any kind of naval or military training.

ARTICLE 190.
On the coming into force of the present Treaty all the wireless stations in the zone referred to in Article 178 shall be handed over to the Principal Allied Powers. Greece and Turkey shall not construct any wireless stations in the said zone.

SECTION III.
AIR CLAUSES.

ARTICLE 191.
The Turkish armed forces must not include any military or naval air forces.
No dirigible shall be kept.

ARTICLE 192.
Within two months from the coming into force of the present Treaty the personnel of the air forces on the rolls of the Turkish land and sea forces shall be demobilised.

ARTICLE 193.
Until the complete evacuation of Turkish territory by the Allied troops, the aircraft of the Allied Powers shall have throughout Turkish territory freedom of passage through the air, freedom of transit and of landing.

ARTICLE 194.
During the six months following the coming into force of the present Treaty the manufacture, importation and exportation of aircraft of every kind, parts of aircraft, engines for aircraft and parts of engines for aircraft shall be forbidden in all Turkish territory.

ARTICLE 195.
On the coming into force of the present Treaty all military and naval aeronautical material must be delivered by Turkey, at her own expense, to the Principal Allied Powers.

Delivery must be completed within six months and must be effected at such places as may be appointed by the Aeronautical Inter-Allied Commission of Control. The Governments of the Principal Allied Powers will decide as to the disposal of this material.

In particular, this material will include all items under the following heads which are or have been in use or were designed for warlike purposes.

Complete aeroplanes and seaplanes, as well as those being manufactured, repaired or assembled.

Dirigibles able to take the air, being manufactured, repaired or assembled.

Plant for the manufacture of hydrogen.

Dirigible sheds and shelters of every kind for aircraft.

Pending their delivery, dirigibles will, at the expense of Turkey be maintained inflated with hydrogen; the plant for the manufacture of hydrogen, as well as the sheds for dirigibles, may, at the discretion of the said Powers, be left to Turkey until the dirigibles are handed over.

Engines for aircraft.

Nacelles and fuselages.

Armament (guns, machine-guns, light machine-guns, bombdropping apparatus, torpedo-dropping apparatus, synchronising apparatus, aiming apparatus).

Munitions (cartridges, shells, bombs loaded or unloaded, stocks of explosives or of material for their manufacture).

Instruments for use on aircraft.

Wireless apparatus and photographic and cinematographic apparatus for use on aircraft.

Component parts of any of the items under the preceding heads.

All aeronautical material of whatsoever description in Turkey shall be considered *primâ facie* as war material, and as such may not be exported, transferred, lent, used or destroyed, but must remain on the spot until such time as the Aeronautical Inter-Allied Commission of Control referred to in Article 202 has given a decision as to its nature; this Commission will be exclusively entitled to decide all such points.

SECTION IV.
INTER-ALLIED COMMISSIONS OF CONTROL AND ORGANISATION.

ARTICLE 196.
Subject to any special provisions in this Part, the military, naval and air clauses contained in the present Treaty shall be executed by Turkey and at her expense under the control of Inter-Allied Commissions appointed for this purpose by the Principal Allied Powers.

The above-mentioned Commissions will represent the Principal Allied Powers in dealing with the Turkish Government in all matters relating to the execution of the military, naval or air clauses. They will communicate to the Turkish authorities the decisions which the Principal Allied Powers have reserved the right to take, or which the execution of the said clauses may necessitate.

ARTICLE 197.
The Inter-Allied Commissions of Control and Organisation may establish their organisations at Constantinople, and will be entitled, as often as they think desirable, to proceed to any point whatever in Turkish territory, or to send sub-commissions, or to authorise one or more of their members to go, to any such point.

ARTICLE 198.
The Turkish Government must furnish to the Inter-Allied Commissions of Control and Organisation all such information and documents as the latter may deem necessary for the accomplishment of their mission, and must supply at its own expense all labour and material which the said Commissions may require in order to ensure

the complete execution of the military, naval or air clauses.

The Turkish Government shall attach a qualified representative to each Commission for the purpose of receiving all communications which the Commission may have to address to the Turkish Government, and of supplying or procuring for the Commission all information or documents which may be required.

ARTICLE 199.

The upkeep and cost of the Inter-Allied Commissions of Control and Organisation and the expenses incurred by their work shall be borne by Turkey.

ARTICLE 200.

The Military Inter-Allied Commission of Control and Organisation will be entrusted on the one hand with the supervision of the execution of the military clauses relating to the reduction of the Turkish forces within the authorised limits, the delivery of arms and war material prescribed in Chapter VI of Section I and the disarmament of the fortified regions prescribed in Chapters VII and VIII of that Section, and on the other hand with the organisation and the control of the employment of the new Turkish armed force.

(I) As the Military Inter-Allied Commission of Control it will be its special duty:

(a) To fix the number of customs officials, local urban and rural police, forest guards and other like officials which Turkey will be authorised to maintain in accordance with Article 170.

(b) To receive from the Turkish Government the notifications relating to the location of the stocks and depots of munitions, the armament of the fortified works, fortresses and forts, the situation of the works or factories for the production of arms, munitions and war material and their operations.

(c) To take delivery of the arms, munitions, war material and plant intended for manufacture of the same, to select the points where such delivery is to be effected, and to supervise the works of rendering things useless and of conversion provided for by the present Treaty.

(2) As the Military Inter-Allied Commission of Organisation it will be its special duty:

(a) To proceed, in collaboration with the Turkish Government, with the organisation of the Turkish armed force upon the basis laid down in Chapters I to IV, Section I of this Part, with the delimitation of the territorial regions provided for in Article 156, and with the distribution of the troops of gendarmerie and the special elements for reinforcement between the different territorial regions;

(b) To control the conditions for the employment, as laid down in Articles 156 and 157, of these troops of gendarmerie and these elements, and to decide what effect shall be given to requests of the Turkish Government for the provisional modification of the normal distribution of these forces determined in conformity with the said Articles;

(c) To determine the proportion by nationality of the Allied and neutral officers to be engaged to serve in the Turkish gendarmerie under the conditions laid down in Article 159, and to lay down the conditions under which they are to participate in the different duties provided for them in the said Article.

ARTICLE 201.

It will be the special duty of the Naval Inter-Allied Commission of Control to visit the building yards and to supervise the breaking-up of the ships, to take delivery of the arms, munitions and naval war material and to supervise their destruction and breaking up.

The Turkish Government must furnish to the Naval Inter-Allied Commission of Control all such information and documents as the latter may deem necessary to ensure the complete execution of the naval clauses, in particular the designs of the warships, the composition of their armaments, the details and models of the guns, munitions, torpedoes, mines, explosives, wireless telegraphic apparatus and in general everything relating to naval war material, as well as all legislative or administrative documents and regulations.

ARTICLE 202.

It will be the special duty of the Aeronautical Inter-Allied Commission of Control to make an inventory of the aeronautical material now in the hands of the Turkish Government, to inspect aeroplane, balloon and motor manufactures and factories producing arms, munitions and explosives capable of being used by aircraft, to visit all aerodromes, sheds, landing grounds, parks and depots on Turkish territory, to arrange, if necessary, for the removal of material and to take delivery of such material.

The Turkish Government must furnish to the Aeronautical Inter-Allied Commission of Control all such information and legislative, administrative or other documents as the Commission may consider necessary to ensure the complete execution of the air clauses, and in particular a list of the personnel belonging to all the Turkish air services and of the existing material as well as of that in process of manufacture or on order, and a complete list of all establishments working for aviation, of their positions, and of all sheds and landing grounds.

ARTICLE 203.

The Military, Naval and Aeronautical Inter-Allied Commissions of Control will appoint representatives who will be jointly responsible for controlling the execution of the operations provided for in paragraphs (1) and (2) of Article 178.

ARTICLE 204.

Pending the definitive settlement of the political status of the territories referred to in Article 89, the decisions of the Inter- Allied Commissions of Control and Organisation will be subject to any modifications which the said Commissions may consider necessary in consequence of such settlement.

ARTICLE 205.

The Naval and Aeronautical Inter-Allied Commissions of Control will cease to operate on the completion of the tasks assigned to them respectively by Articles 201 and 202.

The same will apply to the section of the Military Inter-Allied Commission entrusted with the functions of control prescribed in Article 200 (1).

The section of the said Commission entrusted with the organisation of the new Turkish armed force as provided in Article 200 (2) will operate for five years from the coming into force of the present Treaty. The Principal Allied Powers reserve the right to decide, at the end of this period, whether it is desirable to maintain or suppress this section of the said Commission.

SECTION V.
GENERAL PROVISIONS.

ARTICLE 206.

The following portions of the Armistice of October 30, 1918: Articles 7, 10, 12, 13 and 24 remain in force so far as they are not inconsistent with the provisions of the present Treaty.

ARTICLE 207.

Turkey undertakes from the coming into force of the present Treaty not to accredit to any foreign country any military, naval or air mission, and not to send or allow the departure of such mission; she undertakes, moreover, to take the necessary steps to prevent Turkish nationals from leaving her territory in order to enlist in the army, fleet or air service of any foreign Power, or to be attached thereto with the purpose of helping in its training, or generally to give any assistance to the military, naval or air instruction in a foreign country.

The Allied Powers undertake on their part that from the coming into force of the present Treaty they will neither enlist in their armies, fleets or air services nor attach to them any Turkish national with the object of helping in military training, or in general employ any Turkish national as a military, naval or air instructor. The present provision does not, however, affect the right of France to recruit for the Foreign Legion in accordance with French military laws and regulations.

PART VI.
PRISONERS OF WAR AND GRAVES.
SECTION I.
PRISONERS OF WAR.

[...ARTICLE 208.-217...]

SECTION II.
GRAVES.

[...ARTICLE 218.-225...]

PART VII.
PENALTIES.

ARTICLE 226.

The Turkish Government recognises the right of the Allied Powers to bring before military tribunals persons accused of having committed acts in violation of the laws and customs of war. Such persons shall, if found guilty, be sentenced to punishments laid down by law. This provision will apply notwithstanding any proceedings or prosecution before a tribunal in Turkey. or in the territory of her allies.

The Turkish Government shall hand over to the Allied Powers or to such one of them as shall so request all persons accused of having committed an act in violation of the laws and customs of war, who are specified either by name or by the rank, office or employment which they held under the Turkish authorities.

ARTICLE 227.

Persons guilty of criminal acts against the nationals of one of the Allied Powers shall be brought before the military tribunals of that Power.

Persons guilty of criminal acts against the nationals of more than one of the Allied Powers shall be brought

before military tribunals composed of members of the military tribunals of the Powers concerned.
In every case the accused shall be entitled to name his own counsel.

ARTICLE 228.

The Turkish Government undertakes to furnish all documents and information of every kind, the production of which may be considered necessary to ensure the full knowledge of the incriminating acts, the prosecution of offenders and the just appreciation of responsibility.

ARTICLE 229.

The provisions of Articles 226 to 228 apply similarly to the Governments of the States to which territory belonging to the former Turkish Empire has been or may be assigned, in so far as concerns persons accused of having committed acts contrary to the laws and customs of war who are in the territory or at the disposal of such States.

If the persons in question have acquired the nationality of one of the said States, the Government of such State undertakes to take, at the request of the Power concerned and in agreement with it, or upon the joint request of all the Allied Powers, all the measures necessary to ensure the prosecution and punishment of such persons.

ARTICLE 230.

The Turkish Government undertakes to hand over to the Allied Powers the persons whose surrender may be required by the latter as being responsible for the massacres committed during the continuance of the state of war on territory which formed part of the Turkish Empire on August 1, 1914.

The Allied Powers reserve to themselves the right to designate the tribunal which shall try the persons so accused, and the Turkish Government undertakes to recognise such tribunal.

In the event of the League of Nations having created in sufficient time a tribunal competent to deal with the said massacres, the Allied Powers reserve to themselves the right to bring the accused persons mentioned above before such tribunal, and the Turkish Government undertakes equally to recognise such tribunal.

The provisions of Article 228 apply to the cases dealt with in this Article.

PART VIII.
FINANCIAL CLAUSES.

ARTICLE 231.

Turkey recognises that by joining in the war of aggression which Germany and Austria-Hungary waged against the Allied Powers she has caused to the latter losses and sacrifices of all kinds for which she ought to make complete reparation.

On the other hand, the Allied Powers recognise that the resources of Turkey are not sufficient to enable her to make complete reparation.

In these circumstances, and inasmuch as the territorial rearrangements resulting from the present Treaty will leave to Turkey only a portion of the revenues of the former Turkish Empire, all claims against the Turkish Government for reparation are waived by the Allied Powers, subject only to the provisions of this Part and of Part IX (Economic Clauses) of the present Treaty.

The Allied Powers, desiring to afford some measure of relief and assistance to Turkey, agree with the Turkish Government that a Financial Commission shall be appointed consisting of one representative of each of the following Allied Powers who are specially interested, France, the British Empire and Italy, with whom there shall be associated a Turkish Commissioner in a consultative capacity. The powers and duties of this Commission are set forth in the following Articles.

ARTICLE 232.

The Financial Commission shall take such steps as in its judgment are best adapted to conserve and increase the resources of Turkey.

The Budget to be presented annually by the Minister of Finance to the Turkish Parliament shall be submitted, in the first instance, to the Financial Commission, and shall be presented to Parliament in the form approved by that Commission. No modification introduced by Parliament shall be operative without the approval of the Financial Commission.

The Financial Commission shall supervise the execution of the Budget and the financial laws and regulations of Turkey. This supervision shall be exercised through the medium of the Turkish Inspectorate of Finance, which shall be placed under the direct orders of the Financial Commission, and whose members will only be appointed with the approval of the Commission.

The Turkish Government undertakes to furnish to this Inspectorate all facilities necessary for the fulfilment of its task, and to take such action against unsuitable officials in the Financial Departments of the Government as the Financial Commission may suggest.

ARTICLE 233.

The Financial Commission shall, in addition, in agreement with the Council of the Ottoman Public Debt and the Imperial Ottoman Bank, undertake by such means as may be recognised to be opportune and equitable the regulation and improvement of the Turkish currency.

ARTICLE 234.

The Turkish Government undertakes not to contract any internal or external loan without the consent of the Financial Commission.

ARTICLE 235.

The Turkish Government engages to pay, in accordance with the provisions of the present Treaty, for all loss or damage, as defined in Article 236, suffered by civilian nationals of the Allied Powers, in respect of their persons or property, through the action or negligence of the Turkish authorities during the war and up to the coming into force of the present Treaty.

The Turkish Government will be bound to make to the European Commission of the Danube such restitutions, reparations and indemnities as may be fixed by the Financial Commission in respect of damages inflicted on the said European Commission of the Danube during the war.

ARTICLE 236.

All the resources of Turkey, except revenues conceded or hypothecated to the service of the Ottoman Public Debt (see Annex 1), shall be placed at the disposal of the Financial Commission, which shall employ them, as need arises, in the following manner:

(i) The first charge (after payment of the salaries and current expenses of the Financial Commission, and of the ordinary expenses of such Allied forces of occupation as may be maintained after the coming into force of the present Treaty in territories remaining Turkish) shall be the expenses of the Allied forces of occupation since October 30, 1918, in territory remaining Turkish, and the expenses of Allied forces of occupation in territories detached from Turkey in favour of a Power other than the Power which has borne the expenses of occupation. The amount of these expenses and of the annuities by which they shall be discharged will be determined by the Financial Commission, which will so arrange the annuities as to enable Turkey to meet any deficiency that may arise in the sums required to pay that part of the interest on the Ottoman Public Debt for which Turkey remains responsible in accordance with this Part.

(ii) The second charge shall be the indemnity which the Turkish Government is to pay, in accordance with Article 235, on account of the claims of the Allied Powers for loss or damage suffered in respect of their persons or property by their nationals, (other than those who were Turkish nationals on August 1, 1914) as defined in Article 317, Part IX (Economic Clauses), through the action or negligence of the Turkish authorities during the war, due regard being had to the financial condition of Turkey and the necessity for providing for the essential expenses of its administration. The Financial Commission shall adjudicate on and provide for payment of all claims in respect of personal damage. The claims in respect to property shall be investigated, determined and paid in accordance with Article 287, Part IX (Economic Clauses). The Financial Commission shall fix the annuity to be applied to the settlement of claims in respect of persons as well as in respect of property, should the funds at the disposal of the Allied Powers in accordance with the said Article 287, be insufficient to meet this charge, and shall determine the currency in which the annuity shall be paid.

ARTICLE 237

Any hypothecation of Turkish revenues effected during the war in respect of obligations (including the internal debt) contracted by the Turkish Government during the war is hereby annulled.

ARTICLE 238.

Turkey recognises the transfer to the Allied Powers of any claims to payment or repayment which Germany, Austria, Bulgaria or Hungary may have against her, in accordance with Article 261 of the Treaty of Peace concluded at Versailles on June 28, 1919, with Germany, and the corresponding Articles of the Treaties of Peace with Austria, Bulgaria and Hungary. The Allied Powers agree not to require from Turkey any payment in respect of claims so transferred.

ARTICLE 239.

No new concession shall be granted by the Turkish Government either to a Turkish subject or otherwise without the consent of the Financial Commission.

ARTICLE 240.

States in whose favour territory is detached from Turkey shall acquire without payment all property and possessions situated therein registered in the name of the Turkish Empire or of the Civil List.

ARTICLE 241.

States in whose favour territory has been detached from Turkey, either as a result of the Balkan Wars in 1913, or under the present Treaty, shall participate in the annual charge for the service of the Ottoman Public Debt contracted before November 1, 1914.

The Governments of the States of the Balkan Peninsula and the newly-created States in Asia in favour of whom such territory has been or is detached from Turkey shall give adequate guarantees for the payment of the share of the above annual charge allotted to them respectively.

ARTICLE 242.

For the purposes of this Part, the Ottoman Public Debt shall be deemed to consist of the Debt heretofore governed by the Decree of Mouharrem, together with such other loans as are enumerated in Annex I to this Part. Loans contracted before November 1, 1914, will be taken into account in the distribution of the Ottoman Public Debt between Turkey, the States of the Balkan Peninsula and the new States set up in Asia.

This distribution shall be effected in the following manner:

(1) Annuities arising from loans prior to October 17, 1912 (Balkan Wars), shall be distributed between Turkey and the Balkan States, including Albania, which receive or have received any Turkish territory.

(2) The residue of the annuities for which Turkey remains liable after this distribution, together with those arising from loans contracted by Turkey between October 17, 1912, and November 1, 1914, shall be distributed between Turkey and the States in whose favour territory is detached from Turkey under the present Treaty.

ARTICLE 243.

The general principle to be adopted in determining the amount of the annuity to be paid by each State will be as follows:

The amount shall bear the same ratio to the total required for the service of the Debt as the average revenue of the transferred territory bore to the average revenue of the whole of Turkey (including in each case the yield of the Customs surtax imposed in the year 1907) over the three financial years 1909-10, 1910-11, and 1911-12.

ARTICLE 244.

The Financial Commission shall, as soon as possible after the coming into force of the present Treaty, determine in accordance with the principle laid down in Article 243 the amount of the annuities referred to in that Article, and communicate its decisions in this respect to the High Contracting Parties.

The Financial Commission shall fulfil the functions provided for in Article 134 of the Treaty of Peace concluded with Bulgaria on November 27, 1919.

ARTICLE 245.

The annuities assessed in the manner above provided will be payable as from the date of the coming into force of the Treaties by which the respective territories were detached from Turkey, and, in the case of territories detached under the present Treaty from March 1, 1920; they shall continue to be payable (except as provided by Article 252) until the final liquidation of the Debt. They shall, however, be proportionately reduced as the loans constituting the Debt are successively extinguished.

ARTICLE 246.

The Turkish Government transfers to the Financial Commission all its rights under the provisions of the Decree of Mouharrem and subsequent Decrees.

The Council of the Ottoman Public Debt shall consist of the British, French and Italian delegates, and of the representative of the Imperial Ottoman Bank, and shall continue to operate as heretofore. It shall administer and levy all revenues conceded to it under the Decree of Mouharrem and all other revenues the management of which has been entrusted to it in accordance with any other loan contracts previous to November 1, 1914.

The Allied Powers authorise the Council to give administrative assistance to the Turkish Ministry of Finance, under such conditions as may be determined by the Financial Commission with the object of realising as far as possible the following programme:

The system of direct levy of certain revenues by the existing Administration of the Ottoman Public Debt shall, within limits to be prescribed by the Financial Commission, be extended as widely as possible and applied throughout the provinces remaining Turkish. On each new creation of revenue or of indirect taxes approved by the Financial Commission, the Commission shall consider the possibility of entrusting the administration thereof to the Council of the Debt for the account of the Turkish Government.

The administration of the Customs shall be under a Director-General appointed by and revocable by the Financial Commission and answerable to it. No change in the schedule of the Customs charges shall be made except with the approval of the Financial Commission.

The Governments of France, Great Britain and Italy will decide, by a majority and after consulting the bondholders whether the Council should be maintained or replaced by the Financial Commission or the expiry of the present term of the Council. The decision of the Governments shall be taken at least six months before the date corresponding to the expiry of this period.

ARTICLE 247.
The Commission has authority to propose, at a later date, the substitution for the pledges at present granted to bondholders, in accordance with their contracts or existing decrees, of other adequate pledges, or of a charge on the general revenues of Turkey. The Allied Governments undertake to consider any proposals the Financial Commission might then have to make on this subject.

ARTICLE 248.
All property, movable and immovable, belonging to the Administration of the Ottoman Public Debt, wherever situate, shall remain integrally at the disposal of that body.

The Council of the Debt shall have power to apply the value of any realised property for the purpose of extraordinary amortisation either of the Unified Debt or of the Lots Turcs.

ARTICLE 249.
The Turkish Government agrees to transfer to the Financial Commission all its rights in the Reserve Funds and the Tripoli Indemnity Fund.

ARTICLE 250.
A sum equal to the arrears of any revenues heretofore affected to the service of the Ottoman Public Debt within the territories remaining Turkish, which should have been but have not been paid to the Council of the Debt, shall (except where such territories have been in the military occupation of Allied forces and for the time of such occupation) be paid to the Council of the Debt by the Turkish Government as soon as in the opinion of the Financial Commission the financial condition of Turkey shall permit.

ARTICLE 251.
The Council of the Debt shall review all the transactions of the Council which have taken place during the war. Any disbursements made by the Council which were not in accordance with its powers and duties, as defined by the Decree of Mouharrem or otherwise before the war, shall be reimbursed to the Council of the Debt by the Turkish Government so soon as in the opinion of the Financial Commission such payment is possible. The Council shall have power to review any action on the part of the Council during the war, and to annul any obligation which in its opinion is prejudicial to the interests of the bondholders, and which was not in accordance with the powers of the Council of the Debt.

ARTICLE 252.
Any of the States which under the present Treaty are to contribute to the annual charge for the service of the Ottoman Public Debt may, upon giving six months' notice to the Council of the Debt, redeem such obligation by payment of a sum representing the value of such annuity capitalised at such rate of interest as may be agreed between the State concerned and the Council of the Debt. The Council of the Debt shall not have power to require such redemption.

ARTICLE 253.
The sums in gold to be transferred by Germany and Austria under the provisions of Article 259 (1), (2), (4) and (7) of the Treaty of Peace with Germany, and under Article 210 (1) of the Treaty of Peace with Austria, shall be placed at the disposal of the Financial Commission.

ARTICLE 254.
The sums to be transferred by Germany in accordance with Article 259 (3) of the Treaty of Peace with Germany shall be placed forthwith at the disposal of the Council of the Debt.

ARTICLE 255.
The Turkish Government undertakes to accept any decision that may be taken by the Allied Powers, in agreement when necessary with other Powers, regarding the funds of the Ottoman Sanitary Administration and the former Superior Council of Health, and in respect of the claim of the Superior Council of Health against the Turkish Government, as well as regarding the funds of the Lifeboat Service of the Black Sea and Bosphorus.

The Allied Powers hereby give authority to the Financial Commission to represent them in this matter.

ARTICLE 256.
The Turkish Government, in agreement with the Allied Powers, hereby releases the German Government from the obligation incurred by it during the war to accept Turkish Government currency notes at a specified rate of exchange in payment for goods to be exported to Turkey from Germany after the war.

ARTICLE 257.
As soon as the claims of the Allied Powers against the Turkish Government as laid down in this Part have been satisfied, and Ottoman pre-war Public Debt has been liquidated, the Financial Commission shall determine. The Turkish Government shall then consider in consultation with the Council of the League of Nations whether any

further administrative advice and assistance should in the interests of Turkey be provided for the Turkish Government by the Powers, Members of the League of Nations, and, if so, in what form such advice and assistance shall be given.

ARTICLE 258.

(1) Turkey will deliver, in a seaworthy condition and in such ports of the Allied Powers as the Governments of the said Powers may determine all German ships transferred to the Turkish flag since August 1, 1914; these ships will be handed over to the Reparation Commission referred to in Article 233 of the Treaty of Peace with Germany, any transfer to a neutral flag during the war being regarded in this respect as void so far as concerns the Allied Powers.

(2) The Turkish Government will hand over at the same time as the ships referred to in paragraph (1) all papers and documents which the Reparation Commission referred to in the said paragraph may think necessary in order to ensure the complete transfer of the property in the vessels, free and quit of all liens, mortgages, encumbrances, charges or claims, whatever their nature.

The Turkish Government will effect any re-purchase or indemnisation which may be necessary. It will be the party responsible in the event of any proceedings for the recovery of, or in any claims against, the vessel to be handed over whatever their nature, the Turkish Government being bound in every case to guarantee the Reparation Commission referred to in paragraph (1) against any ejectment or proceedings upon any ground whatever arising under this head.

ARTICLE 259.

Without prejudice to Article 277, Part IX (Economic Clauses) of the present Treaty, Turkey renounces, so far as she is concerned, the benefit of any provisons of the Treaties of Brest-Litovsk and Bucharest or of the Treaties supplementary thereto.

Turkey undertakes to transfer either to Roumania or to the Principal Allied Powers, as the case may be, all monetary instruments, specie, securities and negotiable instruments or goods which she has received under the aforesaid Treaties.

ARTICLE 260.

The legislative measures required in order to give effect to the provisions of this Part will be enacted by the Turkish Government and by the Powers concerned within a period which must not exceed six months from the signature of the present Treaty.

ANNEX I:
THE OTTOMAN PRE-WAR PUBLIC DEBT. (NOVEMBER 5, 1914)
£. T. gold.

Loan	Date of Contract	Interest	Sinking Fund	Original Nominal Capital	Capital outstanding on November 5, 1914[310]	Annuity required for service (including commission).	Period of Amortisation	Bank of Issue.
1	2	3	4	5	6	7	8	9
		Per cent.	Per cent.	£. T. gold.	£. T. gold.	£. T. gold.		
Unified Debt	1903	4	.4644	42,275,772	36,799,840	1,887,375	--	--
Lots Turcs	1870	--	--	15,632,548	10,666,975	270,000	--	--
Osmanié	18/30 April 1890	4	1	4,999,500	2,952,400	249,975	1931	Imperial Ottoman Bank
5 per cent. 1896	29 Feb./12 Mar. 1893	5	.50	3,272,720	2,814,020	180,450	1946	Imperial Ottoman Bank
4 per cent. 1903 Fisheries	3 Oct. 1888 21 Feb-/6 Mar. 1903	4	.50	2,640,000	2,439,228	119,097	1958	Deutsche Bank
Bagdad, Series 1	20 Feb./5 Mar. 1903	4	.87538	2,376,000	2,342,252	97,120	2001	Deutsche Bank
4 per cent. 1904	4/17 Sept. 1903	4	.50	2,750,000	2,594,064	124,059	1960	Imperial Ottoman Bank

---

[310] The figures of the capital outstanding on Nov. 5, 1914, will be replaced at the date of the coming into force of the present Treaty by the figures of the capital remaining outstanding at the date.

4 per cent 1901-5	21 Nov./4 Dec. 1901; 6/19. Nov. 1903; -25 April 8 May 1905	4	.50	5,306,664	4,976,422	239,397	1961	Imperial Ottoman Bank
Tedjhizat-Askerié	4/17 April 1905	4	.50	2,640,000	2,441,340	119,097	1961	Deutsche Bank
Bagdad, Series II	20 May/ 2 June 1908	4	.87538	4,752,000	4,718,120	200,500	2006	Deutsche Bank
Bagdad Series III	20 May /3 June 1908	4	.87538	5,236,000	5,221,700	220,550	2010	Deutsche Bank
4 per cent. 1908	6/19 Sept. 1908	4	.50	4,711,124	4,538,908	212,000	1965	Imperial Ottoman Bank
5 per cent. 1914	13/26 April 1914	5	.50	22,000,000	22,000,000	1,213,025	--	Imperial Ottoman Bank
Docks, Arsenals and Naval Construction	1913	5 ½	1 ½	1,485,00	1,485,00	88,550	1943	National Bank of Turkey
Tombac Priority	26 April /8 May 1893	4	1	1,000,000	664,510	50,250	1934	Imperial Ottoman Bank
Forty millions of francs (Oriental Railways)	1/13 March 1894	4	.35	1,760,000	1,564,192	76,751	1957	Deutsche Bank and its group, including the International Bank
Customs 1902	17/29 May 1886; 28 Sept./11 Oct. 1902	4	.50	8,600,020	7,923,234	387,976	1958	Imperial Ottoman Bank
4 per cent. 1909	30 Sept. /13 Oct. 1999	4	1	7,000,004	6,550,698	350,864	1950	Imperial Ottoman Bank
City of Constantinople Municipal 1909	3/16 Nov. 1909	5	0.50	1,100,00	1,073,490	60,651	1958	National Bank of Turkey
City of Constantinople Municipal 1913	1913	5	0.50	1,100,00	1,094,500	60,500		Banque Périer of Cie
Hodeîda-Sanaa 1911	24 Feb./9 Mar. 1911	4	.098738	1,100,010	1,000,010	40,988	2006	Banque française
Soma – Panderma 1910	20 Nov. /3 Dec. 1910	4	.16715	1,712,304	1,700,644	71,532	1992	Imperial Ottoman Bank
4 per cent. Customs 1911	27 Oct. /9 Nov. 1910	4	1	7,040,000	6,699,880	352,440	1952	Deutsche Bank
City of Bagdad Municipal	1912	6	14.285	33,000	26,070	6,000	--	National Bank of Turkey
Treasury Bonds of the Imperial Ottoman Bank 1912	1912	6	33.333	2,724,893	1,063,664	1,000,003	1915	Imperial Ottoman Bank
Treasury Bonds, Périer and Co.	1913	5	.20	4,400,000	4,400,000[311]	1,100,000	1918	Banque Périer et Cie
Treasury Bonds, 5 per cent. 1911 (purchase of warships)	1911	5	"	1,778,587	1,778,587	125,058	--	National Bank of Turkey
Advance by the Tobacco Régie	....	"	"	1,700,00	890,039	110,000	--	--
Plain of Koniah irrigation	....			818,970	818,970	50,006	1932	Deutsche Bank (Anatolian Railway Co).
Total	....	....	....	161,854,116	143,241,757			

NOTE EXPLANATORY OF ANNEX I.

The figures in columns 5, 6 and 7 are £. T. gold.
Turkey now possesses a paper currency in place of pre-war gold currency. At present rates of exchange the £. T. paper no longer represents the pre-war ratio of the £. T. gold to the currency in which the loans were subscribed, and in which the interest and the amortization payments have to be paid in Europa according to the contract terms of the loans. (*See* Article I of the "Décret-

---

[311] A sum of £. T. 833,147 has been realised upon the security for these Bonds.

Annexe" of September, 1903, and Loan Contracts, *passim*.)
The definition of £. T. gold in these columns does not signify that the provisions for the coupons and sinking funds are to be made in gold, but that the figure in £. T. has to be calculated according to such rate of exchange as will enable the bondholder to be paid in the currency to which he is entitled.

ANNEX II.

1. The Commission shall establish its own rules and procedure.

The Chairmanship shall be held annually by the French, British and Italian Delegates in turn.

Each member shall have the right to nominate a deputy to act for him in his absence.

Decisions shall be taken by the vote of the majority. Abstention from voting will be treated as a vote against the proposal under discussion.

The Commission shall appoint such agents and employees as it may deem necessary for its work, with such emoluments and conditions of service as it may think fit.

The costs and expenses of the Commission shall be paid by Turkey, in conformity with the provisions of Article 236 (i.).

The salaries of the members of the Commission, as well as those of its officials, shall be fixed on a reasonable scale by agreement from time to time between the Governments represented on the Commission.

The members of the Commission shall enjoy the same rights and immunities as are enjoyed in Turkey by duly accredited diplomatic agents of friendly Powers.

2. Turkey undertakes to grant to the members, officials and agents of the Commission full powers to visit and inspect at all reasonable times any place, public works, or undertakings in Turkey, and to furnish to the said Commission all records, documents and information which it may require.

3. The Commission shall be entitled to assume, in agreement with the Turkish Government and independently of any default of the latter in fulfilling its obligations, the control, management and collection of all indirect taxes.

4. No member of the Commission shall be responsible, except to the Government appointing him, for any action or omission in the performance of his duties. No one of the Allied Governments assumes any responsibility in respect of any other Government.

5. The Commission shall publish annually detailed reports on its work, its methods and its proposals for the financial reorganisation of Turkey, as well as regarding its accounts for the period.

6. The Commission shall also take over any other duties which may be assigned to it under the present Treaty or with the assent of the Turkish Government.

PART IX.
ECONOMIC CLAUSES.
SECTION I.
COMMERCIAL RELATIONS.

ARTICLE 261.

The capitulatory regime resulting from treaties, conventions or usage shall be re-established in favour of the Allied Powers which directly or indirectly enjoyed the benefit thereof before August 1, 1914, and shall be extended to the Allied Powers which did not enjoy the benefit thereof on that date.

ARTICLE 262.

The Allied Powers who had post-offices in the former Turkish Empire before August 1, 1914, will be entitled to re-establish post-offices in Turkey.

ARTICLE 263.

The Convention of April 25, 1907, so far as it relates to the rate of import duties in Turkey, shall be re-established in force in favour of all the Allied Powers.

Nevertheless the Financial Commission established in accordance with Article 231, Part VIII (Financial Clauses) of the present Treaty may at any time authorise a modification of these import duties, or the imposition of consumption duties, provided that any duties so modified or imposed shall be applied equally to goods of whatever ownership or origin.

No modification of existing duties or imposition of new duties authorised by the Financial Commission by virtue of this Article shall take effect until after a period of six months from its notification to all the Allied Powers. During this period the Commission shall consider any observations relative thereto which may be formulated by any Allied Power.

ARTICLE 264.

Subject to any rights and exemptions resulting from concession contracts made before August 1, 1914, the Financial Commission shall be entitled to authorise the application by Turkey, in the conditions of equality laid down in Article 263, to the persons or property of the nationals of the Allied Powers of any taxes or duties which shall similarly be imposed on Turkish subjects in the interests of the economic stability and good government of Turkey.

The Financial Commission shall also be entitled to authorise the application, in the same interests and in the same conditions to the nationals of the Allied Powers of any prohibitions on import or export.

No such tax, duty or prohibition shall take effect until after a period of six months from its notification to all the Allied Powers. During this period the Commission shall consider any observations relative thereto that may be formulated by any Allied Power.

ARTICLE 265.

In the case of vessels of the Allied Powers all classes of certificates or documents relating to the vessel which were recognised as valid by Turkey before the war, or which may hereafter be recognised as valid by the principal maritime States, shall be recognised by Turkey as valid and as equivalent to the corresponding certificates issued to Turkish vessels.

A similar recognition shall be accorded to the certificates and documents issued to their vessels by the Governments of new States, whether they have a sea-coast or not, provided that such certificates and documents shall be issued in conformity with the general practice observed in the principal maritime States.

The High Contracting Parties agree to recognise the flag flown by the vessels of an Allied Power or a new State having no sea-coast which are registered at some one specified place situated in its territory; such place shall serve as the port of registry of such vessels.

ARTICLE 266.

Turkey undertakes to adopt all the necessary legislative and administrative measures to protect goods the produce or manufacture of any one of the Allied Powers or new States from all forms of unfair competition in commercial transactions.

Turkey undertakes to prohibit and repress by seizure and by other appropriate remedies the importation, exportation, manufacture, distribution, sale or offering for sale in her territory of all goods bearing upon themselves or their usual get-up or wrappings any marks, names, devices or descriptions whatsoever which are calculated to convey directly or indirectly a false indication of the origin, type, nature or special characteristics of such goods.

ARTICLE 267.

Turkey undertakes, on condition that reciprocity is accorded in these matters, to respect any law, or any administrative or judicial decision given in conformity with such law, in force in any Allied State or new State and duly communicated to her by the proper authorities, defining or regulating the right to any regional appellation in respect of wine or spirits produced in the State to which the region belongs, or the conditions under which the use of any such appellation may be permitted; and the importation, exportation, manufacture, distribution, sale or offering for sale of products or articles bearing regional appellations inconsistent with such law or order shall be prohibited by Turkey and repressed by the measures prescribed in Article 266.

ARTICLE 268.

If the Turkish Government engages in international trade, it shall not in respect thereof have or be deemed to have any rights, privileges or immunities of sovereignty.

SECTION II.
TREATIES.

[...ARTICLE 269. – 281...]

SECTION III.
INDUSTRIAL PROPERTY.

ARTICLE 281.

Subject to the stipulations of the present Treaty, rights of industrial, literary and artistic property, as such property is defined by the International Conventions of Paris and of Berne mentioned in Article 272, shall be re-established or restored, as from the coming into force of the present Treaty, in the territories of the High Contracting Parties, in favour of the persons entitled to the benefit of them at the moment when the state of war commenced, or their legal representatives. Equally, rights which, except for the war, would have been acquired during the war in consequence of an application made for the protection of industrial property, or the publication of a literary or artistic work, shall be recognised and established in favour of those persons who would have been entitled thereto, from the coming into force of the present Treaty.

Nevertheless, all acts done by virtue of the special measures taken during the war under legislative, executive or administrative authority of any Allied Power in regard to the rights of Turkish nationals in industrial, literary or artistic property shall remain in force and shall continue to maintain their full effect.

No claim shall be made or action brought by Turkey or Turkish nationals in respect of the use during the war by the Government of any Allied Power, or by any person acting on behalf or with the assent of such Government, of any rights in industrial, literary or artistic property, nor in respect of the sale, offering for sale or use of any products, articles or apparatus whatsoever to which such rights applied.

Unless the legislation of any one of the Allied Powers in force at the moment of the signature of the present Treaty otherwise directs, sums due or paid in virtue of any act or operation resulting from the execution of the special measures mentioned in the second paragraph of this Article shall be dealt with in the same way as other sums due to Turkish nationals are directed to be dealt with by the present Treaty; and sums produced by any special measures taken by the Turkish Government in respect of rights in industrial, literary or artistic property belonging to the nationals of the Allied Powers shall be considered and treated in the same way as other debts due from Turkish nationals.

Each of the Allied Powers reserves to itself the right to impose such limitations, conditions or restrictions on rights of industrial literary or artistic property (with the exception of trade-marks) acquired before or during the war, or which may be subsequently acquired in accordance with its legislation, by Turkish nationals whether by granting licences, or by the working, or by preserving control over their exploitation, or in any other way, as may be considered necessary for national defence, or in the public interest or for assuring the fair treatment by Turkey of the rights of industrial, literary and artistic property held in Turkish territory by its nationals, or for securing the due fulfilment of all the obligations undertaken by Turkey in the present Treaty. As regards rights of industrial, literary and artistic property acquired after the coming into force of the present Treaty, the right so reserved by the Allied Powers shall only be exercised in cases where these limitations, conditions or restrictions may be considered necessary for national defence or in the public interest.

In the event of the application of the provisions of the preceding paragraph by any Allied Power, there shall be paid reasonable indemnities or royalties, which shall be dealt with in the same way as other sums due to Turkish nationals are directed to be dealt with by the present Treaty.

Each of the Allied Powers reserves the right to treat as void and of no effect any transfer in whole or in part of or other dealing with rights of or in respect of industrial, literary or artistic property effected after August 1, 1914, or in the future, which would have the result of defeating the objects of the provisions of this Article.

The provisions of this Article shall not apply to rights in industrial, literary or artistic property which have been dealt with in the liquidation of businesses or companies under war legislation by the Allied Powers, or which may be so dealt with by virtue of Article 289.

ARTICLE 282

A minimum of one year after the coming into force of the present Treaty shall be accorded to the nationals of the High Contracting Parties, without extension fees or other penalty, in order to enable such persons to accomplish any act, fulfil any formality, pay any fees, and generally satisfy any obligation prescribed by the laws or regulations of the respective States relating to the obtaining, preserving or opposing rights to, or in respect of, industrial property either acquired before August 1, 1914, or which, except for the war, might have been acquired since that date as a result of an application made before the war or during its continuance.

All rights in, or in respect of, such property which may have lapsed by reason of any failure to accomplish any act, fulfil any formality, or make any payment shall revive, but subject in the case of patents and designs to the imposition of such conditions as each Allied Power may deem reasonably necessary for the protection of persons who have manufactured or made use of the subject-matter of such property while the rights had lapsed. Furhter, where rights to patents or designs belonging to Turkish nationals are revived under this Article, they shall be subject in respect of the grant of licences to the same provisions as would have been applicable to them during the war, as well as to all the provisions of the present Treaty.

The period from August 1, 1914, until the coming into force of the present Treaty shall be excluded in considering the time within which a patent should be worked or a trade-mark or design used, and it is further agreed that no patent, registered trade-mark or design in force on August 1, 1914, shall be subject to revocation or cancellation by reason only of the failure to work such patent or use such trade-mark or design for two years after the coming into force of the present Treaty.

ARTICLE 283.

No action shall be brought and no claim made by persons residing or carrying on business within the territories of Turkey on the one part and of the Allied Powers on the other, or persons who are nationals of such Powers respectively, or by any one deriving title during the war from such persons, by reason of any action which has taken place within the territory of the other party between the date of the existence of a state of war and that of the coming into force of the present Treaty, which might constitute an infringement of the rights of industrial property or rights of literary and artistic property, either existing at any time during the war or revived under the provisions of Article 282.

Equally, no action for infringement of industrial, literary or artistic property rights by such persons shall at any time be permissible in respect of the sale or offering for sale for a period of one year after the signature of the present Treaty in the territories of the Allied Powers on the one hand, or Turkey on the other, of products or articles manufactured, or of literary or artistic works published, during the period between the existence of a state of war and the signature of the present Treaty, or against those who have acquired and continue to use them. It is understood, nevertheless, that this provision shall not apply when the possessor of the rights was domiciled or had an industrial or commercial establishment in the districts occupied by Turkey during the war.

ARTICLE 284.

Licences in respect of industrial, literary or artistic property concluded before the war between nationals of the Allied Powers or persons residing in their territory or carrying on business therein on the one part, and Turkish nationals on the other part shall be considered as cancelled as from the date of the existence of a state of war between Turkey and the Allied Power. But in any case the former beneficiary of a contract of this kind shall have the right, within a period of six months after the coming into force of the present Treaty, to demand from the proprietor of the rights the grant of a new licence, the conditions of which in default of agreement between the parties, shall be fixed by the duly qualified tribunal in the country under whose legislation the rights had been acquired, except in the case of licences held in respect of rights acquired under Turkish law. In such cases the conditions shall be fixed by the Arbitral Commission referred to in Article 287. The tribunal or the Commission may, if necessary, fix also the amount which it may deem just should be paid by reason of the use of the rights during the war.

No licence in respect of industrial, literary or artistic property granted under the special war legislation of any Allied Power shall be affected by the continued existence of any licence entered into before the war, but shall remain valid and of full effect, and a licence so granted to the former beneficiary of a licence entered into before the war shall be considered as substituted for such licence.

Where sums have been paid during the war by virtue of a licence or agreement concluded before the war in respect of rights of industrial property or for the reproduction or the representation of literary, dramatic or artistic works, these sums shall be dealt with in the same manner as other debts or credits of Turkish nationals as provided by the present Treaty.

ARTICLE 285.

The inhabitants of territories detached from Turkey under the present Treaty shall, notwithstanding this transfer and the change of nationality consequent thereon, continue to enjoy in Turkey all the rights in industrial, literary and artistic property to which they were entitled under Turkish legislation at the time of the transfer.

Rights of industrial, literary and artistic property which are in force in the territories detached from Turkey under the present Treaty at the moment of the transfer, or which will be re-established or restored in accordance with the provisions of Article 281, shall be recognised by the State to which the said territory is transferred, and shall remain in force in that territory for the same period of time given them under the Turkish law.

ARTICLE 286.

A special convention shall determine all questions relative to the records, registers and copies in connection with the protection of industrial, literary or artistic property, and fix their eventual transmission or communication by the Turkish offices to the offices of the States in favour of which territory is detached from Turkey.

SECTION IV.
PROPERTY, RIGHTS AND INTERESTS.

ARTICLE 287.

The property, rights and interests situated in territory which was under Turkish sovereignty on August 1, 1914, and belonging to nationals of Allied Powers who were not during the war Turkish nationals, or of companies controlled by them, shall be immediately restored to their owners free of all taxes levied by or under the authority of the Turkish Government or authorities, except such as would have been leviable in accordance with the capitulations. Where property has been confiscated during the war or sequestrated in such a way that its owners enjoyed no benefit therefrom, it shall be restored free of all taxes whatever.

The Turkish Government shall take such steps as may be within its power to restore the owner to the possession of his property free from all encumbrances or burdens with which it may have been charged without his assent. It shall indemnify all third parties injured by the restitution.

If the restitution provided for in this Article cannot be effected, or if the property, rights or interests have been damaged or injured, whether they have been seized or not, the owner shall be entitled to compensation. Claims made in this respect by the nationals of Allied Powers or by companies controlled by them shall be investigated and the total of the compensation shall be determined by an Arbitral Commission to be appointed by the Council of the League of Nations. This compensation shall be borne by the Turkish Government and may be charged upon the property of Turkish nationals within the territory or under the control of the claimant's State. So far as it is not met from this source it shall be satisfied out of the annuity referred to in Article 236 (ii), Part VIII.

(Financial Clauses) of the present Treaty.

The above provision shall not impose any obligation on the Turkish Government to pay compensation for damage to property, rights and interests effected since October 30, 1918, in territory in the effective occupation of the Allied Powers and detached from Turkey by the present Treaty. Compensation for any actual damage to such property, rights and interests inflicted by the occupying authorities since the above date shall be a charge on the Allied authorities responsible.

ARTICLE 288.

The property, rights and interests in Turkey of former Turkish nationals who acquire *ipso facto* the nationality of an Allied Power or of a new State in accordance with the provisions of the present Treaty, or any further Treaty regulating the disposal of territories detached from Turkey, shall be restored to them in their actual condition.

ARTICLE 289.

Subject to any contrary stipulations which may be provided in the present Treaty, the Allied Powers reserve the right to retain and liquidate all property, rights and interests of Turkish nationals, or companies controlled by them, within their territories, colonies, possessions and protectorates, excluding any territory under Turkish sovereignty on October 17, 1912.

The liquidation shall be carried out in accordance with the laws of the Allied Power concerned, and the Turkish owner shall not be able to dispose of such property, rights, or interests, or to subject them to any charge, without the consent of that Power.

ARTICLE 290.

Turkish nationals who acquire ipso facto the nationality of an Allied Power or of a new State in accordance with the provisions of the present Treaty, or any further Treaty regulating the disposal of territories detached from Turkey, will not be considered as Turkish nationals within the meaning of the fifth paragraph of Article 281, Articles 282, 284, the third paragraph of Article 287, Articles 289, 291, 292, 293, 301, 302, and 308.

ARTICLE 291.

All property, rights and interests of Turkish nationals within the territory of any Allied Power, excluding any territory under Turkish sovereignty on October 17, 1912, and the net proceeds of their sale, liquidation or other dealing therewith may be charged by that Allied Power with payment of amounts due in respect of claims by the nationals of that Allied Power under Article 287 or in respect of debts owing to them by Turkish nationals.

The proceeds of the liquidation of such property, rights and interests not used as provided in Article 289 and the first paragraph of this Article shall be paid to the Financial Commission to be employed in accordance with the provisions of Article 236 (ii), Part VIII (Financial Clauses) of the present Treaty.

ARTICLE 292.

The Turkish Government undertakes to compensate its nationals in respect of the sale or retention of their property, rights or interests in Allied countries.

ARTICLE 293

The Governments of an Allied Power or new State exercising authority in territory detached from Turkey in accordance with the present Treaty or any other Treaty concluded since October 17, 1912, may liquidate the property, rights and interests of Turkish companies or companies controlled by Turkish nationals in such territory; the proceeds of the liquidation shall be paid direct to the company.

This Article shall not apply to companies in which Allied nationals, including those of the territories placed under mandate, had on August 1, 1914, a preponderant interest.

The provisions of the first paragraph of this Article relating to the payment of the proceeds of liquidation do not apply in the case of railway undertakings where the owner is a Turkish company in which the majority of the capital or the control is held by German, Austrian, Hungarian or Bulgarian nationals either directly or through their interests in a company controlled by them, or was so held on August 1, 1914. In such case the proceeds of the liquidation shall be paid to the Financial Commission.

ARTICLE 294.

The Turkish Government shall, on the demand of the Principal Allied Powers, take over the undertaking, property, rights and interests of any Turkish company holding a railway concession in Turkish territory as it results from the present Treaty, and shall transfer in accordance with the advice of the Financial Commission the said undertaking, property, rights and interests, together with any interest which it may hold in the line or in the undertaking, at a price to be fixed by an arbitrator nominated by the Council of the League of Nations. The amount of this price shall be paid to the Financial Commission and shall be distributed by it, together with any amount received in accordance with Article 293, among the persons directly or indirectly interested in the company, the proportion attributable to the interests of nationals of Germany, Austria, Hungary or Bulgaria being paid to the Reparation Commission established under the Treaties of Peace with Germany, Austria, Hungary and Bulgaria respectively; the proportion of the price attributable to the Turkish Government shall be retained by the Financial Commission for the purposes referred to in Article 236, Part VIII (Financial Clauses) of the present Treaty.

ARTICLE 295.

Until the expiration of a period of six months from the coming into force of the present Treaty, the Turkish Government will effectively prohibit all dealings with the property, rights and interests within its territory which belong, at the date of the coming into force of the present Treaty, to Germany, Austria, Hungary, Bulgaria or their nationals, except in so far as may be necessary for the carrying into effect of the provisions of Article 260 of the Treaty of Peace with Germany or any corresponding provisions in the Treaties of Peace with Austria, Hungary or Bulgaria.

Subject to any special stipulations in the present Treaty affecting property of the said States, the Turkish Government will proceed to liquidate any of the property, rights or interests above referred to which may be notified to it within the said period of six months by the Principal Allied Powers. The said liquidation shall be effected under the direction of the said Powers and in the manner indicated by them. The prohibition of dealings with such property shall be maintained until the liquidation is completed.

The proceeds of liquidation shall be paid direct to the owners, except where the property so liquidated belongs to the German, Austrian, Hungarian or Bulgarian States, in which event the proceeds shall be handed over to the Reparation Commission established under the Treaty of Peace with the State to which the property belonged.

ARTICLE 296.

The Governments exercising authority in territory detached from Turkey in accordance with the present Treaty may liquidate any property, rights and interests within such territory which belong at the date of the coming into force of the present Treaty to Germany, Austria, Hungary, Bulgaria or their nationals, unless they have been dealt with under the provisions of Article 260 of the Treaty of Peace with Germany or any corresponding provisions in the Treaties of Peace with Austria, Hungary or Bulgaria.

The proceeds of liquidation shall be disposed of in the manner provided in Article 295.

ARTICLE 297.

If on the application of the owner the Arbitral Commission provided for in Article 287 is satisfied that the conditions of sale of any property liquidated in virtue of Articles 293, 295 or 296, or measures taken outside its general legislation by the Government exercising authority in the territory in which the property was situated, were unfairly prejudicial to the price obtained, the Commission shall have discretion to award to the owner equitable compensation to be paid by that Government.

ARTICLE 298.

The validity of vesting orders and of orders for the winding-up of businesses or companies and of any other orders, directions decisions or instructions of any court or any department of the Government of any of the Allied Powers made or given, or purporting to be made or given, in pursuance of war legislation with regard to enemy property, rights and interests in their territories is confirmed.

The interests of all persons shall be regarded as having been effectively dealt with by any order, direction, decision or instruction dealing with such property in which they may be interested, whether or not such interests are specifically mentioned in the order, direction, decision or instruction.

No question shall be raised as to the regularity of a transfer of any property, rights or interests dealt with in pursuance of any such order, direction, decision or instruction.

Every action taken with regard to any property, business or company in the territories of the Allied Powers, whether as regards its investigation, sequestration, compulsory administration, use, requisition, supervision or winding-up, the sale or management of property, rights or interests, the collection or discharge of debts, the payment of costs, charges or expenses, or any other matter whatsoever in pursuance of orders, directions, decisions or instructions of any court or of any department of the Government of any of the Allied Powers, made or given, or purporting to be made or given, in pursuance of war legislation with regard to enemy property, rights or interests, is confirmed.

ARTICLE 299.

The validity of any measures taken between October 30, 1918, and the coming into force of the present Treaty by or under the authority of one or more of the Allied Powers in regard to the property, rights and interests in Turkish territory of Germany, Austria, Hungary or Bulgaria or their nationals is confirmed.

Any balance remaining under the control of the Allied Powers as the result of such measures shall be disposed of in the manner provided in the last paragraph of Article 295.

ARTICLE 300.

No claim or action shall be made or brought against any Allied Power or against any person acting on behalf of or under the direction of any legal authority or department of the Government of such a Power by Turkey or by or on behalf of any person wherever resident who on August 1, 1914, was a Turkish national, or who became such after that date, in respect of any act or omission with regard to the property, rights or interests of Turkish nationals during the war or in preparation for the war.

Similarly, no claim or action shall be made or brought against any person in respect of any act or omission under or in accordance with the exceptional war measures, laws or regulations of any Allied Power.

ARTICLE 301.

The Turkish Government, if required, will, within six months from the coming into force of the present Treaty, deliver to each Allied Power any securities, certificates, deeds or documents of title held by its nationals and relating to property, rights or interests which are subject to liquidation in accordance with the provisions of the present Treaty, including any shares, stock, debentures, debenture stock or other obligations of any company incorporated in accordance with the laws of that Power.

The Turkish Government will, at any time on demand of any Allied Power concerned, furnish such information as may be required with regard to such property, rights and interests, or with regard to any transactions concerning such property, rights or interests since July 1, 1914.

ARTICLE 302.

Debts, other than the Ottoman Public Debt provided for in Article 236 and Annex I, Part VIII (Financial Clauses) of the present Treaty, between the Turkish Government or its nationals resident in Turkish territory on the coming into force of the present Treaty (with the exception of Turkish companies controlled by Allied groups or nationals) on the one hand, and the Governments of the Allied Powers or their nationals who were not on August 1, 1914, Turkish nationals or (except in the case of foreign officials in the Turkish service, in regard to their salaries, pensions or official remuneration) resident or carrying on business in Turkish territory, on the other hand, which were payable before the war, or became payable during the war and arose out of transactions or contracts of which the total or partial execution was suspended on account of the war, shall be paid or credited in the currency of such one of the Allied Powers, their colonies or protectorates, or the British Dominions or India, as may be concerned. If a debt was payable in some other currency the conversion shall be effected at the pre-war rate of exchange.

For the purpose of this provision the pre-war rate of exchange shall be defined as the average cable transfer rate prevailing in the Allied country concerned during the month immediately preceding the outbreak of war between the said country and Turkey.

If a contract provides for a fixed rate of exchange governing the conversion of the currency in which the debt is stated into the currency of the Allied Power concerned, then the above provisions concerning the rate of exchange shall not apply.

The proceeds of liquidation of enemy property, rights and interests and the cash assets of enemies, referred to in this Section, shall also be accounted for in the currency and at the rate of exchange provided for above.

The provisions of this Article regarding the rate of exchange shall not affect debts due to or from persons resident in territories detached from Turkey in accordance with the present Treaty.

ARTICLE 303.

The provisions of Articles 287 to 302 apply to industrial literary and artistic property which has been or may be dealt with in the liquidation of property, rights, interests, companies or businesses under war legislation by the Allied Powers, or in accordance with the stipulations of the present Treaty.

SECTION V.
CONTRACTS, PRESCRIPTIONS, JUDGMENTS.

ARTICLE 304.

Subject to the exceptions and special rules with regard to particular contracts or classes of contracts contained in the Annex hereto, any contract concluded between enemies will be maintained or dissolved according to the law of the Allied Power of which the party who was not a Turkish subject on August 1, 1914, is a national, and on the conditions prescribed by that law.

ARTICLE 305.

All periods of prescription or limitation of right of action, whether they began to run before or after the outbreak of war, shall be treated in the territory of the High Contracting Parties, so far as regards relations between enemies, as having been suspended from October 29, 1914, till the coming into force of the present Treaty. They shall begin to run again at earliest three months after the coming into force of the present Treaty. This provision shall apply to the period prescribed for the presentation of interest or dividend coupons or for the

presentation for repayment of securities drawn for repayment or repayable on any other ground.
Having regard to the provisions of the law of Japan, neither the present Article nor Article 304 nor the Annex hereto shall apply to contracts made between Japanese nationals and Turkish nationals.

ARTICLE 306.

As between enemies no negotiable instrument made before the war shall be deemed to have become invalid by reason only of failure within the required time to present the instrument for acceptance or payment, or to give notice of non-acceptance or non-payment to drawers or endorsers, or to protest the instrument, nor by reason of failure to complete any formality during the war.

Where the period within which a negotiable instrument should have been presented for acceptance or for payment, or within which notice of non-acceptance or non-payment should have been given to the drawer or endorser, or within which the instrument should have been protested, has elapsed during the war, and the party who should have presented or protested the instrument or have given notice of non-acceptance or non-payment has failed to do so during the war, a period of not less than three months from the coming into force of the present Treaty shall be allowed within which presentation, notice of non-acceptance or non-payment or protest may be made.

ARTICLE 307.

Judgments given or measures of execution ordered during the war by any Turkish judicial or administrative authority against or prejudicially affecting the interests of a person who was at the time a national of an Allied Power or against or affecting the interests of a company in which such an Allied national was interested shall be subject to revision, on the application of that national, by the Arbitral Commission provided for in Article 287. Where such a course is equitable and possible the parties shall be replaced in the situation which they occupied before the judgment was given or the measure of execution ordered by the Turkish authority. Where that is not possible, the national of an allied power who has suffered prejudice by the judgment or measure of execution shall be entitled to recover such compensation as the Arbitral Commission may consider equitable, such compensation to be paid by the Turkish Government.

Where a contract has been dissolved by reason either of failure on the part of either party to carry out its provisions or of the exercise of a right stipulated in the contract itself the party prejudiced may apply to the Arbitral Commission. This Commission may grant compensation to the prejudiced party, or may order the restoration of any rights in Turkey which have been prejudiced by the dissolution wherever, having regard to the circumstances of the case, such restoration is equitable and possible.

Turkey shall compensate any third party who may be prejudiced by any restitution or restoration effected in accordance with the provisions of this Article.

ARTICLE 308.

All questions relating to contracts concluded before the coming into force of the present Treaty between persons who were or have become nationals of the Allied Powers or of the new States whose territory is detached from Turkey and Turkish nationals shall be decided by the national Courts or the consular Courts of the Allied Power or new State of which one of the parties to the contract is a national, to the exclusion of the Turkish Courts.

ARTICLE 309.

Judgments given by the national or consular Courts of an Allied Power or new State whose territory is detached from Turkey, or orders made by the Arbitral Commission provided for in Article 287, in all cases which, under the present Treaty, they are competent to decide, shall be recognised in Turkey as final, and shall be enforced without it being necessary to have them declared executory

ANNEX

I. *General Provisions.*

1. Within the meaning of Articles 304 to 306 and of the provisions of this Annex, the parties to a contract shall be regarded as enemies when trading between them became impossible in fact, or was prohibited by or otherwise became unlawful under laws, orders or regulations to which one of those parties was subject. They shall be deemed to have become enemies from the date when such trading became impossible in fact or was prohibited or otherwise became unlawful.

2. The following classes of contracts remain in force subject to the application of domestic laws, orders or regulations made during the war by the Allied Powers and subject to the terms of the contracts:
(a) Contracts having for their object the transfer of estates or of real or personal property, where the property therein had passed or the object had been delivered before the parties became enemies;
(b) Leases and agreements for leases of land and houses;
(c) Contracts of mortgage, pledge, or lien;

(d) Contracts between individuals or companies and the State, provinces, municipalities, or other similar juridical persons charged with administrative functions, and concessions granted by the State, provinces, municipalities, or other similar juridical persons charged with administrative functions, subject however to any special provisions relating to concessions laid down in the present Treaty.

When the execution of the contracts thus kept alive would, owing to the alteration of economic conditions, cause one of the parties substantial prejudice, the Arbitral Commission provided for in Article 287 shall be empowered, on the request of the prejudiced party, to grant to him equitable compensation by way of reparation.

II. *Provisions Relating to Certain Classes of Contracts.*
Stock Exchange and Commercial Exchange Contracts.
3(a) Rules made during the war by any recognised Exchange or Commercial Association providing for the closure of contracts entered into before the war by an enemy are confirmed by the High Contracting Parties, as also any action taken thereunder provided:
(1) That the contract was expressed to be made subject to the rules of the Exchange or Association in question;
(2) That the rules applied to all persons concerned;
(3) That the conditions attaching to the closure were fair and reasonable.
(b) The closure of contracts relating to cotton futures which were closed as on July 31, 1914, under the decision of the Liverpool Cotton Association, is also confirmed.

Security.
4. The sale of a security held for an unpaid debt owing by an enemy shall be deemed to have been valid irrespective of notice to the owner if the creditor acted in good faith and with reasonable care and prudence, and no claim by the debtor on the ground of such sale shall be admitted.

Negotiable Instruments.
5. If a person has either before or during the war become liable upon a negotiable instrument in accordance with an undertaking given to him by a person who has subsequently become an enemy, the latter shall remain liable to indemnify the former in respect of his liability, notwithstanding the outbreak of war.

III. *Contracts of Insurance.*
6. The provisions of the following paragraphs shall apply only to insurance and reinsurance contracts between Turkish nationals and nationals of the Allied Powers in the case of which trading with Turkey has been prohibited. These provisions shall not apply to contracts between Turkish nationals and companies or individuals, even if nationals of the Allied Powers, established in territory detached from Turkey under the present Treaty.

In cases where the provisions of the following paragraphs do not apply, contracts of insurance and reinsurance shall be subject to the provisions of Article 304.

Fire Insurance.
7. Contracts for the insurance of property against fire entered into by a person interested in such property with another person who subsequently became an enemy shall not be deemed to have been dissolved by the outbreak of war, or by the fact of the person becoming an enemy, or on account of the failure during the war and for a period of three months thereafter to perform his obligations under the contract, but they shall be dissolved at the date when the annual premium becomes payable for the first time after the expiration of a period of three months after the coming into force of the present Treaty.

A settlement shall be effected of unpaid premiums which became due during the war, or of claims for losses which occurred during the war.

8. Where by administrative or legislative action an insurance against fire effected before the war has been transferred during the war from the original to another insurer, the transfer will be recognised and the liability of the original insurer will be deemed to have ceased as from the date of the transfer. The original insurer will, however, be entitled to receive on demand full information as to the terms of the transfer, and if it should appear that these terms were not equitable, they shall be amended so far as may be necessary to render them equitable.

Furthermore, the insured shall, subject to the concurrence of the original insurer, be entitled to retransfer the contract to the original insurer as from the date of the demand.

Life Insurance.
9. Contracts of life insurance entered into between an insurer and a person who subsequently became an enemy shall not be deemed to have been dissolved by the outbreak of war or by the fact of the person becoming an enemy.

Any sum which during the war became due upon a contract deemed not to have been dissolved under the preceding provision shall be recoverable after the war with the addition of interest at 5 per cent. per annum from the date of its becoming due up to the day of payment.

Where the contract has lapsed during the war owing to non-payment of premiums, or has become void from breach of the conditions of the contract the assured or his representatives or the persons entitled shall have the right at any time within twelve months of the coming into force of the present Treaty to claim from the insurer the surrender value of the policy at the date of its lapse or avoidance.

10. Where contracts of life insurance have been entered into by a local branch of an insurance company established in a country which subsequently became an enemy country, the contract shall, in the absence of any stipulation to the contrary in the contract itself, be governed by the local law, but the insurer shall be entitled to demand from the insured or his representatives the refund of sums paid or claims made or enforced under measures taken during the war, if the making or enforcement of such claims was not in accordance with the terms of the contract itself or was not consistent with the laws or treaties existing at the time when it was entered into.

11. In any case where by the law applicable to the contract the insurer remains bound by the contract, notwithstanding the non-payment of premiums, until notice is given to the insured of the termination of the contract, he shall be entitled where the giving of such notice was prevented by the war to recover the unpaid premiums with interest at 5 per cent. per annum from the insured.

12. Insurance contracts shall be considered as contracts of life assurance for the purpose of paragraphs 9 to 11 when they depend on the probabilities of human life combined with the rate of interest for the calculation of the reciprocal engagements between the two parties.

Marine Insurance.

13. Contracts of marine insurance, including time policies and voyage policies, entered into between an insurer and a person who subsequently became an enemy, shall be deemed to have been dissolved on his becoming an enemy, except in cases where the risk undertaken in the contract had attached before he became an enemy.

Where the risk had not attached, money paid by way of premium or otherwise shall be recoverable from the insurer.

Where the risk had attached, effect shall be given to the contract, notwithstanding the party becoming an enemy, and sums due under the contract either by way of premiums or in respect of losses shall be recoverable after the coming into force of the present Treaty.

In the event of any agreement being come to for the payment, of interest on sums due before the war to or by the nationals of States which have been at war and recovered after the war, such interest shall in the case of losses recoverable under contracts of marine insurance run from the expiration of a period of one year from the date of the loss.

14. No contract of marine insurance with an insured person who subsequently became an enemy shall be deemed to cover losses due to belligerent action by the Power of which the insurer was a national or by the allies of such Power.

15. Where it is shown that a person who had before the war entered into a contract of marine insurance with an insurer who subsequently became an enemy entered after the outbreak of war into a new contract covering the same risk with an insurer who was not an enemy, the new contract shall be deemed to be substituted for the original contract as from the date when it was entered into, and the premiums payable shall be adjusted on the basis of the original insurer having remained liable on the contract only up till the time when the new contract was entered into.

Other Insurances.

16. Contracts of insurance entered before the war between an insurer and a person who subsequently became an enemy, other than contracts dealt with in paragraph 7 to 15, shall be treated in all respects on the same footing as contracts of fire insurance between the same persons would be dealt with under the said paragraphs

Reinsurance.

17. All treatise of reinsurance with a person who became an enemy shall be regarded as having been abrogated by the person becoming an enemy, but without prejudice in the case of life or marine risks which had attached before the war to the right to recover payment after the war for sums due in respect of such risks.

Nevertheless, if, owing to invasion, it has been impossible for the reinsured to find another reinsurer, the treaty shall remain in force until three months after the coming into force of the present Treaty.

When a reinsurance treaty becomes void under this paragraph there shall be an adjustment of accounts between the parties in respect both of premiums paid and payable and of liabilities for losses in respect of life or marine risk which had attached before the war. In the case of risks other than those mentioned in paragraphs 9 to 15, the adjustment of accounts shall be made as at the date of the parties becoming enemies, without regard to claims for losses which may have occurred since that date.

18. The provisions of paragraph 17 will extend equally to reinsurances existing at the date of the parties becoming enemies of particular risks undertaken by the insurer in a contract of insurance against any risk other than

life or marine risks.

19. Reinsurance of life risks effected by particular contracts and not under any general treaty remain in force.

20. In case of a reinsurance effected before the war of a contract of marine insurance, the cession of a risk which had been ceded to the reinsurer shall, if it had attached before the outbreak of war, remain valid and effect be given to the contract, notwithstanding the outbreak of war; sums due under the contract of reinsurance in respect either of premiums or of losses shall be recoverable after the war.

21. The provisions of paragraphs 14 and 15 and the last part of paragraph 13 shall apply to contracts for the reinsurance of marine risks.

SECTION VI.
COMPANIES AND CONCESSIONS.

ARTICLE 310.

In application of the provisions of Article 287, Allied nationals and companies controlled by Allied groups or nationals holding concessions granted before October 29, 1914, by the Turkish government or by any Turkish local authority in territory remaining Turkish under the present Treaty, or holding concessions which may be assigned to them by the Financial Commission in virtue of Article 294, shall be replaced by such Government or authorities in complete possession of the rights resulting from the original concession contract and any subsequent agreements prior to October 29, 1914. The Turkish Government undertakes to adapt such contracts or agreements to the new economic conditions, and to extend them for a period equal to the interval between October 29, 1914, and the coming into force of the present Treaty. In cases of dispute with the Turkish Government the matter shall be submitted to the Arbitral Commission referred to in Article 287.

All legislative or other provisions, all concessions and all agreements subsequent to October 29, 1914, and prejudicial to the rights referred to in the preceding paragraph shall be declared null and void by the Turkish Government.

The concessionnaires referred to in this Article may, if the Financial Commission approves, abandon the whole or part of the compensation accorded to them by the Arbitral Commission under the conditions laid down in Article 287 for damage or loss suffered during the war, in exchange for contractual compensation.

ARTICLE 311 .

In territories detached from Turkey to be placed under the authority or tutelage of one of the Principal Allied Powers, Allied nationals and companies controlled by Allied groups or nationals holding concessions granted before October 29, 1914, by the Turkish Government or by any Turkish local authority shall continue in complete enjoyment of their duly acquired rights and the Power concerned shall maintain the guarantees granted or shall assign equivalent ones.

Nevertheless, any such Power, if it considers that the maintenance of any of these concessions would be contrary to the public interest, shall be entitled, within a period of six months from the date on which the territory is placed under its authority or tutelage, to buy out such concession or to propose modifications therein; in that event it shall be bound to pay to the concessionnaire equitable compensation in accordance with the following provisions.

If the parties cannot agree on the amount of such compensation, it will be determined by Arbitral Tribunals composed of three members, one designated by the State of which the concessionnaire or the holders of the majority of the capital in the case of a company is or are nationals, one by the Government exercising authority in the territory in question, and the third designated, failing agreement between the parties, by the Council of the League of Nations.

The Tribunal shall take into account, from both the legal and equitable standpoints, all relevant matters, on the basis of the maintenance of the contract adapted as indicated in the following paragraph.

The holder of a concession which is maintained in force shall have the right, within a period of six months after the expiration of the period specified in the second paragraph of this Article, to demand the adaptation of his contract to the new economic conditions, and in the absence of agreement direct with the Government concerned the decision shall be referred to the Arbitral Commission provided for above.

ARTICLE 312.

In all territories detached from Turkey, either as a result of the Balkan Wars in 1913, or under the present Treaty, other than those referred to in Article 311, the State which definitively acquires the territory shall *ipso facto* succeed to the duties and charges of Turkey towards concessionnaires and holders of contracts, referred to in the first paragraph of Article 311, and shall maintain the guarantees granted or assign equivalent ones.

This succession shall take effect, in the case of each acquiring State, as from the coming into force of the Treaty under which the cession was effected. Such State shall take all necessary steps to ensure that the concessions may be worked and the carrying out of the contracts proceeded with without interruption.

Nevertheless, as from the coming into force of the present Treaty, negotiations may be entered into between the acquiring States and the holders of contracts or concessions, with a view to a mutual agreement for bringing such concessions and contracts into conformity with the legislation of such States and the new economic conditions. Should agreement not have been reached within six months, the State or the holders of the concessions or contracts may submit the dispute to an Arbitral Tribunal constituted as provided in Article 311.

ARTICLE 313.

The application of Articles 311 and 312 shall not give rise to any award of compensation in respect of the right to issue paper money.

ARTICLE 314.

The Allied Powers shall not be bound to recognise in territory detached from Turkey the validity of the grant of any concession granted by the Turkish Government or by Turkish local authorities after October 29, 1914, nor the validity of the transfer of any concession effected after that date. Any such concessions and transfers may be declared null and void, and their cancellation shall give rise to no compensation.

ARTICLE 315.

All concessions or rights in concessions granted by the Turkish Government since October 30, 1918, and all such concessions or rights granted since August 1, 1914, in favour of German, Austrian, Hungarian, Bulgarian or Turkish nationals or companies controlled by them, until the date of the coming into force of the present Treaty, are hereby annulled.

ARTICLE 316.

(a) Any company incorporated in accordance with Turkish law and operating in Turkey which is now or shall hereafter be controlled by Allied nationals shall have the right, within five years from the coming into force of the present Treaty, to transfer its property, rights and interests to another company incorporated in accordance with the law of one of the Allied Powers whose nationals control it; and the company to which the property, rights and interests are transferred shall continue to enjoy the same rights and privileges as the other company enjoyed under the laws of Turkey and the terms of the present Treaty, subject to meeting obligations previously incurred.

The Turkish Government undertakes to modify its legislation so as to allow companies of Allied nationality to hold concessions or contracts in Turkey.

(b) Any company incorporated in accordance with Turkish law and operating in territory detached from Turkey, which is now or hereafter shall be controlled by Allied nationals, shall, in the same way and within the same period, have the right to transfer its property, rights and interests to another company incorporated in accordance with the law either of the State exercising authority in the territory in question or of one of the Allied Powers whose nationals control it. The company to which the property, rights and interests are transferred shall continue to enjoy the same rights and privileges as the other company enjoyed, including those conferred on it by the present Treaty.

(c) In Turkey companies of Allied nationality to which the property, rights and interests of Turkish companies shall have been transferred in virtue of paragraph (a) of this Article, and, in territories detached from Turkey, companies of Turkish nationality controlled by Allied groups or nationals and companies of nationality other than that of the State exercising authority in the territory in question to which the property, rights and interests of Turkish companies shall have been transferred in virtue of paragraph (b) of this Article, shall not be subjected to legislative or other provisions or to taxes, imposts or charges more onerous than those applied in Turkey to similar companies possessing Turkish nationality, and in territory detached from Turkey to those possessing the nationality of the State exercising authority therein.

(d) The companies to which the property, rights and interests of Turkish companies are transferred in virtue of paragraphs (a) and (b) of this Article shall not be subjected to any special tax on account of this transfer.

SECTION VII.
GENERAL PROVISION.

ARTICLE 317.

The term "nationals of the Allied Powers," wherever used in this Part or in Part VIII (Financial Clauses), covers:

(1) All nationals, including companies and associations, of an Allied Power or of a State or territory under the protectorate of an Allied Power;

(2) The protected persons of the Allied Powers whose certificate of protection was granted before August 1, 1914;

(3) Turkish financial, industrial and commercial companies controlled by Allied groups or nationals, or in which such groups or nationals possessed the preponderant interest on August 1, 1914

(4) Religious or charitable institutions and scholastic establishments in which nationals or protected persons of

the Allied Powers are interested.

The Allied Powers will communicate to the Financial Commission, within one year from the coming into force of the present Treaty, the list of companies, institutions and establishments in which they consider that their nationals possess a preponderant interest or are interested.

PART X.
AERIAL NAVIGATION.
[...ARTICLE 318.-327...]

PART XI.
PORTS, WATERWAYS AND RAILWAYS.
SECTION I.
GENERAL PROVISIONS.

ARTICLE 328.

Turkey undertakes to grant freedom of transit through her territories on the routes most convenient for international transit, either by rail, navigable waterway or canal, to persons, goods, vessels, carriages, wagons and mails coming from or going to the territories of any of the Allied Powers, whether contiguous or not; for this purpose the crossing of territorial waters shall be allowed. Such persons, goods, vessels, carriages, wagons and mails shall not be subjected to any transit duty or to any undue delays or restrictions, and shall be entitled in Turkey to national treatment as regards charges, facilities and all other matters.

Goods in transit shall be exempt from all customs or other similar duties.

All charges imposed on transport in transit shall be reasonable having regard to the conditions of the traffic. No charge, facility or restriction shall depend directly or indirectly on the ownership or the nationality of the ship or other means of transport on which any part of the through journey has been, or is to be, accomplished.

ARTICLE 329.

Turkey undertakes neither to impose nor to maintain any control over transmigration traffic through her territories beyond measures necessary to ensure that passengers are *bonâ fide* in transit; nor to allow any shipping company or any other private body, corporation or person interested in the traffic to take any part whatever in, or to exercise any direct or indirect influence over, any administrative service that may be necessary for this purpose.

ARTICLE 330.

Turkey undertakes to make no discrimination or preference, direct or indirect, in the duties, charges and prohibitions relating to importations into or exportations from her territories, or, subject to any special provisions in the present Treaty, in the charges and conditions of transport of goods or persons entering or leaving her territories, based on the frontier crossed, or on the kind, ownership or flag of the means of transport (including aircraft) employed, or on the original or immediate place of departure of the vessel, wagon or aircraft or other means of transport employed, or its ultimate or intermediate destination, or on the route of or places of transshipment on the journey, or on whether any port through which the goods are imported or exported is a Turkish port or a port belonging to any foreign country, or on whether the goods are imported or exported by sea, by land or by air.

Turkey particularly undertakes not to establish against the ports and vessels of any of the Allied Powers any surtax or any direct or indirect bounty for export or import by Turkish ports or vessels, or by those of another Power, for example, by means of combined tariffs. She further undertakes that persons or goods passing through a port or using a vessel of any of the Allied Powers shall not be subjected to any formality or delay whatever to which such persons or goods would not be subjected if they passed through a Turkish port or a port of any other Power, or used a Turkish vessel or a vessel of any other Power.

ARTICLE 331.

All necessary administrative and technical measures shall be taken to expedite, as much as possible, the transmission of goods across the Turkish frontiers and to ensure their forwarding and transport from such frontiers irrespective of whether such goods are coming from or going to the territories of the Allied Powers or are in transit from or to those territories, under the same material conditions in such matters as rapidity of carriage and care *en route* as are enjoyed by other goods of the same kind carried on Turkish territory under similar conditions of transport .

In particular, the transport of perishable goods shall be promptly and regularly carried out, and the customs formalities shall be effected in such a way as to allow the goods to be carried straight through by trains which make connection.

ARTICLE 332.

The seaports of the Allied Powers are entitled to all favours and to all reduced tariffs granted on Turkish railways or navigable waterways for the benefit of Turkish ports (without prejudice to the rights of concessionaires) or of any port of another Power.

ARTICLE 333

Subject to the rights of concessionaires, Turkey may not refuse to participate in the tariffs or combinations of tariffs intended to secure for ports of any of the Allied Powers advantages similar to those granted by Turkey to her own ports or the ports of any other Power.

SECTION II.
NAVIGATION.
CHAPTER I.
FREEDOM OF NAVIGATION.

ARTICLE 334.

The nationals of any of the Allied Powers as well as their vessels and property shall enjoy in all Turkish ports and on the inland navigation routes of Turkey at least the same treatment in all respects as Turkish nationals, vessels and property.

In particular, the vessels of any one of the Allied Powers shall be entitled to transport goods of any description and passengers to or from any ports or places in Turkish territory to which Turkish vessels may have access, under conditions which shall not be more onerous than those applied in the case of national vessels, they shall be treated on a footing of equality with national vessels as regards port and harbour facilities and charges of every description, including facilities for stationing, loading and unloading, tonnage duties and charges, harbour, pilotage, lighthouse, quarantine and all analogous duties and charges of whatsoever nature levied in the name of or for the profit of the Government, public functionaries, private individuals, corporations or establishments of any kind.

In the event of Turkey granting a preferential regime to any of the Allied Powers or to any other foreign Power, this regime shall be extended immediately and unconditionally to all the Allied Powers.

There shall be no restrictions on the movement of persons or vessels other than those arising from prescriptions concerning customs, police, public health, emigration, and immigration and those relating to the import and export of prohibited goods. Such regulations must be reasonable and uniform and must not impede traffic unnecessarily.

CHAPTER II.
PORTS OF INTERNATIONAL CONCERN

ARTICLE 335.

The following Eastern ports are declared ports of international concern and placed under the regime defined in the following Articles of this section;
Constantinople, from St. Stefano to Dolma Bagtchi;
Haidar Pasha;
Smyrna;
Alexandretta;
Haifa;
Basra;
Trebizond (in the conditions laid down in Article 352);
Batum (subject to conditions to be subsequently fixed).
Free zones shall be provided in these ports.
Subject to any provisions to the contrary in the present Treaty, the regime laid down for the above ports shall not prejudice the territorial sovereignty.

(1) Navigation.
ARTICLE 336

In the ports declared of international concern the nationals, goods and flags of all States Members of the League of Nations shall enjoy complete freedom in the use of the port. In this connection and in all respects they shall be treated on a footing of perfect equality, particularly as regards all port and quay facilities and charges, including facilities for berthing, loading and discharging, tonnage dues and charges, quay, pilotage, lighthouse, quarantine and all similar dues and charges of whatsoever nature, levied in the name of or for the profit of the Government, public functionaries, private individuals, corporations or establishments of every kind, no distinction being made between the nationals, goods and flags of the different States and those of the State under whose sovereignty or authority the port is placed.

There shall be no restrictions on the movement of persons or vessels other than those arising from regulations concerning customs, police, public health, emigration and immigration and those relating to the import and export of prohibited goods. Such regulations must be reasonable and uniform and must not impede traffic unnecessarily.

(2) Dues and Charges.
ARTICLE 337.

All dues and charges for the use of the port or of its approaches, or for the use of facilities provided in the port, shall be levied under the conditions of equality prescribed in Article 336, and shall be reasonable both as regards their amount and their application, having regard to the expenses incurred by the port authority in the administration, upkeep and improvement of the port and of the approaches thereto, or in the interests of navigation.

Subject to the provisions of Article 54, Part III (Political Clauses) of the present Treaty all dues and charges other than those provided for in the present Article or in Articles 338, 342, or 343 are forbidden.

ARTICLE 338.

All customs, local octroi or consumption dues, duly authorised, levied on goods imported or exported through a port subject to the international regime shall be the same, whether the flag of the vessel which effected or is to effect the transport be the flag of the State exercising sovereignty or authority over the port or any other flag. In the absence of special circumstances justifying an exception on account of economic needs, such dues must be fixed on the same basis and at the same tariffs as similar duties levied on the other customs frontiers of the State concerned. All facilities which may be accorded by such State over other land or water routes or at other ports for the import or export of goods shall be equally granted to imports and exports through the port subject to the international regime.

(3) Works.
ARTICLE 339.

In the absence of any special arrangement relative to the execution of works for maintaining and improving the port, it shall be the duty of the State under whose sovereignty or authority the port is placed to take suitable measures to remove any obstacle or danger to navigation and to secure facilities for the movements of ships in the port.

ARTICLE 340.

The State under whose sovereignty or authority the port is placed must not undertake any works liable to prejudice the facilities for the use of the port or of its approaches.

(4) Free Zones
ARTICLE 341.

The facilities granted in a free zone for the erection or use of warehouses and for packing and unpacking goods shall be in accordance with trade requirements for the time being. All goods allowed to be consumed in the free zone shall be exempt from customs, excise and all other duties of any description whatsoever apart from the statistical duty provided for in Article 342. Unless otherwise provided in the present Treaty, it shall be within the discretion of the State under whose sovereignty or authority the port is placed to permit or to prohibit manufacture within the free zone. There shall be no discrimination in regard to any of the provisions of this Article either between persons belonging to different nationalities or between goods of different origin or destination.

ARTICLE 342.

No duties or charges, other than those provided for in Article 336, shall be levied on goods arriving in the free zone or departing therefrom, from whatever foreign country they come or for whatever foreign country they are destined, other than a statistical duty which shall not exceed 1 per mille *ad valorem*. The proceeds of this statistical duty shall be devoted exclusively to the maintenance of the service dealing with the statistics relating to the traffic of the free zone.

ARTICLE 343.

Subject to the provisions of Article 344, the duties referred to in Article 338 may be levied under the conditions laid down in that Article on goods coming from or going to the free zone on their importation into the territory of the State under whose sovereignty or authority the port is placed or on their exportation from such territory respectively.

ARTICLE 344.

Persons, goods, postal services, ships, vessels, carriages, wagons and other means of transport coming from or going to the free zone, and crossing the territory of the State under whose sovereignty or authority the port is placed, shall be deemed to be in transit across that State if they are going to or coming from the territory of any other State whatsoever.

(5) Dispute
ARTICLE 345.
Subject to the provisions contained in Article 61, Part III (Political Clauses), differences which may arise between interested States with regard to the interpretation or to the application of the dispositions contained in Articles 335 to 344, as well as, in general, any differences between interested States with regard to the use of the ports, shall be settled in accordance with the conditions laid down by the League of Nations.

Differences with regard to the execution of works liable to prejudice the facilities for the use of the port or of its approaches shall be dealt with by an accelerated procedure, and may be the object of an expression of opinion, or of a provisional decision which may prescribe the suspension or the immediate suppression of the said works, without prejudice to the ultimate opinion or decision in the case.

CHAPTER III.
CLAUSES RELATING TO THE MARITSA AND THE DANUBE
ARTICLE 346.
On a request being made by one of the riparian States to the Council of the League of Nations, the Maritsa shall be declared an international river, and shall be subject to the regime of international rivers laid down in Articles 332 to 338 of the Treaty of Peace concluded with Germany on June 28, 1919.

ARTICLE 347
On a request being made to the Council of the League of Nations by any riparian State, the Maritsa shall be placed under the administration of an International Commission, which shall comprise one representative of each riparian State and one representative of Great Britain, one of France and one of Italy.

ARTICLE 348.
Without prejudice to the provisions of Article 133, Part III (Political Clauses), Turkey hereby recognises and accepts all the dispositions relating to the Danube inserted in the Treaties of Peace concluded with Germany, Austria, Hungary and Bulgaria and the regime for that river resulting therefrom.

CHAPTER IV.
CLAUSES GIVING TO CERTAIN STATES THE USE OF CERTAIN PORTS.
ARTICLE 349
In order to ensure to Turkey free access to the Mediterranean and Ægean Seas, freedom of transit is accorded to Turkey over the territories and in the ports detached from Turkey.

Freedom of transit is the freedom defined in Article 328, until such time as a General Convention on the subject shall have been concluded, whereupon the dispositions of the new Convention shall be substituted therefor. Special conventions between the States or Administrations concerned will lay down, as regards Turkey with the assent of the Financial Commission, the conditions of the exercise of the right accorded above, and will settle in particular the method of using the ports and the free zones existing in them, the establishment of international (joint) services and tariffs, including through tickets and way-bills, and the application of the Convention of Berne of October 14, 1890, and its supplementary provisions, until its replacement by a new Convention.

Freedom of transit will extend to postal, telegraphic and telephonic services.

ARTICLE 350.
In the port of Smyrna Turkey will be accorded a lease in perpetuity, subject to determination by the League of Nations, of an area which shall be placed under the general regime of free zones laid down in Articles 341 to 344, and shall be used for the direct transit of goods coming from or going to that State.

The delimitation of the area referred to in the preceding paragraph, its connection with existing railways, its equipment and exploitation, and in general all the conditions of its utilisation, including the amount of the rental, shall be decided by a Commission consisting of one delegate of Turkey, one delegate of Greece, and one delegate appointed by the League of Nations. These conditions shall be susceptible of revision every ten years in the same manner.

ARTICLE 351.
Free access to the Black Sea by the port of Batum is accorded to Georgia, Azerbaijan and Persia, as well as to Armenia. This right of access will be exercised in the conditions laid down in Article 349.

ARTICLE 352.
Subject to the decision provided for in Article 89, Part III (Political Clauses), free access to the Black Sea by the port of Trebizond is accorded to Armenia. This right of access will be exercised in the conditions laid down in Article 349.

In that event Armenia will be accorded a lease in perpetuity, subject to determination by the League of Nations, of an area in the said port which shall be placed under the general regime of free zones laid down in Articles

34x to 344, and shall be used for the direct transit of goods coming from or going to that State.

The delimitation of the area referred to in the preceding paragraph, its connection with existing railways, its equipment and exploitation, and in general all the conditions of its utilisation, including the amount of the rental, shall be decided by a Commission consisting of one delegate of Armenia, one delegate of Turkey, and one delegate appointed by the League of Nations. These conditions shall be susceptible of revision every ten years in the same manner.

SECTION III.
RAILWAYS.
CHAPTER I.
CLAUSES RELATING TO INTERNATIONAL TRANSPORT

ARTICLE 353.

Subject to the rights of concessionaire companies, goods coming from the territories of the Allied Powers and going to Turkey and vice versa, or in transit through Turkey from or to the territories of the Allied Powers, shall enjoy on the Turkish railways as regards charges to be collected (rebates and drawbacks being taken into account), facilities and all other matters, the most favourable treatment applied to goods of the same kind carried on any Turkish lines, either in internal traffic or for export, import or in transit, under similar conditions of transport, for example as regards length of route.

International tariffs established in acordance with the rates referred to in the preceding paragraph and involving through way bills shall be established when one of the Allied Powers shall require it from Turkey.

ARTICLE 354

From the coming into force of the present Treaty Turkey agrees, under the reserves indicated in the second paragraph of this Article, to subscribe to the conventions and arrangements signed at Berne on October 14, 1890, September 20, 1893, July 16, 1895, June 16, 1898, and September 19, 1906, regarding the transportation of goods by rail.

If within five years from the date of the coming into force of the present Treaty a new convention for the transportation of passengers, luggage and goods by rail shall have been concluded to replace the Berne Convention of October 14, 1890, and the subsequent additions referred to above, this new convention and the supplementary provisions for international transport by rail which may be based on it shall bind Turkey, even if she shall have refused to take part in the preparation of the convention or to subscribe to it. Until a new convention shall have been concluded, Turkey shall conform to the provisions of the Berne Convention and the subsequent additions referred to above, and to the current supplementary provisions.

ARTICLE 355.

Subject to the rights of concessionaire companies, Turkey shall be bound to co-operate in the establishment of through-ticket services (for passengers and their luggage) which shall be required by any of the Allied Powers to ensure their communication by rail with each other and with all other countries by transit across the territories of Turkey; in particular Turkey shall, for this purpose, accept trains and carriages coming from the territories of the Allied Powers and shall forward them with a speed at least equal to that of her best long-distance trains on the same lines. The rates applicable to such through services shall not in any case be higher than the rates collected on Turkish internal services for the same distance, under the same conditions of speed and comfort.

The tariffs applicable under the same conditions of speed and comfort to the transportation of emigrants going to or coming from ports of the Allied Powers and using the Turkish railways shall not be at a higher kilometric rate than the most favourable tariffs (drawbacks and rebates being taken into account) enjoyed on the said railways by emigrants going to or coming from any other ports.

ARTICLE 356.

Turkey shall not apply specially to such through services, or to the transportation of emigrants going to or coming from the ports of the Allied Powers, any technical, fiscal or administrative measures, such as measures of customs examination, general police, sanitary police, and control, the result of which would be to impede or delay such services.

ARTICLE 357

In case of transport partly by rail and partly by internal navigation, with or without through way-bill, the preceding Articles shall apply to the part of the journey performed by rail.

CHAPTER II.
ROLLING STOCK.

ARTICLE 358.

Turkey undertakes that Turkish wagons used for international traffic shall be fitted with apparatus allowing:
(1) Of their inclusion in goods trains on the lines of such of the Allied Powers as are parties to the Berne Convention of May 15, 1886, as modified on May 18, 1907, without hampering the action of the continuous brake which may be adopted in such countries within ten years of the coming into force of the present Treaty and
(2) Of the acceptance of wagons of such countries in all goods trains on the Turkish lines.
The rolling-stock of the Allied Powers shall enjoy on the Turkish lines the same treatment as Turkish rolling stock as regards movement, upkeep and repair.

CHAPTER III.
TRANSFERS OF RAILWAY LINES.

ARTICLE 359.

Subject to any special provisions concerning the transfer of ports and railways, whether owned by the Turkish Government or private companies, situated in the territories detached from Turkey under the present Treaty, and to the financial conditions relating to the concessionaires and the pensioning of the personnel, the transfer of railways will take place under the following conditions:
(1) The works and installations of all the railroads shall be left complete and in as good condition as possible.
(2) When a railway system possessing its own roiling stock is situated in its entirety in transferred territory, such stock shall be left complete with the railway, in accordance with the last inventory before October 30, 1918, and in a normal state of upkeep, Turkey being responsible for any losses due to causes within her control.
(3) As regards lines, the administration of which will in virtue of the present Treaty be divided, the distribution of the rolling stock shall be made by agreement between the administrations taking over the several parts thereof. This agreement shall have regard to the amount of the material registered on those lines in the last inventory before October 30, 1918, the length of track (sidings included) and the nature and amount of the traffic. Failing agreement the points in dispute shall be settled by an arbitrator designated by the League of Nations who shall also, if necessary, specify the locomotives, carriages and wagons to be left on each section, the conditions of their acceptance, and such provisional arrangements as he may judge necessary to ensure for a limited period the current maintenance in existing workshops of the transferred stock.
(4) Stocks of stores, fittings and plant shall be left under the same conditions as the rolling stock.

ARTICLE 360.

The Turkish Government abandons whatever rights it possesses over the Hedjaz railway, and accepts such arrangements as shall be made for its working, and for the distribution of the property belonging to or used in connection with the railway, by the Governments concerned. In any such arrangements the special position of the railway from the religious point of view shall be fully recognised and safeguarded.

CHAPTER IV.
WORKING AGREEMENTS.

ARTICLE 361.

When, as a result of the fixing of new frontiers, a railway connection between two parts of the same country crosses another country, or a branch line from one country has its terminus in another, the conditions of working, if not specifically provided for in the present Treaty, shall be laid down in a convention between the railway administrations concerned. If the administrations cannot come to an agreement as to the terms of such convention, the points of difference shall be decided by an arbitrator appointed as provided in Article 359.
The establishment of all new frontier stations between Turkey and the contiguous Allied States or new States, as well as the working of the lines between those stations, shall be settled by agreements similarly concluded.

ARTICLE 362.

A standing conference of technical representatives nominated by the Governments concerned shall be constituted with powers to agree upon the necessary joint arrangements for through traffic working, wagon exchange, through rates and tariffs and other similar matters affecting railways situated on territory forming part of the Turkish Empire on August 1, 1914.

SECTION IV.
MISCELLANEOUS.
CHAPTER I.
HYDRAULIC SYSTEM.

ARTICLE 363

In default of any provision to the contrary, when as the result of the fixing of a new frontier the hydraulic system (canalisation inundation, irrigation, drainage or similar matters) in a State is dependent on works executed within the territory of another State, or when use is made on the territory of a State, in virtue of pre-war usage, of water or hydraulic power the source of which is on the territory of another State, an agreement shall be made between the States concerned to safeguard the interests and rights acquired by each of them.

Failing an agreement, the matter shall be regulated by an arbitrator appointed by the Council of the League of Nations.

CHAPTER II.
TELEGRAPHS AND TELEPHONES.

ARTICLE 364

Turkey undertakes on the request of any of the Allied Powers to grant facilities for the erection and maintenance of trunk telegraph and telephone lines across her territories.

Such facilities shall comprise the grant to any telegraph or telephone company nominated by any of the Allied Powers of the right:

(a) To erect a new line of poles and wires along any line of railway or other route in Turkish territory;
(b) To have access at all times to such poles and wires or wires placed by agreement on existing poles, and to take such steps as may be necessary to maintain them in good working order;
(c) To utilise the services of their own staff for the purpose of working such wires.

All questions relating to the establishment of such lines, especially as regards compensation to private individuals, shall be settled in the same conditions as are applied to telegraph or telephone lines established by the Turkish Government itself.

ARTICLE 365.

Notwithstanding any contrary stipulations in existing treaties, Turkey undertakes to grant freedom of transit for telegraphic correspondence and telephonic communications coming from or going to any one of the Allied Powers, whether contiguous with her or not, over such lines as may be most suitable for international transit and in accordance with the tariffs in force. This correspondence and these communications shall be subjected to no unnecessary delay or restriction; they shall enjoy in Turkey national treatment in regard to every kind of facility, and especially in regard to rapidity of transmission. No payment, facility or restriction shall depend directly or indirectly on the nationality of the transmitter or the addressee.

Where, in consequence of the provisions of the present Treaty, lines previously entirely on Turkish territory traverse the territory of more than one State, pending the revision of telegraph rates by a new international telegraphic convention, the through charges shall not be higher than they would have been if the whole of the territory traversed had remained under Turkish sovereignty, and the apportionment of the through charges between the States traversed shall be dealt with by agreement between the administrations concerned.

CHAPTER III.
SUBMARINE CABLES.

[...ARTICLE 366.-367...]

CHAPTER IV.
EXECUTORY PROVISIONS.

ARTICLE 368.

Turkey shall carry out the instructions given her, in regard to transport, by an authorised body acting on behalf of the Allied Powers:

(1) For the carriage of troops under the provisions of the present Treaty, and of material, ammunition and supplies for army use;
(2) As a temporary measure, for the transportation of supplies for certain regions, as well as for the restoration, as rapidly as possible, of the normal conditions of transport, and for the organisation of postal and telegraphic services.

SECTION V.
DISPUTES AND REVISION OF PERMANENT CLAUSES.
ARTICLE 369.
Unless otherwise specifically provided for in the present Treaty, disputes which may arise between interested Powers with regard to the interpretation and application of this Part of the present Treaty shall be settled as provided by the League of Nations.

ARTICLE 370.
At any time the League of Nations may recommend the revision of such of these Articles as relate to a permanent administrative regime.

ARTICLE 371.
The stipulations of Articles 328 to 334, 353 and 355 to 357 shall be subject to revision by the Council of the League of Nations at any time after three years from the coming into force of the present Treaty.

Subject to the provisions of Article 373 no Allied Power can claim the benefit of any of the stipulations of the Articles enumerated above on behalf of any portion of its territories in which reciprocity is not accorded in respect of such stipulations.

SECTION VI.
SPECIAL PROVISIONS.
ARTICLE 372.
Without prejudice to the special obligations imposed on her by the present Treaty for the benefit of the Allied Powers, Turkey undertakes to adhere to any General Conventions regarding the international regime of transit, waterways, ports or railways which may be concluded, with the approval of the League of Nations, within five years of the coming into force of the present Treaty.

ARTICLE 373.
Unless otherwise expressly provided in the present Treaty, nothing in this Part shall prejudice more extensive rights conferred on the nationals of the Allied Powers by the Capitulations or by any arrangements which may be substituted therefor.

PART XII.
LABOUR.

See Part XIII, Treaty of Versailles.

PART XIII.
MISCELLANEOUS PROVISIONS.
ARTICLE 415.
Turkey undertakes to recognise and to accept the conventions made or to be made by the Allied Powers or any of them with any other Power as to the traffic in arms and in spirituous liquors, and also as to the other subjects dealt with in the General Acts of Berlin of February 26, 1885, and of Brussels of July 2, 1890, and the conventions completing or modifying the same.

ARTICLE 416.
The High Contracting Parties declare and place on record that they have taken note of the Treaty signed by the Government of the French Republic on July 17, 1918, with His Serene Highness the Prince of Monaco, defining the relations between France and the Principality.

ARTICLE 417.
Without prejudice to the provisions of the present Treaty, Turkey undertakes not to put forward directly or indirectly against any Allied Power any pecuniary claim based on events which occurred at any time before the coming into force of the present Treaty.

The present stipulation will bar completely and finally all claims of this nature, which will be thenceforward extinguished, whoever may be the parties in interest.

ARTICLE 418.
Turkey accepts and recognises as valid and binding all decrees and orders concerning Turkish ships and goods and all orders relating to the payment of costs made by any Prize Court of any of the Allied Powers, and undertakes not to put forward any claim arising out of such decrees or orders on behalf of any Turkish national. The Allied Powers reserve the right to examine in such manner as they may determine all decisions and orders of Turkish Prize Courts, whether affecting the property rights of nationals of those Powers or of neutral Powers.

Turkey agrees to furnish copies of all the documents constituting the record of the cases, including the decisions and orders made, and to accept and give effect to the recommendations made after such examination of the cases.

ARTICLE 419.

With a view to minimising the losses arising from the sinking of ships and cargoes in the course of the war, and to facilitating the recovery of ships and cargoes which can be salved and the adjustment of the private claims arising with regard thereto, the Turkish Government undertakes to supply all the information in its power which may be of assistance to the Governments of the Allied Powers or to their nationals with regard to vessels sunk or damaged by the Turkish naval forces during the period of hostilities.

ARTICLE 420.

Within six months from the coming into force of the present Treaty the Turkish Government must restore to the Governments of the Allied Powers the trophies, archives, historical souvenirs or works of art taken from the said Powers or their nationals, including companies and associations of every description controlled by such nationals, since October 29, 1914.

The delivery of the articles will be effected in such places and conditions as may be laid down by the Governments to which they are to be restored.

ARTICLE 421.

The Turkish Government will, within twelve months from the coming into force of the present Treaty, abrogate the existing law of antiquities and take the necessary steps to enact a new law of antiquities which will be based on the rules contained in the Annex hereto, and must be submitted to the Financial Commission for approval before being submitted to the Turkish Parliament. The Turkish Government undertakes to ensure the execution of this law on a basis of perfect equality between all nations.

ANNEX.

1. "Antiquity" means any construction or any product of human activity earlier than the year 1700.
2. The law for the protection of antiquities shall proceed by encouragement rather than by threat.

Any person who, having discovered an antiquity without being furnished with the authorisation referred to in paragraph 5, reports the same to an official of the competent Turkish Department, shall be rewarded according to the value of the discovery.

3. No antiquity may be disposed of except to the competent Turkish Department, unless this Department renounces the acquisition of any such antiquity.

No antiquity may leave the country without an export licence from the said Department.

4. Any person who maliciously or negligently destroys or damages an antiquity shall be liable to a penalty to be fixed.
5. No clearing of ground or digging with the object of finding antiquities shall be permitted, under penalty of fine, except to persons authorised by the competent Turkish Department.
6. Equitable terms shall be fixed for expropriation, temporary or permanent, of lands which might be of historical or archæological interest.
7. Authorisation to excavate shall only be granted to persons who show sufficient guarantees of archæological experience. The Turkish Government shall not, in granting these authorisations, act in such a way as to eliminate scholars of any nation without good grounds.
8. The proceeds of excavations may be divided between the excavator and the competent Turkish Department in a proportion fixed by that Department. If division seems impossible for scientific reasons, the excavator shall receive a fair indemnity in lieu of a part of the find.

ARTICLE 422.

All objects of religious, archæological, historical or artistic interest which have been removed since August 1, 1914, from any of the territories detached from Turkey will within twelve months from the coming into force of the present Treaty be restored by the Turkish Government to the Government of the territory from which such objects were removed.

If any such objects have passed into private ownership, the Turkish Government will take the necessary steps by expropriation or otherwise to enable it to fulfil its obligations under this Article.

Lists of the objects to be restored under this Article will be furnished to the Turkish Government by the Governments concerned within six months from the coming into force of the present Treaty.

ARTICLE 423.

The Turkish Government undertakes to preserve the books, documents and manuscripts from the Library of the Russian Archæological Institute at Constantinople which are now in its possession, and to deliver them to such authority as the Allied Powers, in order to safeguard the rights of Russia, reserve the right to designate. Pending such delivery the Turkish Government must allow all persons duly authorised by any of the Allied Powers to have free access to the said books, documents and manuscripts.

ARTICLE 424.

On the coming into force of the present Treaty, Turkey will hand over without delay to the Governments concerned archives, registers, plans, title-deeds and documents of every kind belonging to the civil, military, financial, judicial or other forms of administration in the transferred territories. If any one of these documents, archives, registers, title-deeds or plans is missing, it shall be restored by Turkey upon the demand of the Government concerned.

In case the archives, registers, plans, title-deeds or documents referred to in the preceding paragraph, exclusive of those of a military character, concern equally the administrations in Turkey, and cannot therefore be handed over without inconvenience to such administrations, Turkey undertakes, subject to reciprocity, to give access thereto to the Governments concerned.

The Turkish Government undertakes in particular to restore to the Greek Government the local land registers or any other public registers relating to landed property in the districts of the former Turkish Empire transferred to Greece since 1912, which the Turkish authorities removed or may have removed at the time of the evacuation. In cases where the restitution of one or more of such registers is impossible owing to their disappearance or for any other reason, and whenever necessary for purposes of verification of titles produced to the Greek authorities, the Greek Government shall be entitled to take any necessary copies of the entries in the Central Land Registry at Constantinople.

ARTICLE 425.

The Turkish Government undertakes, subject to reciprocity, to afford to the Governments exercising authority over territory detached from Turkey, or of which the existing status is recognised by Turkey under the present Treaty, access to any archives and documents of every description relating to the administration of Wakfs in such territory, or to particular Wakfs, wherever situated, in which persons or institutions established in such territory are interested.

ARTICLE 426.

All judicial decisions given in Turkey by a judge or court of an Allied Power between October 30, 1918, and the coming into force of the new judicial system referred to in Article 136, Part III (Political Clauses) shall be recognised by the Turkish Government, which undertakes if necessary to ensure the execution of such decisions.

ARTICLE 427.

Subject to the provisions of Article 46, Part III (Political Clauses) Turkey hereby agrees so far as concerns her territory as delimited in Article 27 to accept and to co-operate in the execution of any decisions taken by the Allied Powers, in agreement where necessary with other Powers, in relation to any matters previously dealt with by the Constantinople Superior Council of Health and the Turkish Sanitary Administration which was directed by the said Council.

ARTICLE 428.

As regards the territories detached from Turkey under the present Treaty, and in any territories which cease in accordance with the present Treaty to be under the suzerainty of Turkey, Turkey hereby agrees to accept any decisions in conformity with the principles enunciated below taken by the Allied Powers, in agreement where necessary with other Powers, in relation to any matters previously dealt with by the Constantinople Superior Council of Health or the Turkish Sanitary Administration which was directed by the said Council, or by the Alexandria Sanitary, Maritime and Quarantine Board.

The principles referred to in the preceding paragraph are as follows:

(a) Each Allied Power will be responsible for maintaining and conducting in accordance with the provisions of international sanitary conventions its own quarantine establishments in any territory detached from Turkey which is placed under its control, whether the Allied Power be in sovereign possession, or act as mandatory or protector, or be responsible for the administration, of the territory in question;

(b) Such measures for the sanitary control of the Hedjaz pilgrimage as have hitherto been carried out by, or under the direction of, the Constantinople Superior Council of Health or the Turkish Sanitary Administration, or by the Alexandria Sanitary, Maritime and Quarantine Board, will henceforth be undertaken by the Allied Powers under whose sovereignty, mandate, protection or responsibility will pass those territories in which the various quarantine stations and sanitary establishments necessary for the execution of such measures are situated. The measures will be in conformity with the provisions of international sanitary conventions, and in order to secure complete uniformity in their execution each Allied Power concerned in the sanitary control of the pilgrimage will be represented on a coordinating Pilgrimage Quarantine Committee placed under the supervision of the Council of the League of Nations.

ARTICLE 429.
The High Contracting Parties agree that, in the absence of a subsequent agreement to the contrary, the Chairman of any Commission established by the present Treaty shall in the event of an equality of votes be entitled to a second vote.

ARTICLE 430.
Except where otherwise provided in the present Treaty, in all cases where the Treaty provides for the settlement of a question affecting particularly certain States by means of a special Convention to be concluded between the States concerned, it is understood by the High Contracting Parties that difficulties arising in this connection shall, until Turkey is admitted to membership of the League of Nations, be settled by the Principal Allied Powers.

ARTICLE 431.
Subject to any special provisions of the present Treaty, at the expiration of a period of six months from its coming into force, the Turkish laws must have been modified and shall be maintained by the Turkish Government in conformity with the present Treaty.

Within the same period, all the administrative and other measures relating to the execution of the present Treaty must have been taken by the Turkish Government.

ARTICLE 432.
Turkey will remain bound to give every facility for any investigation which the Council of the League of Nations, acting if need be by a majority vote, may consider necessary, in any matters relating directly or indirectly to the application of the present Treaty.

ARTICLE 433.
The High Contracting Parties agree that Russia shall be entitled, on becoming a Member of the League of Nations, to accede to the present Treaty under such conditions as may be agreed upon between the Principal Allied Powers and Russia, and without prejudice to any rights expressly conferred upon her under the present Treaty.

The present Treaty, in French, in English, and in Italian, shall be ratified. In case of divergence the French text shall prevail, except in Parts I (Covenant of the League of Nations) and XII (Labour), where the French and English texts shall be of equal force. The deposit of ratifications shall be made at Paris as soon as possible. Powers of which the seat of the Government is outside Europe will be entitled merely to inform the Government of the French Republic through their diplomatic representative at Paris that their ratification has been given; in that case they must transmit the instrument of ratification as soon as possible.

A first procès-verbal of the deposit of ratifications will be drawn up as soon as the Treaty has been ratified by Turkey on the one hand, and by three of the Principal Allied Powers on the other hand.

From the date of this first procès-verbal the Treaty will come into force between the High Contracting Parties who have ratified it.

For the determination of all periods of time provided for in the present Treaty this date will be the date of the coming into force of the Treaty.

In all other respects the Treaty will enter into force for each Power at the date of the deposit of its ratification. The French Government will transmit to all the signatory Powers a certified copy of the procès-verbaux of the deposit of ratifications.

IN FAITH WHEREOF the above-named Plenipotentiaries have signed the present Treaty.

Done at Sevrès, the tenth day of August one thousand nine hundred and twenty, in a single copy which will remain deposited in the archives of the French Republic, and of which authenticated copies will be transmitted to each of the Signatory Powers.

(L. S.) GEORGE GRAHAME.
(L. S.) GEORGE H. PERLEY.
(L. S.) ANDREW FISHER.
(L. S.) GEORGE GRAHAME.
(L. S.) R. A. BLANKENBERG.
(L. S.) ARTHUR HIRTZEL.
(L. S.) A. MILLERAND.
(L. S.) F. FRANÇOIS-MARSAL.
(L. S.) JULES CAMBON. (L. S.) PALÉOLOGUE.
(L. S.) BONIN.
(L. S.) MARIETTI.

(L. S.) K:. MATSUI.
(L. S.) A. AHARONIAN.
(L. S.) J. VAN DEN HEUVEL.
(L. S.) ROLIN JAEQUEMYNS,
(L. S.) E. K. VENIZELOS.
(L. S.) A. ROMANOS.

(L. S.) MAURICE ZAMOYSKI.
(L. S.) ERASME PILTZ
(L. S.) AFFONSO COSTA.

(L. S.) D. J. GUIKA.

(L. S.) STEFAN OSUSKY.

(L. S.) HADI.
(l.. S.) DR. RIZA TEWFIK.
(L. S.) RÉCHAD HALISS.

8.3. Der Vertrag von Lausanne vom 24. Juli 1923

TREATY OF PEACE WITH TURKEY - SIGNED AT LAUSANNE - JULY 24, 1923

THE BRITISH EMPIRE, FRANCE, ITALY, JAPAN, GREECE, ROUMANIA and the SERB-CROAT-SLOVENE STATE, of the one part,

and TURKEY, of the other part;

Being united in the desire to bring to a final close the state of war which has existed in the East since 1914,
Being anxious to re-establish the relations of friendship and commerce which are essential to the mutual well-being of their respective peoples,
And considering that these relations must be based on respect for the independence and sovereignty of States,
Have decided to conclude a Treaty for this purpose, and have appointed as their Plenipotentiaries:

HIS MAJESTY THE KING OF THE UNITED KINGDOM OF GREAT BRITAIN AND IRELAND AND OF THE BRITISH DOMINIONS BEYOND THE SEAS, EMPEROR OF INDIA:
> The Right Honourable Sir Horace George Montagu Rumbold, Baronet, G.C.M.G., High Commissioner at Constantinople;

THE PRESIDENT OF THE FRENCH REPUBLIC:
> General Maurice Pelle, Ambassador of France, High Commissioner of the Republic in the East, Grand Officer of the National Order of the Legion of Honour;

HIS MAJESTY THE KING OF ITALY:
> The Honourable Marquis Camillo Garroni, Senator of the Kingdom, Ambassador of Italy, High Commissioner at Constantinople, Grand Cross of the Orders of Saints Maurice and Lazarus, and of the Crown of Italy;
> M. Giulio Cesare Montagna, Envoy Extraordinary and Minister Plenipotentiary at Athens, Commander of the Orders of Saints Maurice and Lazarus, Grand Officer of the Crown of Italy;

HIS MAJESTY THE EMPEROR OF JAPAN:
> Mr. Kentaro Otchiai, Jusammi, First Class of the Order of the Rising Sun, Ambassador Extraordinary and Plenipotentiary at Rome;

HIS MAJESTY THE KING OF THE HELLENES:
> M. Eleftherios K. Veniselos, formerly President of the Council of Ministers, Grand Cross of the Order of the Saviour;
> M. Demetrios Caclamanos, Minister Plenipotentiary at London, Commander of the Order of the Saviour;

HIS MAJESTY THE KING OF ROUMANIA:
> M. Constantine I. Diamandy, Minister Plenipotentiary;
> M. Constantine Contzesco, Minister Plenipotentiary;

HIS MAJESTY THE KING OF THE SERBS, THE CROATS AND THE SLOVENES:
> Dr. Miloutine Yovanovitch, Envoy Extraordinary and Minister Plenipotentiary at Berne;

THE GOVERNMENT OF THE GRAND NATIONAL ASSEMBLY OF TURKEY:
> Ismet Pasha, Minister for Foreign Affairs, Deputy for Adrianople;
> Dr. Riza Nour Bey, Minister for Health and for Public Assistance, Deputy for Sinope;
> Hassan Bey, formerly Minister, Deputy for Trebizond;

Who, having produced their full powers, found in good and due form, have agreed as follows:

TREATY OF LAUSANNE - PART 1

POLITICAL CLAUSES

ARTICLE 1.

From the coming into force of the present Treaty, the state of peace will be definitely re-established between the British Empire, France, Italy, Japan, Greece, Roumania and the Serb-Croat-Slovene State of the one part, and Turkey of the other part, as well as between their respective nationals. Official relations will be resumed on both sides and, in the respective territories, diplomatic and consular representatives will receive, without prejudice to such agreements as may be concluded in the future, treatment in accordance with the general principles of international law.

SECTION I.
I. TERRITORIAL CLAUSES.
ARTICLE 2.
From the Black Sea to the Ægean the frontier of Turkey is laid down as follows:
(1) *With Bulgaria*:
From the mouth of the River Rezvaya, to the River Maritza, the point of junction of the three frontiers of Turkey, Bulgaria and Greece:
the southern frontier of Bulgaria as at present demarcated;
(2) *With Greece*:
Thence to the confluence of the Arda and the Maritza:
the course of the Maritza;
then upstream along the Arda, up to a point on that river to be determined on the spot in the immediate neighbourhood of the village of Tchorek-Keuy:
the course of the Arda;
thence in a south-easterly direction up to a point on the Maritza, 1 kilom. below Bosna-Keuy:
a roughly straight line leaving in Turkish territory the village of Bosna-Keuy. The village of Tchorek-Keuy shall be assigned to Greece or to Turkey according as the majority of the population shall be found to be Greek or Turkish by the Commission for which provision is made in Article 5, the population which has migrated into this village after the 11th October, 1922, not being taken into account;
thence to the Ægean Sea:
the course of the Maritza.

ARTICLE 3.
From the Mediterranean to the frontier of Persia, the frontier of Turkey is laid down as follows:
(1) *With Syria*:
The frontier described in Article 8 of the Franco-Turkish Agreement of the 20th October, 1921;
(2) *With Iraq*:
The frontier between Turkey and Iraq shall be laid down in friendly arrangement to be concluded between Turkey and Great Britain within nine months.
In the event of no agreement being reached between the two Governments within the time mentioned, the dispute shall be referred to the Council of the League of Nations.
The Turkish and British Governments reciprocally undertake that, pending the decision to be reached on the subject of the frontier, no military or other movement shall take place which might modify in any way the present state of the territories of which the final fate will depend upon that decision.

ARTICLE 4.
The frontiers described by the present Treaty are traced on the one-in-a-million maps attached to the present Treaty. In case of divergence between the text and the map, the text will prevail. [See Introduction.]

ARTICLE 5.
A Boundary Commission will be appointed to trace on the ground the frontier defined in Article 2 (2). This Commission will be composed of representatives of Greece and of Turkey, each Power appointing one representative, and a president chosen by them from the nationals of a third Power.
They shall endeavour in all cases to follow as nearly as possible the descriptions given in the present Treaty, taking into account as far as possible administrative boundaries and local economic interests.
The decision of the Commission will be taken by a majority and shall be binding on the parties concerned.
The expenses of the Commission shall be borne in equal shares by the parties concerned.

ARTICLE 6.
In so far as concerns frontiers defined by a waterway as distinct from its banks, the phrases "course" or "channel" used in the descriptions of the present Treaty signify, as regards non-navigable rivers, the median line of the waterway or of its principal branch, and, as regards navigable rivers, the median line of the principal channel of navigation. It will rest with the Boundary Commission to specify whether the frontier line shall follow any changes of the course or channel which may take place, or whether it shall be definitely fixed by the position of the course or channel at the time when the present Treaty comes into force.
In the absence of provisions to the contrary, in the present Treaty, islands and islets lying within three miles of the coast are included within the frontier of the coastal State.

ARTICLE 7.
The- various States concerned undertake to furnish to the Boundary Commission all documents necessary for its task, especially authentic copies of agreements fixing existing or old frontiers, all large scale maps in exist-

ence, geodetic data, surveys completed but unpublished, and information concerning the changes of frontier watercourses. The maps, geodetic data, and surveys, even if unpublished, which are in the possession of the Turkish authorities, must be delivered at Constantinople with the least possible delay from the coming into force of the present Treaty to the President of the Commission.

The States concerned also undertake to instruct the local authorities to communicate to the Commission all documents, especially plans, cadastral and land books, and to furnish on demand all details regarding property, existing economic conditions and other necessary information.

ARTICLE 8.

The various States interested undertake to give every assistance to the Boundary Commission, whether directly or through local authorities, in everything that concerns transport, accommodation, labour, materials (sign posts, boundary pillars) necessary for the accomplishment of its mission.

In particular, the Turkish Government undertakes to furnish, if required, the technical personnel necessary to assist the Boundary Commission in the accomplishment of its duties.

ARTICLE 9.

The various States interested undertake to safeguard the trigonometrical points, signals, posts or frontier marks erected by the Commission.

ARTICLE 10.

The pillars will be placed so as to be intervisible. They will be numbered, and their position and their number will be noted on a cartographic document.

ARTICLE 11.

The protocols defining the boundary and the maps and documents attached thereto will be made out in triplicate, of which two copies will be forwarded to the Governments of the limitrophe States, and the third to the Government of the French Republic, which will deliver authentic copies to the Powers who sign the present Treaty.

ARTICLE 12.

The decision taken on the 13th February, 1914, by the Conference of London, in virtue of Articles 5 of the Treaty of London of the 17th-30th May, 1913, and 15 of the Treaty of Athens of the 1st-14th November, 1913, which decision was communicated to the Greek Government on the 13th February, 1914, regarding the sovereignty of Greece over the islands of the Eastern Mediterranean, other than the islands of Imbros, Tenedos and Rabbit Islands, particularly the islands of Lemnos, Samothrace, Mytilene, Chios, Samos and Nikaria, is confirmed, subject to the provisions of the present Treaty respecting the islands placed under the sovereignty of Italy which form the subject of Article 15.

Except where a provision to the contrary is contained in the present Treaty, the islands situated at less than three miles from the Asiatic coast remain under Turkish sovereignty.

ARTICLE 13.

With a view to ensuring the maintenance of peace, the Greek Government undertakes to observe the following restrictions in the islands of Mytilene, Chios, Samos and Nikaria:

(1) No naval base and no fortification will be established in the said islands.

(2) Greek military aircraft will be forbidden to fly over the territory of the Anatolian coast. Reciprocally, the Turkish Government will forbid their military aircraft to fly over the said islands.

(3) The Greek military forces in the said islands will be limited to the normal contingent called up for military service, which can be trained on the spot, as well as to a force of gendarmerie and police in proportion to the force of gendarmerie and police existing in the whole of the Greek territory.

ARTICLE 14.

The islands of Imbros and Tenedos, remaining under Turkish sovereignty, shall enjoy a special administrative organisation composed of local elements and furnishing every guarantee for the native non-Moslem population in so far as concerns local administration and the protection of persons and property. The maintenance of order will be assured therein by a police force recruited from amongst the local population by the local administration above provided for and placed under its orders.

The agreements which have been, or may be, concluded between Greece and Turkey relating to the exchange of the Greek and Turkish populations will not be applied to the inhabitants of the islands of Imbros and Tenedos.

ARTICLE 15.

Turkey renounces in favour of Italy all rights and title over the following islands: Stampalia (Astrapalia), Rhodes (Rhodos), Calki (Kharki), Scarpanto, Casos (Casso), Piscopis (Tilos), Misiros (Nisyros), Calimnos (Kalymnos), Leros, Patmos, Lipsos (Lipso), Simi (Symi), and Cos (Kos), which are now occupied by Italy, and the islets dependent thereon, and also over the island of Castellorizzo.

ARTICLE 16.

Turkey hereby renounces all rights and title whatsoever over or respecting the territories situated outside the frontiers laid down in the present Treaty and the islands other than those over which her sovereignty is recognised by the said Treaty, the future of these territories and islands being settled or to be settled by the parties concerned.

The provisions of the present Article do not prejudice any special arrangements arising from neighbourly relations which have been or may be concluded between Turkey and any limitrophe countries.

ARTICLE 17.

The renunciation by Turkey of all rights and titles over Egypt and over the Soudan will take effect as from the 5th November, 1914.

ARTICLE 18.

Turkey is released from all undertakings and obligations in regard to the Ottoman loans guaranteed on the Egyptian tribute, that is to say, the loans of 1855, 1891 and 1894. The annual payments made by Egypt for the service of these loans now forming part of the service of the Egyptian Public Debt, Egypt is freed from all other obligations relating to the Ottoman Public Debt.

ARTICLE 19.

Any questions arising from the recognition of the State of Egypt shall be settled by agreements to be negotiated subsequently in a manner to be determined later between the Powers concerned. The provisions of the present Treaty relating to territories detached from Turkey under the said Treaty will not apply to Egypt.

ARTICLE 20.

Turkey hereby recognises the annexation of Cyprus proclaimed by the British Government on the 5th November, 1914.

ARTICLE 21.

Turkish nationals ordinarily resident in Cyprus on the 5th November, 1914, will acquire British nationality subject to the conditions laid down in the local law, and will thereupon lose their Turkish nationality. They will, however, have the right to opt for Turkish nationality within two years from the coming into force of the present Treaty, provided that they leave Cyprus within twelve months after having so opted.

Turkish nationals ordinarily resident in Cyprus on the coming into force of the present Treaty who, at that date, have acquired or are in process of acquiring British nationality in consequence of a request made in accordance with the local law, will also thereupon lose their Turkish nationality.

It is understood that the Government of Cyprus will be entitled to refuse British nationality to inhabitants of the island who, being Turkish nationals, had formerly acquired another nationality without the consent of the Turkish Government.

ARTICLE 22.

Without prejudice to the general stipulations of Article 27, Turkey hereby recognises the definite abolition of all rights and privileges whatsoever which she enjoyed in Libya under the Treaty of Lausanne of the 18th October, 1912, and the instruments connected therewith.

2. SPECIAL PROVISIONS.

ARTICLE 23.

The High Contracting Parties are agreed to recognise and declare the principle of freedom of transit and of navigation, by sea and by air, in time of peace as in time of war, in the strait of the Dardanelles, the Sea of Marmora and the Bosphorus, as prescribed in the separate Convention signed this day, regarding the regime of the Straits. This Convention will have the same force and effect in so far as the present High Contracting Parties are concerned as if it formed part of the present Treaty.

ARTICLE 24.

The separate Convention signed this day respecting the regime for the frontier described in Article 2 of the present Treaty will have equal force and effect in so far as the present High Contracting Parties are concerned as if it formed part of the present Treaty.

ARTICLE 25.

Turkey undertakes to recognise the full force of the Treaties of Peace and additional Conventions concluded by the other Contracting Powers with the Powers who fought on the side of Turkey, and to recognise whatever dispositions have been or may be made concerning the territories of the former German Empire, of Austria, of Hungary and of Bulgaria, and to recognise the new States within their frontiers as there laid down.

ARTICLE 26.

Turkey hereby recognises and accepts the frontiers of Germany, Austria, Bulgaria, Greece, Hungary, Poland, Roumania, the Serb-Croat-Slovene State and the Czechoslovak State, as these frontiers have been or may be determined by the Treaties referred to in Article 25 or by any supplementary conventions.

ARTICLE 27.

No power or jurisdiction in political, legislative or administrative matters shall be exercised outside Turkish territory by the Turkish Government or authorities, for any reason whatsoever, over the nationals of a territory placed under the sovereignty or protectorate of the other Powers signatory of the present Treaty, or over the nationals of a territory detached from Turkey.

It is understood that the spiritual attributions of the Moslem religious authorities are in no way infringed.

ARTICLE 28.

Each of the High Contracting Parties hereby accepts, in so far as it is concerned, the complete abolition of the Capitulations in Turkey in every respect.

ARTICLE 29.

Moroccans, who are French nationals ("ressortissants") and Tunisians shall enjoy in Turkey the same treatment in all respects as other French nationals ("ressortissants").

Natives ("ressortissants") of Libya shall enjoy in Turkey the same treatment in all respects as other Italian nationals ("ressortissants").

The stipulations of the present Article in no way prejudge the nationality of persons of Tunisian, Libyan and Moroccan origin established in Turkey.

Reciprocally, in the territories the inhabitants of which benefit by the stipulations of the first and second paragraphs of this Article, Turkish nationals shall benefit by the same treatment as in France and in Italy respectively.

The treatment to which merchandise originating in or destined for the territories, the inhabitants of which benefit from the stipulations of the first paragraph of this Article, shall be subject in Turkey, and, reciprocally, the treatment to which merchandise originating in or destined for Turkey shall be subject in the said territories shall be settled by agreement between the French and Turkish Governments.

SECTION II.
NATIONALITY.

ARTICLE 30.

Turkish subjects habitually resident in territory which in accordance with the provisions of the present Treaty is detached from Turkey will become *ipso facto*, in the conditions laid down by the local law, nationals of the State to which such territory is transferred.

ARTICLE 31.

Persons over eighteen years of age, losing their Turkish nationality and obtaining *ipso facto* a new nationality under Article 30, shall be entitled within a period of two years from the coming into force of the present Treaty to opt for Turkish nationality.

ARTICLE 32.

Persons over eighteen years of age, habitually resident in territory detached from Turkey in accordance with the present Treaty, and differing in race from the majority of the population of such territory shall, within two years from the coming into force of the present Treaty, be entitled to opt for the nationality of one of the States in which the majority of the population is of the same race as the person exercising the right to opt, subject to the consent of that State.

ARTICLE 33.

Persons who have exercised the right to opt in accordance with the provisions of Articles 31 and 32 must, within the succeeding twelve months, transfer their place of residence to the State for which they have opted.

They will be entitled to retain their immovable property in the territory of the other State where they had their place of residence before exercising their right to opt.

They may carry with them their movable property of every description. No export or import duties may be imposed upon them in connection with the removal of such property.

ARTICLE 34.

Subject to any agreements which it may be necessary to conclude between the Governments exercising authority in the countries detached from Turkey and the Governments of the countries where the persons concerned are resident, Turkish nationals of over eighteen years of age who are natives of a territory detached from Turkey under the present Treaty, and who on its coming into force are habitually resident abroad, may opt for the nationality of the territory of which they are natives, if they belong by race to the majority of the population of that territory, and subject to the consent of the Government exercising authority therein. This right of option must be exercised within two years from the coming into force of the present Treaty.

ARTICLE 35.

The Contracting Powers undertake to put no hindrance in the way of the exercise of the right which the persons concerned have under the present Treaty, or under the Treaties of Peace concluded with Germany, Austria, Bulgaria or Hungary, or under any Treaty concluded by the said Powers, other than Turkey, or any of them, with Russia, or between themselves, to choose any other nationality which may be open to them.

ARTICLE 36.

For the purposes of the provisions of this Section, the status of a married woman will be governed by that of her husband, and the status of children under eighteen years of age by that of their parents.

SECTION III.
PROTECTION OF MINORITIES.

ARTICLE 37.

Turkey undertakes that the stipulations contained in Articles 38 to 44 shall be recognised as fundamental laws, and that no law, no regulation, nor official action shall conflict or interfere with these stipulations, nor shall any law, regulation, nor official action prevail over them.

ARTICLE 38.

The Turkish Government undertakes to assure full and complete protection of life and liberty to all inhabitants of Turkey without distinction of birth, nationality, language, race or religion.

All inhabitants of Turkey shall be entitled to free exercise, whether in public or private, of any creed, religion or belief, the observance of which shall not be incompatible with public order and good morals.

Non-Moslem minorities will enjoy full freedom of movement and of emigration, subject to the measures applied, on the whole or on part of the territory, to all Turkish nationals, and which may be taken by the Turkish Government for national defence, or for the maintenance of public order.

ARTICLE 39.

Turkish nationals belonging to non-Moslem minorities will enjoy the same civil and political rights as Moslems.

All the inhabitants of Turkey, without distinction of religion, shall be equal before the law.

Differences of religion, creed or confession shall not prejudice any Turkish national in matters relating to the enjoyment of civil or political rights, as, for instance, admission to public employments, functions and honours, or the exercise of professions and industries.

No restrictions shall be imposed on the free use by any Turkish national of any language in private intercourse, in commerce, religion, in the press, or in publications of any kind or at public meetings.

Notwithstanding the existence of the official language, adequate facilities shall be given to Turkish nationals of non-Turkish speech for the oral use of their own language before the Courts.

ARTICLE 40.

Turkish nationals belonging to non-Moslem minorities shall enjoy the same treatment and security in law and in fact as other Turkish nationals. In particular, they shall have an equal right to establish, manage and control at their own expense, any charitable, religious and social institutions, any schools and other establishments for instruction and education, with the right to use their own language and to exercise their own religion freely therein.

ARTICLE 41.

As regards public instruction, the Turkish Government will grant in those towns and districts, where a considerable proportion of non-Moslem nationals are resident, adequate facilities for ensuring that in the primary schools the instruction shall be given to the children of such Turkish nationals through the medium of their own language. This provision will not prevent the Turkish Government from making the teaching of the Turkish language obligatory in the said schools.

In towns and districts where there is a considerable proportion of Turkish nationals belonging to non-Moslem minorities, these minorities shall be assured an equitable share in the enjoyment and application of the sums which may be provided out of public funds under the State, municipal or other budgets for educational, religious, or charitable purposes.

The sums in question shall be paid to the qualified representatives of the establishments and institutions concerned.

ARTICLE 42.

The Turkish Government undertakes to take, as regards non-Moslem minorities, in so far as concerns their family law or personal status, measures permitting the settlement of these questions in accordance with the customs of those minorities.

These measures will be elaborated by special Commissions composed of representatives of the Turkish Government and of representatives of each of the minorities concerned in equal number. In case of divergence, the Turkish Government and the Council of the League of Nations will appoint in agreement an umpire chosen from amongst European lawyers.

The Turkish Government undertakes to grant full protection to the churches, synagogues, cemeteries, and other religious establishments of the above-mentioned minorities. All facilities and authorisation will be granted to the pious foundations, and to the religious and charitable institutions of the said minorities at present existing in Turkey, and the Turkish Government will not refuse, for the formation of new religious and charitable institutions, any of the necessary facilities which are guaranteed to other private institutions of that nature.

ARTICLE 43.

Turkish nationals belonging to non-Moslem minorities shall not be compelled to perform any act which constitutes a violation of their faith or religious observances, and shall not be placed under any disability by reason of their refusal to attend Courts of Law or to perform any legal business on their weekly day of rest.

This provision, however, shall not exempt such Turkish nationals from such obligations as shall be imposed upon all other Turkish nationals for the preservation of public order.

ARTICLE 44.

Turkey agrees that, in so far as the preceding Articles of this Section affect non-Moslem nationals of Turkey, these provisions constitute obligations of international concern and shall be placed under the guarantee of the League of Nations. They shall not be modified without the assent of the majority of the Council of the League of Nations. The British Empire, France, Italy and Japan hereby agree not to withhold their assent to any modification in these Articles which is in due form assented to by a majority of the Council of the League of Nations.

Turkey agrees that any Member of the Council of the League of Nations shall have the right to bring to the attention of the Council any infraction or danger of infraction of any of these obligations, and that the Council may thereupon take such action and give such directions as it may deem proper and effective in the circumstances.

Turkey further agrees that any difference of opinion as to questions of law or of fact arising out of these Articles between the Turkish Government and any one of the other Signatory Powers or any other Power, a member of the Council of the League of Nations, shall be held to be a dispute of an international character under Article 14 of the Covenant of the League of Nations. The Turkish Government hereby consents that any such dispute shall, if the other party thereto demands, be referred to the Permanent Court of International Justice. The decision of the Permanent Court shall be final and shall have the same force and effect as an award under Article 13 of the Covenant.

ARTICLE 45.

The rights conferred by the provisions of the present Section on the non-Moslem minorities of Turkey will be similarly conferred by Greece on the Moslem minority in her territory.

TREATY OF LAUSANNE - PART II

FINANCIAL CLAUSES.
SECTION I.
OTTOMAN PUBLIC DEBT.

ARTICLE 46.

The Ottoman Public Debt, as defined in the Table annexed to the present Section, shall be distributed under the conditions laid down in the present Section between Turkey, the States in favour of which territory has been detached from the Ottoman Empire after the Balkan wars of 1912-13, the States to which the islands referred to in Articles 12 and 15 of the present Treaty and the territory referred to in the last paragraph of the present Article have been attributed, and the States newly created in territories in Asia which are detached from the Ottoman Empire under the present Treaty. All the above States shall also participate, under the conditions laid down in the present Section, in the annual charges for the service of the Ottoman Public Debt from the dates referred to in Article 53.

From the dates laid down in Article 53, Turkey shall not be held in any way whatsoever responsible for the shares of the Debt for which other States are liable.

For the purpose of the distribution of the Ottoman Public Debt, that portion of the territory of Thrace which was under Turkish sovereignty on the 1st August, 1914, and lies outside the boundaries of Turkey as laid down by Article 2 of the present Treaty, shall be deemed to be detached from the Ottoman Empire under the said Treaty.

ARTICLE 47.

The Council of the Ottoman Public Debt shall, within three months from the coming into force of the present Treaty, determine, on the basis laid down by Articles 50 and 51, the amounts of the annuities for the loans referred to in Part A of the Table annexed to the present Section which are payable by each of the States concerned, and shall notify to them this amount.

These States shall be granted an opportunity to send to Constantinople delegates to check the calculations made for this purpose by the Council of the Ottoman Public Debt.

The Council of the Debt shall exercise the functions referred to in Article 134 of the Treaty of Peace with Bulgaria of the 27th November, 1919.

Any disputes which may arise between the parties concerned as to the application of the principles laid down in the present Article shall be referred, not more than one month after the notification referred to in the first paragraph, to an arbitrator whom the Council of the League of Nations will be asked to appoint; this arbitrator shall give his decision within a period of not more than three months. The remuneration of the arbitrator shall be determined by the Council of the League of Nations, and shall, together with the other expenses of the arbitration, be borne by the parties concerned. The decisions of the arbitrator shall be final. The payment of the annuities shall not be suspended by the reference of any disputes to the above-mentioned arbitrator.

ARTICLE 48.

The States, other than Turkey, among which the Ottoman Public Debt, as defined in Part A of the Table annexed to this Section is attributed, shall, within three months from the date on which they are notified, in accordance with Article 47, of their respective shares in the annual charges referred to in that Article, assign to the Council of the Debt adequate security for the payment of their share. If such security is not assigned within the above-mentioned period, or in the case of any disagreement as to the adequacy of the security assigned, any of the Governments signatory to the present Treaty shall be entitled to appeal to the Council of the League of Nations.

The Council of the League of Nations shall be empowered to entrust the collection of the revenues assigned as security to international financial organisations existing in the countries (other than Turkey) among which the Debt is distributed. The decisions of the Council of the League of Nations shall be final.

ARTICLE 49

Within one month from the date of the final determination under Article 47 of the amount of the annuities for which each of the States concerned is liable, a Commission shall meet in Paris to determine the method of carrying out the distribution of the nominal capital of the Ottoman Public Debt as defined in Part A of the Table annexed to this Section. This distribution shall be made in accordance with the proportions adopted for the division of the annuities, and account shall be taken of the terms of the agreements governing the loans and of the provisions of this Section.

The Commission referred to in the first paragraph shall consist of a representative of the Turkish Government, a representative of the Council of the Ottoman Public Debt, a representative of the debt other than the Unified Debt and the Lots Turcs; each of the Governments concerned shall also be entitled to appoint a representative. All questions in regard to which the Commission may be unable to reach agreement shall be referred to the arbitrator referred to in the fourth paragraph of Article 47.

If Turkey shall decide to create new securities in respect of her share, the distribution of the capital of the Ottoman Public Debt shall be made in the first instance as it affects Turkey by a Committee consisting of the representative of the Turkish Government, the representative of the Council of the Ottoman Public Debt and the representative of the debt other than the Unified Debt and the Lots Turcs. The new securities shall be delivered to the Commission, which shall ensure their delivery to the bondholders upon such terms as will provide for the release of Turkey from liability and the rights of the bondholders towards the other States which are liable for a share of the Ottoman Public Debt. The securities issued in respect of the share of each State in the Ottoman Public Debt shall be exempt in the territory of the High Contracting Parties from all stamp duties or other taxes which would be involved by such issue.

The payment of the annuities for which each of the States concerned is liable shall not be postponed as a consequence of the provisions of the present Article in regard to the distribution of the nominal capital.

ARTICLE 50.

The distribution of the annual charges referred to in Article 47 and of the nominal capital of the Ottoman Public Debt mentioned in Article 49 shall be effected in the following manner:

(1) The loans prior to the 17th October, 1912, and the annuities of such loans shall be distributed between the Ottoman Empire as it existed after the Balkan wars of 1912-13, the Balkan States in favour of which territory was detached from the Ottoman Empire after those wars, and the States to which the islands referred to in Arti-

cles 12 and 15 of the present Treaty have been attributed; account shall be taken of the territorial changes which have taken place after the coming into force of the treaties which ended those wars or subsequent treaties.

(2) The residue of the loans for which the Ottoman Empire remained liable after this first distribution and the residue of the annuities of such loans, together with the loans contracted by that Empire between the 17th October, 1912, and the 1st November, 1914, and the annuities of such loans shall be distributed between Turkey, the newly created States in Asia in favour of which a territory has been detached from the Ottoman Empire under the present Treaty, and the State to which the territory referred to in the last paragraph of Article 46 of the said Treaty has been attributed.

The distribution of the capital shall in the case of each loan be based on the capital amount outstanding at the date of the coming into force of the present Treaty.

ARTICLE 51.

The amount of the share in the annual charges of the Ottoman Public Debt for which each State concerned is liable in consequence of the distribution provided for by Article 50 shall be determined as follows:

(1) As regards the distribution provided for by Article 50 (1), in the first place the share of the islands referred to in Articles 12 and 15 and of the territories detached from the Ottoman Empire after the Balkan wars, taken together, shall be fixed. The amount of this share shall bear the same proportion to the total sum of the annuities to be distributed in accordance with Article 50 (1) as the average total revenue of the above mentioned islands and territories, taken as a whole, bore to the average total revenue of the Ottoman Empire in the financial years 1910-1911 and 1911-1912, including the proceeds of the customs surtaxes established in 1907.

The amount thus determined shall then be distributed among the States to which the territories referred to in the preceding paragraph have been attributed, and the share for which each of these States will thus be made liable shall bear the same proportion to the total amount so distributed as the average total revenue of the territory attributed to each State bore in the financial years 1910-11 and 1911-12 to the average total revenue of the territories detached from the Ottoman Empire after the Balkan Wars and the islands referred to in Articles 12 and 15. In calculating the revenues referred to in this paragraph, customs revenues shall be excluded.

(2) As regards the territories detached from the Ottoman Empire under the present Treaty (including the territory referred to in the last paragraph of Article 46), the amount of the share of each State concerned shall bear the same proportion to the total sum of the annuities to be distributed in accordance with Article 50 (2) as the average total revenue of the detached territory (including the proceeds of the Customs surtax established in 1907) for the financial years 1910-11 and 1911-12 bore to the average total revenue of the Ottoman Empire, excluding the territories and islands referred to in paragraph (1) of this Article.

ARTICLE 52.

The advances referred to in Part B of the Table annexed to the present Section shall be distributed between Turkey and the other States referred to in Article 46 under the following conditions:

(1) As regards the advances referred to in the Table which existed on the 17th October, 1912, the capital amount, if any, outstanding at the date of the coming into force of the present Treaty, together with the interest from the dates mentioned in the first paragraph of Article 53 and the repayments made since those dates, shall be distributed in accordance with the provisions of Article 50 (1) and Article 51 (1).

(2) As regards the amounts for which the Ottoman Empire remains liable after the first distribution and the advances referred to in the Table which were contracted by the said Empire between the 17th October, 1912, and the 1st November, 1914, the capital amount, if any, outstanding at the date of the coming into force of the present Treaty, together with the interest from the 1st March, 1920, and the repayments made since that date, shall be distributed in accordance with the provisions of Article 50 (2) and Article 51 (2).

The Council of the Ottoman Public Debt shall, within three months from the coming into force of the present Treaty, determine the amount of the share in these advances for which each of the States concerned is liable, and notify them of such amount.

The sums for which States other than Turkey are liable shall be paid by those States to the Council of the Debt and shall be paid by the Council to the creditors, or credited to the Turkish Government up to the amount paid by Turkey, by way of interest or repayment, for the account of those States.

The payments referred to in the preceding paragraph shall be made by five equal annuities from the coming into force of the present Treaty. Such portion of these payments as is payable to the creditors of the Ottoman Empire shall bear interest at the rates laid down in the contracts governing the advances; the portion to be credited to the Turkish Government shall be paid without interest.

ARTICLE 53.

The annuities for the service of the loans of the Ottoman Public Debt (as defined in Part A of the Table annexed to this Section) due by the States in favour of which a territory has been detached from the Ottoman Empire after the Balkan wars, shall be payable as from the coming into force of the treaties by which the respective territories were transferred to those States. In the case of the islands referred to in Article 12, the annuity shall be payable as from the 1st/14th November, 1913, and, in the case of the islands referred to in Article 15, as from the 17th October, 1912. The annuities due by the States newly created in territories in Asia detached from the Ottoman Empire under the present Treaty, and by the State to which the territory referred to in the last paragraph of Article 46 has been attributed, shall be payable as from the 1st March, 1920.

ARTICLE 54.

The Treasury Bills of 1911, 1912 and 1913 included in Part A of the Table annexed to this Section shall be repaid, with interest at the agreed rate, within ten years from the dates fixed by the contracts.

ARTICLE 55.

The States referred to in Article 46, including Turkey, shall pay to the Ottoman Debt Council the amount of the annuities required for the service of their share of the Ottoman Public Debt (as defined in Part A of the Table annexed to this Section) to the extent that such annuities have remained unpaid as from the dates laid down by Article 53. This payment shall be made, without interest, by means of twenty equal annuities from the coming into force of the present Treaty.

The amount of the annuities paid to the Council of the Debt by the States other than Turkey shall, to the extent that they represent payments made by Turkey for the account of those States, be credited to Turkey on account of the arrears with which she is debited.

ARTICLE 56.

The Council of the Administration of the Ottoman Public Debt shall no longer include delegates of the German, Austrian and Hungarian bondholders.

ARTICLE 57.

Limits of time fixed for the presentation of coupons of or claims for interest upon the loans and advances of the Ottoman Public Debt and the Turkish Loans of 1855, 1891 and 1894 secured on the Egyptian tribute, and the limits of time fixed for the presentation of securities of these loans drawn for repayment, shall, on the territory of the High Contracting Parties, be considered as having been suspended from the 29th October, 1914, until three months after the coming into force of the present Treaty.

ANNEX I TO SECTION I.

Table of the Ottoman Pre-War Public Debt (November 1, 1914).

Part A.

Loan	Date of Contract	Interest %	Date of Redemption	Bank of Issue
1	2	3	4	5
Unified Debt	1-14.9.1903--8-21.6.1906	4		
Lots turcs	5.1.1870			
Osmanie	18-30.4.1890	4	1931	Imperial Ottoman Bank
Tombac priority	26.4-8.5.1893	4	1954	Imperial Ottoman Bank
40,000,000fr (Oriental Railways)	1-13.3.1894	4	1957	Deutsche Bank and its group, Including International Bank and two French banks.
5%, 1896	29.2-12.3.1896	5	1946	Imperial Ottoman Bank
Customs, 1902	17-29.5.1886-28.9-11.10.1902	4	1958	Imperial Ottoman Bank
4%, 1903 (Fisheries)	3.10.1888-21.2-6.3.1903.	4	1958	Deutsche Bank
Bagdad, Series I	20.2-5.3.1903	4	2001	Deutsche Bank
4%, 1904	4-17.9.1903	4	1960	Imperial Ottoman Bank
4%, 1901-1905	21.11-4.12.1901-6.11.1903-25.4-8.5.1905	4	1961	Imperial Ottoman Bank
Tedjhizat-Askerie	4-17.4.1905	4	1961	Deutsche Bank
Bagdad, Series II	20.5-2.6.1908	4	2006	Deutsche Bank
Bagdad, Series III	20.5-2.6.1908	4	2010	Deutsche Bank
4%, 1908	6-19.9.1908	4	1965	Imperial Ottoman Bank
4%, 1909	30.9-13.10.1909	4	1950	Imperial Ottoman Bank

Soma-Panderma	20.11-3.12.1910	4	1992	Imperial Ottoman Bank
Hodeida-Sanaa	24.2-9.3.1911	4	2006	Banque francaise
Customs 1911	27.10-9.11.1910	4	1952	Deutsche Bank and its group
Plain of Koniah irrigation	5-18.1913		1932	
Docks, arsenals and naval constructions	19.11-2 12.1913	5 1/2	1943	
5%, 1914	13-26.4.1914	5	(1962)	Imperial Ottoman Bank
Avance Régie des Tabacs	4.8.1913			
Treasury Bills, 5% 1911 (purchase of warships)	13-7.1911	5	1916[312]	National Bank of Turkey
Treasury Bills, Imperial	8.21.11.1912	6	1915*	Imperial Ottoman Bank
Treasury Bills, 1913 (induding the bills issued directly)	19.1-1.2.1913	5	1918*	Périer and Co.

Part B.

Advance	Date of Contract	Interest	Original Nominal Capital £ T.
Bagdad Railway Company	3/16 June, 1908	7	300,000
Lighthouse Administration	5/18 August, 1904	8	55,000
Lighthouse Administration	5/18 July, 1907	7	300,000
Constanza Cable Company	27/9 October, 1904	4	17,335
Tunnel Company			3,000
Orphan's Fund	Various dates		153,147
Deutsche Bank	13/26 August, 1912	5.5	33,000
Lighthouse Administration	3/16 April, 1913	7	500,000
Anatolia Railway Company	23/5 March, 1914	6	200,000

SECTION II.
MISCELLANEOUS CLAUSES.
ARTICLE 58.

Turkey, on the one hand, and the other Contracting Powers (except Greece) on the other hand, reciprocally renounce all pecuniary claims for the loss and damage suffered respectively by Turkey and the said Powers and by their nationals (including juridical persons) between the 1st August, 1914, and the coming into force of the present Treaty, as the result of acts of war or measures of requisition, sequestration, disposal or confiscation.

Nevertheless, the above provisions are without prejudice to the provisions of Part III (Economic Clauses) of the present Treaty.

Turkey renounces in favour of the other Contracting Parties (except Greece) any right in the sums in gold transferred by Germany and Austria under Article 259 (I) of the Treaty of Peace of the 28th June, I9I9, with Germany, and under Article 210 (I) of the Treaty of Peace of the 10th September, 1919, with Austria.

The Council of the Administration of the Ottoman Public Debt is freed from all liability to make the payments which it was required to make by the Agreement of the 20th June, 1331 (3rd July, 1915) relating to the first issue of Turkish currency notes or by the words inscribed on the back of such notes.

Turkey also agrees not to claim from the British Government or its nationals the repayment of the sums paid for the warships ordered in England by the Ottoman Government which were requisitioned by the British Government in 1914, and renounces all claims in the matter.

ARTICLE 59.

Greece recognises her obligation to make reparation for the damage caused in Anatolia by the acts of the Greek army or administration which were contrary to the laws of war.

On the other hand, Turkey, in consideration of the financial situation of Greece resulting from the prolongation of the war and from its consequences, finally renounces all claims for reparation against the Greek Govern-

---

[312] See Article 54

ment.

ARTICLE 60.

The States in favour of which territory was or is detached from the Ottoman Empire after the Balkan wars or by the present Treaty shall acquire, without payment, all the property and possessions of the Ottoman Empire situated therein.

It is understood that the property and possessions of which the transfer from the Civil List to the State was laid down by the Iradés of the 26th August, 1324 (8th September, 1908) and the 20th April, 1325 (2nd May, 1909), and also those which, on the 30th October, 1918, were administered by the Civil List for the benefit of a public service, are included among the property and possessions referred to in the preceding paragraph, the aforesaid States being subrogated to the Ottoman Empire in regard to the property and possessions in question. The Wakfs created on such property shall be maintained.

The dispute which has arisen between the Greek and Turkish Governments relating to property and possessions which have passed from the Civil List to the State and are situated in territories of the former Ottoman Empire transferred to Greece either after the Balkan wars, or subsequently, shall be referred to an arbitral tribunal at The Hague, in accordance with the special protocol No. 2 annexed to the Treaty of Athens of the 1st-4th November, 1913. The terms of reference shall be settled between the two Governments.

The provisions of this Article will not modify the juridical nature of the property and possessions registered in the name of the Civil List or administered by it, which are not referred to in the second and third paragraphs above.

ARTICLE 61.

The recipients of Turkish civil and military pensions who acquire under the present Treaty the nationality of a State other than Turkey, shall have no claim against the Turkish Government in respect of their pensions.

ARTICLE 62.

Turkey recognises the transfer of any claims to payment or repayment which Germany, Austria, Bulgaria or Hungary may have against her, in accordance with Article 261 of the Treaty of Peace concluded at Versailles on the 28th June, 1919, with Germany, and the corresponding articles of the Treaties of Peace of the 10th September, 1919, with Austria; of the 27th November, 1919, with Bulgaria; and of the 4th June, 1920 with Hungary.

The other Contracting Powers agree to release Turkey from the debts for which she is liable on this account.

The claims which Turkey has against Germany, Austria, Bulgaria and Hungary, are also transferred to the aforesaid Contracting Powers.

ARTICLE 63.

The Turkish Government, in agreement with the other Contracting Powers, hereby releases the German Government from the obligation incurred by it during the war to accept Turkish Government currency notes at a specified rate of exchange in payment for goods to be exported to Turkey from Germany after the war.

TREATY OF LAUSANNE – PART III
ECONOMIC CLAUSES.

ARTICLE 64.

In this part, the expression "Allied Powers" means the Contracting Powers other than Turkey.

The term "Allied nationals" includes physical persons, companies and associations of the Contracting Powers other than Turkey, or of a State or territory under the protection of one of the said Powers.

The provisions of this Part relating to "Allied nationals" shall benefit persons who without having the nationality of one of the Allied Powers, have, in consequence of the protection which they in fact enjoyed at the hands of these Powers, received from the Ottoman authorities the same treatment as Allied nationals and have, on this account, been prejudiced.

SECTION I.
PROPERTY, RIGHTS AND INTERESTS.

ARTICLE 65.

Property, rights and interests which still exist and can be identified in territories remaining Turkish at the date of the coming into force of the present Treaty, and which belong to persons who on the 29th October, 1914, were Allied nationals, shall be immediately restored to the owners in their existing state.

Reciprocally, property, rights and interests which still exist and can be identified in territories subject to the sovereignty or protectorate of the Allied Powers on the 29th October, 1914, or in territories detached from the Ottoman Empire after the Balkan wars and subject to-day to the sovereignty of any such Power, and which belong to Turkish nationals, shall be immediately restored to the owners in their existing state. The same provision shall apply to property, rights and interests which belong to Turkish nationals in territories detached from the Ottoman Empire under the present Treaty, and which may have been subjected to liquidation or any other exceptional measure whatever on the part of the authorities of the Allied Powers.

All property, rights and interests situated in territory detached from the Ottoman Empire under the present Treaty, which, after having been subjected by the Ottoman Government to an exceptional war measure, are now in the hands of the Contracting Power exercising authority over the said territory, and which can be identified, shall be restored to their legitimate owners, in their existing state. The same provision shall apply to immovable property which may have been liquidated by the Contracting Power exercising authority over the said territory. All other claims between individuals shall be submitted to the competent local courts.

All disputes relating to the identity or the restitution of property to which a claim is made shall be submitted to the Mixed Arbitral Tribunal provided for in Section V of this Part.

ARTICLE 66.

In order to give effect to the provisions of the first and second paragraphs of Article 65 the High Contracting Parties will, by the most rapid procedure, restore the owners to the possession of their property, rights and interests free from any burdens or encumbrances with which such property, rights and interests may have been charged without the consent of the said owners. It will be the duty of the Government of the Power effecting the restitution to provide for the compensation of third parties who may have acquired the property directly or indirectly from the said Government and who may be injured by this restitution. Disputes which may arise in connection with such compensation shall be dealt with by the ordinary courts.

In all other cases it will be open to any third parties who may be injured to take action against whoever is responsible, in order to obtain compensation.

In order to give effect to these provisions all acts of transfer or other exceptional war measures, which the High Contracting Parties may have carried out in respect of enemy property, rights and interests, shall be immediately cancelled and stayed when liquidation has not yet been completed. Owners who make claims shall be satisfied by the immediate restitution of their property, rights and interests as soon as these shall have been identified.

When at the date of the signature of the present Treaty the property, rights and interests, the restitution of which is provided for in Article 65. have been liquidated by the authorities of one of the High Contracting Parties, that Party shall be discharged from the obligation to restore the said property, rights and interests by payment of the proceeds of the liquidation to the owner. If, on application being made by the owner, the Mixed Arbitral Tribunal provided for by Section V finds that the liquidation was not effected in such conditions as to ensure the realisation of a fair price, it will have the power, in default of agreement between the parties, to order the addition to the proceeds of the liquidation of such amount as it shall consider equitable. The said property, rights and interests shall be restored if the payment is not made within two months from the agreement with the owner or from the decision of the Mixed Arbitral Tribunal mentioned above.

ARTICLE 67.

Greece, Roumania and the Serb-Croat-Slovene State on the one hand, and Turkey on the other hand undertake mutually to facilitate, both by appropriate administrative measures and by the delivery of all documents relating thereto, the search on their territory for, and the restitution of, movable property of every kind taken away, seized or sequestrated by their armies or administrations in the territory of Turkey, or in the territory of Greece, Roumania or the Serb-Croat-Slovene State respectively, which are actually within the territories in question.

Such search and restitution will take place also as regards property of the nature referred to above seized or sequestrated by German, Austro-Hungarian or Bulgarian armies or administrations in the territory of Greece, Roumania or the Serb-Croat-Slovene State, which has been assigned to Turkey or to her nationals, as well as to property seized or sequestrated by the Greek, Roumanian or Serbian armies in Turkish territory, which has been assigned to Greece, Roumania or the Serb-Croat-Slovene State or to their nationals.

Applications relating to such search and restitution must be made within six months from the coming into force of the present Treaty.

ARTICLE 68.

Debts arising out of contracts concluded, in districts in Turkey occupied by the Greek army, between the Greek authorities and administrations on the one hand and Turkish nationals on the other, shall be paid by the Greek Government in accordance with the provisions of the said contracts.

ARTICLE 69.

No charge, tax or surtax to which, by virtue of the privileges which they enjoyed on the 1st August, 1914, Allied nationals and their property were not subject, shall be collected from Allied subjects or their property in respect of the financial years earlier than the financial year 1922-23.

If any sums have been collected after the 15th May, 1923, in respect of financial years earlier than the financial year 1922-1923, the amount shall be refunded to the persons concerned, as soon as the present Treaty comes into force. No claim for repayment shall be made as regards sums encashed before the 15th May, 1923.

ARTICLE 70.

Claims based on Articles 65, 66 and 69 must be lodged with the competent authorities within six months, and, in default of agreement, with the Mixed Arbitral Tribunal within twelve months, from the coming into force of the present Treaty.

ARTICLE 71.

The British Empire, France, Italy, Roumania and the Serb-Croat-Slovene State or their nationals having begun claims or suits with regard to their property, rights and interests against the Ottoman Government before the 29th October, 1914, the provisions of this Section will not prejudice such claims or suits.

Claims or suits begun against the British, French, Italian, Roumanian or Serb-Croat-Slovene Governments by the Ottoman Government or its nationals will similarly not be prejudiced. These claims or suits will be continued against the Turkish Government and against the other Governments mentioned in this Article under the conditions existing before the 29th October, 1914, due regard being had to the abolition of the Capitulations.

ARTICLE 72.

In the territories which remain Turkish by virtue of the present Treaty, property, rights and interests belonging to Germany, Austria, Hungary and Bulgaria or to their nationals, which before the coming into force of the present Treaty have been seized or occupied by the Allied Governments, shall remain in the possession of these Governments until the conclusion of arrangements between them and the German, Austrian, Hungarian and Bulgarian Governments or their nationals who are concerned. If the above-mentioned property, rights and interests have been liquidated, such liquidation is confirmed.

In the territories detached from Turkey under the present Treaty, the Governments exercising authority there shall have power, within one year from the coming into force of the present Treaty, to liquidate the property, rights and interests belonging to Germany, Austria, Hungary and Bulgaria or to their nationals.

The proceeds of liquidations, whether they have already been carried out or not, shall be paid to the Reparation Commission established by the Treaty of Peace concluded with the States concerned, if the property liquidated belongs to the German, Austrian, Hungarian or Bulgarian State. In the case of liquidation of private property, the proceeds of liquidation shall be paid to the owners direct.

The provisions of this Article do not apply to Ottoman limited Companies.

The Turkish Government shall be in no way responsible for the measures referred to in the present Article.

SECTION II.
CONTRACTS, PRESCRIPTIONS AND JUDGMENTS.

ARTICLE 73.

The following classes of contracts concluded, before the date mentioned in Article 82, between persons who thereafter became enemies as defined in that Article, remain in force subject to the provisions of the contracts and to the stipulations of the present Treaty:

(a) Contracts for the sale of real property, even if all formalities may not have been concluded, provided that delivery did in fact take place before the date on which the parties became enemies as defined in Article 82.

(b) Leases and agreements for leases of land and houses entered into between individuals.

(c) Contracts between individuals regarding the exploitation of mines, forests or agricultural estates.

(d) Contracts of mortgage, pledge or lien.

(e) Contracts constituting companies, excepting "sociétés en 'nom collectif'" which do not constitute, under the law to which they are subject, an entity separate from that of the persons of which they are composed (partnerships).

(f) Contracts, whatever may be their purpose, concluded between individuals or companies and the State, provinces, municipalities or other similar juridical persons charged with administrative functions.

(g) Contracts relating to family status.

(h) Contracts relating to gifts or bounties of any kind whatever.

This Article cannot be invoked in order to give to contracts a validity different from that which they had in themselves when they were concluded.

It does not apply to concessionary contracts.

ARTICLE 74.

Insurance contracts are governed by the provisions of the Annex to this Section.

ARTICLE 75.

Contracts other than those specified in Articles 73 and 74 and other than concessionary contracts, which were entered into between persons who subsequently became enemies, shall be considered as having been annulled as from the date on which the parties became enemies.

Nevertheless, either of the parties to the contract shall have power, within three months from the coming into force of the present Treaty, to require the execution of the contract, on condition of paying, where the circumstances demand it, to the other party compensation calculated according to the difference between the conditions prevailing at the time when the contract was concluded and those prevailing at the time when its maintenance is required. In default of agreement between the parties, this compensation shall be fixed by the Mixed Arbitral Tribunal.

ARTICLE 76.

The validity of all compromises entered into before the coming into force of the present Treaty between nationals of the Contracting Powers, parties to contracts specified in Articles 73 to 75, particularly those providing for the cancellation, the maintenance, the methods of execution, or the modification of such contracts, including agreements relating to the currency of payment or the rate of exchange, is confirmed.

ARTICLE 77.

Contracts between Allied and Turkish nationals concluded after the 30th October, 1918, remain in force and will be governed by the ordinary law.

Contracts duly concluded with the Constantinople Government between the 30th October, 1918, and the 16th March, 1920, also remain in force and will be governed by the ordinary law.

All contracts and arrangements duly concluded after the 16th March, 1920, with the Constantinople Government concerning territories which remained under the effective control of the said Government, shall be submitted to the Grand National Assembly of Turkey for approval, if the parties concerned make application within three months from the coming into force of the present Treaty. Payments made under such contracts shall be duly credited to the party who has made them.

If approval is not granted, the party concerned shall, if the circumstances demand it, be entitled to compensation corresponding to the direct loss which has been actually suffered; such compensation, in default of an amicable agreement, shall be fixed by the Mixed Arbitral Tribunal.

The provisions of this Article are not applicable either to concessionary contracts or to transfers of concessions.

ARTICLE 78.

All disputes which already exist, or may arise within the period of six months mentioned below, relating to contracts, other than concessionary contracts, between parties who subsequently became enemies, shall be determined by the Mixed Arbitral Tribunal, with the exception of disputes which, in accordance with the laws of neutral Powers are within the competence of the national courts of those Powers. In the latter case, such disputes shall be determined by the said national courts, to the exclusion of the Mixed Arbitral Tribunal. Applications relating to disputes which, under this Article, are within the competence of the Mixed Arbitral Tribunal, must be presented to the said Tribunal within a period of six months from the date of its establishment.

After the expiration of this period, disputes which have not been submitted to the Mixed Arbitral Tribunal shall be determined by the competent courts in accordance with the ordinary law.

The provisions of this Article do not apply to cases in which all the parties to the contract resided in the same country during the war and there freely disposed of their persons and their property, nor to disputes in respect of which judgment was given by a competent court before the date on which the parties became enemies.

ARTICLE 79.

All periods whatever of prescription or limitation of right of action, whether they began to run before or after the outbreak of war, shall be treated, in the territory of the High Contracting Parties so far as regards relations between enemies, as having been suspended from the 29th October, 1914, until the expiration of three months after the coming into force of the present Treaty.

This provision applies, in particular, to periods of time allowed for the presentation of interest or dividend coupons, or for the presentation for payment of securities drawn for redemption or repayable on any other ground.

As regards Roumania, the above-mentioned periods shall be considered as having been suspended as from the 27th August 1916.

ARTICLE 80.

As between enemies no negotiable instrument made before the war shall be deemed to have become invalid by reason only of failure within the required time to present the instrument for acceptance or payment, or to give notice of non-acceptance or non-payment to drawers or endorsers, or to protest the instrument, nor by reason of failure to complete any formality during the war.

When the period within which a negotiable instrument should have been presented for acceptance or payment, or within which notice of non-acceptance or non-payment should have been given to the drawers or endorsers, or within which the instrument should have been protested, has expired during the war, and when the party who should have presented or protested the instrument or given notice of non-acceptance or non-payment, has failed to do so during the war, a period of three months from the coming into force of the present Treaty shall be allowed within which the presentation, notice of non-acceptance or non-payment, or protest may be made.

ARTICLE 81.

Sales effected during the war in order to realise pledges or mortgages created before the war as security for debts which have become payable, shall be deemed valid, although it may not have been possible to perform all the formalities required for notifying the debtor, subject to the express right of the said debtor to summon the creditor before the Mixed Arbitral Tribunal to render accounts, failing which the creditor will be liable to be cast in damages.

It shall be the duty of the Mixed Arbitral Tribunal to settle the accounts between the parties, to investigate the conditions under which the property pledged or mortgaged was sold, and to order the creditor to make good any loss suffered by the debtor as a result of the sale if the creditor acted in bad faith or if he did not take all steps in his power to avoid having recourse to a sale or to cause the sale to be conducted in such conditions as to ensure the realisation of a fair price.

The present provision is applicable only between enemies and does not extend to transactions referred to above which may have been carried out after the 1st May, 1923.

ARTICLE 82.

For the purposes of the present Section, the parties to a contract shall be regarded as enemies from the date on which trading between them became impossible in fact or was prohibited or became unlawful under laws, orders or regulations to which one of the parties was subject.

By way of exception to Articles 73-75, 79 and 80, contracts shall be governed by the ordinary law if they were concluded within the territory of one of the High Contracting Parties between enemies (including companies) or their agents, if this territory was an enemy country for one of the contracting parties who remained there during the war and was there able to dispose freely of his person and property.

ARTICLE 83.

The provisions of this Section do not apply between Japan and Turkey; matters dealt with in this Section shall, in both of these countries, be determined in accordance with the local law.

ANNEX.
[...I. LIFE ASSURANCE....]
[...II. MARINE INSURANCE...]
[...III. FIRE AND OTHER INSURANCES...]

SECTION III.
DEBTS.

ARTICLE 84.

The High Contracting Parties are in agreement in recognising that debts which were payable before the war or which became payable during the war under contracts entered into before the war, and which remained unpaid owing to the war, must be settled and paid, in accordance with the provisions of the contracts, in the currency agreed upon, at the rate current in its country of origin.

Without prejudice to the provisions of the Annex to Section II of this part, it is agreed that where payments to be made under a pre-war contract are represented by sums collected during the war in whole or in part in a currency other than that mentioned in the said contract, such payments can be made by handing over the sums actually collected, in the currency in which they were collected. This provision shall not affect settlements inconsistent with the foregoing provisions arrived at by voluntary agreement between the parties before the coming into force of the present Treaty.

ARTICLE 85.

The Ottoman Public Debt is by general agreement left outside the scope of this Section and of the other Sections of this Part (Economic Clauses).

SECTION IV.
INDUSTRIAL, LITERARY AND ARTISTIC PROPERTY.

ARTICLE 86.

Subject to the stipulations of the present Treaty, rights of industrial, literary and artistic property as they existed on the 1st August, 1914, in accordance with the law of each of the contracting countries, shall be re-established or restored as from the coming into force of the present Treaty in the territories of the High Contracting Parties in favour of the persons entitled to the benefit of them at the moment when the state of war commenced, or of their legal representatives. Equally, rights which, but for the war, could have been acquired during the war, by means of an application legally made for the protection of industrial property or of the publication of a literary or artistic work, shall be recognised and established in favour of those persons who would have been entitled thereto, from the coming into force of the present Treaty.

Without prejudice to the rights which are required to be restored in accordance with the above provision, all acts (including the grant of licences) done by virtue of the special measures taken during the war by a legislative, executive or administrative authority of an Allied Power in regard to the rights of Turkish nationals in respect of industrial, literary or artistic property, shall remain in force and continue to have their full effect. This provision applies *mutatis mutandis* to corresponding measures taken by Turkish authorities in regard to the rights of the nationals of any Allied Power.

ARTICLE 87.

A minimum of one year from the coming into force of the present Treaty shall be granted, without surtax or penalty of any kind, to Turkish nationals in the territory of each of the other Contracting Powers, and to the nationals of these Powers in Turkey, within which they may accomplish any act, fulfil any formality, pay any fees, and generally satisfy any obligation prescribed by the laws and regulations of the respective States for preserving or obtaining or opposing the grant of rights to industrial property which had already been acquired on the 1st August, 1914, or which, but for the war, might have been acquired since that date by means of an application made before or during the war.

Rights to industrial property which have lapsed by reason of any failure to accomplish any act, fulfil any formality, or pay any fees shall be revived, but subject, in the case of patents and designs, to the adoption of such measures as each Power may deem reasonably necessary for the protection of the rights of third parties who have exploited or made use of patents or designs since they had lapsed.

The period from the 1st August, 1914, until the coming into force of the present Treaty shall be excluded in calculating the time within which a patent has to be exploited or a trade-mark or design used, and it is further agreed that no patent, trade-mark or design in force on the 1st August, 1914, shall be subject to revocation or cancellation by reason only of the failure to exploit such patent or use such trade-mark or design, for two years after the coming into force of the present Treaty.

ARTICLE 88.

No action shall be brought and no claim made on the one hand by Turkish nationals or persons residing or carrying on business in Turkey, and on the other hand by nationals of the Allied Powers or persons residing or carrying on their business in the territory of these Powers, nor by third parties having derived title during the war from such persons, by reason of any occurrence which has taken place within the territory of the other party, between the date of the beginning of a state of war and that of the coming into force of the present Treaty, which might be held to constitute an infringement of rights of industrial property or rights of literary or artistic property either existing at any time during the war, or revived under the provisions of Article 86.

Among the occurrences referred to above are included the use by the Governments of the High Contracting Parties, or by any person acting on their behalf, or with their consent, of rights of industrial, literary or artistic property, as well as the sale, the offering for sale or the use of products, apparatus, or any articles whatsoever to which these rights apply.

ARTICLE 89.

Licences for the use of industrial property, or for the reproduction of literary or artistic works, granted before the war by or to nationals of the Allied Powers or persons residing in their territories or carrying on business therein, on the one hand, to or by Turkish nationals on the other hand, shall be considered as cancelled as from the date of the beginning of a state of war between Turkey and the Allied Power concerned. But in any case, the former beneficiary of a licence of this kind shall have the right within a period of six months from the coming into force of the present Treaty to require from the proprietor of the rights the grant of a new licence, the conditions of which, in default of agreement between the parties, shall be fixed by the Mixed Arbitral Tribunal referred to in Section V of this Part. The Tribunal shall have the power, where the circumstances demand it, to fix at the same time the amount which it considers fair payment for the use of the property during the war.

ARTICLE 90

The inhabitants of territories detached from Turkey under the present Treaty shall, notwithstanding this transfer and the change of nationality consequent thereon, continue in complete enjoyment in Turkey of all the rights in industrial, literary and artistic property to which they were entitled under Ottoman law at the time of transfer.

Rights of industrial, literary and artistic property which are in existence in territories detached from Turkey under the present Treaty at the time of separation, or which are re-established or restored by the provisions of Article 86, shall be recognised by the State to which the said territory is transferred, and shall remain in existence in that territory for the same period of time as that which they would have enjoyed under Ottoman law.

ARTICLE 91

All grants of patents and registrations of trade-marks, as well as all registrations of transfers or assignments of patents or trade marks which have been duly made since the 30th October, 1918, by the Imperial Ottoman Government at Constantinople or elsewhere, shall be submitted to the Turkish Government and registered, if the parties concerned make an application within three months from the coming into force of the present Treaty. Such registration shall have effect as from the date of the original registration.

SECTION V.
MIXED ARBITRAL TRIBUNAL.

ARTICLE 92.

Within three months from the date of the coming into force of the present Treaty, a Mixed Arbitral Tribunal shall be established between each of the Allied Powers, on the one hand, and Turkey, on the other hand.

Each of these Tribunals shall be composed of three members, two being appointed respectively by each of the Governments concerned, who shall be entitled to designate several persons from whom, according to the case in question, they will choose one to sit as a member of the Tribunal. The president shall be chosen by agreement between the two Governments concerned.

In case of failure to reach agreement within two months from the coming into force of the present Treaty, the president shall be appointed, upon the request of one of the Governments concerned, from among nationals of Powers which remained neutral during the war, by the President of the Permanent Court of International Justice at The Hague.

If within the said period of two months one of the Governments concerned does not appoint a member to represent it on the Tribunal, the Council of the League of Nations will have power to proceed to the appointment of such member upon the request of the other Government concerned.

If a member of the Tribunal should die or resign or for any reason become unable to perform his duties, he shall be replaced by the method laid down for his appointment, the above period of two months running from the date of death, resignation or inability as duly verified.

ARTICLE 93.

The seat of the Mixed Arbitral Tribunals shall be at Constantinople. If the number and character of the cases justify it, the Governments concerned shall be entitled to create in each Tribunal one or more additional Sections, the seat of which shall be in whatever place may be convenient. Each of these Sections shall be composed of a vice-president and two members appointed as laid down in the second, third, fourth and fifth paragraphs of Article 92.

Each Government shall appoint one or more agents to represent it before the Tribunal.

If, after three years from the establishment of a Mixed Arbitral Tribunal, or of one of its Sections, such Tribunal or Section has not finished its work, and if the Power on whose territory such Tribunal or Section has its seat so requests, the seat shall be removed from such territory.

ARTICLE 94.

The Mixed Arbitral Tribunals established pursuant to Articles 92 and 93 shall decide all questions within their competence under the present Treaty.

Decisions shall be taken by a majority.

The High Contracting Parties agree to regard the decisions of the Mixed Arbitral Tribunals as final and conclusive, and to render them binding upon their nationals, and to ensure their enforcement in their respective territories as soon as the decisions of the Tribunals are notified to them, without it being necessary to have them declared executory.

The High Contracting Parties further undertake that their Tribunals and authorities shall directly assist the fixed Arbitral Tribunals in every way that is in their power, particularly as regards the transmission of notices and the collection of evidence.

ARTICLE 95.

The Mixed Arbitral Tribunals shall be guided by justice, equity and good faith.

Each Tribunal will determine the language to be used before it, and shall order such translations to be made as are necessary to ensure that the proceedings are completely understood; it will lay down rules and time limits for the procedure to be observed. These rules must be based on the following principles:

(1) The procedure shall include the presentation of a memorial and a counter-memorial respectively, with the option of presenting a reply and a rejoinder. If either of the parties asks for leave to present an oral argument he will be permitted to do so; in such case the other party will have the same right.

(2) The Tribunal shall have full power to order enquiries, the production of documents, and expert examinations, to make a view, to demand any information, to hear any witnesses and to ask the parties or their representatives for any verbal or written explanations.

(3) Subject to any contrary provision in the present Treaty, no claim shall be admitted after the expiry of a period of six months from the establishment of the Tribunal, except upon express authority contained in a decision of the said Tribunal and justified as an exceptional measure by considerations relating to distance or *force majeure*.
(4) It shall be the duty of the Tribunal to hold as many sittings each week as may be needed for the prompt despatch of its business, except during vacations, which shall not exceed a total of eight weeks a year.
(5) Judgment must always be given within at most two months from the end of the hearing, after which the Tribunal will at once proceed to consider its judgment.
(6) Oral arguments, if any, shall be heard in public, and in all cases judgment shall be delivered in public.
(7) Each Mixed Arbitral Tribunal shall be entitled to hold sittings elsewhere than in the place where its seat is established, if it considers it advantageous for the despatch of business.

ARTICLE 96.

The Governments concerned shall appoint by agreement a Secretary-General for each Tribunal, and shall each attach to him one or more Secretaries. The Secretary-General and the Secretaries shall be under the orders of the Tribunal, which with the consent of the Governments concerned shall be entitled to engage any persons whose assistance it may need.

The Secretariat of each Tribunal shall have its offices at Constantinople. The Governments concerned shall have power to establish additional offices in such other places as may be convenient.

Each Tribunal shall keep in its Secretariat the records, papers and documents relating to the cases submitted to it, and upon the completion of its duties it shall deposit them in the archives of the Government of the country where its seat is established. These archives shall always be accessible to the Governments concerned.

ARTICLE 97.

Each Government shall pay the emoluments of the member of the Mixed Arbitral Tribunal whom it appoints, as well as those of any agent or secretary appointed by it.

The emoluments of the President and those of the Secretary-General shall be fixed by agreement between the Governments concerned, and these emoluments and the general expenses of the Tribunal shall be paid in equal shares by the two Governments.

ARTICLE 98.

The present section shall not apply to cases between Japan and Turkey, which, according to the terms of the present Treaty, would fall within the competence of the Mixed Arbitral Tribunal. Such cases shall be settled by agreement between the two Governments.

SECTION VI.
TREATIES.

[…ARTICLE 99.-100…]

TREATY OF LAUSANNE – PART IV

COMMUNICATIONS AND SANITARY QUESTIONS.
SECTION I.
COMMUNICATIONS.

[…ARTICLE 101.-113…]

SECTION II.
SANITARY QUESTIONS.

[…ARTICLE 114.-118…]

PART V.
MISCELLANEOUS PROVISIONS.
SECTION I.
PRISONERS OF WAR.

[…ARTICLE 119.-123…]

SECTION II.
GRAVES.

[…ARTICLE 124.-136…]

SECTION III.
GENERAL PROVISIONS.
ARTICLE 137.
Subject to any agreements concluded between the High Contracting Parties, the decisions taken and orders issued since the 30th October, 1918, until the coming into force of the present Treaty, by or in agreement with the authorities of the Powers who have occupied Constantinople, and concerning the property, rights and interests of their nationals, of foreigners or of Turkish nationals, and the relations of such persons with the authorities of Turkey, shall be regarded as definitive and shall give rise to no claims against the Powers or their authority.

All other claims arising from injury suffered in consequence of any such decisions or orders shall be submitted to the Mixed Arbitral Tribunal.

ARTICLE 138.
In judicial matters, the decisions given and orders issued in Turkey from the 30th October, 1918, until the coming into force of the present Treaty by all judges, courts or authorities of the Powers who have occupied Constantinople, or by the Provisional Mixed Judicial Commission established on the 8th December, 1921, as well as the measures taken in execution of such decisions or orders, shall be regarded as definitive, without prejudice, however, to the terms of paragraphs IV and VI of the Amnesty Declaration dated this day.

Nevertheless, in the event of a claim being presented by a private person in respect of damage suffered by him in consequence of a judicial decision in favour of another private person given in a civil matter by a military or police court, this claim shall be brought before the Mixed Arbitral Tribunal, which may in a proper case, order the payment of compensation or even restitution of the property in question.

ARTICLE 139.
Archives, registers, plans, title-deeds and other documents of every kind relating to the civil, judicial or financial administration, or the administration of Wakfs, which are at present in Turkey and are only of interest to the Government of a territory detached from the Ottoman Empire, and reciprocally those in a territory detached from the Ottoman Empire which are only of interest to the Turkish Government, shall reciprocally be restored.

Archives, registers, plans, title-deeds and other documents mentioned above which are considered by the Government in whose possession they are as being also of interest to itself, may be retained by that Government, subject to its furnishing on request photographs or certified copies to the Government concerned.

Archives, registers, plans, title-deeds and other documents which have been taken away either from Turkey or from detached territories shall reciprocally be restored in original, in so far as they concern exclusively the territories from which they have been taken.

The expense entailed by these operations shall be paid by the Government applying therefor.

The above stipulations apply in the same manner to the registers relating to real estates or Wakfs in the districts of the former Ottoman Empire transferred to Greece after 1912.

ARTICLE 140.
Prizes made during the war between Turkey and the other Contracting Powers prior to the 30th October, 1918, shall give rise to no claim on either side. The same shall apply to seizures effected after that date, for violation of the armistice, by the Powers who have occupied Constantinople.

It is understood that no claim shall be made, either by the Governments of the Powers who have occupied Constantinople or their nationals, or by the Turkish Government or its nationals, respecting small craft of all kinds, vessels of light tonnage, yachts and lighters which any of the said Governments may, between the 29th October, 1914, until the 1st January, 1923, have disposed of in their own harbours or in harbours occupied by them. Nevertheless, this stipulation does not prejudice the terms of paragraph VI of the Amnesty Declaration dated this day, nor the claims which private persons may be able to establish against other private persons in virtue of rights held before the 29th October, 1914.

Vessels under the Turkish flag seized by the Greek forces after the 30th October, 1918, shall be restored to Turkey.

ARTICLE 141.
In accordance with Article 25 of the present Treaty, Articles 155, 250 and 440 and Annex III, Part VIII (Reparation) of the Treaty of Peace of Versailles, dated the 28th June, 1919, the Turkish Government and its nationals are released from any liability to the German Government or to its nationals in respect of German vessels which were the object during the war of a transfer by the German Government or its nationals to the Ottoman Government or its nationals without the consent of the Allied Governments, and at present in the possession of the latter.

The same shall apply, if necessary, in the relations between Turkey and the other Powers which fought on her side.

ARTICLE 142.

The separate Convention concluded on the 30th January, 1923, between Greece and Turkey, relating to the exchange of the Greek and Turkish populations, will have as between these two High Contracting Parties the same force and effect as if it formed part of the present Treaty.

ARTICLE 143.

The present Treaty shall be ratified as soon as possible.

The ratifications shall be deposited at Paris.

The Japanese Government will be entitled merely to inform the Government of the French Republic through their diplomatic representative at Paris when their ratification has been given; in that case, they must transmit the instrument of ratification as soon as possible.

Each of the Signatory Powers will ratify by one single instrument the present Treaty and the other instruments signed by it and mentioned in the Final Act of the Conference of Lausanne, in so far as these require ratification.

A first *procès-verbal* of the deposit of ratifications shall be drawn up as soon as Turkey, on the one hand, and the British Empire, France, Italy and Japan, or any three of them, on the other hand, have deposited the instruments of their ratifications.

From the date of this first *procès-verbal* the Treaty will come into force between the High Contracting Parties who have thus ratified it, Thereafter it will come into force for the other Powers at the date of the deposit of their ratifications.

As between Greece and Turkey, however, the provisions of Articles 1, 2 (2) and 5-11 inclusive will come into force as soon as the Greek and Turkish Governments have deposited the instruments of their ratifications, even if at that time the *procès-verbal* referred to above has not yet been drawn up.

The French Government will transmit to all the Signatory Powers a certified copy of the *procès-verbaux* of the deposit of ratifications.

In faith whereof the above-named Plenipotentiaries have signed the present Treaty.

Done at Lausanne, the 24th July, 1923, in a single copy, which will be deposited in the archives of the Government of the French Republic, which will transmit a certified copy to each of the Contracting Powers.

(L.S.) HORACE RUMBOLD.
(L.S.) PELLÉ.
(L.S) GARRONI.
(L.S.) G. C. MONTAGNA.
(L.S.) K. OTCHIAI.
(L-S.) E. K. VENISELOS.
(L.S.) D. CACLAMANOS.
(L.S.) CONST. DIAMANDY.
(L.S.) CONST. CONTZESCO.
(   ) ....
(L.S.) M. ISMET.
(L.S.) DR. RIZA NOUR.
(L.S.) HASSAN.

8.4. Konvention über die Regime der Meerengen vom 24. Juli 1923

THE CONVENTION RELATING TO THE REGIME OF THE STRAITS AND TURKEY

THE BRITISH EMPIRE, FRANCE, ITALY, JAPAN, BULGARIA, GREECE, ROUMANIA, RUSSIA, the SERB-CROAT-SLOVENE STATE and TURKEY, being desirous of ensuring in the Straits freedom of transit and navigation between the Mediterranean Sea and the Black Sea for all nations, in accordance with the principle laid down in Article 23 of the Treaty of Peace signed this day,
And considering that the maintenance of that freedom is necessary to the general peace and the commerce of the world,
Have decided to conclude a Convention to this effect, and have appointed as their respective Plenipotentiaries:

HIS MAJESTY THE KING OF THE UNITED KINGDOM OF GREAT BRITAIN AND IRELAND AND OF THE BRITISH DOMINIONS BEYOND THE SEAS, EMPEROR OF INDIA:
    The Right Honourable Sir Horace George Montagu Rumbold, Baronet, G.C.M.G., High Commissioner at Constantinople;

THE PRESIDENT OF THE FRENCH REPUBLIC:
    General Maurice Pellé, Ambassador of France, High Commissioner of the Republic in the East, Grand Officer of the National Order of the Legion of Honour;

HIS MAJESTY THE KING OF ITALY:
    The Honourable Marquis Camillo Garroni, Senator of the Kingdom, Ambassador of Italy, High Commissioner at Constantinople, Grand Cross of the Orders of Saints Maurice and Lazarus, and of the Crown of Italy;
    M. Giulio Cesare Montagna, Envoy Extraordinary and Minister Plenipotentiary at Athens, Commander of the Order of Saints Maurice and Lazarus, Grand Officer of the Crown of Italy;

HIS MAJESTY THE EMPEROR OF JAPAN:
    Mr. Kentaro Otchiai, Jusammi, First Class of the Order of the Rising Sun, Ambassador Extraordinary and Plenipotentiary at Rome;

HIS MAJESTY THE KING OF THE BULGARIANS:
    M. Bogdan Morphoff, formerly Minister of Railways, Posts and Telegraphs;
    M. Dimitri Stancioff, Doctor of Law, Envoy Extraordinary and Minister Plenipotentiary at London, Grand Cross of the Order of Saint Alexander;

HIS MAJESTY THE KING OF THE HELLENES:
    M. Eleftherios K. Veniselos, formerly President of the Council of Ministers, Grand Cross of the Order of the Saviour;
    M. Demetrios Caclamanos, Minister Plenipotentiary at London, Commander of the Order of the Saviour;

HIS MAJESTY THE KING OF ROUMANIA:
    M. Constantine I. Diamandy, Minister Plenipotentiary;
    M. Constantine Contzesco, Minister Plenipotentiary;

RUSSIA:
    M. Nicolas Ivanovitch Iordanski;

HIS MAJESTY THE KING OF THE SERBS, THE CROATS AND THE SLOVENES:
    Dr. Miloutine Yovanovitch, Envoy Extraordinary and Minister Plenipotentiary at Berne;

THE GOVERNMENT OF THE GRAND NATIONAL ASSEMBLY OF TURKEY:
    Ismet Pasha, Minister for Foreign Affairs, Deputy for Adrianople;
    Dr. Riza Nour Bey, Minister for Health and for Public Assistance, Deputy for Sinope;
    Hassan Bey, formerly Minister, Deputy for Trebizond;

Who, having produced their full powers, found in good and due form, have agreed as follows:

ARTICLE 1.

The High Contracting Parties agree to recognise and declare the principle of freedom of transit and of navigation by sea and by air in the Strait of the Dardanelles, the Sea of Marmora and the Bosphorus, hereinafter comprised under the general term of the "Straits."

ARTICLE 2.

The transit and navigation of commercial vessels and aircraft, and of war vessels and aircraft in the Straits in time of peace and in time of war shall henceforth be regulated by the provisions of the attached Annex.

ANNEX.

Rules for the Passage of Commercial Vessels and Aircraft, and of War Vessels and Aircraft through the Straits.

1. *Merchant Vessels, including Hospital Ships, Yachts and Fishing Vessels and non-Military Aircraft.*
(a) *In Time of Peace.*
Complete freedom of navigation and passage by day and by night under any flag and with any kind of cargo, without any formalities, or tax, or charge whatever (subject, however, to international sanitary provisions) unless for services directly rendered, such as pilotage, light, towage or other similar charges, and without prejudice to the rights exercised in this respect by the services and undertakings now operating under concessions granted by the Turkish Government.
To facilitate the collection of these dues, merchant vessels passing the Straits will communicate to stations appointed by the Turkish Government their name, nationality, tonnage and destination.
Pilotage remains optional.

(b) *In Time of War, Turkey being Neutral.*
Complete freedom of navigation and passage by day and by night under the same conditions as above. The duties and rights of Turkey as a neutral Power cannot authorise her to take any measures liable to interfere with navigation through the Straits, the waters of which, and the air above which, must remain entirely free in time of war, Turkey being neutral just as in time of peace.
Pilotage remains optional.

(c) *In Time of War, Turkey being a Belligerent.*
Freedom of navigation for neutral vessels and neutral non-military aircraft, if the vessel or aircraft in question does not assist the enemy, particularly by carrying contraband, troops or enemy nationals. Turkey will have the right to visit and search such vessels and aircraft, and for this purpose aircraft are to alight on the ground or on the sea in such areas as are specified and prepared for this purpose by Turkey. The rights of Turkey to apply to enemy vessels the measures allowed by international law are not affected.
Turkey will have full power to take such measures as she may consider necessary to prevent enemy vessels from using the Straits. These measures, however, are not to be of such a nature as to prevent the free passage of neutral vessels, and Turkey agrees to provide such vessels with either the necessary instruction or pilots for the above purpose.

2. *Warships, including Fleet Auxiliaries, Troopships, Aircraft Carriers and Military Aircraft.*
(a) *In Time of Peace.*
Complete freedom of passage by day and by night under any flag, without any formalities, or tax, or charge whatever, but subject to the following restrictions as to the total force:
The maximum force which any one Power may send through the Straits into the Black Sea is not to be greater than that of the most powerful fleet of the littoral Powers of the Black Sea existing in that sea at the time of passage; but with the proviso that the Powers reserve to themselves the right to send into the Black Sea, at all times and under all circumstances, a force of not more than three ships, of which no individual ship shall exceed 10,000 tons.
Turkey has no responsibility in regard to the number of war vessels which pass through the Straits.
In order to enable the above rule to be observed, the Straits Commission provided for in Article 10 will, on the 1st January and the 1st July of each year, enquire of each Black Sea littoral Power the number of each of the following classes of vessel which such Power possesses in the Black Sea: Battle-ships, battle-cruisers, aircraft-carriers, cruisers, destroyers, submarines, or other types of vessels as well as naval aircraft; distinguishing between the ships which are in active commission and the ships with reduced complements, the ships in reserve and the ships undergoing repairs or alterations.
The Straits Commission will then inform the Powers concerned that the strongest naval force in the Black Sea comprises: Battleships, battle-cruisers, aircraft carriers, cruisers, destroyers, submarines, aircraft and units of other types which may exist. The Straits Commission will also immediately inform the Powers concerned when, owing to the passage into or out of the Black Sea of any ship of the strongest Black Sea force, any alteration in tha force has taken place.
The naval force that may be sent through the Straits into the Black Sea will be calculated on the number and type of the ships of war in active commission only.

(b) *In Time of War, Turkey being Neutral.*
Complete freedom of passage by day and by night under any flag, without any formalities, or tax, or charge whatever, under the same limitations as in paragraph 2 (a).
However, these limitations will not be applicable to any belligerent Power to the prejudice of its belligerent rights in the Black Sea.
The rights and duties of Turkey as a neutral Power cannot authorise her to take any measures liable to interfere with navigation through the Straits, the waters of which, and the air above which, must remain entirely free in time of war, Turkey being neutral, just as in time of peace.
Warships and military aircraft of belligerents will be forbidden to make any capture, to exercise the right of visit and search, or to carry out any other hostile act in the Straits
As regards revictualling and carrying out repairs, war vessels will be subject to the terms of the Thirteenth Hague Convention of 1907, dealing with maritime neutrality.
Military aircraft will receive in the Straits similar treatment to that accorded under the Thirteenth Hague Convention of 1907 to warships, pending the conclusion of an international Convention establishing the rules of neutrality for aircraft.

(c) *In Time of War, Turkey being Belligerent.*
Complete freedom of passage for neutral warships, without any formalities, or tax, or charge whatever, but under the same limitations as in paragraph 2 (a).
The measures taken by Turkey to prevent enemy ships and aircraft from using the Straits are not to be of such a nature as to prevent the free passage of neutral ships and aircraft, and Turkey agrees to provide the said ships and aircraft with either the necessary instructions or pilots for the above purpose.
Neutral military aircraft will make the passage of the Straits at their own risk and peril, and will submit to investigation as to their character. For this purpose aircraft are to alight on the ground or on the sea in such areas as are specified and prepared for this purpose by Turkey.

3. (a) The passage of the Straits by submarines of Powers at peace with Turkey must be made on the surface.
(b) The officer in command of a foreign naval force, whether coming from the Mediterranean or the Black Sea, will communicate, without being compelled to stop, to a signal station at the entrance to the Dardanelles or the Bosphorus, the number and the names of vessels under his orders which are entering the Straits.
These signal stations shall be notified from time to time by Turkey; until such signal stations are notified, the freedom of passage for foreign war vessels in the Straits shall not thereby be prejudiced, nor shall their entry into the Straits be for this reason delayed.
(c) The right of military and non-military aircraft to fly over the Straits, under the conditions laid down in the present rules, necessitates for aircraft:
(i) Freedom to fly over a strip of territory of five kilometres on each side of the narrow parts of the Straits;
(ii) Liberty, in the event of a forced landing, to alight on the coast or on the sea in the territorial waters of Turkey.

4. *Limitation of Time of Transit for Warships.*
In no event shall warships in transit through the Straits, except in the event of damage or peril of the sea, remain therein beyond the time which is necessary for them to effect their passage, including the time of anchorage during the night if necessary for safety of navigation.

5. *Stay in the Ports of the Straits and of the Black Sea.*
(a) Paragraphs 1, 2 and 3 of this Annex apply to the passage of vessels, warships and aircraft through and over the Straits and do not affect the right of Turkey to make such regulations as she may consider necessary regarding the number of men-of-war and military aircraft of any one Power which may visit Turkish ports or aerodromes at one time, and the duration of their stay.
(b) Littoral Powers of the Black Sea will also have a similar right as regards their ports and aerodromes.
(c) The light-vessels which the Powers at present represented on the European Commission of the Danube maintain as *stationnaires* at the mouths of that river as far up as Galatz will be regarded as additional to the men-of-war referred to in paragraph 2, and may be replaced in case of need.

6. *Special Provisions relating to Sanitary Protection.*
Warships which have on board cases of plague, cholera or typhus, or which have had such cases on board during the last seven days, and warships which have left an infected port within less than five times 24 hours must pass through the Straits in quarantine and apply by the means on board such prophylactic measures as are necessary to prevent any possibility of the Straits being infected.
The same rule shall apply to merchant ships having a doctor on board and passing straight through the Straits without calling at a port or breaking bulk.

Merchant ships not having a doctor on board shall be obliged to comply with the international sanitary regulations before entering the Straits, even if they are not to call at a port therein.

Warships and merchant vessels calling at one of the ports in the Straits shall be subject in that port to the international sanitary regulations applicable in the port in question.

ARTICLE 3.

With a view to maintaining the Straits free from any obstacle to free passage and navigation, the provisions contained in Articles 4 to 9 will be applied to the waters and shores thereof as well as to the islands situated therein, or in the vicinity.

ARTICLE 4.

The zones and islands indicated below shall be demilitarised:

(1) Both shores of the Straits of the Dardanelles and the Bosphorus over the extent of the zones delimited below:

Dardanelles:

On the north-west, the Gallipoli Peninsula and the area south-east of a line traced from a point on the Gulf of Xeros 4 kilometres north-east of Bakla-Burnu, reaching the Sea of Marmora at Kumbaghi and passing south of Kavak (this village excluded);

On the south-east, the area included between the coast and a line 20 kilometres from the coast, starting from Cape Eski-Stamboul opposite Tenedos and reaching the Sea of Marmora at a point on the coast immediately north of Karabigha.

Bosphorus (without prejudice to the special provisions relating to Constantinople contained in Article 8):

On the east, the area extending up to a line 15 kilometres from the eastern shore of the Bosphorus;

On the west, the area up to a line 15 kilometres from the western shore of the Bosphorus.

(2) All the islands in the Sea of Marmora, with the exception of the island of Emir Ali Adasi.

(3) In the Ægean Sea, the islands of Samothrace, Lemnos, Imbros, Tenedos and Rabbit Islands.

ARTICLE 5.

A Commission composed of four representatives appointed respectively by the Governments of France, Great Britain, Italy and Turkey shall meet within 15 days of the coming into force of the present Convention to determine on the spot the boundaries of the zone laid down in Article 4 (1).

The Governments represented on that Commission will pay the salaries of their respective representatives.

Any general expenses incurred by the Commission shall be borne in equal shares by the Powers represented thereon.

ARTICLE 6

Subject to the provisions of Article 8 concerning Constantinople, there shall exist, in the demilitarised zones and islands, no fortifications, no permanent artillery organisation, no submarine engines of war other than submarine vessels, no military aerial organisation, and no naval base.

No armed forces shall be stationed in the demilitarised zones and islands except the police and gendarmerie forces necessary for the maintenance of order; the armament of such forces will be composed only of revolvers, swords, rifles and four Lewis guns per hundred men, and will exclude any artillery.

In the territorial waters of the demilitarised zones and islands, there shall exist no submarine engines of war other than submarine vessels.

Notwithstanding the preceding paragraphs Turkey will retain the right to transport her armed forces through the demilitarised zones and islands of Turkish territory, as well as through their territorial waters, where the Turkish fleet will have the right to anchor.

Moreover, in so far as the Straits are concerned, the Turkish Government shall have the right to observe by means of aeroplanes or balloons both the surface and the bottom of the sea. Turkish aeroplanes will always be able to fly over the waters of the Straits and the demilitarised zones of Turkish territory, and will have full freedom to alight therein, either on land or on sea.

In the demilitarised zones and islands and in their territorial waters, Turkey and Greece shall similarly be entitled to effect such movements of personnel as are rendered necessary for the instruction outside these zones and islands of the men recruited therein.

Turkey and Greece shall have the right to organise in the said zones and islands in their respective territories any system of observation and communication, both telegraphic, telephonic and visual. Greece shall be entitled to send her fleet into the territorial waters of the demilitarised Greek islands, but may not use these waters as a base of operations against Turkey nor for any military or naval concentration for this purpose.

ARTICLE 7.

No submarine engines of war other than submarine vessels shall be installed in the waters of the Sea of Marmora.

The Turkish Government shall not install any permanent battery or torpedo tubes, capable of interfering with the passage of the Straits, in the coastal zone of the European shore of the Sea of Marmora or in the coastal zone on the Anatolian shore situated to the east of the demilitarised zone of the Bosphorus as far as Darije.

ARTICLE 8.

At Constantinople, including for this purpose Stamboul, Pera, Galata, Scutari, as well as Princes' Islands, and in the immediate neighbourhood of Constantinople, there may be maintained for the requirements of the capital, a garrison with a maximum strength of 12,000 men. An arsenal and naval base may also be maintained at Constantinople.

ARTICLE 9.

If, in case of war, Turkey, or Greece, in pursuance of their belligerent rights, should modify in any way the provisions of demilitarisation prescribed above, they will be bound to re-establish as soon as peace is concluded the regime laid down in the present Convention.

ARTICLE 10.

There shall be constituted at Constantinople an International Commission composed in accordance with Article 12 and called the "Straits Commission."

ARTICLE 11.

The Commission will exercise its functions over the waters of the Straits.

ARTICLE 12.

The Commission shall be composed of a representative of Turkey, who shall be President, and representatives of France, Great Britain, Italy, Japan, Bulgaria, Greece, Roumania, Russia, and the Serb-Croat-Slovene State, in so far as these Powers are signatories of the present Convention, each of these Powers being entitled to representation as from its ratification of the said Convention.

The United States of America, in the event of their acceding to the present Convention, will also be entitled to have one representative on the Commission.

Under the same conditions any independent littoral States of the Black Sea which are not mentioned in the first paragraph of the present Article will possess the same right.

ARTICLE 13.

The Governments represented on the Commission will pay the salaries of their representatives. Any incidental expenditure incurred by the Commission will be borne by the said Governments in the proportion laid down for the division of the expenses of the League of Nations.

ARTICLE 14.

It will be the duty of the Commission to see that the provisions relating to the passage of warships and military aircraft are carried out; these provisions are laid down in paragraphs 2, 3 and 4 of the Annex to Article 2.

ARTICLE 15.

The Straits Commission will carry out its functions under the auspices of the League of Nations, and will address to the League an annual report giving an account of its activities, and furnishing all information which may be useful in the interests of commerce and navigation; with this object in view the Commission will place itself in touch with the departments of the Turkish Government dealing with navigation through the Straits.

ARTICLE 16.

It will be the duty of the Commission to prescribe such regulations as may be necessary for the accomplishment of its task.

ARTICLE 17.

The terms of the present Convention will not infringe the right of Turkey to move her fleet freely in Turkish waters.

ARTICLE 18.

The High Contracting Parties, desiring to secure that the demilitarisation of the Straits and of the contiguous zones shall not constitute an unjustifiable danger to the military security of Turkey, and that no act of war should imperil the freedom of the Straits or the safety of the demilitarised zones, agree as follows:

Should the freedom of navigation of the Straits or the security of the demilitarised zones be imperilled by a violation of the provisions relating to freedom of passage, or by a surprise attack or some act of war or threat of war, the High Contracting Parties, and in any case France, Great Britain, Italy, and Japan, acting in conjunction, will meet such violation, attack, or other act of war or threat of war, by all the means that the Council of the League of Nations may decide for this purpose.

So soon as the circumstance which may have necessitated the action provided for in the preceding paragraph shall have ended, the regime of the Straits as laid down by the terms of the present Convention shall again be strictly applied.

The present provision, which forms an integral part of those relating to the demilitarisation and to the freedom of the Straits, does not prejudice the rights and obligations of the High Contracting Parties under the Covenant of the League of Nations.

ARTICLE 19.

The High Contracting Parties will use every possible endeavour to induce non-signatory Powers to accede to the present Convention.

This adherence will be notified through the diplomatic channel to the Government of the French Republic, and by that Government to all signatory or adhering States. The adherence will take effect as from the date of notification to the French Government.

ARTICLE 20.

The present Convention shall be ratified. The ratification shall be deposited at Paris as soon as possible.

The Convention will come into force in the same way as the Treaty of Peace signed this day. In so far as concerns those Powers who are not signatories of this Treaty and who at that date shall not yet have ratified the present Convention, this Convention will come into force as from the date on which they deposit their respective ratifications, which deposit shall be notified to the other Contracting Powers by the French Government.

In faith whereof the above-named Plenipotentiaries have signed the present Convention.

Done at Lausanne the 24th July, 1923, in a single copy which will remain deposited in the archives of the Government of the French Republic, and of which authenticated copies will be transmitted to each of the Contracting Powers.

(L.S.)HORACE RUMBOLD.
(L.S.) PELLÉ
(L.S.) GARRONI.
(L.S.)G. C. MONTAGNA.
(L.S.)K. OTCHIAI.
(L.S.)B. MORPHOFF.
(L.S.) STANCIOFF
(L.S.)E. K. VENISÉLOS.
(L.S.)D. CACLAMANOS.
(L.S.)CONST. DIAMANDY.
(L.S.)CONST. CONTZESCO.
(......) ....
(......) ....
(L.S.)M. ISMET.
(L.S.)DR. RIZA NOUR.
(L.S.) HASSAN.

8.5. Konvention über den Austausch der griechischen und türkischen Bevölkerung vom 30. Januar 1923

CONVENTION CONCERNING THE EXCHANGE OF GREEK AND TURKISH POPULATIONS

The Government of the Grand National Assembly of Turkey and the Greek Government have agreed upon the following provisions:

Article 1
As from the 1st May, 1923, there shall take place a compulsory exchange of Turkish nationals of the Greek Orthodox religion established in Turkish territory, and of Greek nationals of the Moslem religion established in Greek territory.

These persons shall not return to live in Turkey or Greece respectively without the authorisation of the Turkish Government or of the Greek Government respectively.

Article 2
The following persons shall not be included in the exchange provided for in Article 1:
(a) The Greek inhabitants of Constantinople.
(b) The Moslem inhabitants of Western Thrace.

All Greeks who were already established before the 30th October, 1918, within the areas under the Prefecture of the City of Constantinople, as defined by the law of 1912, shall be considered as Greek inhabitants of Constantinople.

All Moslems established in the region to the east of the frontier line laid down in 1913 by the Treaty of Bucharest shall be considered as Moslem inhabitants of Western Thrace.

Article 3
Those Greeks and Moslems who have already, and since the 18th October, 1912, left the territories the Greek and Turkish inhabitants of which are to be respectively exchanged, shall be considered as included in the exchange provided for in Article 1.

The expression "emigrant" in the present Convention includes all physical and juridical persons who have been obliged to emigrate or have emigrated since the 18th October, 1912.

Article 4
All able-bodied men belonging to the Greek population, whose families have already left Turkish territory, and who are now detained in Turkey, shall constitute the first instalment of Greeks sent to Greece in accordance with the present Convention.

Article 5
Subject to the provisions of Articles 9 and 10 of the present Convention, the rights of property and monetary assets of Greeks in Turkey or Moslems in Greece shall not be prejudiced in consequence of the exchange to be carried out under the present Convention

Article 6
No obstacle may be placed for any reason whatever in the way of the departure of a person belonging to the populations which are to be exchanged. In the event of an emigrant having received a definite sentence of imprisonment, or a sentence which is not yet definitive, or of his being the object of criminal proceedings, he shall be handed over by the authorities of the prosecuting country to the authorities of the country whither he is going, in order that he may serve his sentence or be brought to trial.

Article 7
The emigrants will lose the nationality of the country which they are leaving, and will acquire the nationality of the country of their destination, upon their arrival in the territory of the latter country.

Such emigrants as have already left one or other of the two countries and have not yet acquired their new nationality, shall acquire that nationality on the date of the signature of the present Convention.

Article 8
Emigrants shall be free to take away with them or to arrange for the transport of their movable property of every kind, without being liable on this account to the payment of any export or import duty or any other tax.

Similarly, the members of each community (including the personnel of mosques, tekkes, meddresses, churches, convents, schools, hospitals, societies, associations and juridical persons, or other foundations of any nature whatever) which is to leave the territory of one of the Contracting States under the present Convention, shall have the right to take away freely or to arrange for the transport of the movable property belonging to their communities.

The fullest facilities for transport shall be provided by the authorities of the two countries, upon the recommendation of the Mixed Commission provided for in Article 11.

Emigrants who may not be able to take away all or part of their movable property can leave it behind. In that event, the local authorities shall be required to draw up, the emigrant in question being given an opportunity to be heard, an inventory and valuation of the property left by him. *Procès-verbaux* containing the inventory and the valuation of the movable property left by the emigrant shall be drawn up in four copies, one of which shall be kept by the local authorities, the second transmitted to the Mixed Commission provided for in Article 11 to serve as the basis for the liquidation provided for by Article 9, the third shall be handed to the Government of the country to which the emigrant is going, and the fourth to the emigrant himself.

Article 9

Immovable property, whether rural or urban, belonging to emigrants, or to the communities mentioned in Article 8, and the movable property left by these emigrants or communities, shall be liquidated in accordance with the following provisions by the Mixed Commission provided for in Article 11.

Property situated in the districts to which the compulsory exchange applies and belonging to religious or benevolent institutions of the communities established in a district to which the exchange does not apply, shall likewise be liquidated under the same conditions.

Article 10

The movable and immovable property belonging to persons who have already left the territory of the High Contracting Parties and are considered, in accordance with Article 3 of the present Convention, as being included in the exchange of populations, shall be liquidated in accordance with Article 9. This liquidation shall take place independently of all measures of any kind whatever, which, under the laws passed and the regulations of any kind made in Greece and Turkey since the 18th October, 1912, or in anyother way, have resulted in any restriction on rights of ownership over the property in question, such as confiscation forced sale, etc. In the event of the property mentioned in this Article or in Article 9 having been submitted to a measure of this kind, its value shall be fixed by the Commission provided for in Article 11, as if the measures in question had not been applied.

As regards expropriated property, the Mixed Commission shall undertake a fresh valuation of such property, if it has been expropriated since the 18th October, 1912, having previously belonged to persons liable to the exchange of populations in the two countries, and is situated in territories to which the exchange applies. The Commission shall fix for the benefit of the owners such compensation as will repair the injury which the Commission has ascertained. The total amount of this compensation shall be carried to the credit of these owners and to the debit of the Government on whose territory the expropriated property is situated.

In the event of any persons mentioned in Articles 8 and 9 not having received the income from property, the enjoyment of which they have lost in one way or another, the restoration of the amount of this income shall be guaranteed to them on the basis of the average yield of the property before the war, and in accordance with the methods to be laid down by the Mixed Commission.

The Mixed Commission provided for in Article 11, when proceeding to the liquidation of Wakf property in Greece and of the rights and interests connected therewith, and to the liquidation of similar foundations belonging to Greeks in Turkey, shall follow the principles laid down in previous Treaties with a view to fully safeguarding the rights and interests of these foundations and of the individuals interested in them.

The Mixed Commission provided for in Article 11 shall be entrusted with the duty of executing these provisions.

Article 11

Within one month from the coming into force of the present Convention a Mixed Commission shall be set up in Turkey or in Greece consisting of four members representing each of the High Contracting Parties, and of three members chosen by the Council of the League of Nations from among nationals of Powers which did not take part in the war of 1914-1918. The Presidency of the Commission shall be exercised in turn by each of these three neutral members.

The Mixed Commission shall have the right to set up, in such places as it may appear to them necessary, Sub-Commissions working under its order. Each such Sub-Commission shall consist of a Turkish member, a Greek member and a neutral President to be designated by the Mixed Commission. The Mixed Commission shall decide the powers to be delegated to the Sub-Commission.

Article 12

The duties of the Mixed Commission shall be to supervise and facilitate the emigration provided for in the present Convention and to carry out the liquidation of the movable and immovable property for which provision is made in Articles 9 and 10.

The Commission shall settle the methods to be followed as regards the emigration and liquidation mentioned above.

In a general way the Mixed Commission shall have full power to take the measures necessitated by the execution of the present Convention and to decide all questions to which this Convention may give rise.

The decisions of the Mixed Commission shall be taken by a majority.

All disputes relating to property, rights and interests which are to be liquidated shall be settled definitely by the Commission.

Article 13

The Mixed Commission shall have full power to cause the valuation to be made of the movable and immovable property which is to be liquidated under the present Convention, the interested parties being given a hearing or being duly summoned so that they may be heard.

The basis for the valuation of the property to be liquidated shall be the value of the property in gold currency.

Article 14

The Commission shall transmit to the owner concerned a declaration stating the sum due to him in respect of the property of which he has been dispossessed, and such property shall remain at the disposal of the Government on whose territory it is situated.

The total sums due on the basis of these declarations shall constitute a Government debt from the country where the liquidation takes place to the Government of the country to which the emigrant belongs. The emigrant shall in principle be entitled to receive in the country to which he emigrates, as representing the sums due to him, property of a value equal to and of the same nature as that which he has left behind.

Once every six months an account shall be drawn up of the sums due by the respective Governments on the basis of the declarations as above.

When the liquidation is completed, if the sums of money due to both sides correspond, the accounts relating thereto shall be balanced. If a sum remains due from one of the Governments to the other Government after a balance has been struck, the debit balance shall be paid in cash. If the debtor Government requests a postponement in making this payment, the Commission may grant such postponement, provided that the sum due be paid in three annuities at most. The Commission shall fix the interest to be paid during the period of postponement.

If the sum to be paid is fairly large and requires longer postponement, the debtor Government shall pay in cash a sum to be fixed by the Mixed Commission, up to a maximum of 20 per cent. of the total due, and shall issue in respect of the balance loan certificates bearing such interest as the Mixed Commission may fix, to be paid off within 20 years at most. The debtor Government shall assign to the service of these loans pledges approved by the Commission, which shall be administered and of which the revenues shall be encashed by the International Commission in Greece and by the Council of the Public Debt at Constantinople. In the absence of agreement in regard to these pledges, they shall be selected by the Council of the League of Nations.

Article 15

With a view to facilitating emigration, funds shall be advanced to the Mixed Commission by the States concerned, under conditions laid down by the said Commission.

Article 16

The Turkish and Greek Governments shall come to an agreement with the Mixed Commission provided for in Article 11 in regard to all questions concerning the notification to be made to persons who are to leave the territory of Turkey and Greece under the present Convention, and concerning the ports to which these persons are to go for the purpose of being transported to the country of their destination.

The High Contracting Parties undertake mutually that no pressure direct or indirect shall be exercised on the populations which are to be exchanged with a view to making them leave their homes or abandon their property before the date fixed for their departure. They likewise undertake to impose on the emigrants who have left or who are to leave the country no special taxes or dues. No obstacle shall be placed in the way of the inhabitants of the districts excepted from the exchange under Article 2 exercising freely their right to remain in or return to those districts and to enjoy to the full their liberties and rights of property in Turkey and in Greece. This provision shall not be invoked as a motive for preventing the free alienation of property belonging to inhabitants of the said regions which are excepted from the exchange, or the voluntary departure of those among these inhabitants who wish to leave Turkey or Greece.

Article 17

The expenses entailed by the maintenance and working of the Mixed Commission and of the organizations dependent on it shall be borne by the Governments concerned in proportions to be fixed by the Commission.

Article 18

The High Contracting Parties undertake to introduce in their respective laws such modifications as may be necessary with a view to ensuring the execution of the present Convention.

Article 19

The present Convention shall have the same force and effect as between the High Contracting Parties as if it formed part of the Treaty of Peace to be concluded with Turkey. It shall come into force immediately after the ratification of the said Treaty by the two High Contracting Parties.

In faith whereof, the undersigned Plenipotentiaries, whose respective full Powers have been found in good and due form, have signed the present Convention.

Done at Lausanne, the 30th January, 1923, in three copies, one of which shall be transmitted to the Greek Government, one to the Government of the Grand National Assembly of Turkey, and the third shall be deposited in the archives of the Government of the French Republic, which shall deliver certified copies to the other Powers signatory of the Treaty of Peace with Turkey.

(L.S.) E. K. VENISELOS
(L.S.) D. CACLAMANOS
(L.S.) ISMET
(L.S.) DR. RIZA NOUR
(L.S.) HASSAN

PROTOCOL

The undersigned Turkish Plenipotentiaries, duly authorized to that effect, declare that, without waiting for the coming into force of the Convention with Greece of even date, relating to the exchange of the Greek and Turkish populations, and by way of exception to Article 1 of that Convention, the Turkish Government, on the signature of the Treaty of Peace, will release the able-bodied men referred to in Article 4 of the said Convention, and will provide for their departure.

Done at Lausanne, the 30th January, 1923.
ISMET
DR. RIZA NOUR
HASSAN

ibidem-Verlag

Melchiorstr. 15

D-70439 Stuttgart

info@ibidem-verlag.de

www.ibidem-verlag.de
www.ibidem.eu
www.edition-noema.de
www.autorenbetreuung.de